Memoirs of A Life Insurance Icon: Khuda Buksh

Memoirs of A Life Insurance Icon: Khuda Buksh

Compiled by: Muhammad Rahim

Editors

Roushanara Rahman
Hossain Mir Mosharraf
Mosleh Uddin Ahmed
Shazzadur Rahman
Tanisha Bukth
Shafique Khan
Bazlur Rahim

Copyright © 2010 by Muhammad Rahim.

Library of Congress Control Number: 2010907520
ISBN: Softcover   978-1-4500-5168-2

All rights reserved. No part of this book may be reproduced or transmitted in any form or by any means, electronic or mechanical, including photocopying, recording, or by any information storage and retrieval system, without permission in writing from the copyright owner.

    Originally published as বীমাবিদ খোদা বকস্ স্মারকগ্রন্থ *Khuda Buksh Commemorative Volume*

    © 2009 by Khuda Buksh Memorial Trust and Foundation, Dhaka, Bangladesh 2009

    Cover design by Ashraful Hassan Arif

    The part of the book has been translated from Bengali to English by Abdus Samad and Arnab Banerjee.

This book was printed in the United States of America.

To order additional copies of this book, contact:
Xlibris Corporation
1-888-795-4274
www.Xlibris.com
Orders@Xlibris.com
65810

Contents

Preface xv
Introduction xvii
Abbreviations xxi

PART I

Bangladesh Insurance Personnel Interviews and Memoirs

Khuda Buksh: Life Insurance was His Mission 3
The Image of an Insurer 11
Khuda Buksh: As I have Seen Him 16
Insurance, Insurance, Insurance was His Day and Night Dream 22
Khuda Buksh: His Contributions in Insurance are Simply Incomparable ... 27
Khuda Buksh: My Friend, Philosopher and Guide 31
Khuda Buksh: A Man with Exception 34
Khuda Buksh Sahib Gave us Proper Guidance all the Time 42
Khuda Buksh: He was the Heart of Life Insurance Business 46
The Unforgettable Khuda Buksh 48
Insurance is Unimaginable Without Khuda Buksh 52
Every Moment he Thought of Nothing but Insurance 60
Khuda Buksh: A Builder of Salesman 63
A Creditable Life Insurance Personality 67
The Memories of Old Days 72
Insurance was his Day and Night Dream 76
Khuda Buksh: The Vacuum has not been Filled 80
Life Insurance and Khuda Buksh 82
A Man who Never Bowed His Head to Unjust Demands 85

PART II

Pakistan Insurance Personnel Interviews and Memoirs

Khuda Buksh: Fair, Loving, Trusted and Respected Leader 95
Where's the Business? 97
A Boss Without Bossing 108
A Man Thinking of Insurance, Dreaming of Insurance and Sleeping with
Insurance in His Conscience 110
If your Man has Committed a Wrong Thing You Have to Fulfill that Promise .. 113
There was no Team Leader Better than Him in all of Pakistan 117
If Bangladesh had not Come into Existence 120
If I Would have the Opportunity to Work Again with Mr. Khuda Buksh! 124
Even Today, my Inspiration is Khuda Buksh . . . It is Almost 30 Years! 128
Even After so Many Years I Still Remember Him. That is His Greatness 137
Khuda Buksh: Who Treated me as His Own Son, His Child 143
What I Remember of Khuda Buksh 146
I Wouldn't Compare Anybody with Khuda Buksh 149
How are you Babu? 153

PART III

Interviews and Memoirs of Friends, Associates and Family Members

A Respected Person 163
One-Day Memoir 165
Brother Khuda Buksh: To Whose Incomparable Nobility I am Indebted 167
A Good Man's Memoir 172
Khuda Buksh: An Enlightened Individual 175
He was our Guardian, Friend and Well Wisher 180
He did the Right Thing by Employing People from His own District 182
My Beloved Father 185
Glancing Beyond the Picture 187
That Large-Hearted Man 189
Our Beloved Uncle: Khuda Buksh 192
A Man in Action 195
Mr. Khuda Buksh: Someone we can Never Forget 197
A Pleasure Seeking Palmist 199
Helping Anyone was a Part of His Life 201
An Ethical Will of Action 205
An Icon of Life Insurance: A Personal Reminiscence 208
A Granddaughter's Perspective 212

My Father's Memoir	214
A Great Soul Indeed!	224
My Untold Stories	232
Khuda Buksh: The Pioneer of Life Insurance in Bangladesh	242

PART IV
Articles and Newsletters by Khuda Buksh

My Memoir	265
A Reminiscence: When I Look Back	269
Selling Life Insurance Successfully – A Career	274
30 Progressive Years – EFU 1932 to 1962	279
Life Insurance Selling – A profession	282
Record Rs 35 Cr. Business in 1965 by Eastern Federal	286
Foreword: On 2nd all Pakistan EFU Convention	292
The G.M's Visualization of a Field Officer	294
Foreword: Symposium on Life Insurance in Pakistan	296
Foreword: On to Ultima Thule	298
Your Duty is Onerous	301
The GM's Message to the EFU Field Force	304
How to Win Precious Reward	306
Obligation to Nationalised Industry	308
Nationalisation of Insurance: An Appraisal	311
Chronology	316

APPENDICES

Appendix A Wolfram W. Karnowski's Letter to Muhammad Rahim	327
Appendix B A Dialogue about the Late Khuda Buksh	328
Appendix C Dialogue of an Insurance Giant	331
Appendix D A Clarion Call	333
Appendix E Mymensingh Accords Hearty Welcome to the GM	334
Appendix F An Open Letter to all Members of the Field Force	336
Appendix G Khuda Buksh is Commissioned a Kentucky Colonel	337
Appendix H Rotary News on Khuda Buksh's Death	338
Appendix I As I See it	339
Appendix J A Story and Few Quotes from Publications: 1967-2010	341
Appendix K A Brief Profile of the Contributors	343
Acknowledgements	351
Index	353

Khuda Buksh (1912-1974)

To my mother, Zobeda Khatun

Editors' Note

This book was originally published in English and Bengali by Khuda Buksh Trust and Foundation, Bangladesh, in February 2009. To make the material accessible to a broader range of readers and researchers, it is presented here in English.

Preface

RENOWNED, FAMOUS AND celebrated insurance specialist Khuda Buksh (1912-1974) himself is an institution, an organization. He was the father of insurance industry in the region of our country. He can be appellated as an omniscient without any hesitation. In the very age of British period in the third decade of the last century, he engaged himself fully in a challenging profession of life insurance. His coming to the profession was an extraordinary event among Bengali Muslims who were hostile to life insurance. This personal desire helped him in large expansion of insurance industry in the present land of Bangladesh in the Pakistani era as a result of which the successful progression of this industry became possible in independent Bangladesh.

After the completion of his institutional academics in Damudya of Shariatpur district and in Kolkata, he joined Oriental Government Security Life Assurance Company in the year of 1935. Not only he took the insurance profession as his occupation but also his aim was far-reaching in deeper sense. He was focused and determined in reaching his goal. In effect, industrious and prompt Khuda Buksh's promotion had never been late in whatever company he worked in India, Pakistan and Bangladesh. Moreover, he set his proof of success in work in all cases; he became a legend in insurance business. All these causes helped him to become a proper 'wizard of insurance'. In 1973, Khuda Buksh retired from the post of managing director, Jiban Bima Corporation, Bangladesh.

However, evaluating Khuda Buksh in terms of the timeline of his professional life is not sufficient. As devotion to work, timeliness and sense of responsibility were among his major qualities, so proverbial was his popularity in case of providing leadership and his organizational skills. His involvement in social life was innate which made many people attracted and devoted to him. Sympathy and Compassion was inseparable from the characteristics of his nature. This noble-hearted man unified his personal and family life with his working life. For this reason, presence of this higher official was certain in necessity and in time of trouble of any of his colleagues. He was widely honored in the expansion of insurance industry due to the simultaneous assemblage of his patience and firmness.

While in a discussion to erect a 'monument' in memory of insurance specialist Khuda Buksh, a renowned journalist commented, "There is no necessity to build a memorial for him. The history of insurance in Bangladesh itself is his memorial". He also added, "He had no equal, no parallel and no rival". Insurance and Khuda Buksh are synonymous!

This benevolent man always used to remember those with gratefulness whoever helped or cooperated him by any means at any phase of his life. He had a great power in mass communication. Khuda Buksh could easily endear any newly met person in little time. Along with his mother tongue, he also had envious command over the English language. As a result of his love for Bengali language, he took the initiative to publish other papers along with all booklets and premium records of the insurance industry there. For all these uniqueness in his nature, Khuda Buksh was able to get friendship and company of many people including politicians, litterateurs, journalists and social workers.

Although he had left this world more than three decades ago, the proof that he had not lost in the fathom of past, that his idealism is refulgent even today is the publication of this book. Khuda Buksh's dedication for his nation and country has been embodied through the opinions by the authors in the essays written in the book, their experience and paying homage and it does not become difficult to realize from this what a person of great stature he was.

The Khuda Buksh Memorial Trust and Foundation has done the mammoth task of retrieving a rare gem like Khuda Buksh from the great ocean of human resources in the country in search of our national heritage and the root on behalf of the entire nation that the entire Bengali community should have done together earlier.

It is my belief that the publication of this commemorative book will be helpful to the present generation to build a plan for their coming future by knowing an honest, tireless, humble and friend-loving person in Bengali community of near past.

February 2009   M. Harunur Rashid

Introduction

IN BANGLADESH, KHUDA Buksh was himself an institution. He was the first managing director of Jiban Bima Corporation. He took his last breath on 13 May 1974, more than three decades ago. In 2000, twenty-six years after his demise, the Khuda Buksh Memorial Trust and Foundation, founded by the family members of Khuda Buksh, planned to publish a book in the memory of Buksh in May 2003. The idea of publishing a book in the memory of Khuda Buksh came from his two sons, Muhammad Rahim and Bazlur Rahim in 1974. But due to some practical problems, this idea did not materialize then. The project went in steps through various adversities and changes. We were so much involved that we hardly realized when eight years had passed.

The Khuda Buksh Memorial Trust and Foundation is organizing, within its means, various programs like medical aid to the destitute and donations to the educational institutions. During the last seven years, we have enriched ourselves in stages with information pertaining to the publication of the memoir.

Though we knew a little bit about his personal life, we had no knowledge whatsoever about his world of insurance or the vast realms of his work, even three decades after his death. The Foundation didn't have adequate information to publish a detailed work on his life. On top of that, it was the foundation's first endeavor to publish a book. Most of the contemporaries of Khuda Buksh were dead or untraceable by then. Much of the information and documents had been lost. Rarely do the family members of the dead preserve his detailed belongings. It is obvious that the emergence and demands of the new generation have gradually replaced the old ways.

Yet we started. Many of the top honchos of the insurance world today made it there with the help of Khuda Buksh. We talked to some of them and made a list of names of people we wanted to interview. We proceeded according to the list. Informing them about the memoir, we requested that every body contribute a few lines. Within a few days we realized that it was hard for them to accurately recollect memories so old; many changes had occurred in their own lives, and they had also witnessed the deaths of many great men. One can write about the experiences of life only if they are intense enough and leave an indelible mark. So we changed our plans. We approached them with a questionnaire and a recorder. We recorded all the available information through the question-answer sessions. Using the dictation prepared from the recordings, we made an initial draft. Then we finalized the draft and handed it over to the interviewees for further editing.

The project was taking too much time, and we had our other assignment to complete. Hence we became apprehensive when some of the listed personalities departed from this world without our knowledge. At the same time we felt both pain and joy to observe that some of them were departing while leaving behind old and valuable information for us. Such was our working condition. So from this aspect the readers should consider this book to be unique. This was also the main reason behind the delay in publication. We express our gratitude to the insurance experts of this nation who took the trouble of remembering Khuda Buksh, and helped us with valuable information which was needed to compose the "Biography."

Khuda Buksh was the general manager of the life insurance department of the Eastern Federal Union Insurance Company Ltd. (EFU) of Pakistan. It meant that in his work he spanned what was then East and West Pakistan. Parallel to that, it should also be mentioned that The EFU was one of the big insurance companies in Asia then. So the book could not be completed without the memories of some of his colleagues who are still alive and reside in present-day Pakistan. This realization further expanded our span of work. The now separate nations, geographical distance and language barrier made our job more complicated. It took us quite some years to frame the questionnaire for the interviews in Pakistan, select the right people, organize the interviews and convert the results into publishable details. Yet we are grateful to those insurance experts who in spite of the partition left no stones unturned to recall and respect the fond memories of Khuda Buksh in unison, thus proving that the legacy of this great man was unaffected by politics.

Khuda Buksh started his career in Kolkata as an agent of the Oriental Government Security Life Assurance Company of the undivided India. As far as we know, he was the first among the Bengal Muslim community who embraced insurance as a full-time profession. He was so involved in his profession that he sent his family to Dhaka and himself worked there in West Bengal even after the partition. As a reward for his efficiency, he was promoted to the post of insurance inspector. He had spent more than two decades in Kolkata, which included both his professional and educational career. This book would be regarded complete in every aspect if the writings of his colleagues and well-wishers in Kolkata could be included in it. But Bangladesh was declared an independent nation in 1971, a new national designation for the third time. Besides, nearly half a century had passed since 1971. All these factors, together, made it impossible for us to track the original company records, and so we had to restrict our efforts from taking a bigger expansion. We consider ourselves lucky that the well-wishers of Khuda Buksh from every sphere of life other than insurance were able to remember and supply detailed information about him.

Even though his field of work was insurance, from the records we came to know that he was quite popular amongst people from all walks of life. We express our gratitude to those who, in spite of being busy, gave us time. We are also grateful to the family and relatives of Khuda Buksh. In fact, we got to know him even better as a person in learning about his various activities as a family man.

The first part of the memoir has been taken from the book *The EFU Saga* by German insurance specialist and former colleague of Khuda Buksh, Wolfram W. Karnowski. When Karnowski was requested, he expressed his pleasure over the inclusion of his writings in the memoir, and we are grateful to him for that. He was the first man in national and international circles who did a materialistic discussion on the life and career of Khuda Buksh. For this reason, we decided to include his writings at the beginning of the memoir.

For interested readers, we further inform them that after reading the book *The EFU Saga*, Muhammad Rahim has been doing intensive research on Khuda Buksh, life insurance, Eastern Federal and other related subjects for the past six years. The outcome of his research is the book *Khuda Buksh:The Pioneer of Life Insurance in Bangladesh*, which is expected to be published in Bangladesh.

In this context, it must be mentioned that we have not intentionally humiliated or hurt anybody, dead or alive, in this book. We have consciously tried to avoid any damaging comments or remarks. We request that readers let us know of any such objectionable material which we might have overlooked and help us to rectify the problem in the subsequent editions.

It is evident that all of us involved in the various stages of editing and publication of the memoir weren't interested in insurance. Yet while executing the project, we have developed respect for the achievements of Buksh in totality. To us it was not a mere memoirs of an insurance icon. We as a nation have forgotten many such personalities and would have probably done so with Buksh. But we have made a sincere endeavor to rise above such narrowness of vision and portrayed Khuda Buksh as a personality to be remembered. There might be mistakes in our compilation, but we feel that we have done justice to history on the publication of the memoir even three decades after his demise. May the soul of Khuda Buksh rest in peace!

February 2009

Shazzadur Rahman
On behalf of the Editorial Board

Abbreviations

ALICO	American Life Insurance Company
CSP	Civil Service of Pakistan
DIT	Dhaka Improvement Trust
EFU	Eastern Federal Union Insurance Company Limited
EPCIS	East Pakistan Co-operative Insurance Society
EPR	East Pakistan Rifles
JBC	Jiban Bima Corporation
KBSS	Khuda Buksh Smriti Sangsad
KBMT&F	Khuda Buksh Memorial Trust and Foundation
OGSLA	Oriental Government Security Life Assurance Company
PECHS	Pakistan Employees Cooperative Housing Society
PFS	Pakistan Foreign Service

PART I

Bangladesh Insurance Personnel Interviews and Memoirs

Khuda Buksh: Life Insurance was His Mission

Wolfram W. Karnowski[1]

IT WAS A beautiful, sunny afternoon when Mr. Zubaidur Rahim, eldest son of late Mr. Khuda Buksh, picked us up from our Hotel in Dhaka to have an early dinner with his family and his mother, Begum Buksh, widow of a man who had been a close colleague of mine way back in the 60s. This was in March 1998. My wife and I had come here again after more than thirty five years, the first time ever after this part of the world had been renamed and was now called Bangladesh. I had been visiting Dhaka and Chittagong rather frequently during my tenure of office with the 'old' EFU. By 'old' suggesting that this was before Life insurance was nationalised and both the 'twins', General Insurance and Life still working under one roof. I had always liked it.

The climate was so much different from the one prevailing in Karachi. And this was not only so in meteorological terms. The people were different and so was the political climate. I always found the typical Bengalis much softer, even more warm-hearted than many of their countrymen in Punjab and Sindh. Outgoing lively and sort of electrified. To the extent that there is a sense of nervousness around them which sometimes becomes unbearable and yet makes them so loveable, so wonderfully unpredictable. A 'real' Bengali, – if such specie would ever exist, would never be able to sit still, not even for a moment. There would be always some part of his body in action, either his feet, his hands, or just his ever wandering, ever

---

[1]Former Senior Executive, Munich Reinsurance Company (Munichre), Munich, Germany. For details, see Appendix K.

questioning eyes. Most of the Bengalis I know or have known would qualify for such a generalising assessment. If it is offensive, I sincerely apologies. This is surely the last thing I ever would like to be. It is meant to express my great love and admiration for the proud people of Bengal who over centuries have contributed so much to the intellectual political development of the Indian subcontinent and were rarely rewarded for their courage,-but rather more often severely punished for their outright determination to put self respect before cheap and easy and short term profits.

Zubaidur Rahim reminded me of his father, my old colleague and friend, Khuda Buksh. The same stature, same friendliness and smile. The moment you met him you knew, you were in trustworthy hands, had nothing to worry. A very good feeling indeed.

His father was the Chief of EFU's Life Department when I joined this company in early 1960. I had heard a lot about him, had been told that he was an outstanding salesman, a man who even in his dreams would only be able to think of life insurance. People said that he was totally obsessed by it. Very much a Bengali, with a small body and a big heart for almost everyone, but particularly for those people who, like him, just could not think of anything else but life insurance.

Mr. Khuda Buksh was born in 1912 in Faridpur, a small place in East Bengal that has produced quite a number of outstanding people, amongst them Mr. Mujibur Rahman, the 'father of Bangladesh', a man well known to him as they were both coming from the same place. His early life would be representative for the majority of people living in this part of India at that time. He was born into a very poor family[2]. His father was a worker in a rice godown and was never offered any opportunity whatsoever for furthering his professional horizon. Khuda Buksh got his early education in his home village, where he passed the entrance examination with honors in mathematics. He went for further education to Calcutta and got himself enrolled at the Islamia College from where he obtained further degrees. And again, he stood first in First Division. He joined the prestigious Presidency College in Calcutta but could not pursue his higher studies because he fell seriously ill. During all this time he stayed as a 'paying guest' with the family of a middle class man. But instead of paying them normal dues he used to tutor their children, which proved to be of great help to him because there was only very little support forthcoming from his father who had to struggle very hard to make physical survival possible. Even that proved to be hard enough and had it not been or the fact that there was some land which his father had inherited and which was gradually disposed off, Khuda Buksh would have never had this opportunity to get even this much of education.

At the advice of one of his teachers he accepted a job as librarian of the Presidency College with a salary of 10 Taka, which even by the standard of those days, was not much of a salary at all. He has often told his children about these very difficult times and he was never ashamed of where he came from. I remember him mentioning

---

[2][Ed. Not true]

this more than once when talking to his field officers and workers, stressing that was the real picture of his early life and a good example for others who start from a similar situation and may sometimes feel disheartened about it.

He worked there until he joined the Oriental Government Security Life Assurance Company in Calcutta, a very reputable insurer in those days. This was in 1934[3]. He was then 26 years of age[4] and became the first Muslim ever to join the field force of the prestigious organization. His salary then was fixed at 30 Taka, an increase of 300% over the previous one. A good friend of his had given him this advice, saying that he had witnessed him for quite some time and had come to the conclusion that the way how his friend dealt with people and with his highly developed sense of persuasive power, he would make an excellent insurance salesman. And this friend of his proved to be more than correct. Khuda Buksh became a highly successful sales professional of this company and stayed with them for 17 years until such time that he decided to migrate to Pakistan, which he did. He settled down in Dacca, the then capital of East Pakistan and joined Eastern Federal. This was in 1952. The company was in urgent need of a capable man who would be able to develop its life insurance business in East Pakistan as successfully as the Wisaluddin clan had done in the Western part of the country. He became the company's Manager for East Pakistan and developed it really almost from scratch. It was Mr. E.C Iven, the then Deputy General Manager of EFU who through some common friends had come to know about this dynamic sales professional and who then hired him. Very soon Khuda Buksh became a household name in this part of the country and he was the natural choice when EFU's top position in the Life Department became vacant. He moved to Karachi somewhere around 1959[5] but did not give up his home in Dacca, which also remained the main domicile of his family. His wife occasionally joined him in Karachi, a city that never came really close to his heart. He always felt like a stranger, who however, did not matter much because, as his son tells me, he hardly left his jacket and his trousers before midnight. Every day. And still, I never found him tired. Never. He was so much entangled in his work, so enthusiastic about it. Life insurance was his mission. He really believed in the necessity of this product, did never consider this simply an economic proposition primarily devised as a means to earn commission for the agent involved. This is how, I think, he and Mr. Bhimjee, his boss for many years, were very similar to each other, were speaking the same language. Both wanted the message of life insurance to reach even the remotest corner of East and West Pakistan. Both were convinced that by doing so they were rendering a social service to the country. Zubaidur Rahim said, "My father very often used to tell me that if one wants to succeed in selling whatever product it may be, one has to be convinced about its quality and also that those who buy it get value

---

[3][Ed. Correct year 1935]

[4][Ed. Correct age 24 years]

[5][Ed. Correct year 1960]

for their money. I have always followed that excellent advice in whatever marketing exercise I had to do in my career. And he had also told me that the most important thing to do if one wants to make a successful career, in whatever line of business ever, is to develop personal relationships on all possible levels. To build up human relations on a very personal level is the main key for success, and now looking back at my own career, I think that this was the most decisive piece of advice which was ever given to me."

Together with Mr. S.M Moinuddin, he was promoted to General Manager in 1965. The one occupying the top position on the General Business side, he the man in charge of the ever growing Life operation. His great services to EFU and Pakistan's Insurance Industry as a whole thus duly recognized by the company he had helped to build up to such an enormous size and strength. I was on my way out from the company then, but I still remember how happy and satisfied he was when this announcement was made.

Himself being of rather small physical stature he rose to the occasion and became a very big name in the field of Life Insurance, a profession he loved with all the vigor and determination he possessed. But in his outward appearance he remained the same humble man, he had always been, and whose simplicity and sincerity made him look much bigger than his body would otherwise allow him to be.

There were temptations though. To be the chief of EFU's life operations and be the man who carried that huge responsibility made him a very important and really big man, regardless of whosoever this position occupies. These were the days of President Ayub Khan and irrespective of certain irritations between the Eastern and Western wings of the country; both got along with each other reasonably well. East Pakistan, of course, and rightly so, I think, notoriously blaming the West for taking an undue and unfair of whatever the country had to offer in terms of capital and important Government posts. Ayub, so people say, was at least aware of this unsatisfactory situation and tried to achieve some sort of powering balance between the two. When he was looking for a suitable candidate for the highly prestigious position as Federal Minister of Commerce, the name of Khuda Buksh was recommended to him. For the obvious reason that not only did he fulfil the prerequisite credential of being a Bengali from Faridpur District, but his name had become so well known in the whole country that he seemed to be a most suitable candidate for such a position.

Whosoever might have been responsible for such a proposal certainly had done the wrong thing for the right reasons. Khuda Buksh knew that if there was ever something he definitely did not want to be, this was to be a politician. And the brave man that he was, he went to Islamabad, met President Ayub Khan and told him: "Sir, you are bestowing a great, unexpected honor on me. I shall remain grateful to you until the end of my life. But I have to tell you, in all humbleness, this is no job for me. I am not a politician. And, if you don't mind, Sir, this is only a temporary job, something I hated to do all my life," And Ayub Khan obviously took it lightly and asked our friend whether he would be able to suggest a suitable person for this job, somebody from East Pakistan, preferably from Faridpur. And he suggested the name of an old friend, Mr. Wahiduzzaman, who indeed then was appointed and graciously agreed to preside over one of the very big conventions held by another great institution of the country, the Eastern Federal Union.

One of the great things about this remarkable man was that he never really openly boasted about whatever he was able to achieve. We, his immediate colleagues in those days, were; of course, not aware of the advances made to him by the then President of Pakistan. We were only wondering why the then Commerce Minister, Mr. Wahiduzzaman, was making quite a few flattering remarks about his old school mate from Faridpur, praising him even more than the man who was really running the show, as anyone attending the Convention could see for himself, Mr. Roshen Ali Bhimjee, Khuda Buksh's boss and a fast friend of Wahiduzzaman. But in hindsight his decision had also turned out to be an extremely clever move, for the job offered to him would have been really only of a very temporary nature. A little over a year later President Ayub relinquished power to General Yahya Khan and indirectly also paved the way for a man he had pampered so very much, Zulfiquar Ali Bhutto. Apart from these deliberations, Khuda Buksh, of course, was the best man to judge that he was not made for such type of a job. And even his closest friends would have found it difficult to imagine seeing Khuda Buksh amongst that circle of men who were right in the centre of political power. Yes, he was a man with extreme willpower. And he was all his life very proud to be Bengali. He made that very clear, even to those who were not really that anxious to be told. I distinctly remember that even in our Management Meeting in EFU, Khuda Buksh was the one who all the time tried to drive the message home that, according to him and many other leading Bengali business men and politicians, the contribution of East Pakistan towards the overall development of Pakistan should be more adequately recognized. To some extent he was even carrying his arguments with a certain amount of aggressiveness, which one would never expect coming from a man of his stature. He did this with a lot of personal drive and utmost determination. But even when critical, he was never politicizing issues. I remember having always given him full marks for that attitude. He never seemed to be really interested in politics for the sake of it. Yes, when East Pakistani members of the Central Government or the General Assembly visited Mr. Bhimjee or attended official functions held by EFU, in which he, of course, prominently figured, then one could see how proud he was that the visiting VIP was a man of his tribe, but he never tried to rub shoulders with them. There was always this certain aura of independence and dignity around him, self-respect, of which he had a lot. He, however, also expected the same amount of respect shown to him. Like most persons of a comparatively low stature he had his moments, stopping short of showing signs of an inferiority complex, giving the impression of getting a bit moody. But it never lasted, he was easily to be cheered up again.

His son narrates a very typical incident which, I think, serves as a good example of what I am trying to drive at, "My father" he said, "was a very humble man throughout his life, even then, when he had become rather an important man in the eyes of the people around him. He never became a rich man because he had far too many obligations towards poorer people. He very generously supported a school. He virtually had no vices, did not smoke. His only hobbies were soccer game. Sometimes he went to the 9 o'clock shows. And he was fond of reading but only books on insurance, actuarial books. And he was a very loving father, I could give you many examples just to prove that point. Very often do I think now that I really have lost in him a very great man. Let me give you a description of just one very typical incident. I had just joined Muslim Commercial Bank in Dhaka. The office was not far away from his, just around the corner. The new one, I mean, the one near Gulshed[6] Cinema. It was in the afternoon, around 4.30 PM. He was suddenly standing in my office, holding some keys in his hand. They were the keys for a brand-new car, parked just opposite the office. And he turned on one of his brightest smiles, gave me the keys and said : "this, son, is for my prestige. You must come to your office every day in this new car." It shows you his attitude towards life and the sincerity and selflessness with which he treated those dear and close to him."

His decision to leave EFU in 1969 and to form his own company in the eastern wing of the country was a great loss for the company he had successfully helped to grow into the leading and dominating position it then held, but it was at the same time a great gain for East Pakistan which soon should become Bangladesh, a nation of their own. Many people, of course, were wondering why one of the most successful and gifted senior executives EFU had ever produced so far should have decided to leave the vehicle of his success.

His son, Zubaidur Rahim, believes what close friends of his father had told him, that Khuda Buksh and Bhimjee had some major dispute about the company's investment policy. About a plot of land which was bought in Dhaka without prior consent of the Chief Executive. I would not buy this particular theory nor would I necessarily be inclined to bite the first one. Bhimjee has always been very conscious about the special sentiments of the people of East Pakistan and to see a beautiful building to coming up in Dhaka immediately after the one he was planning in Rawalpindi would be completed was a dream very close to his heart. And as I have discussed already in some other context Mr. Bhimjee was mentally anyhow much closer to East Pakistan's leading elite politicians than to their counterparts in the Western wing. I, therefore, think that neither of these two suggestions given as why Khuda Buksh unexpectedly decided to leave EFU after 17 highly satisfactory and successful years do really do justice to what he did. I could well imagine that he simply thought that if some important people felt that he would be capable to direct

---

[6] [Ed. Correct name Gulistan]

the country's economic policy, he would definitely have the necessary ability to be his own, master and head an insurance company of his own.

Whatever the reason, fact is that in April 1969 he floated a new company called Federal Life and General Assurance Company. And even after he had left EFU, I was told by many who should and would know, he spoke never a bad word about his old, beloved company nor did he utter a single bad word about Mr. Bhimjee whom for so many years he had genuinely admired. "He never spoke about it, never gave us the reasons why he had decided to leave EFU, the company he had loved so much," says his son." Whatever my guesses, are the result of what I have been told by others, friends of my father, never by himself."

The Head Office of his new company was located in Dhaka and some seven or eight leading and big industrialists and businessmen from East Pakistan were behind this move which seemed to be crowned with immediate success. Because after one year the company declared a dividend to its shareholders.

This fortunate development, very unfortunately, was not allowed to last long. The turmoil and upheaval in East Pakistan started and finally Bangladesh came into being. Insurance was nationalized and four Insurance Corporations were formed, two for Life and two for General. Mujibur Rahman, the father of the new country, a man whom he knew since his childhood because both came from the same area, Faridpur, had consulted Khuda Buksh on the future of the country's insurance industry and had made him Chairman[7] of one of the Corporations.

After 17 months it was felt those four corporations were too many, so a decision was taken to close down two of them. Khuda Buksh, who without any question was considered to be the senior most insurance official in the country, was appointed Managing Director of the Jiban Beema Corporation, the Life Insurance Body. This was on the 13th of May 1973. Exactly one year thereafter, on 12th of May 1974[8] he fell sick and was rushed to the hospital. He spent some time there and appeared to recover well. However, he had a second, very massive attack and he left this world on the 30th of May 1974[9], at the comparatively young age of 62. He was thus not allowed to reap the final laurels of his work and success. There were long obituaries appearing in all newspapers and magazines of the country. He was hailed as one of the great sons of the Bengali soil and in his honour and memory a large photo is displayed at the Insurance Institute of Dhaka.

People still speak very highly of him. His son is rightly proud of the fact that whenever his profession brings him in contact with important Government officials, bureaucrats and business tycoons and he is asked by them as to his family background, people get out of their chairs whenever he tells them that he is the son of late Mr. Khuda Buksh, and they tell him what a wonderful man he was and what he has

---

[7] [Ed. Correct designation Director]
[8] [Ed. Correct date 12th April 1974]
[9] [Ed. Correct date 13th May 1974]

done for the country even at a time when it did not yet exist as a national entity. And people would always immediately try to assist him for the sake and memory of his late father.

Could there be a nicer epitaph for a human soul than this!

[Reprinted from *The EFU Saga, 2001* with permission from the author, Wolfram W. Karnowski. All rights reserved.]

The Image of an Insurer

M. Harunur Rashid[10]

IT WAS A period of transition for Bengali Muslims when Khuda Buksh started his career. In those days, the Muslims lagged far behind the Hindus in all aspects, be it education or business. Ninety-five percent of the Muslims earned a livelihood through cultivation. The Zaminderi system was in vogue then, but all except a few were Muslim Zamainders. Since the Hindus were firmly established in the trades and commerce, the Muslims had little chance to have a job in those commercial organizations. As a result, the educated section of the young Muslim people tried their best to have a job under the government. Only a handful of young people chose private firms as their place of duty.

Khuda Buksh had extraordinary talent as a student. It was then almost next to impossible to for the Muslim students to get into the Presidency College, Calcutta. In the '30s, Presidency College was one of the best educational institutions in India. Khuda Buksh Sahib studied there for some time (he could not sit for the BA examination, owing to his illness). He also worked as librarian of the collage. Later, he joined Oriental Government Security Life Assurance (OGSLA) Company as an agent. I think he could have gotten a good government job. But why he took up a private and challenging job like insurance is still a mystery to me. Ten to one, he chose insurance because of his challenging mentality.

In 1952, he joined Eastern Federal Union Insurance Company Limited (EFU) in Dhaka. I was then a senior officer of that company. He used to talk to us regarding his past life. He also frequently mentioned the name of Mr. Atahar Ali Sahib, a reputed insurance personality. Mr. Atahar Ali was indeed a top insurance worker in

---

[10]Former, Executive Director, United Insurance Company limited, Dhaka, Bangladesh. For details, see Appendix K.

India. Mr. Khuda Buksh said that it was Mr. Atahar Ali who inspired him to take up insurance business. Mr. Atahar hailed from Barisal and worked in Calcutta.

Then there was another top insurer named Syed Shamsher Ali. It was the period of the '40s. The Muslims were just rising from their hibernation. The Muslim League Government was established in the then individual Bengal. A.K. Fazlul Haque became the Chief Minister of individual Bengal, and he was also Minister for Education for a short while. Fazlul Haque contributed much to the education and jobs of the Muslims. He did his best to create a separate entity for them. To be frank, Fazlul Haque was behind all-round flourishing of the Muslims today.

Khuda Buksh started his career in that very age. It can be said undoubtedly that there were only a handful of Bengali Muslims rich enough to buy an insurance policy. This was why people were reluctant to buy an insurance policy. Moreover, Muslim fundamentalism always discouraged insurance as un-Islamic. As such, it was troublesome for the Muslims to buy policies. Even in the midst of such a difficult situation, Khuda Buksh had the boldness to get down to this risky business.

Khuda Buksh joined his career as a field worker at the OGSLA, the best of its kind in India. He was a very meritorious student, as I told earlier. I know little about his clients, I yet think he managed to collect a considerable number of Hindu clients in Calcutta and thus established himself as a man of repute. Being a Muslim, it was really a tactful job to collect Hindu clients in a fairly hostile environment like Calcutta.

It is true that Khuda Buksh made a name for himself as a first class insurer in Calcutta even before partition. And this was circulated throughout Pakistan.

On the fifteenth of August, 1947, only three insurance companies were under Muslim ownership:

1. The Eastern Federal Union Insurance Company Limited (EFU), established in 1932 in Calcutta.
2. Muslim Insurance Company, established in 1934 in Lahore, and
3. Habib Insurance Company, established in the '40s in Bombay.

EFU was headquartered in Calcutta before Pakistan came into being. Habib Insurance Company was transferred to Pakistan in black and white. But even after the birth of Pakistan, EFU's head office was in Calcutta up to April 1950. EFU, however, opened two branch offices in Dhaka and Chittagong then. Mentionably, EFU transferred its registered office to Chittagong just before partition.

Habib Insurance Company employed only a few commission-based chief agents in East Pakistan. On the other hand, Muslim Insurance Company had several branches here in East Pakistan, but the company was financially insolvent. So, the branch manager was in no position to fully pay the workers.

But EFU had a strong financial base, which is why it was able to retain its branch offices and employees. Over and above, it was prepared to appoint dexterous insurance workers on regular basis. It was then that EFU made effort to take Khuda Buksh.

Early in 1952, EFU was a non-Bengali organization, and naturally the managers were also non-Bengalis. Mr. Jamaluddin, a West Pakistani gentleman, came to work as senior life manager of East Pakistan. He joined Dhaka office in 1951 but unfortunately died on 8 January 1952. This caused a vacuum at EFU's Dhaka branch. In the circumstances, EFU authorities contacted Khuda Buksh in Calcutta and managed to send him to Karachi to discuss job affairs with higher authorities. He was then inspector at OGSLA. Everything was okayed in Karachi and on the second of July 1952, Khuda Buksh joined as life manager of EFU's East Pakistan branch.[11]

I was ill, and I could not go to office on the day Khuda Buksh joined EFU branch office, at Johnson Road, south of Victoria Park (now Bahadur Shah Park). But I learned later that there was a sensation among the officers and field workers on the occasion of his joining.

Here, mention may be made of one thing. In those days, the number of persons willing to buy an insurance policy was limited. There was fundamentalist propaganda against insurance, and so agents or chief agents could not make a good profit in the business. And the agents were not paid properly. This discouraged the workers, and they frequently quit the profession. After the appointment as the life manager of EFU, Khuda Buksh realized the actual situation and started a new system. He encouraged young people to come to the profession. He gave them salary-based appointment letters. Since everyone got salary in time, there was an air of security among the employees. He managed to arrange training courses for the employees. He arranged salary-based jobs for all the employees, whether or not the company was making money. In the field of insurance, this system was unique in East Pakistan. No other company maintained this. As a result, the educated section was motivated to come to the profession.

He tried his best to retain the employees up to the last. He did not let them go easily. A few examples will further clarify the matter.

If anyone left the company, he used to keep him under close observation. I can recall, I left EFU and joined Khyber Insurance Company in 1961. It was a general insurance company. Once, American Life Insurance Company (ALICO) wanted me to be the head of their East Pakistan branch. Eventually, I submitted my resignation letter to Khyber Insurance.

Khuda Buksh was then in Karachi. When he heard of what I was doing, he talked to me from there over the telephone thus, "You must not leave Khyber Insurance Company and you must not join ALICO." Because ALICO was his rival, so he did not want me to join ALICO. And, accordingly, I did not join ALICO.

---

[11] A background story of this period is depicted in page 303 under the chapter "Great Contributors" in the *The EFU Saga*, written by W. W. Karnowaski.

In another incident, a senior EFU officer was trying to join another company. After hearing this, he visited the residence of that officer on the morrow. When the officer came out of the house, he saw that Khuda Buksh was standing before him. This put him by surprise. Khuda Buksh then took the man in his car to the office. And he took all necessary measures so that the man considered it unwise to leave EFU. Insurance policy, be it big or small, or the client be in any financial position, he used to visit the client's house with the agent or the chief agent. Personally, I have seen some such incidents.

In the fifties he lived at Gandaria in Dhaka. Once, in the afternoon I visited his friend Dr. M.A. Waheed's chamber along with a client for his medical checkup. The chamber was adjacent to a road. Incidentally, he was driving along that road at that time. His wife and son were in the car. When he found me sitting in the doctor's chamber with a client, he drove to his residence outright and put his wife and son there. He returned then and came to the doctor's chamber. The client's check-up being over, he took him and me to his residence. He talked to the client for long about the merits of insurance. I chuckled to see his patience. Never before in my life I have seen anyone talking so patiently about insurance.

He was damn hardy – he scarcely distinguished between day and night. He was what we call workaholic. In January 1953, I contacted a senior secretary of East Pakistan government. And I was to take Khuda Buksh to the secretary's Minto road residence. It was the month of Ramadan. It was raining heavily that morning. I was thinking anxiously, how I would take the doctor and Khuda Buksh to the client's residence in the rain. I saw suddenly that Khuda Buksh had arrived in his car, ignoring heavy rainfall. I was very surprised. He then took us to the secretary's Minto road residence. The secretary was extremely pleased with Mr. Khuda Buksh, and we had a big business that day.

As he was relentless to the workers, so was he kind and sympathetic towards them. In one case, he dismissed a worker for embezzlement. Subsequently, he was requested by colleagues to reinstate the worker on the ground that if the worker was dismissed, the members of his family would starve to death. He at once rehabilitated the worker. Such incidents bear testimony to his sympathetic mind. His sympathy and empathy towards his staff were really unprecedented.

Before the joining of Khuda Buksh at EFU, policies used to be issued from Karachi. It caused unusual delay. To avoid this problem, Khuda Buksh increased manpower so in order that policy renewal, premium, et cetera and other necessary arrangements could be done from East Pakistan. It certainly bears testimony to his extraordinary foresight. Consequently, insurance business went on increasing, and a good number of new jobs were also created. It undoubtedly gave East Pakistan insurance business a new dimension. His abilities, however, were recognized, and he was called to Karachi. He was made life manager of EFU (all Pakistan life section), and subsequently he was made DGM and general manager. He had to travel all over Pakistan after taking over the new responsibility.

In 1969, he took leave of EFU on personal grounds and established Federal Life and General Insurance Company. After the war of liberation in 1971, a new dimension was added to the insurance business. All the insurance companies were nationalized, and a national insurance corporation was established. Four insurance companies worked under the corporation, namely Surma, Rupsha, Karnofuli, and Tista.

In March 1973, Mr. A.H.M. Kamruzzaman became the commerce minister and reorganized insurance companies within a short time. Only one Jiban Bima Corporation and a single Sadharan Bima Corporation were established. The government appointed Mr. Khuda Buksh the first Managing Director of Jiban Bima Corporation. To keep the company going and to keep it financially stable, he worked day and night. He was as restless as a bee. Eventually, this hard work told upon his health.

Possibly on the twenty-seventh of November, 1973, he departed from insurance profession for life. But the way in which he was released pained him much. As a matter of fact, a very haphazard situation got the upper hand after the independence of Bangladesh. The people at insurance business began to demand undue advantages from him, which, as a man of character, he was in no position to comply with. And naturally he did not take defeat. In such a situation, a movement was crystallized against him. He was almost on the verge of giving up going to his office. When such was the situation, Mr. Moyeedul Islam returned to Bangladesh from Karachi, and he was given the post of the managing director. Khuda Buksh was released by the Government of Bangladesh.

When he departed, I was general manager of Jiban Bima. I was at Jiban Bima at first and later, I joined as general manager of General Insurance. At one point during my stay at Jiban Bima, I had conflict of opinions with him, but ultimately a friendly relation grew between us. It was by his choice that he brought me from General Insurance and appointed me to the post of general manager, Jiban Bima. I was present on the day he was released. At the time of handing over charges to Mr. Moyeedul Islam Sahib, he said, "I sacrificed my whole life for insurance, and I am to go thus today." It was indeed a painful experience for me.

There is no denying the fact that it was because of Khuda Buksh's untiring efforts that insurance industry made a mark in Bangladesh. I don't think that insurance industry could have made such a sharp rise without him.

Khuda Buksh: As I have Seen him

Mosleh Uddin Ahmed[12]

IN 1950, AN elderly gentleman named Ainuddin Ahmed came to our Barisal residence. He was a bearded, good-looking fellow. I saw that my father was showing him much respect and cordial hospitality. I came to know later that he was my father's teacher. And the name which was being frequently quoted in their discussion was "Khuda Buksh."

I had the opportunity of seeing the repeatedly discussed person, that is, Khuda Buksh, in 1956. That year, he came to Barisal on an official tour. I passed the matriculation that year and got myself admitted into a college. He was then the life manager of Eastern Federal Union Insurance Company (EFU), East Pakistan. Earlier, he was in the Oriental Government Security Life Assurance Company, Kolkata. Khuda Buksh was a bit junior to my father. Both studied at the same school at Damodya under Faridpur district (now Shariatpur). Khuda Buksh went to school from his Damodya house, and my father lived at the school hostel. Mr. Ainuddin Ahmed was a teacher and the hostel superintendent of the school.

When I heard the name Khuda Buksh, it occurred to me that he would be robust figure. I don't know why. But our ocular meeting proved wrong. He was in fact a diminutive figure, well-dressed, resourceful, and attractive. He was a fluent speaker, and he walked very fast. He was always shipshape. He seemed to retain a vast potential and special magical power.

Whenever Khuda Buksh went to Barisal, he would visit our place, though sometimes for a short period of time. I regarded him as an ideal man at first sight.

---

[12]Former Managing Director, Express Insurance Limited, Dhaka, Bangladesh. For details, see Appendix K.

After appearing in the matriculation examination, I had a time to relax for a period of three months (till the publication of the results). That, in my opinion, was a dark stage in my life. In that period, I mixed with a special group of wicked boys, and the companionship pushed me out of control. This undesirable friendship with blackguards of the society almost caused an end to my studies. On an official visit, Khuda Buksh came to Barisal exactly at this time. As usual, he came to our house. In course of discussion, he asked my father about me. My father could hardly utter a word, as his voice was choked in despondency. He could only say, "My son has totally gone astray. He has given up his studies. I am now in a fix as to what to do about him." I was hearing the discussion secretly from an adjacent room. Khuda Buksh took pity on my father and said simply, "But your son was not like that. Possibly he has gone astray because of bad company. If you please, I can take him to Dhaka and provide him with a job under my company. When he will be involved in works, he will face the reality and realize his blunder. And perhaps he will get admitted into a night class and resume his studies."

He opined that it was an urgency to detach me from bad company. Father said to him, "If you think it wise, take him from here immediately. I am fully in agreement with you that if he stays here, he could never carry on his studies. Moreover, things will go from bad to bad."

And I had to come to Dhaka that very month. I had an interview and subsequently got a clerical job at EFU. After my joining there on the tenth of July, 1961, I took the profession very sincerely. I found that in insurance, one could rise very rapidly. Ninety percent of the cars parked then at Jinnah Avenue (now Bangabandhu Avenue) belonged to the EFU officers.

Though my job was very small, Khuda Buksh called me on various occasions. He always called me "Milu." Incidentally, I can mention here that one of his sons' name is "Milu."

Soon after my joining, I noticed with a surprise that he always motivated even the commonest worker in marketing – so forcefully that it brought him considerable income. I also noticed that many people were buying cars and houses overnight. Being well fed, well-dressed, and buying houses in aristocratic sections of the city all became easy and regular acts of EFU agents and field workers.

Khuda Buksh was a true altruist; he had an altruistic heart. He arranged the marriage of countless number of marriageable daughters. I cannot remember such an incident in which he heard the news of somebody's illness but he did not go to see him. His presence was almost guaranteed at the *janaza* (a prayer for salvation of a departed soul before burial of a body) or *qulkhani* (a prayer for departed soul within 40 days after death) of the relatives or neighbors. And on marriage ceremonies, his presence was a certainty.

On many occasions, he had to visit West Pakistan and many other European cities, including London. When he would return to Dhaka from any foreign land, an unprecedented thing would happen. It would be seen that a good number of field workers were at the airport to newly welcome him. Such an event was un-thought of, not only then but even today. This generally happens only in case of very popular political figures. The puny man would almost be covered with garlands. This remains and will remain ever fresh in the minds of many like me as a very strange affair.

This is a general propensity that a person would go to his own house after returning from a foreign country. But surprisingly, he did quite the opposite Suppose he landed at the airport at noon. From there he would go to his office direct, not to his residence. He was a genuine insurer from top to toe. He had little respite to think over anything expect insurance. Khuda Buksh and insurance had the same meaning.

Thirty-seven local and foreign insurance companies then worked in Pakistan. EFU's yearly business were greater than those of all other companies combined. They simply envied EFU. And it was Khuda Buksh who was at the root of this creditable performance of the company. If anyone in his company sold an insurance policy, he would instantly send him a congratulation letter. At that period, telephone was not handy, and fax or other technological advantages were not available. There was a system of sending air mail letters, but that, too, was limited to a few particular places of the country. It was apparent that such letters of praise inspired them greatly.

He had a particular style of his own to motivate field workers to go on working in full swing. Suppose, someone among the workers applied for taka 2,000 [$420] for the wedding of his daughter. He used to call him and say, "What will you do with such a small amount? You better take 5,000 [$1,050], and you need not come back until you have finished all the related works. Arrange your daughter's marriage in a big way. And after returning, start working with full vigor. You will find that your income has increased to a large extent. You won't be in debt for long." And people were so much fascinated with his words and advice. And what is more, they would be really benefited by following his advice. And after all, the company itself would be benefited. Allah gave him such a fascinating and magnetic attractiveness which I have never seen in anyone else.

Occasionally, he would be on official tour, which definitely inspired field workers, and they would get an instantaneous solution of their problems. If someone asked for some money, he would propose to give him a larger amount and said, "I am not giving this from my own pocket. This is just an advance from your future earning. Work vigorously and pay it later on. I want your problem to be solved first."

He was an extraordinary popular personality. Whoever the man or whatever his profession, Khuda Buksh was known to everyone. The capacity he earned to persuade people was, in short, extraordinary. Very few people could refuse an insurance proposal offered by him. His excellent organizing capacity and sky-skill popularity were the causes of envy of the West Pakistani EFU officers.

He had conflict of opinions with EFU's managing director Roshen Ali Bhimjee. Mr. Bhimjee started to treat him in such a nasty manner that it became difficult for him to stay at EFU. So, in early 1969, he resigned, almost suddenly. His resignation was the result of the conflict of personalities. Of course, it was not in political sense. On many occasions, it was seen that managing director Bhimjee and Khuda Buksh both joined a party where everyone was eager to take care of Khuda Buksh, leaving Bhimjee in a corner; or everyone was all agog to listen to the speech of Khuda Buksh. Higher authorities could not bear this.

It was he who purchased land at Dilkusha Commercial Area – Jiban Bima Tower stands there today. Even in those days, the project involved an amount of Tk. *four and a quarter crores* [$8.92 million]. A drawing was prepared for the twenty-four-story building and multifarious plans were there. He was able to persuade the higher authorities that permanent properties should be set up in the eastern wing of the country in order that as in other fields, East Pakistani people do not consider themselves deprived of insurance facilities. The building plan he prepared was unique; there was not such a planned building in the whole of Pakistan. Facilities proposed in the plan were a spinning top floor, a luxurious auditorium with multilingual address system, et cetera. He also got the plan of the building passed from Dhaka Improvement Trust (DIT).

The foundation stone of the building was laid on the second of January, 1970. But he was then no longer at EFU. The foundation stone was laid by Mr. Nasiruddin, the most veteran EFU worker. Construction works was started, but after a few days, it came to a halt, owing to the political disturbances of the country. Subsequently, after the liberation of Bangladesh, Jiban Bima Corporation building was built in a slightly modified version of the original plan.

After deciding to depart from EFU, he started working to establish a new company. On the twenty-ninth of May, 1969, the newly established company started its journey. It takes me by surprise to think how rapidly he started the functioning of the new company. This also bears testimony to his extraordinary organizing capacity.

I, too, left EFU and joined his company. First, he discouraged me to join his company, because it might be unwise to leave the largest insurance company of Pakistan. Secondly, his company was new, and everything was unpredictable. Moreover, insurance business was not so good because of political unrest. He told me to think again before leaving a stable job and setting foot in the path of uncertainty. I told him that it was he who had brought me to the insurance business and since he was no longer at EFU, I was also ill prepared to stay at EFU, as I will always feel a kind of pangs of separation. I knew in my mind that whatever business he would put his hands in was bound to be a success. He, however, took me to his company. Political movement started in full swing a few days after the establishment of his company. And even in the midst of a host of troubles, his company was proceeding well. Many Bengalis then surrendered their policies at EFU and started to buy policies at Federal Life.

The later history is quite different. The country became independent. After the nationalization of all the insurance companies, Jiban Bima Corporation and Sadharan Bima Corporation were established. And Khuda Buksh was made the managing director of Jiban Bima Corporation. Soon after independence, a state of anarchy prevailed over the country. Most organizations were nationalized overnight. Trade unions began to demand undue and unlawful advantages. *Gherao* (act of surrounding/besieging) and strike became an everyday affair. Khuda Buksh never experienced this before. In these circumstances, he himself was hesitating whether he would leave his job.

At one stage, the government appointed Mr. Moyeedul Islam as the managing director of Jiban Bima Corporation. Formerly, he was the managing director of Pakistan Insurance Corporation. He returned to Dhaka after the Bangladesh Liberation War. In 1973, Khuda Buksh was released, and Moyedul Islam was given appointment. Soon after his release, the workaholic became ill. I never even saw him sick, but he was taken ill suddenly and died within a month. I saw that even after his departure, he used to come to Bangabandhu Avenue parking lot, talked to this or that man for some time, and left. I think that he did so because he was in no position to bear the degradation of the insurance corporation he helped build himself. This is my personal assumption that after his departure, he was vehemently shocked mentally. This caused his illness and later, death.

Like me, others should be pained to consider one thing. I have heard that, hearing his death news, all the insurance companies in Pakistan declared a holiday. But the news failed to create any reaction in his own country. The land of Jiban Bima tower was bought mainly under his dynamic guidance and painstaking effort. Some people even thought of naming the tower "Khuda Buksh Tower." But in this land of strange characteristics, this could not be materialized. And for proper reason, politicians always got the upper hand in these matters.

I started working at EFU as a clerk. I was studying at night. When I took leave of EFU, I was then assistant superintendent. After getting in to service, I took my works seriously. When recommendations for works would go to Khuda Buksh at year end, he once called the workers and said, "What's the matter? Why do you always call Moslehuddin such a good man? Is it because his father is my friend?" They said, "No, sir, we don't know that his father is your friend. But the fact is that the boy is really sincere in his works." Later, he took me to Karachi for higher training.

Once, he himself called me, just to examine me. I was a bit frightened. The big boss was calling. Have I made any mistake? Given my post, it was not customary for him to call me direct. He handed over me a complain letter of a policy holder and said, "Read it." When I finished reading, he said, "What should be done?" I replied, "The complain of the writer must be ascertained by examining the ledger." He then told me to write a reply and show it to him. I examined the papers and prepared a reply. Then I went to him with the letter. I came back. He called me again a bit later and said, "Your writing is not bad." He then made some modifications in the letter and returned it to the superintendent. He then told him, "From now onwards you will make all the letter draftings of your department by him. Then you will see them and make necessary modifications." This created me a big chance to learn.

I always tried to follow him. After joining Federal Life, I had an opportunity to come in close contact with him. Many ask me now, "How do you keep contact with so many people?" Even some members of my family complain, "Need you go everywhere, or is it necessary?" I have learnt all these from him. When someone becomes ailing, when somebody dies, when anybody invites me, I go everywhere.

He regarded me as his son. It was he who rescued me from a wrong course. He brought me from Barisal and provided me with a job in his company. All my success and whatever I have got in my life are due to his untiring efforts to see me happy. Were it not for his kindness, what would happen to me, only Allah knows. Some of my young friends in Barisal had to suffer imprisonment. And it could happen to me, too!

Insurance, Insurance, Insurance was His Day and Night Dream

C.M. Rahman[13]

IT'S A GREAT pleasure to recollect a personality like Mr. Khuda Buksh. We were intimately connected with each other and worked very closely for several years. I knew Mr. Khuda Buksh for quite a long time. When I was studying Bachelor of Commerce, "insurance" was my major subject. During my preparation for the final exam, I wanted to know more about certain aspects of life insurance. In those days, very few people studied insurance, and the opportunity to learn about the subject was very meagre. So I decided to consult Mr. Khuda Buksh.

When I went to meet him and entered his room, Mr. Khuda Buksh stood up, came to the door, and received me. I was overwhelmed with his vast knowledge on the subject and with his charming personality. Though I was just a student and much younger in age, he was very helpful, courteous, and kind to me. We had a long conversation. I don't really remember it, but I still remember that I left with a lot of admiration for him as well as for his depth of knowledge on insurance.

I came in close contact with him after I joined East Pakistan Co-operative Insurance Society (EPCIS). After I joined, he told me that he was instrumental to my joining EPCIS. The management of EPCIS approached Mr. Khuda Buksh to find a competent person for the Life department, and he thought of me as the best choice. At that time, I was working in Habib Insurance Company Ltd. He, along with a member of the Board of Directors of EPCIS, met my general manager at

---

[13]Former, Managing Director, Jiban Bima Corporation, Bangladesh

Karachi and inquired about me. I was invited to join EPCIS as the head of the Life Department in October 1962.

In October 1964, when I almost decided to leave EPCIS, Mr. Khuda Buksh phoned me from Karachi and reminded me of my promise to him that if I had ever decided to leave EPCIS, I would join his company. He further told me that he was sending me the air ticket, and he would be at the airport to receive me. One can realize from this small incident how forward-looking he was and how much he loved his company. On the following night of my joining Eastern Federal Union Insurance Company Ltd., there was a dinner party of the company at Beech Luxury Hotel, where Mr. Khuda Buksh introduced me to the managing director, Roshen Ali Bhimjee, a very popular name in the insurance industry of Pakistan. I knew Mr. Bhimjee for quite some time. He told me that it was in his knowledge that I worked very hard in establishing the Life Department of EPCIS and desired me to rest and enjoy life in Karachi for three months at the company's cost, and that my wife would receive my pay check in Dhaka. This demonstrates the working environment and the attitude of the top management towards its officers.

The environment of Eastern Federal was not the employer-employee relationship. It was like a family. It impressed me so much, and that kind of management attitude allowed you to give your best for the company. This is how I started and worked in a family-like environment, till I left EFU in 1972. In 1972, I migrated to the newborn Bangladesh.

When I joined EFU insurance company as a manager of the head office in Karachi, Mr. Khuda Buksh was the general manager for life insurance. So, obviously, I was the only senior East Pakistani executive in the head office except Mr. Khuda Buksh. Due to my direct appointment as manager in the head office, there were a lot of hard feelings among the many contenders for this post. So, naturally, there were lots of wind directed against my appointment.

Mr. Khuda Buksh joined EFU in 1952 as manager, East Pakistan. An extremely hardworking and a devoted insurance sales manager, Mr. Khuda Buksh built up a strong field force all over East Pakistan and became champion in life insurance in East Pakistan. That was why EFU used to underwrite more new insurance business from East Pakistan than from West Pakistan.

Mr. Khuda Buksh was very well connected amongst the high Government officials, professionals, politicians, educationalists, et cetera. He was also a popular Rotarian. His noble disposition, simplicity in life, unflinching fidelity, and stern sense of duty won the love and respect from everybody, whoever came in contact with him.

I may recall an incident which reflects his management style. Once, we were traveling together. One of our field officers had a small car, and he was standing by the road. It was giving some trouble. Mr. Khuda Buksh got down from his car and immediately asked him, "Why don't you change your car? Buy a new car!" I asked Mr. Khuda Buksh, "You offer such a big concession for him, and you offer him to buy a car at the company's advance money? But can you justify this?" Khuda Buksh looked at me and said, "This man has great potential as a salesman. So I am giving you opportunity to utilize his potential to the best of his ability. So it is an encouragement for him, and this is a very positive step to increase business." I was fully convinced that he was right.

We used to live together, so I could see him throughout the day and night. He was a very simple person. He used to take care of me in every aspect. Very simple in his habit, very honest, very sincere and very helpful, and always smiling. I have never seen him in disturbed mind. He was always smiling, always talking, and so devoted to his profession. Around the clock, whenever he used to meet people, he used to talk about insurance, insurance, insurance – that was his day and night dream.

In those days, for an East Pakistani to rule over, to manage a life insurance field force of West Pakistan was not an easy task. Particularly, the field management itself is a very difficult management, because these field officers are not under any service rule, and they are not under any strict control of the management. Yet, Mr. Khuda Buksh could win the heart of all the field officers in East and West Pakistan and constituted a strong, efficient field force. Eastern Federal was the number one company in Pakistan in those days.

Whenever there was any dispute or clash between the company and its employees, Mr. Khuda Buksh applied his own personal relationship. I knew at Dhaka some of our senior field officers resigned. He went to their home to persuade them to come back and join Eastern Federal. So, that was his approach. He used to solve the problem by his personal approach. There was another very important aspect to Mr. Khuda Buksh's management. He used to establish relationships not only with the person himself, but with all his family members. He used to visit their home, talk to his wife and children, and establish a family link so that if he used to fail to persuade an officer to rejoin, he used to persuade his wife to convince him to join back at Eastern Federal. This shows how much he used to like his institution and his own people.

He introduced in the company a sense of competition amongst the individuals and amongst various field officers teams ... At the same time, there were a group of people who used to work under each individual senior field officer as a unit. He used to introduce competition from time to time and reward them by different types of prizes. He also used to reward individuals who used to do brilliantly well by giving a car advance or other facilities.

The phenomenal progress of EFU could be divided into two parts. First, the growth of new life insurance business: in this sector, Mr. Khuda.Buksh was an undisputed leader, and right from the managing director to everybody appreciated him. As a mark of appreciation, we have seen that after closing the year, when Mr. Khuda Buksh returned to his headquarters at Karachi, everybody used to be present at the Karachi airport to receive him. So, it signifies that he was the person responsible for the business growth. Now, this growth itself is not all in all for the overall growth of a life insurance company. In other sectors, there were lots of contribution met by other senior executives of the company.

When Mr. Khuda Buksh was general manager for life, I was manager of the Life Head Office of EFU. So, after him, I was the only senior East Pakistani executive in the head office. Besides us, Mr. Mohammed Ahmed of Premier Insurance was the only senior East Pakistani insurance executive in West Pakistan. Unfortunately, the attitudes of the people of West Pakistan towards those from East Pakistan were not favorable. They used to look down upon them and were reluctant to appreciate their good work or to give them their due. This gave birth to regional disparity at the national level.

Here I may recall a small incident. I was a participant of the Fourteenth Session of the Pakistan Administrative Staff College, Lahore in 1967. This was the highest academic institute for the civil servants of the Government of Pakistan. Senior Officers like Mr. S.B. Awan, Chief Secretary of North West Frontier Province, and Mr. Alauddin Ahmed and S.B. Chowdhury, Secretaries of the Government of East Pakistan, were amongst the participants of my course mates in the Fourteenth Session.

In every provincial Headquarter, there was a Chapter of the ex-participants of the College that used to meet once a month to hold discussions on contemporary national issues. In late 1970, our Karachi Chapter held a discussion meeting on the issue of "Regional Disparity in Pakistan." This was a burning political issue at that time. The speaker was a retired Secretary of the Government of Pakistan who also worked as provincial Secretary in East Pakistan. At the outset, the speaker outlined the history of disparity in Pakistan and then tried to say that in reality it was a hypothetical issue. He said that as far back as in the early 1950s, the Members of Parliament from East Pakistan used to come to attend the Parliament together with some Dhaka University professors. These professors used to tutor those parliament members to speak on economic disparities committed to East Pakistan. He tried to give the impression that the parliamentarians at the instance of some disgruntled university professors voiced their lies on the regional disparity. He was not appreciative of deprivation of East Pakistan due to the vast disparity in economic development, distribution of foreign exchange, recruitment in civil administration and armed forces, et cetera. At the time of the question and answer session, I stood up and said, "If the apprehension of the East Pakistani Parliamentarians about the growing economic disparity was heeded, then the matter would not have grown up to the present serious situation threatening the very unity of the country. It was also very unfortunate that what the professors of Dhaka University could visualize as far back as in early 1950s, neither the West Pakistani parliamentarians nor the Government of Pakistan could appreciate it. Now, when a document no less than the revised Constitution of Pakistan of 1962 itself admitted the prevalence of wide disparity between East and West Pakistan, there is no scope to deny it." My statement came like throwing cold water on a burning carnage. The speaker did not expect that an East-Pakistani participant could be present there and soon corrected the motion.

In fact, this sort of attitude prevailed in most of the Government Offices as well as in the armed forces. This also cast a similar shadow in the private organizations. When Mr. Khuda Buksh was posted in Karachi as the Life Manager of Pakistan, he faced a lot of non-cooperation and humiliation. But he was not a character to be daunted.

I had the opportunity of talking with Mr. Bhimjee. In those days, I was very close to both Mr. Khuda Buksh and Mr. R.A. Bhimjee. They had sometimes complained against each other, and both of them used to tell me about their feelings. Mr. Khuda Buksh retired on attainment of retirement age. Mr. Bhimjee offered his financial help to establish a jute mill in East Pakistan, but Mr. Khuda Buksh felt this was to mislead him and to make him stay away from his insurance profession. He did not accept the proposal, and he established another new life insurance company.

It was not a surprise to me, because Mr. Khuda Buksh used to discuss with me how he was progressing about registration of a new life insurance company. He also discussed with me about selection of his senior executives, like Mr. M.A. Samad and others. I felt very happy that such a big insurance giant would start a life insurance company in East Pakistan, which was definitely going to be a pride for East Pakistanis.

I think Mr. Khuda Buksh's absence was more felt in East Pakistan. In West Pakistan, since the highest management knew of his resignation, they already made very elaborate arrangement; and immediately after his retirement, they made changes at the top level to cope with the business and other insurance services in the head office rather than the regional offices in Pindi and Lahore. So, there everything was quite normal. But in East Pakistan, because of his management, his absence was more felt in East Pakistan than in West Pakistan.

I was working for the company, and that was my motto. I was not working for either Mr. Bhimjee nor Mr. Khuda Buksh. As a senior executive, my loyalty was with the company. But still the personal relationship was always there. I had excellent personal relationship with Mr. Khuda Buksh as well as with Mr. Bhimjee. Once, it so happened that after Mr. Khuda Buksh left the company, on the following year after business closing, there was a dinner at Mr. Bhimjee's house; and while we were taking drinks in his lawn, all of the senior officers of West Pakistan were there present. Suddenly, Mr. Bhimjee told me, "Mr. Rahman, you were very close to Mr. Khuda Buksh, but that is not going to harm you."

Khuda Buksh: His Contributions in Insurance are Simply Incomparable

A.R. Chowdhury[14]

I JOINED EFU AS an agent in 1948. We heard from before that someone from Kolkata would come here. It was our general assumption that those who were unable to stay in Kolkata were coming here. Then came Khuda Buksh. And by dint of his moral courage and ability to work, he conquered our hearts.

When Khuda Buksh joined EFU, the general insurance staff remained unpaid because of shortage of funds. He raised the income of life insurance, and with that amount, he paid the salaries of the general staff. There was a time when we heard that Eastern Federal will be abolished for shortage of money. But after his joining, the situation improved.

Khuda Buksh joined EFU in 1952 at the age of about forty. He would show much affection to me. He took me to his house, to Rawalpindi (Pakistan), and there is no such place in the country where he did not take me. Among the Bengalis, he took me to many places more frequently than others.

It was his contribution that led me to the zenith of the insurance profession. What more I can say about a dynamic insurance giant? Moreover, nowadays I am

---

[14]Former, General Manager, Jiban Bima Corporation, Chittagong Branch, Bangladesh. For details, see Appendix K.

short of memory. I have never seen such a dedicated, devoted insurance worker in my life. We have failed to even go near him.

EFU's activities in Chittagong were not very extensive. There was no electricity at Halishahar. A party from there opened an insurance company. It was Siddiqur Rahman agency. He arranged car for us. My salary was then 125 taka [$26 per month] only. One day he said to me, "Chowdhury Sahib, buy a car." But how was it possible? He raised my salary to taka 400 [$84 per month], and we had to collect premiums amounting to taka 30,000 [$6,300], which was really unimaginable. He assured me and said, "No. No, you won't have to face any problem." He got a new contract signed and gave me a car. He said, "You pay fifty percent, and I'll pay the rest." Lastly, he paid two-thirds, and I paid the rest. And we had a car for twenty-five hundred taka [$525]. Gradually, the number of agents started to increase, and so did our business.

He was simply uncompromising throughout his life. He lifted many poor families to higher positions. They managed to buy cars and houses all because of him. The contributions he has made in insurance are simply incomparable. People from all walks of life were connected to him. He was a very familiar figure everywhere. The chief justice of East Pakistn was then S.M Morshed (Syed Mahboob Morshed); chief secretary was Safiul Azam Sahib. Both of them had intimacy with him.

Frankly speaking, he gave birth to insurance in Bangladesh. From the religious point of view, insurance was then prohibited. From such a difficult situation, he managed to bring insurance to such a height. There was no such place even in West Pakistan where he did not pay visit and build insurance workers. It is generally seen that workers patiently wait for political figures. He was the only exception in this field, because people waited for him wherever he went. Even the people who would not buy a policy would wait just to have a glimpse of him. They used to ask, "Who is Khuda Buksh? We have heard of him so many times. We would like to see him." He was so uncommonly popular. And people from all walks of life will meet him eagerly.

Once in Karachi, Khuda Buksh said to me, "You need not stay in a hotel; you will stay at my residence." So I stayed at his residence. At one occasion, there were number of guests, including journalists in his residence. I was called. I came, putting on a simple shirt, and took my seat in a vacant chair. A bearer came and said to me, "Sir, you haven't put on a tie!" I said, "Tie? I even don't know how to wear a tie!" Khuda Buksh noticed it and said, "Don't you know how to wear a tie? Okay, come with me." So saying, he took me to his dressing room and helped me to wear a tie. He loved me so dearly.

During my stay at Karachi, once I was taken ill seriously. Khuda Buksh personally visited Dr. Sayeed Khan and called him. I have never seen such a person in my life. I have never seen such a person among the politicians, businessmen, and even the religious-minded.

If any claim would come, he directed to pay it instantly, without any delay. If he knew, he would say, "Huda Sahib, (Referring to EFU, Manager, administration) here is a claim. Pay it immediately."

Once a gentleman came to buy an insurance policy amounting to taka one *lac* [$21,000]. Soon after his coming, he drank a glass of water. Khuda Buksh asked me, "Chowdhury Sahib, would he buy a policy?" He then said to the gentleman, "You are going to buy a big policy. But do you know how much the premium would come to?" The gentleman asked Khuda Buksh, "Is your name Khuda Buksh? Are you born here in this country?" The gentleman actually thought that he was being considered incapable of paying the premium. The gentleman was a close friend of Fazlul Kader Chowdhury (Speaker, Pakistan Assembly). However, at the time of preparing necessary papers, Khuda Buksh asked him his name, et cetera. The gentleman suddenly flew into a rage and asked, "Why are you asking me so many questions? Just write Fazlul Kader Chowdhury."

This was how he compelled the guy to buy an insurance policy. He hit him at such a point that the gentleman had no alternative but to buy an insurance policy. Khuda Buksh later told him, "Okay, you need not write anything, just put your signature here." The man was milder than before and said, "Yes, your men know everything about me. And Chowdhury Sahib knows everything too well."

We already did some groundwork whenever we heard that Khuda Buksh would come to Chittagong. Everyone knew it to be Khuda Buksh's company. Soon after his arrival, he would arrange various discussion meetings.

If someone would be his agent, Khuda Buksh went to him and encouraged him ... He inspired him, saying, "You have to build a house, buy a car," et cetera, et cetera.

One day, he came to my residence and told my wife, "What? Chowdhury Sahib lives here in this situation? Where is the carpet?" He personally went to Amin Carpet company and bought a carpet for me. He said to me, "You pay later."

I put my signature on the deed of EFU Bhaban land (now Jiban Bima Bhaban). Khuda Buksh Sahib also signed on the deed. Most probably, Azim Rahim (later MD of EFU General, East Pakistan) also signed. It was Khuda Buksh who told me to put my signature. However, I have forgotten the year.

K.F. Haider was then general manager. Khuda Buksh came to EFU in 1952, and Roshan Ali Bhimjee in 1960. Following his joining, a conflict of personalities started to keep shape between them.

When Khuda Buksh was at the point of leaving EFU, Bhimjee gave him an offer. Bhimjee came to East Pakistan. I didn't understand what was in his mind, but it appeared to me that he wanted Khuda Buksh to remain at EFU. Bhimjee called some of us. He said to me, "Khuda Buksh Sahib wants to leave. What will be the problem if he goes?" I said, "We will be ruined if he goes." He said, "I will not let him go easily. Some of you go to his residence." I, along with a few others, visited his residence. Ahmed Ali (Regional Manager, EFU) was with us. We told him about the wishes of Bhimjee. Khuda Buksh, however, gave some conditions, which he did not tell us. He told about it to Justice Abdus Sattar (subsequently President of Bangladesh). Later, I knew that one of the conditions was that Bhimjee should keep his hands off from the affairs of East Pakistan. Khuda Buksh said "And if I am given the absolute power to take decisions about the affairs of East Pakistan, I will not leave EFU; I will stay on." Bhimjee, however, was in no position to comply with the conditions of Khuda Buksh, but he tried to the best of his capacity to retain Khuda Buksh up to the eleventh hour. But I do not know whether it was a show.

In 1969, he came direct to my residence from the airport. This was why some people complained to Roshen Ali Bhimjee against me, because Khuda Buksh had established Federal Life by that time.

He has sacrificed his whole life for the sake of insurance He was a real master in conquering a man's heart. Just as Sheikh Mujib was a giant politician, so was he in the world of insurance.

There was no trade union at EFU. But a trade union was formed after EFU was merged into a corporation, after the independence of Bangladesh. And soon after that, some people among us went severely against him. For this reason and he became sick and was mentally hurt. None had dared to talk rudely in his presence. I was present when Khuda Buksh was last insulted. He received impolite treatment from union leaders when a person gave lecture in a seriously insulting manner standing on a table. I no longer remember his name and do not wish to remember.

May God keep his soul in peace!

Khuda Buksh: My Friend, Philosopher and Guide

Mujib-ud-Doula[15]

I JOINED EASTERN FEDERAL Union Insurance Company (EFU) as assistant manager in 1964. Before that, I was working in Homeland Insurance. I had purchased a car with a loan from Homeland. The person from whom I had purchased the car was a government officer. He sold the car and left for Australia. He had purchased the car with a loan from the government. I did not know that he had not repaid the loan. So, the government seized the car and took it away. That means it was a huge loss for me. At this stage, when I was considering leaving Homeland, American Insurance offered a loan to me for the purchase of a car. But that would be a bank loan for which there would be an interest. About such a time, I got acquainted with the late Mr. Khuda Buksh. He told me, "We will also provide a loan for the purchase of a car, and on that, we will not charge any interest."

So, I thought that suited me. Besides, there was still my pending loan of Tk. 11,000 [$2,310] from Homeland for the purchase of my previous car. Thereafter, my terms were finalized with him. Next day, I went to his office. When I went there, he called the Accounts Officer, the late Mr. Atiqullah, and instructed him, "Please write a check for Tk. 11,000, and I will sign it." But I still hadn't got my appointment. Then Mr. Atiqullah wrote the check and brought it, which Mr. Khuda Buksh immediately signed and handed to me, saying, "Cash it from United Bank [now Janata Bank] which is just next door."

---

[15]Former Managing Director, Meghna Life Insurance Company Limited, Dhaka, Bangladesh. For details, see Appendix K.

I have mentioned this incident in order to illustrate how he facilitated my resignation from Homeland after repayment of their loan of Tk. 11,000. This is the way I got acquainted with Khuda Buksh, joined Eastern Federal and came close to him. After appointing me, he went to Karachi. Before leaving, he simply gave me one advice, "work according to your judgment and decision. I know about you. If you make any mistake, I'll be responsible for it. So, you should take responsibility, and work according to your decision." I got so encouraged by his words that I felt very confident. Since that time until he formed his own company, I got the opportunity to work with him in EFU. I consider him as my friend, philosopher, and guide. Regarding matters related to me, this statement is fully applicable to him.

I must mention something here. From a long time before I joined EFU, Mr. Shamsul Huda had been working there as Administrative Manager. Sometime before I went there, he had resigned and had decided not to stay with EFU. However, the day I joined, Mr. Shamsul Huda returned and started working in the office. Probably, he had assumed that EFU couldn't go on without him. So, when I joined, he changed his mind and returned to EFU.

In those days, it wasn't always possible to buy a car as desired. It was necessary to obtain prior permission from the government. Previously, I had already lost a car, and the people on the ministerial level knew about it. Then I wrote a fresh application and got its approval. When I received the approval, Mr. Khuda Buksh was in Karachi. I telephoned him in Karachi and asked, "Sir, I received a permit for a car. Please tell me what I should do now." He told me to direct the call to Mr. Huda. Then he instructed Mr. Huda to lend me Tk. 11,000 for the car. From these incidents, we can realize his ability to take instant decision and his trust in people.

When he formed Federal Life, I did all the necessary paperwork. As I had been with Swiss Insurance Training Center in 1962, I knew everyone at Swiss Insurance Company. Besides, I helped to complete the insurance agreement with Federal Life Assurance through correspondence. I was also supposed to go to Federal Life as he had advised me to do, but it didn't materialize, because the other Assistant Manager of Eastern Federal, Mr. Siddiqui, was in Chittagong at that time. He was facing some difficulties there and wanted to be transferred to Dhaka. Mr. Khuda Buksh then told me, "As Mr. Siddiqui is going through such problems, I have to take him." To that, I also responded, "Since he has such problems, please take him. I don't have any problems. You can take me when you need to." But my joining Federal Life never materialized, and I stayed on with Eastern Federal.

Mr. Khuda Buksh was a very friendly person. He had friendship with people from different strata of society. He knew all the CSP officers of that time. Almost all those who got posted in West Pakistan or those who went to Karachi for training, used to put up initially at the house of Mr. Khuda Buksh. As other members of his family lived in Dhaka, his large house in Karachi remained almost empty.

We regarded him as a super salesman. In Eastern Federal, he rose from the position of a salesman to general manager and later became the managing director of Federal Life. We considered him as one of the greatest insurance magnets in Asia.

When he was the general manager of the Life Section of Eastern Federal, its head office was in Karachi. All investments of the company were made in Karachi. But he wanted them to be shifted to East Pakistan. On this issue, he used to have difference of opinion with the then managing director, Mr. Bhimjee. I think when it was about to reach a climax, he resigned from EFU and founded Federal Life.

Incidentally, it should be mentioned here that preparations were underway to build EFU Bhobon (building) where the present Life Insurance Bhobon stands. The foundation stone of EFU building had been laid on 30 January 1970. Its construction was started on 25 March 1971. On that night, a large number of laborers were on the site, and thus a lot of laborers embraced death in the shootings on 28 March. Then the construction of EFU was stopped.

A disorganized state prevailed immediately after the creation of Bangladesh. Trade unions started to lay down such unsystematic programs that it was not possible for him to continue work in a proper way. The misdeeds of trade unions had been then giving rise to unrest. Ultimately, he had to leave life insurance.

I feel that Mr. Khuda Buksh could foresee his future by divine insight. I am mentioning this, because just a few weeks before his demise, he suddenly came to my house. My house was at Jhigatola at that time. He lived in Dhanmondi. He was no longer in life insurance. I was surprised by his sudden visit to my house. He said, "I'm just going around to meet everyone," I didn't realize that he would pass away just after about a week. Later, I felt that probably he knew it coming. That's why he was going around meeting those he loved most and had affection for.

Khuda Buksh:
An Exceptional Personality

Hedayet-ul Islam Khan[16]

I PASSED THE INTERMEDIATE Arts (IA) exam, then I visited EFU office in 1956 with a reference. I found ten, twelve young men there. They were given papers and questions for an exam. Khuda Buksh asked me, "Have you given an application?" I said, "No." He said, "Give an application and avail yourself of the opportunity to sit for the examination."

I did so. That day was Saturday. The next day was holiday. I met him on Monday. He asked me, "Are you willing to serve at a salary of taka 125 [$26/month]?" I replied that I had a chance to have a job in a government office at the salary of taka 130 [$27]. I told him that I would let him know after two, three days. He said, "No, you won't be given any time." I said, "I'll get medical facilities there." He said, "Here, too, you'll get medical facilities.' Actually, he spoke so tactfully that at one stage, he convinced me that the job in the insurance was better, though I hardly knew anything about insurance. He asked me no question. I thought that such a man was insisting me so much, and in the circumstances what could I do except doing job here? My exam result was not so good; I got almost fifty percent marks. However, I joined the next day as a clerk.

I started to work. He refused to grant me leave. I also did not take leave. I also did not take the yearly leaves allowed for me. This was because of the fact that if we took leave, he would be displeased. To make me experienced, he frequently allowed me to change sections; thus I changed five sections in six months. In the

---

[16]Former Managing Director, Homeland Insurance Company., Dhaka, Bangladesh,

meantime, I made many mistakes, and I was also heavily scolded by him for this. Then everything could be done in English. I was only an intermediate, and as such it was quite natural that I would make a few mistakes. After correcting my mistakes, he used to advise me, "Can't you buy a grammar book from footpath and read it?" There was a typist who came to EFU from Calcutta. He would type my drafts. But the letter which I gave him for typing would be corrected. He typed it according to his own method. One day Khuda Buksh told me, "Do you compare the typed letter with your original letter?" I said, "No." He advised me to compare it and said that the typist was changing my letter. He also said that it was evidently wrong. He advised me to tell him to type exactly whatever was in my letter, right or wrong. He also said, "If your letter is wrong, I will correct it. Otherwise, you won't be able to learn." I said, "Okay, I'll give you the typed letter along with the draft." This was one example of how I learned from him.

Khuda Buksh himself supervised the development section. It was a very important section indeed. I worked with him as an in-charge. I was doing so many faults that I had to stand before him most of the time to give an explanation. My table was at the corner of the office, and his chamber was in another corner. He called me with the help of a peon. The situation was such that I had to go to his chamber all day long and come back. He used to ask, why the fault was here, why that fault was there, et cetera. Anyone who takes an insurance policy falls under the jurisdiction of this section. And all the complains are made here in this section. Sometimes he would become seriously enraged.

At one point I saw that he was no longer scolding me. Rather he was talking in my favor. I, too, continued to work up to 9 p.m. everyday. There was no overtime. One day, he went out from office but came back again, seeing the light in the office. He said to us, "You work here for so long?" I said, "Yes." He said, "Don't you eat?" We replied, "No." He said, "Go down and bring *parota* (bread fried in oil) and kabob. If you work at night, have some food every day." Parota and kabab cost one taka and two annas. He told us to give him the bill. He then went away.

I kept myself engaged in office works so deeply that I had little time to study. But my degree was a necessity. There was an unwritten rule at EFU that if you work here, you could not read. But I got myself admitted without giving him an intimation. The office broke at 5.30 p.m. but classes would begin at 5.00 p.m. I missed the first period, and availed myself of the opportunity of the next classes. Nobody in the office knew this. I, however, needed a few days' leave during the exam.

One day, I went to him and said to him, "Sir, I want to sit for the exam." (I was trembling with fear). He said, "What exam?" I replied, "BA exam." He said, "Okay, sit for the exam." There is an instruction not to study. But there is no instruction not to sit for the exam. If you can pass, well and good. He granted me leave – only for the days of the exams. I sat for the exam and got over. Four of us worked together. Two of them were graduates; another guy and I were non-graduates. Those two graduates went elsewhere. The rest of us stayed on.

One day, he said to me, "You have got over the BA exam with much difficulty. I have started an officer's training course in Karachi. I want to send you there with the first batch. Two will go from here." However, letters came from Karachi.

I got married by the time. Three months ago. My residence was here. My wife went to the airport with me to see me off. I had never been to Karachi, never boarded a plane. Khuda Buksh appeared suddenly. I said, "Here is my wife." He talked to her and said, "I am taking your husband. Don't worry. I will return him to you again."

I said, "Sir, are you coming?" He said, "I may come tomorrow or day after tomorrow. Rest assured."

We arrived in Karachi at 1 a.m. We were taken to a hotel. I thought it was unnecessary to stay at such a good hotel, spending so much money. When we told them, they said, Khuda Buksh told them to take us into a first class hotel. I was thinking about the payment. Who would pay the bill? They said, "Khuda Buksh Sahib knows everything. It is our responsibility to look after you until he comes."

I went to the office the next day. I could see the difference. How beautiful their office was. We actually had limitations. We underwent three months' training. Khuda Buksh's residence was at a distance. Yet he came to us occasionally to see whether we were in any difficulty, whether we required to send money to Dhaka.

One day, I said to him, "I did not go to your residence even for a day." He said, "Do you like to come to my residence? Okay, let us go today." He took me to his residence, fed me, and took me back to the hotel at about 10.30 p.m. These human qualities of him were beyond my expectation. I could not think of a person who could do such things. He did these with cordiality.

I was given taka 800 [$160] as a weekly grant. I found that it was much more than my salary. I also did not pay the hotel bill. I was thinking how much the bill would come to at the time of our departure. One day I talked to him about my grant. He said, "If you think your grant is too much, if you don't like to take 800 taka, take 400 taka from now." I said, "What will happen to the money I took so long?" He said, "It will be decided later on."

This is not actually a fact. I worked as an assistant superintendent. But he sent me to Karachi as a superintendent. I did not know that, nor did any one in Dhaka know that. There was a gulf of difference between the post of an assistant superintendent and the post of a superintendent. Salary also greatly differed. And there was difference in grants. When the training was at a finishing stage, he let me know this and told me not to say this to anyone after my return to Dhaka. He said, "There are a dozen of others who are equal to you in rank. If they hear this, they will surely take to heart. I am coming some days later. Then, along with others, I will declare you as superintendent." Those who underwent training were all superintendents. So, if I were sent as an assistant superintendent, it could certainly create a trouble for those people. Considering this, he made me superintendent. Otherwise, it could clearly create a complex problem. Such profound was his foresight. I am doubtful if anyone does so today.

I have learnt from him devotion to work and integrity. I can cite an event here:

I was very young then. I had just joined my job. We got only two days' leave at the time of Eid, the Eid day and the day after Eid day. My parents lived at Kishoreganj then. A train left Dhaka at 3 p.m., but the office was up to 5:30 p.m. I was thinking of getting leave earlier. I went to him and asked for leave, a bit frightened. He said, "Leave, but why?" I said, "A train starts at 3:30 p.m.; if I can go out at 3, I can avail the train." He said, "All right, but what's your problem if you don't go?" I said, "I belong to a mess. They have already gone. They will also return earlier. I don't require a key for my room. But I don't have a key with me now, nor do I have the place to sleep at night. What should I do now?" He said, "Okay. Be seated." He called the peon and told him to call the driver. He then upheld the receiver and told his wife at the residence, "A guest of mine will stay at our residence tonight." He then told the driver, "You will take him with us when we go." He also said to me, "I think you don't have any objection to be my guest. Since you are in difficulty, be my guest for tonight." I was then caught red-handed. I felt like a fish out of water. He said, "Why did you tell a lie?" I kept mum. He continued, "Never tell a lie to your boss. Remember, never, whatever difficulty you are in. If you do so, his trust in you will surely fade." I said, "I am in the wrong, sir. I'll never do so." He said, "I understand that you'll not do so with me. But bear in mind, whoever be your boss, wherever you work, never tell a lie to your boss."

I have kept my word. I have worked at many places for long. But I never told a lie. I did not tell a lie to the chairman even when I was working as the Managing Director. This is really true. And this helped me in many ways. I had to face trouble occasionally, but I profited more from this.

He worked at EFU for seventeen years. He was an intermediate, but he was quite dexterous in insurance business. As a matter of fact, a man should not be judged merely by his academic qualifications. He was so good at English that none could even go near him. His pronunciation was close to those of a Bengali, but he had extreme boldness in speech. He had the speech, manners, and qualities necessary for establishing himself to the West Pakistanis.

Jiban Bima *Bhaban's* (building) land was bought during Khuda Buksh's stay at EFU. An investment board was then formed for East Pakistan. The chairman of the board (East-West combined) was Kazi Anwarul Haque. He was the chief secretary of East Pakistan. Then came Justice Abdus Sattar (subsequently President of Bangladesh).

EFU's investment board was independent. And the managing director was related to it. And the general manager was not related. In the field of decision making, Khuda Buksh was not related. But he was related to implementation of the decision already taken. The plot of Jiban Bima was Khuda Buksh's selection.

During that time Pakistan had a reputation in hockey then. So, the design of the bhaban was made in imitation of a hockey stick and a ball. The tower is the ball. The lower portion is the stick.

Khuda Buksh left EFU following a conflict between the then managing director and himself. The then managing director passed a negative comment against policy of selling life insurance policies in Dhaka. This comment cut him to the quick. In fact he helped turn his company into one of the best insurance companies in Pakistan, where he is providing a negative comment on selling life insurance. An irony of fate, indeed!

Bhimji Sahib said this when he was speaking to the field officers on the fourth floor of Dienfa building. He made such a comment in presence of Khuda Buksh. I also attended the meeting. This caused his emotional suffering and mental distress. He decided in his mind that he would no longer be at EFU. However, he stopped coming to office.

I went to his residence one day. He said, "A few field officers are coming to meet me. They want me to set up a new company." I saw the field officers who came later on. I used to work with them. Then he took me in his car and drove me to a Dhanmondi residence. It was the residence of Abdul Jabbar Mehman. He told me there, "Hedayet Sahib, if you want to establish a company, you'll have to sell shares. I'll see if I can collect some money." It was then that I came to know that he was going to build up a new company. The works of the new company was started by Moslehuddin Sahib and Nurul Haq Sahib. However, the company he established was named Federal Life Assurance Company Limited. Both of them joined there.

One day he left me get down from his car at a place near Gulistan, where he intended to set up his new office. He said to me, "You get a high salary, but now I am not in a position to give you as much as they are giving you. I will take you in time." I said, "It's all right, sir."

In May 1969, Khuda Buksh's new company started to function. During crackdown in 1971, new sale of policies almost came to a halt. New premiums hardly came. It was a period of predicament. He was thrown into a really financial hardship.

In May that year, I was terminated from Eastern Federal. They said to me, "Your service is no longer required." The date was 15 May 1971. I provided remarkable services to the EFU. Even at the moment when nobody was present, I received the cash. I was not absent even for a single day up to the fifteenth of May. In spite of all these services, they terminated me. I was sacked because they thought that it is I who have passed the law and advised Khuda Buksh to set up a new company.

Rayer Bazar was then the killing ground. I purchased a car with a loan from EFU. I kept the car here. The area was isolated and unfrequented by people. One day, after 16 December, I happened to meet him. He said, "Hedayet Sahib, you join again." I said, "No, sir, I won't serve any longer." He said, "No, no, don't do that, you join again."

I, however, joined again, as a freedom fighter. After a few days, the insurance companies turned into corporations. In the very corporation act, it was stated that "Khuda Buksh will be the Managing Director of Jiban Bima Corporation." The name of a person is not mentioned in an act. But his name was in the act.

However, he became my boss once again, and I took the responsibility of the claim department. The process of nationalization was going on then. One day he called me and said, "Today is Friday. You will sit at my chamber from today."

Mr. Moslehuddin used to sit by him. Mr. M.A. Samad also sat beside him. I did not go to office for two days. I was thinking how I would sit in his chamber. On the day I went to office, Moslehuddin Sahib told me that there was extra chair at the chamber, and he told me to sit there. The next day Khuda Buksh called me and said, "Didn't you keep my word?" I said, "Why, sir?" He said, "Didn't you sit at my chamber?" I said, "Such and such persons are already seated there; as such, how could I sit there?" He said, "I urge you to sit at my chamber." The next day I went right into his chamber and sat there. This mentality of his clearly indicates how dearly he loved me.

In the meantime, the dominance of trade unions set in. Those who were appointed by him, and all his acquaintances became leaders and chiefs of the association. They were the leaders of influence. He had conflict with them. They could not stand him. They said that whatever the demands, he would have to comply with that unquestioningly. Small companies (thirty-two companies under Jiban Bima) increased the salaries of the employees according to their wishes, and they were taking the same even coming under the corporation. Things were still to come to a harmonious system. On the other hand, Eastern Federal was yet to do so, and many more people worked here. So, the leaders started to create pressure in various ways. Their demand was – give him promotion, raise his salary and so on. He simply did not tolerate this. But everyone says that he has cheated people. They say that he did not uplifted them, et cetera. But he can not unduly raise a person without qualifications. Those who are at the lowest level of insurance are non-graduates. So, how could he raise them, without breaking the rule? So long as his company was a private one, he could do that. But after nationalization, he was not in a position to do whatever he liked. It was the non-qualified section of the employees who raised the stormy movement and made him disrupted with their illegal demands.Once he went to Adamjee building to talk to the Company people. But they were reluctant to hear him. Meanwhile, some unruly fellows stood up on the table and made insulting comments to him.

I was not at Adamjee that day. He was returning in his car. I met him. He extended his hand towards me and said, "Those whom I gave appointment, who worked under me, unduly insulted me today. I am going today. I'll not come back tomorrow. It is only you whom I am relating this. I got such treatments from those for whom I did everything. These are my countrymen!"

Not that he was released, not even that he himself resigned. The fact was that from that day, he never came to Jiban Bima. Jiban Bima's head office was then at Homeland Building.

In my opinion, Khuda Buksh gave appointment to many non-qualified persons from his region. So, people from other areas did have little respect for him. Incidentally, mention may be made of the fact that he gave jobs to many people of his locality and Abdur Razzk Sahib's area. But I have not seen anyone acknowledge this.

Khuda Buksh Sahib, A. Rahim Sahib, M.A. Samad Sahib, Moyeedul Islam Sahib: all were managing directors of Jiban Bima. All of them left Jiban Bima, being extremely disappointed with the activities of the trade unions. Even today, one cannot work in a proper order because of the unlawful influence of the trade unions. Now someone from the government got the appointment. A joint secretary from the home ministry is the managing director now.

I remember many events [involving Khuda Buksh].

Once, I saw a person, sitting at our office for a long time. I asked him, "What's the matter?"

He said, "I have come to your office. I am in trouble, having an insurance policy."

I asked, "What's your problem?"

He said, "Brother, I am a fat man. Your field officer told me, since you are a fat man, you can't get an insurance policy. So, get an insurance policy for your wife. As such, he has insured my wife with an insurance policy. I have paid the money. Now my wife is dead. Now he says that I'll not get the insurance money. We are people of Dhaka, and he is so cunning to cheat me! So I am waiting for the big boss. I want to know what he says."

I asked, "When did your wife die?"

He said, "Nearly one month ago."

I said, "When did you take an insurance?"

He said, "About two months ago."

"What was her disease?" I asked again.

He said, "She was dying for many days."

I said, "If she was dying for many days, how can you get the money?"

"But your field officer did not say that. He simply said, give us the money and we insure her."

I called upon the peon and told him to take the man in to meet Khuda Buksh. I thought it unwise to make a meaningless hue and cry. The man went in and came out a few minutes later. He was raising a hue and cry.

I said, "what happened?"

He said, "Oh! what a man you have kept sitting there. Is he a man? Angel, angel. I can very well call him an angel. He has come from the heaven. Can an insurance company run without such a man? He only said, 'You will get the money, go home now.' He is a man made of gold. My wife is dead, but I have no sorrow. Now I really get peace after talking with him."

Such was the case that he has gone to *janaja* (prayer for salvation of a departed soul before burial of the body) of the insured person and has taken the check with him. I, however, did not like such a thing. The wife of the deceased used to say, "What check? My husband is dead, what good is it to write my signature now? Why have you come with the check at such a moment?" Most people would be displeased. But Khuda Buksh would say, "This is the time when they need help most. So this must be done. This will raise their morale. And the relatives also think that he has the insurance."

He always said, "Never make delay in giving the claim." The necessary papers of the policy holders who died in 1971 were not available and not found in proper order. He would say, "Always pay the money. In it, there is no loss for you but a great benefit for them. What a great benefit it is for a widow or her children. Don't give them the trouble of coming repeatedly."

And I always tried to follow him to the letter.

I have worked with Khuda Buksh for a considerably long period of time. But for his help, I could not have reached at this stage of my life. What he has done for me is not easy to do for others. I did not have any blood-relation with him, nor did I hail from his village.

Khuda Buksh Sahib Gave us Proper Guidance all the Time

Siddiquallah Miah[17]

I GOT ACQUAINTED WITH Khuda Buksh Sahib in 1965 for the first time. I was then serving as a patent designer under the Ministry of Industries. Hai Sahib, secretary of the Chandpur District Samity, M. Ahmed Ali Sahib, and some other people were then working as development officers at the Eastern Federal Union Insurance Company. Occasionally, I used to visit them. Consequent upon such frequent visits, profound intimacy grew between us; and moreover, I was given an insurance agency. Within one hundred days of my having the agency, I was introduced to Khuda Buksh Sahib.

As far as I can remember, it happened in 1967. After my having got the agency, I sold out six policies at the rate of Tk. ten thousand [$2,100] each and deposited a premium worth Tk. 600 [$1,260]. Khuda Buksh Sahib was then probably the general manager of the company. My extraordinary performance elated Hai Sahib, who took me to Khuda Buksh. Soon, I found myself in the cordial grip of Khuda Buksh, who said, "You did a wonderful job, you are a very prospective fellow." It was thus when I was introduced to him, and we had a hearty discussion afterwards. He said, "You join straight to EFU." What difference does it make to have or leave an upper division job of Tk. 200 [$42] per month under the central government?

Some days later, I was waiting in front of the Bardhaman house for a bus or a rickshaw. It was raining. All of a sudden, a Volkswagen stopped before me. The door opened; Khuda Buksh overhung his head and called me by the name "Siddiquallah Sahib!

---

[17]Former Manager, Jiban Bima Corporation, Dhaka, Bangladesh

Siddiquallah Sahib! Siddiquallah Sahib! Where will you go? Just get on!" Khuda Buksh was then a godlike fellow to us. We served him greatly. He, too, gave us great honor.

He was driving the car. He allowed me to sit by him. I was living with my family in a tin roofed house at Azimpur. I said to him, "Sir, please drop me at the corner of New Market." He said, "It is not your duty, it is not your lookout. Since I am driving the car, it is my duty." He dropped me exactly in front of the gate of my residence and said, "One day I will come and talk to your wife." That day, I was really surprised. A man like Khuda Buksh speaks to me like this! From that very day, I puzzled my head, thinking about whether I will work for Eastern Federal.

Meanwhile, the central government gave me a promotion and made residential arrangements for me at the Azimpur colony. Later, I was transferred to Karachi. Many at Eastern Federal got the news. Both Hai Sahib and Kashem Sahib hailed from Comilla. I had a few meetings with them about this. Some men of my acquaintance said to me, "Why would you quit a central government job? The Ayub Khan government has provided you with a quarter, you will get an allowance and other facilities," et cetera.

In the meantime, on 1 May 1968, I was released from the Dhaka office, and I was given Tk. 5,500 as travel allowance for going to Karachi. In this situation, I bought my tickets, made the necessary arrangements, and went to my village home to take leave of them, my dearest and nearest ones. In my absence, Khuda Buksh Sahib did not sit idle. One day he, along with Hai Sahib and Ahmed Ali Sahib, appeared at my house. My wife entertained them with white pilaf and king sized *Koi* (a variety of fish famous for deliciousness when fried).

Khuda Buksh, in the meantime, convinced my wife, telling her that Siddiquallah Sahib would not have to do any work. "We'll just give him Tk. 500 [$105] per month from the company. What he has to do is give his consent, putting his signature on a paper." Seeing Khuda Buksh and hearing his confirming speeches, my wife was mentally prepared to accept his proposal. Besides, as Mr. Hai and Mr. Ahmed Ali both hailed from Comilla, personalizing my wife was a bit easier.

In such a situation, I quit my government job. I got my appointment at Eastern Federal on 1 May 1968. I became a development officer.

Khuda Buksh Sahib was deeply affectionate towards me. He supervised my task and gave me necessary cooperation from time to time. Having made an account at year's end, it was revealed that after making salaries the year round, the office still owed me Tk. 11,000. Khuda Buksh Sahib then asked me whether I intended to have a promotion. But some of my friends advised me not to take the promotion right now. He, however, arranged for my salary increase.

My job at Eastern Federal was a stage of outstanding success. Khuda Buksh Sahib took great care of me, and he used to give me necessary instructions at different times. One day, he called me in his chamber; in addition to salary, he gave me a lump sum of Tk. 22,000 [$4,622] in cash. What is more, he gave me a promotion and made me the chief development officer. Then there were three chief development officers in Pakistan, me, Majid Sahib and someone else (whose name I have forgotten).

Later, I got a promotion and was made the agency manager, and a car was allotted to me. A Toyota car then cost approximately Tk. 20,000 to 30,000 [$4,200 to $6,300]. But I could not own the car, because in the meantime, the war of independence began. Firing took place at East Pakistan Rifles (EPR, currently Bangladesh Rifles) gate. Considering my living in Dhaka quite unsafe, I moved my family members from Azimpur to my uncle's residence at Mugdapara. From there, I moved to my village home. For nine months, I was there at home, and after independence, I returned to Dhaka.

After independence of Bangladesh, Jiban Bima Corporation was established. Those who were very cunning and foxy at that time divided the corporation among themselves. When the country was still Pakistan, I was agency manager, and my salary was Tk. 1,200 per month [$252]. We thought that since the country had become independent, our position in the country would be decided as per rule. We were the salesmen. All people in East and West Pakistan knew us well. But we could hardly realize how a handful of cunning guys – much junior to us in service position – became directors.

When Khuda Buksh Sahib departed from Eastern Federal, we wept for him. Many workers in the office cried for him on the day of his departure. To us, no pain was greater than this. I think Khuda Buksh Sahib has left behind manifold examples in the insurance industry which are still followed by many.

Harunur Rashid Sahib was above me in position. When he and Abdus Samad Sahib became the members of the Diabetic Society, they invited me every year during election to deliver a speech about them.

But for the sympathetic cooperation of Mr. Khuda Buksh and Mr. Hai, my present name and fame in Dhaka would be hardly possible. Currently, I am a life member of Bangladesh Diabetic Society, Red Crescent Society, Bangladesh Cancer Society, and many other institutions. Besides, I am general secretary of greater Comilla Samity, President of Chadpur District Samity. Again, I have been occupying big positions in many other institutions. And all these have been possible thanks to the sympathetic cooperation of big people like Khuda Buksh Sahib, Hai Sahib, and Ahmed Ali Sahib.

At that time, we generally had to deal with cases worth Tk. 2000 to 3000. Khuda Buksh Sahib had an extraordinary good habit. Whenever we gained a good policy holder, he called us in his chamber then and there and thanked us cordially. He also called in Siddiquallah Sahib (me), Ahmed Ali Sahib, and others.

I have performed Hajj twice; I have allowed my father to do the same. During Hajj, I have prayed for Khuda Buksh Sahib, Ahmed Ali Sahib, and Hai Sahib. Besides, on special days, I pray for Khuda Buksh Sahib from the depth of my heart. I'll never forget him.

I was not a big officer, but Jiban Bima still bears my name and fame. Many of our times have retired now, yet whenever someone goes to the office, he will certainly be told about Khuda Buksh Sahib and us. This is because we bear no defamation at Jiban Bima and Eastern Federal. We have never oversold or undersold a policy; our sales were always accurate.

I have earned some qualities from Khuda Buksh. We've never treated badly a policy holder, never played false, never told a lie; and we've distributed money profusely. We used to lead a decent life, about which Khuda Buksh Sahib gave us proper guidance all the time. He always reminded us not to speak exaggeratingly. And owing to all of this, we could make a rapid headway in the insurance business. If I could not make progress in insurance then, my children today would have been virtually non-existent.

I don't know who says what today, but it was rare a opportunity to get in close to him, and be dear to him. I am really gladdened to learn that memoirs are going to be published on Khuda Buksh Sahib. Please let me know if I can be of any use in this regard. I feel myself fortunate to be able to do anything for him.

Khuda Buksh: He was the Heart of Life Insurance Business

Nazmul Haq Siddiqui[18]

KHUDA BUKSH HAD great affection for me. I was at the Premier Insurance Company before joining Eastern Federal. At Eastern Federal, I had the pleasure to work under him at two divisions. I was at Rajshahi in 1964. Then I was given a promotion and sent to Chittagong. I was there for a long time.

Truly speaking, Khuda Buksh was the greatest organizer of the country. Insurance is a business of promise of the long term, and it was extremely difficult to organize it. Despite this, he was a great success in this field. He knew how to get things done, and how to love people. He was really a very good person.

He was a trailblazer in organizing insurance in Bangladesh. He properly accomplished the work wherever he put his hand. His hand-picked workers toiled tirelessly to perform the task. There were a large number of field workers and organizers in insurance, and at the zenith was Khuda Buksh. As a man, he was excellent, as he always helped others in performing their tasks. He alienated himself with the low ranking officers and workers.

Khuda Buksh trusted me deeply. He was all agog to fulfill insurance demands of the clients without any delay. I remember such an incident. After the death of an insurance policy holder, Khuda Buksh talked with me over the phone. He told me that the body of the deceased had been brought out of the medical college hospital. He further told me to go immediately to his house to pay the insurance check. In accordance with his instructions, I went to Bajitpur with the dead body, attended

---

[18]Former Deputy General Manager, Jiban Bima Corporation. For details, see Appendix K.

the *janaza* and handed over the insurance check to his family, and returned to my work place.

I consider him an extraordinary success in the field of insurance. As a man, his greatest achievement was strict adherence to rules. In this case, he was really uncompromising.

Even the most successful person on earth is not always respected – there were a host of reasons behind his departing from Eastern Federal. First, he was unable to comply with what they said. Another reason was that some senior officers of EFU wanted him removed in order that they could occupy his position. Again, to the West Pakistani officers, the importance of Khuda Buksh was possibly at a low ebb. I also resigned the very day Khuda Buksh said goodbye to Eastern Federal. I do not think anyone of Eastern Federal had any sacrificing tendency for him.

In the sixth decade, Eastern Federal turned into a leading insurance company of Pakistan, thanks to a single man, and the person was Khuda Buksh. Khuda Buksh supervised the affairs of *Jiban Bima* (life insurance). On the other hand, Bhimjee supervised both Jiban Bima and *Sadharan Bima* (general insurance).

In 1967, I published a book named Jiban Bima. I dedicated the book to Khuda Buksh. I respected him for the fact that he contributed matchlessly to make the honor of the insurance men sky-high. In this field, he was incomparable. In this field of activity, he was above the common level. In fact, in the insurance business of the country, he was the nucleus.

The Unforgettable Khuda Buksh

A.B.M. Nurul Haq[19]

I JOINED EASTERN FEDERAL Union Insurance Company Limited (EFU) in 1964. In that period there were more than 52 insurance companies in Pakistan. Among the prominent companies besides EFU were Muslim Insurance Company, Habib Insurance Company, Khyber Insurance Company, and Homeland Insurance Company.

After appearing for the M.A. examination in Dhaka University, I was working as a teacher at Cantonment School. Seeing the advertisement in the newspaper, I met Khuda Buksh at the EFU regional office at Jinnah Avenue (now Bangabandhu Avenue). No sooner had I sent my slip than I was called. He said to me, "Would you like to do a job? OK, see me at my residence tomorrow." That day was a Sunday, so far as I can recall. His residence was at Eskaton Garden. I met him the next day and he received me very effusively. I was overwhelmed with his cordiality. I was served light refreshment in a really hospitable manner. Later he said to me, "I can provide you with a job here or even in a bank. Now, which one do you prefer?"

May be, for some reason, he liked me. It was a big thing for an insurance personality to collect a man of ability and he had the qualities to do so. The Muslims had little interest in coming to the insurance profession. But just as the hunter knows where the prey is, and how to catch it, so did Mr. Khuda Buksh know how to select the fittest person. He brought many Bengalis to the insurance profession in that period. He managed to give big posts to many Bengalees in West Pakistan. He could realize the qualities of a man at every outset.

I thought, since he was there, it would be better for me to work there. I gave vent to my feelings to him. He appointed me as a special representative at the

---

[19]Managing Director, Global Insurance Ltd, Dhaka, Bangladesh. For details, see Appendix K.

development branch. I tried my best but the work did not suit me. I then told him to work elsewhere in the office. A week later he brought me to office as a junior officer. I started working in this way.

I stayed with him from then. I took preparations for Civil Service examination. He said, "You stay here. It will be better for you." I stayed on. Now I see it was a wise decision. Those who became secretaries are now retired, and they are now looking for jobs. But I am free from such tension. Within two years I got a promotion and at the time of my next promotion he told me, "I am not in a position to give you promotion this year; I will see what I can do next year." Such was my relation of affection with him.

In 1969, he departed from the EFU following conflict of opinions with the office authorities. It was his lifelong goal to establish Bengalis. He took many people to Karachi. He became General Manager of EFU. It was indeed a big post for a Bengali. I was then at a much lower position. I think that he was removed from the office following a conflict with the authorities, and the conflict resulted from his affinity with the Bengalis, which the West Pakistanis vehemently disliked.

As a matter of fact, a situation was created, and it made him compelled to depart from EFU. It was actually a conflict between Bengalees and non-Bengalees. When he was thinking about his future plans after leaving EFU, I used to visit his Dhanmondi residence. In fact, I respected him very much. Sometimes, when he took me somewhere, he introduced me thus: "This is a son of mine." It is still bright in my memory.

He started a new company named Federal Life and General Insurance Company Limited. The office was at 4 Bangabandhu Avenue (former Jinnah Avenue). I frequently visited him at his office. He used to say, "If it is disclosed that you visit my office, you will be dismissed." I replied, "There is nothing to worry. I won't serve there; I am going to work here."

I came out of EFU suddenly. It was around April, May 1969. He said, "What's up?" I said, "Sir, I have given up my job." He said, "Is it so? OK, I see what can be done." So saying, he let me sit in his office. But I was still in the dark about the name of the post, salary, et cetera. It was in fact the result of my natural and spontaneous obedience to him. Not only I, but many others had this obedience.

One month later, he made me the company secretary. I was only 26 or 27 years old, but it was a big post. After appointing me to the post, he said, "You are the Walajahi of Federal Life." S.A. Walajahi was then EFU's secretary. He compared me with him. This is how he motivated people and brought to light their instinctive qualities. The relationship between us came to such a stage that whatever he did, he let me know. He used to say, "You have come at my old age."

In 1971, my residence was at Azimpur, and he lived at Dhanmondi. Because of an unfavorable situation, he stayed in the office only for a short time. On his way back from the office, he took me to his car and dropped me at Azimpur.

He used to say many things about the situations of the country. The Kali temple at racecourse was demolished by the westerners. He said, "See, they won't last long. What they are doing are wrong."

I can recall an incident. Ataur Rahman Kahan was the chairman of Federal Life & General Insurance Company Limited. By July, August 1971, Tikka Khan's forces arrested him. Khuda Buksh then went to Tikka Khan to get the release of Ataur Rahman Kahan. What I want to mean is that he had incredible boldness. It was a period when it required extraordinary guts for a Bangalee to meet a Pakistani military officer to recommend a Bangalee's release.

Federal Life & General Insurance Company Limited functioned well up to 26 March 1972. After that, all the insurance companies were nationalized. He was the director of Jatiya Bima Corporation. I was made officer-in-charge of the corporation.

On the fourteenth of May, 1973, the Government appointed him as the Managing Director of the newly formed Jiban Bima Corporation. I was given the post of secretary. After the independence of Bangladesh, insurance workers raised undue financial demands in many institutions. Even at Jiban Bima, an opportunist group raised their heads. There was a movement against Khuda Buksh, too. Maybe he was trying to do something the workers disliked. Moreover, there were conflicts among groups that contributed to the movement.

He was at Jiban Bima for less than a year. The government was looking for a new face to tackle the situation. Mr. Moyeedul Islam was the managing director of Pakistan Insurance Corporation. After his return from Pakistan, he was made MD, and Khuda Buksh was released. This was mentally shocking for him. I have always thought about how it happened. I think he was so profoundly involved in insurance that he could not think of anything other than insurance. Detachment from insurance was indeed unbearable for him.

Moreover, those whom he provided with jobs, whom he gave support, also went against him. This also pained him much. Occasionally, he talked with me about this.

He knew English well. He also wrote good English. In fact, the root of commercial correspondence is that you must speak through a letter. He used to speak through letters, and it was very effective. In spite of heavy pressure at work, he used to come to my table . . . He had extraordinary administrative capability.

Khuda Buksh always wanted everyone to make money and be well off. People nowadays are reluctant to do good to others. But he was quite opposite to this. Sometimes, he asked somebody straightforwardly, "Have you bought a house?"

He arranged the marriage of many girls. He used to be on the lookout for suitable boys for marriageable daughters of his friends and relatives. And whenever he found one, he married her off with the boy. He had some extraordinary qualities. I was fortunate enough to learn many things from him. I am also highly successful in insurance business, and he had considerable contribution in this regard.

He helped his boyhood teacher and village people a lot. Every year, that teacher would come to his residence and stayed there for over a month. To bring up a man, to socialize him – these things he did with seriousness. He used to take me to the Rotary Club meetings. This meant he wanted me to grow up. Later on, I also became a Rotarian. Interestingly, he was known to so many people that it was a wonder. Occasionally, he made steamer journey for official work. All the passengers knew him well, and those who are still alive remember him. It is really surprising – more so because he was not a political figure.

He had good relationships with journalists. Each year, on the occasion of Bengali New Year's Day, he invited VIPs along with veteran journalists at his residence. I also attended many times. I also took part in arrangements. Persons like Abdus Salam of *Observer*, Moinul Hossain of *Ittefaq*, Zahur Hossain Chowdhury of *Sangbad*, A.B.M. Musa, Kamal Lohani, and many other veteran journalists used to attend. Only Bengali dishes were served. With his death on the thirteenth of May, 1974, this yearly occasion, too, has come to a close.

Insurance is Unimaginable Without Khuda Buksh

Hossain Mir Mosharraf[20]

"We cannot dedicate-we cannot consecrate-we cannot
Hollow this ground. The brave men, living
And dead, who struggled here, have consecrated
It far above our poor power to add or detract."
[From Abraham Lincoln's Gettysburg speech]

ICON AND WIZARD of life insurance, the father of life insurance, and crownless king of life insurance of then East Pakistan, Khuda Buksh Sahib (1912-1974) was a man of charismatic personality. He lived all his life under three standards: the Union Jack of British India, the moon-and-star-studded Pakistan flag, and the red and green flag of Bangladesh. His life began from Damodya, a green shady village under Shariatpur district where birds sang and cuckoos cooed. This was Khuda Buksh, an ever-smiling guy of uncommon magnanimity. Khuda Buksh's contribution to the insurance industries of India, Pakistan, and Bangladesh was matchless and was regarded as a legend. He made history and secured his place in history; "Khuda Buksh" and "life insurance" are tantamount.

In his eventful working life (1935-1973), Khuda Buksh came into close association with five insurance companies:

---

[20]Former General Manager (Administration and Public Relations) Jiban Bima Corporation. For details, see Appendix K.

- Oriental Government Security Life Assurance Company
- Eastern Federal Union Insurance Company
- Federal Life and General Assurance Company
- Jatiya Jiban Bima Corporation
- Jiban Bima Corporation

There was a time when the game of football was tantamount to Mohammedan, "newspaper" meant *The Azad*, and life insurance was another name for Khuda Buksh. In those days, people ridiculed insurance agents as brokers. People were even unwilling to marry their daughters with them. It was exactly in such a moment that he took insurance as a profession. It was then British India. After partition, he popularized life insurance among the East Pakistani intellectuals and educated section of people. It was he who transformed insurance into a respectable profession.

My career began at Homeland Insurance Company. Its office was at 37 Jinnah Avenue. Later, I joined EFU on 1 May 1963. It was at Dienfa Bhaban, 7 Jinnah Avenue.

It was a great fortune for me that at EFU, I started working under Khuda Buksh's direct supervision from the very outset. This was why I had the rare opportunity to see him closely. The endless riches of his life have completely drenched my heart.

Just as the sea could not be put into a water pitcher, so in such a limited scope, the vast story of a simplistic yet colorful, multidimensional Khuda Buksh could not be completely told.

Before independence, as many as thirty-seven insurance companies worked in the country. But it was generally said that EFU was the largest insurance company in Asia after Japan. The saying was virtually a slogan. EFU was undoubtedly a big company.

There was another saying that every second man insured in Pakistan is insured with EFU. There is no denying the fact that EFU was one of the largest insurance companies in the subcontinent. Though EFU turned into a insurance giant, it had little difference in planning with other insurance companies. In fact, the man who made the difference was Mr. Khuda Buksh.

It is still a surprise to think what an extraordinarily tactful insurer he was! On many occasions, I have seen him selling off an insurance proposal form in the course of talking. For example, he asked someone, "Well, how do you spell your name?" And he used to write it himself on the form. And sometimes it was seen that the form had been filled up in the course of discussion. He told the client only to put his signature on it. And sometimes, he himself paid the premium and told the client to pay it later.

He often visited other district towns on official duties. On such occasions, he would host gorgeous tea parties. People from the elite to the university teachers and students used to attend. And from here, he took many to the insurance business. To grow interest among them regarding insurance, he would sometimes give them an amount of money as an advance or give them a large amount for buying a car. These he did to invite interest among people regarding the insurance business.

He really was a humanist. He had great empathy for people. He kept himself informed about the family affairs, even those of the field officers.

His chamber was at the first floor of Dianfa Bhaban, 7 Jinna Avenue (now Bangabandhu Avenue). Once, a day laborer came to his chamber with a basket in hand. He had a tattered *lungi* (akind of loin-cloth) on his person. It was apparent that he was a poverty stricken guy. Khuda Buksh's personal staff tried to drive the guy away. Hearing the hue and cry, Khuda Buksh came out and heard the guy patiently. When he heard that the poor man needed a lungi and a basket, he took out some money from his pocket and handed him the money.

Once, I went to Karachi for an EFU training. Khuda Buksh was then working in Karachi as the manager (life), EFU. And he would go to Rawalpindi for business promotion. He had extremely busy schedule and would fly to Rawalpindi the next day. In spite of such a press of works, he arranged for us a full course dinner at night at the five star Karachi Intercontinental. We sat on the "Top of the Roof" [restaurant]. Khuda Buksh served dishes with his own hands. On the way back, he gave heavy tips to drivers. On his return from Rawalpindi, he took me to various places whenever he had time. Sometimes at Clifton beach, another day at Karachi Rotary Club, the other day at Karachi Boat Club or Sindh Club. I noticed that like in East Pakistan, he was equally popular in West Pakistan.

One day, Khuda Buksh took me to Savar to see a plot of land belonging to his friend. The plot was surrounded with barbed wire. The caretaker lived at a tin shed in the middle. Suited, booted Khuda Buksh sat down on the *hogla* (mat). I was astonished. On the way back, he bought five kilograms of *pantoa* (bell shaped sweet-meat) and *roshogolla* (a sweet and juicy drop made of curd and flour). I said to him, "Sir, what will you do with so much sweets?" Khuda Buksh replied smilingly, "Shouldn't I give you two kilograms?" Later, he bought some more for the driver also. Incidentally, I can say that there are plenty of cars in Dhaka today. But it was not so in the past. Khuda Buksh's car was an eye-catcher. It was a huge car with a giant bonnet. It was a Mercedes Benz, and so far as I can recall, the number was 7733. There was a scintillating star burning brightly over the bonnet, made of hardened steel.

And so was the personality of Khuda Buksh, as if made of hardened steel. When the question of principal came, he never budged; he was uncompromising, unmoving, and unfaltering. He could only be compared to an unsheathed sword that will break but not bend. On the question of principal, he could steadfastly and resolutely give up all the advantages and hug uncertainty, whatever the consequences. And the uncertain path itself reinstated him again and again. And destiny let him meet the people. And the people were his vast insurance workers and field force. He was a fluent speaker; he fascinated a vast audience with his mesmerizing speech. And everyone listened with a pin-drop silence. Statistics were there in his speech, but it never sounded boring. His mode of speaking was polished.

Once, it happened that Rajshahi divisional manager M.A. Sattar (martyred in the war of liberation) was not on speaking terms with Khuda Buksh. It was out of vanity on the part of M.A. Sattar. And the news was passing around that Mr. M.A. Sattar would depart from EFU and join another company. Khuda Buksh decided that he would eliminate his (M.A. Sattar's) vanity without even uttering a word. And what is more, he would not let him leave EFU. Khuda Buksh went to Rajshahi, and he took me as his companion. From Dhaka, we flew to Ishwardi. A car from the Rajshahi office came, and it took us to Rajshahi. We stayed at the Rajshahi Circuit House. Khuda Buksh said to me, "You meet M.A. Sattar's wife without delay and tell her that I have been suffering from indigestion. So, I won't take any food cooked at the Circuit House. And you tell *bhabi* (M.A. Sattar's wife) to send gruel-rice and *magur*-fish (a variety of cat fish)

We did not see Sattar Sahib for a while. At lunch hour, we saw him at the Circuit house. His tiffin carrier was filled to capacity with food. Both Khuda Buksh and M.A. Sattar were smiling. And the period of vanity was over. Mr. M.A. Sattar stayed at EFU.

He often told a story regarding meeting insurance demands. Someone has jumped from the fifteenth story of a building with a view to committing suicide. He has an insurance. The check of his insurance will be handed to him through the windows before his body touches the ground. Though it is a joke, the reality is that on many occasions, I have seen Khuda Buksh hand over the check of the deceased person at his residence before his burial. I also have seen him hand over the check at the graveyard.

In the then Pakistan, all the documents of insurance were in English. It was he who first took the initiative of transforming those into Bengali. He gave me the task of rendering those papers into Bengali, which I tried to perform responsibly.

He also gave much emphasis on training, which other companies did not do. He made Mr. A.F.M. Safiyyullah (son of Dr. Md. Sahidullah) training advisor for the training of the field inspectors. Besides, he brought Mr. P.M. Rebello, a reputed insurance personality of India, for the training of East Pakistani insurance workers. In those days, there were no university courses on insurance.

Because of the rise of Bengali nationalism, EFU's managing director, Mr. Roshen Ali Bhimjee, became dependent on West Pakistani officers. Consequently, he became alienated from Khuda Buksh, mentally. This is why Khuda Buksh left EFU and formed Federal Life and General Assurance Company.

At the time of leaving EFU, Khuda Buksh was the general manager (life) and Mr. S.M. Moinuddin was general manager (general). After independence, all insurance companies were merged, and several companies were formed, namely Surma Jiban Bima Corporation and Rupsa Jiban Bima Corporation. General Insurance corporation were transformed into Tista and Karnofuli. The mother organization, Jatiya Bima Corporation, had four directors, of whom Khuda Buksh was one.

However, a few companies like ALICO then worked in East Pakistan. Even after independence, they continued their business here. And the government did not nationalize them. Foreign general insurance companies, however, were nationalized. In fact, the companies left out by Pakistanis were nationalized by the Bangladesh government. Mentionable foreign insurance companies were ALICO (USA), Prudential Insurance Company (UK), and Norwich Union Insurance Company (UK). In the face of the unjust demands of a section of workers, Khuda Buksh was removed from the post of managing director of Jiban Bima. In his place, Mr. Moyeedul Islam was given the appointment. An able-bodied person, virtually the legend of insurance, had to go in this way. It shocked him deeply. It was indeed a painful experience for him. In fact, he departed from EFU because of idealistic differences. He left Jiban Bima for the same reason.

Each year, on the first day of the Bengali new year, he arranged lunch for the journalists. Most were Bangalee dishes. Among the items were vegetables, *bharta* (dish of boiled vegetables, fish etc kneaded to soft, moist mass and mixed with spices), *shutki* (driedfish), *rui, katla, pangas* (kind of very large fish), *pabda* (a particular species of fish; *callichurus pabda*), lobster, curd, sweets, cheese and what not! On many occasions, I helped him arrange the lunch. The occasion turned into a bond of friendship among journalists. The first two letters, K and B, are needed to write the name Khuda Buksh. Many called him simply Khuda Buksh. Many on their first visit to EFU asked, "Is Khuda Buksh in?" I have heard that even his sons called him Khuda Buksh. This naturally created a sense of laughter, which he seemed to enjoy to his heart's content. He indeed was a loving father. He had considerable zeal for education. He, however, had little time to study a variety of subjects. His constant thinking was about the development of insurance.

Once, a discussion took place between Khuda Buksh and myself regarding Shakespeare, the great English playwright. He said:

> French author Victor Hugo and his son were once banished on a sea shore. Hugo said to his son, 'How would we spend so many days here?' The son replied, 'By seeing the beauty of the sea.' When asked by the son how Hugo would spend his time, Hugo replied that he would spend twelve years by reading Shakespeare. In fact, the sea is a prime subject in Shakespeare's writings. He often quoted from Shakespeare, "Life is a tale told by an idiot, full of sound and fury, signifying nothing."

He provided a lot of people with jobs. He also arranged the marriage of many girls. He was a member of the Dhaka Rotary Club. It was then extremely difficult to become a Rotarian. The general rule was that only one person could be a Rotarian from one profession, and the insurance profession was represented by Khuda Buksh.

A subsequent direction from Rotary headquarters, USA, came that two members might be taken, one from insurance (life) and the other from insurance (general). Golam Mowla's (later became MD of Sadharan Bima Corporation) becoming a Rotarian.

He could write and read excellent English and Bengali. He used simple words. So, nobody needed to use the dictionary. His English was equally as smart as he. In fact, Khuda Buksh was not only a name, he was a symbol of honesty, sincerity, devotion, and patriotic zeal. We can very well call him an institution. He arranged the livelihood of thousands of people. He turned many unemployed young men into self-dependent guys. It was Khuda Buksh's untiring efforts that made many people owners of houses and cars. He lit the light of hope among the despondent. He helped bring to light the inner man. He was by far one of the best examples of humanity and unparalleled in magnanimity.

Man was the focus of his spirit and all his activities. And love of man was the central philosophy of his life. His Dhanmondi residence was virtually an orphanage. Most of the poor relatives frequently visited his residence. He provided Mr. Ainuddin Ahmed, his boyhood teacher, with a financial grant all through his life. I heard later after the death of Khuda Buksh, Ainuddin Sahib used to visit Khuda Buksh's Dhaka residence and stay for over a month at a time.

Khuda Buksh's range of public relationships was extensive and simply vast. He had unhindered communications in all areas of the society. I have seen many veteran politicians visit his place. Not only that, many artists, litterateurs, journalists, intellectuals, and social workers visited his house.

I cannot exactly remember the day and date. I can only recall that it was a day of the '60s. Khuda Buksh took me to M.A. Hassan building at Jinnah Avenue. He went there for an important piece of business. After finishing, he came to the first floor. And the Alpha Insurance Company office was there. Alpha had general insurance business. The East Pakistan head of the company was Sheikh Mujibur Rahman. He was not yet "Bangabandhu." Gazi Ghulam Mustafa (subsequently chairman, Bangladesh Red Cross) was his Personal Secretary (PS). The PS opened the door of the chamber. Khuda Buksh entered. I followed him. Sheikh Mujibur Rahman stood up and shook hands with Khuda Buksh. They exchanged greetings. They talked. At one stage, Khuda Buksh stood up to bid adieu. Sheikh Mujib said, "I can't let you go just now. Lunch will be served from the house. And you must take lunch with me." I still remember the moment. Fine rice, fried bitter gourd, magur fish, thickly cooked "mug" dal, curd, and porridge were served.

Once, I was flying to Chittagong with Khuda Buksh in a Fokker Friendship plane. It was half-an-hour's journey. Finding him lonely, I told him to say something about his philosophy of life. Khuda Buksh said to me, smiling, "Why do you want to know? Do you like to write something about me?" I smiled and said, "You should write your autobiography." Khuda Buksh started writing his autobiography, but the task was unfinished.

I was then the editor of the *Field Force* magazine of EFU. Khuda Buksh's autobiography was being published in that magazine for some time. But unfortunately, he was busier than the busiest, and as such the publication stopped one time. I still bear the brunt of this failure. However, the weather was rough, the plane was flying at full speed, and Khuda Buksh started to say about the philosophy of his life. He quoted from the Bible, "Life means love, love has patience, love is kindness, love never envies, never boasts, never treats badly, never self-seeks, never becomes angry. Love glorifies truth, tolerates everything. Love is willing to trust everyone, hopeful of everything and remains static at every stage. Love never ends." I remembered, I listened to him virtually spellbound.

When people got insured with EFU, they used to say, "I got insured with Khuda Buksh." Actually, EFU meant Khuda Buksh, Khuda Buksh meant EFU.

Khuda Buksh was the dream merchant. He created dreams among people; he created the dream of a bright future, of a happy, peaceful life of golden days. And people bought insurance with the expectation that insurance money would bring their dream to reality. And how painstakingly eager he was to provide the service of insurance at everyone's doorstep! He frequently wrote personal letters to policy holders, reminding them to pay the premium in time. He behaved as if the policy holders were the members of his family. In his colorful life, Khuda Buksh got the blessings of many orphans and widows, as many of them were saved from imminent danger with the money obtained from insurance. Girls from poor families were married off, boys got higher education, and ill luck reversed with the insurance money, got unexpectedly like a sudden flare of light.

Khuda Buksh's sense of humor was unbelievably sharp, his wit matchless. Once, I asked Khuda Buksh in a lonely moment, "Why did you come to the world of insurance?" Smilingly, Khuda Buksh replied, "If you ask, I have no answer, but if you don't, I know the answer." Hardly have I seen such a modern and smart guy. He was impossibly affectionate. He was good as a man, good as a neighbor, good as a father, and good as a husband. He was modest, calm, and steadfast. Nowadays, a gentleman is a rarity. He was polite from head to foot, from top to toe. A gentleman can disagree without being disagreeable, and he was a fine example of this. His childlike, smiling face sometimes reminded me of the Semitic Masseur.

Khuda Buksh gave everything to everyone, without any expectation in return. If the history of insurance be put in black and white in this land of Bangladesh, covering an area of one lac forty thousand kilometers, the name of Khuda Buksh must be written not in letters of gold but in letters of platinum. Khuda Buksh was virtually the lighthouse of our insurance industry. Just as Hamlet cannot be imagined without the price of Denmark, so insurance is unimaginable without Khuda Buksh.

I still remember his last days. He was ailing and bedridden at a cabin at the Dhaka Medical College Hospital. I saw him there along with reputed editor-journalist Mothhar Hossain Siddiqui. Former Prime Minister Tajuddin Ahmed had met him a few moments earlier. We met him at the hospital. Khuda Buksh said to us that just after getting well, he would arrange a lunch at his residence for the journalists. He also told us to prepare a list of the expected guests and show it to him. Motahar Hossain Siddiqui was then at the public relations section of Jaban Bima Corporation. He was once the regional director of EFU's public relations. He is no more now.

Hearing of the death-news of Khuda Buksh, a journalist said, "He was our banyan tree." That banyan tree left us forever, quite unexpectedly, on 13 May 1974. The big shady banyan tree, the symbol of ultimate reliability is gone. He was an optimist. He never broke down. Even in the midst of great hopelessness and despair, he was an optimist. Even in the event of his physical breakdown, he was an optimist. Death has taken him away, but his inspiration remains. Such optimism would be the lifeblood of the future generation.

Epitaph

As long as the sun will rise
And the moon will shed its ray,
We will never forget Khuda Buksh
Not even for a day.

– Hossain Mir Musharraf

Every Moment he Thought of Nothing Except Insurance

A.J. Mehman[21]

ONCE *THE MILLAT* magazine was being published from the courthouse street. I was then working as an apprentice there. One day, somebody took me to Muslim Insurance Company. I frequented that office for some days. In course of time, I often heard the names of EFU and Khuda Buksh, wherever I went. Everybody seemed to know everything about Khuda Buksh. It appeared that Khuda Buksh was a household name.

One day, a friend of mine told me that he would buy an insurance policy from EFU. Then I talked to Khuda Buksh about this matter over the telephone. I introduced myself and also expressed that I was interested to work in his company, and it would be of great help if he would be kind enough get my friend insured. He assured me and took necessary particulars from me. The next morning, Mr. M. A. Rahim driving a Morris Minor, came to Fazlul Haque Hall where I was staying. I introduced myself and took agency from him. Thus my work in insurance started. As far as I remember it happened in 1954.

After a few days, I first met Mr. Khuda Buksh. Later I found that insurance policies were being bought one after another. But another thing took place. Somebody else took my commission. I was deeply upset at the incident. One day I met Zainul Abedin, an income tax advocate. He took me at the American Life Insurance Company (ALICO) and helped me to complete few life insurance policies. That is, he completed a few life insurance policies with the people whose favor I solicited

---

[21]Editor, the *Bank-Bima,* Dhaka Bangladesh. For details se appendix K.

for insurance. I insured Mr. Hamidul Haque Chowdhury's life (Owner *the Pakistan Observer*/then Foreign Minister of Pakistan) and got about two to three thousand taka [$420 to $630] from that source. I bought a rickshaw and made private and I continued to work for the ALICO up to 1966. Later, I became secretary general of American Life Field Officer's Association.

ALICO built an office at Motijheel Commercial area in 1966. Some of the agents thought that we might be given some space to do our office work. But the management told us that there would be no development office. We were very disappointed, and a group of us resigned from ALICO. At the same time, we realized that it was evidently wrong for us to work for a foreign company like ALICO. After my resignation, I met Khuda Buksh, he told me to work at EFU, and employed me as an agency manager as I held that position in ALICO.

Khuda Buksh was then the general manager of EFU for all Pakistan. He worked hard day and night. He employed a good number of workers, and he managed good manners. He carefully avoided whatever might cause a jolt in the minds of those with whom he had to work. His main objective was to flourish in the insurance business.

I have had little conflict with Khuda Buksh. Once I lost several businesses, one after another. I let him know this. He said, "You'll continue to gain and lose in business, throughout your life. This is the reality. Go ahead, nothing to worry."

He had considerable contribution to the rise of Mr. M.A. Samad. Mr. Samad was the life manager of Great Eastern Insurance Company. Khuda Buksh brought him. He even gave him his personal car. This took me by surprise. Khuda Buksh wanted that everyone of his company be solvent enough to buy cars and houses. And this would make him feel proud. To him it was an incongruity that he himself would drive a big car, and his workforce would look at it hopelessly.

This was my personal assumption, that I will be able to do good in the field. And he admired my extraordinary ability of dashing-pushing. He also made me a member of Dhaka Club. It was his realization that I had a very good circle of friends. I had been a member of Dhaka Club from the Pakistani period, and am now a life member. He always thought of the progress of the company. He thought that if a handful of men, say, five persons, be made members of the Dhaka Club, everyone would say that they all belong to Khuda Buksh's company.

Every moment, he thought of nothing except insurance. So far as I can assume, he did not do much about his family. But he bought things while he would visit another house. I have never seen anyone do so but him.

Why Khuda Buksh resigned from EFU – it is still a surprise to me. But some say that in 1967, during the second All Pakistan EFU convocation in Dhaka, something caused a problem there. I do not exactly remember what really happened. His resignation from the EFU came as a surprise to everyone.

After the liberation of Bangladesh, he called me to join the newly formed Surma Jiban Bima Corporation, thinking that I would be able to give it a life by dint of my moral courage and dexterity. And when Jiban Bima Corporation was formed, he became the first managing director of the Jiban Bima Corporation. He selected me as in-charge of group insurance division. During this time I had direct contact with him. After that we became very close. He had a particular fondness for me. And I. too, had a deep sense of regard for him. He used to perform all group work, group payment and accounting through me.

He was a very social-minded person. He used to attend that *namaj-e-janaza* (prayer for salvation of a departed soul before burial of the body of deceased person) of his acquaintance. One day, early in the morning he rang me up and told me that a university teacher had died and he was going to attend his janaza. Later, he told me to send him the money earned through his group insurance. Whenever he found that someone was out of sight for a fairly long period of time, or someone was ill or not paying the premium, he would meet him. In such visits, I accompanied him many times. Sometimes he drove the car himself.

I consider him beyond criticism, whoever ever blamed him or was critical about him, he mixed with him with a vengeance.

Wisaluddin was the chief of ALICO of Pakistan. I also have seen top personalities like Golam Mowla, Moyeedul Islam and others. But never have I seen a formidable insurance personality like Khuda Buksh.

He suddenly realized that he was no longer needed. This possibly hastened his death. Even after his departure from EFU, he could avail himself of the opportunity to establish another company. But in independent Bangladesh, there was no scope for setting up a new company after his release from Jiban Bima Corporation. It would have been proper for him because of his age or ill health. But he had to go when he was still green and vigorous. A workaholic like him was considered superfluous, and verily this was for him the cause of a deep mental shock.

Khuda Buksh:
A Builder of Salesman

Quazi Abdur Rashid[22]

WHEN KHUDA BUKSH joined EFU, the condition of the office was really miserable. EFU's office was then on the first floor of the Provincial Book Depot. It was opposite Victoria Park (now Bahadur Shah Park). The staircase to the second floor could not be accessed directly from the main road; a lane had to be crossed. It was a simple office with very ordinary furniture and little decoration. Some of the employees sat in the room close to the entrance of the office. Apart from this, there were two small rooms, one of which was occupied by Khuda Buksh. He joined as the life manager of East Pakistan branch and started to sit at such an office. From this modest situation, EFU evolved to become the largest and most famous insurance company under the leadership of Khuda Buksh.

When Khuda Buksh, a short stature person became the manager of EFU, not everybody accepted him from the heart. But gradually they realized that Khuda Buksh was a workaholic and that the well being of the company was always uppermost in his mind. This forced them to change their initial opinions.

In Kolkata, Khuda Buksh obtained vast knowledge and experience about the life insurance selling in the field. From his experience, he knew very well how a novice could be transformed into an efficient agent through appropriate training. He did not simply keep knowledge to himself. He shared his knowledge and experience and imparted to the newly recruited agents for their training. That is why I feel that being trained under him was a totally different experience. The matters such as – how

---

[22]Former Chief Development Officer, Jiban Bima Corporation, Dhaka, Bangladesh.

to communicate with a client, how to deal with him, how is his financial position, whether he will be able to run the policy after accepting the proposal – such things had to be studied seriously. What kind of service is to be given after the proposal, also was the subject of training.

At the time of recruiting agents and development officers, he would see the type of their proposals. That is, he evaluated a field agent or an officer by observing whether the agents were going to service holders or businessman. He could identify their standard by scanning the standard of the proposal. Sometimes he allowed a lot of time to agents. He delayed in giving them appointment letters. But it could not be said that he was unnecessarily causing the delay. In fact, he tactfully allowed them time just for the sake of teaching them. Whenever anyone came to his for an appointment letter, he said, "Not today, please come tomorrow; I am busy now," et cetera, et cetera. Actually, he thus studied the agents, analyzed their success or failure and, above all, their patience.

When he found that an agent was failing to do good business or was unable to sell a policy to a client, he wanted to know his problem. The agent then told the real story, "Sir, I am pursuing a client for long, but not being able to 'manage' him," and that was enough to cut the agent's work in half." He would say to the agent, "Okay, you do the program and take me to the client."

I have seen many such incidents. An agent was expecting that if Khuda Buksh accompanied him, the client would buy a policy worth Tk. 10,000 [$2,100] at the best. Surprisingly, a policy worth Tk.100,000 to 200,000 [$21,000 to $42,000] would be sold. His acquaintances were so large and he knew so many people that it was really astonishing. I myself was once pursuing a client for two years. In spite of the best of my ability, I failed to make him buy a policy. The client was financially solvent. The client was tantalizing me. I was then in the horns of a dilemma. When such was the situation, one day I told Khuda Buksh everything. He said, "Okay, you take me to him one day."

After making an appointment, I took him to the client's house. After introduction, Khuda Buksh started talking about everything from family affairs to illness. The conversation continued with cups of tea, without mentioning anything about insurance. I was almost run down when at a point Khuda Buksh said to me, "Oh, your policy."

The client's father was bedridden upstairs, completely paralyzed. We went upstairs to see his father. He was old, and his age would not allow him to buy a policy. He said, "Let my son buy a policy." Khuda Buksh said to me, "Make an account of a policy worth taka two lakhs [$42,000]." At last, the gentleman had a policy amounting to taka eighty thousand [$16,800]. Along with that, he gave us a check for premium. It happened in 1965. In this way, he helped many agents get business success, and he never claimed any credit for the same.

Khuda Buksh had a completely different approach whenever he contacted people. He had an extraordinary convincing capacity. He paid death claims of policies unhesitatingly. Whenever, a death claim came, he waived many things as soon as possible. He tried to pay the money quickly. In this regard he always said, "Never show any excuse when the question of paying the claim arises. A man has run the policy throughout his life. He is dead now. If, in such a critical situation, the family does not get the money, no one will buy any insurance policy in future."

During the 1967 convention, a conflict ensued between Roshan Ali Bhimjee and Khuda Buksh. It grew up eventually. The crux of the question was about investment in East Pakistan. EFU was reluctant to invest in East Pakistan, because Roshan Ali Bhimjee opposed such an investment. Bhimji Sahib also intervened in the field of some appointments. Khuda Buksh was unyielding, and consequently the distance between Roshan Ali Bhimjee was widening. Later, it was seen that Bhimjee Sahib was taking various decisions without letting Khuda Buksh know it. In such a situation, Khuda Buksh went to West Pakistan. He sent me a small slip with a bearer. In it, he wrote, "I'm going to retire."

Khuda Buksh did not resign. It will be wrong to say that he resigned. He actually retired. There were difference of opinions between Bhimjee Sahib and Khuda Buksh, and it was to some extent disregarded. When he first joined EFU, then the collection of premium amounted to taka three or four lakhs [$63,000 or $84,000]. He was able to raise it to over taka one crore [$2.1 million] within a year, which was undoubtedly a breakthrough. Khuda Buksh and his field force gave a new life to Eastern Federal, as a result EFU became a household name in Pakistan.

After retiring in Karachi, he returned to Dhaka and started working hastily towards establishing a new company. The company's prospectus was printed at the Paramount press. The owner of the press, Badal, was my close friend. The prospectus was printed within a very short time. There appeared a problem as to the bank deposit. The bank was unwilling to give clearance because of the shortage of Tk. 5,000. Khuda Buksh rang me up and said, "There is a shortage; what now?" One month before the incident, I deposited an amount with a view to buying a plot at Baridhara. I surrendered the application and got back the money and gave Khuda Buksh that amount. The directors of the company were: Ashraf Ali Chowdhury, M.A. Hassan, A.R. Khan, M.A. Rakib, former Minister Wahiduzzaman, Habibur Rahman, Aminur Rahman Khan, M. Ahmed, Ataul Hoq., Iftekharul Alam, and Sahabuddin Ahmed Chowdhury. Ataur Rahman Khan was the chairman.

I have never seen him taking any wrong decision. In official, family, or social matters, he was never seen to have taken any wrong decision. Sometimes, I objected face to face, but ultimately I consented.

I joined his new company even at the cost of a considerable personal loss. Even after that, Kasem Sahib and Mozaffer Sahib came to me many times and insisted me to stay on at EFU. They allured me in many ways. It was not possible on my part to comply with their request. However, there is no denying the fact that Mozaffer Sahib taught me many things.

After opening the new company, Khuda Buksh did not have to face any major obstacle, though there were financial problems. He tried his best to give the company an impressive shape and recruited people needed for the purpose. The anti-Ayub movement in 1969 and non-cooperation movement in 1971 created such an attitude among the Bengalis that they were against working in West Pakistani companies. For this, the new company could recruit people without much difficulty. Among the Khulna groups, one belonged to Habib Insurance Company. Jahangir Sahib left Habib Insurance Company and joined Federal Life with his full group. In this way, Nur Hossain from Rajshahi, Nazimudding from Khustia, M.A. Samad from Rangpur, Mokbul Hossain from Bogra, and Dinajpur joined Federal Life. In spite of being newly established, there was hardly any shortage of manpower in the company. Everyone from to bottom worked very hard to keep the company running. Their hard labor was crowned with success.

After Bangladesh got independence, all insurance companies, including EFU, were nationalized. It is quite natural to quit if somebody finds that he is being subjected to disregard and neglect at the very place where he invested the best part of his life. It appeared to him that it was better for him to depart rather than to remain in his way.

There were few people who went againt Khuda Buksh at EFU. After his departure from EFU, they did not get anything from management worth mentioning. They, however, realized their fault, and they confessed to Khuda Buksh. It is difficult to recollect the painful events after a long time.

Throughout his life, Khuda Buksh faced difficulties with boldness. He knew that life itself is a challenge, and better did he know that both weal and woe are mixed up in human life. The cloud in the sky cannot block the rays of the sun for long. Everyone can find in the border of patches of cloud a sunny lining indicating that sunlight will soon be seen. Khuda Buksh was a student of nature that taught him to rise above all meanness and made him think that every cloud has a silver lining.

May God keep his soul in peace! I

A Creditable Insurance Personality

S.R. Khan[23]

KHUDA BUKSH: THE name is more sufficient. No honorific titles are required to be put before or after the name. In the whole of Pakistan, he was unparalleled in reputation in the field of insurance, and he was simply unmatched. And it is doubtful whether anyone would be able to attain such a spectacular height in the profession in future. In fact, he was a mighty insurance personality – to put in a nutshell. He brought about the renaissance of insurance in the then Pakistan. We, Muslims, have little propensity to save something against a rainy day, let alone buy an insurance. And in an effort to put an end to such averseness, he tried his utmost best. Language fails to express how avidly he worked day and night for the economic emancipation of his countrymen. And he had to stand the toil and moil of life steadfastly and with a smiling face for the sake of doing this. He had to run between the two wings of the country to achieve his objectives, practically like a shuttlecock. He had to stay for a considerable part of his time in London. He wanted to bring sophistication to insurance.

It was his realization that life insurance will get its foothold in the lower section of the society only after it becomes widely popular among the big guns of the day. The educated section of the society have seen that people from other religions have a liking for insurance and as such feel secured by being insured. And the affluent among those get themselves insured and also preach the various benefits of insurance everywhere in order that the common people make the best use of it. I also have seen that the Chief Justice of East Pakistan, S.M. Morshed (deceased) and Chief Secretary Mr. Safiul Azam (deceased) were his bosom friends.

---

[23]Former Managing Director, Sunflower Life Insurance Company Limited, Dhaka, Bangladesh.

The man whose close companionship I deeply remember at this very outset of my career is Khuda Buksh. My fascination for him skyrocketed when, after leaving my government job, I joined EFU and went to him to get my first month's salary. It took me by surprise to see that he gave me double the amount and said that I had left a government job and moreover I had a son, so to lead a happy, peaceful life, I would require a considerable amount. I realized later that he actually bound me in the insurance business with his fascinating charisma. I also understood that a man of insurance business must lead a high life. He always led a high life and inspired us to do the same. To live under his dynamic guidance, to explore and learn, was a life-changing challenge that a man like me will never forget. In this situation, your mind will open and flourish. And he was one of a handful of people who used a Mercedes Benz, a symbol of aristocracy.

In spite of being a top insurer, he always kept close contact with ordinary insurance workers like us. He did not set any regulations to meet him. We used to meet him anytime and discussed freely about various problems. It still takes me by surprise to think that he came to my residence to inspire a young blood like me from as far as Gandaria. This exceptional and extraordinary characteristic of him fascinated all. He actually had a progressive mentality, and he retained an unimaginably vast potential.

An endless flow of events is crowding my mind as I have started to talk in memory of an insurance giant like Khuda Buksh.

Once, my father-in-law came to see him in his office on the first floor. Khuda Buksh sir said to me, "He is senior to me, so it would be better for me to go down to meet him." In fact, my father-in-law was ten years older than him. Perhaps destiny bound them together, and so Khuda Buksh sir passed away on the thirteenth of May, 1974 and my father-in-law died on the first September of the same year – keeping a distance of less than four months. My father-in-law once commented on Khuda Buksh sir, "He can do five to six things at a time."

In the office meeting, Khuda Buksh sir one day said, "I saw S.R. Khan one day at Gulshan going somewhere on a rickshaw, and so I gave him a car; just one year and one day after I started my job." In another meeting, he said, "None has been able to come close to S.R. Khan in selling insurance policies to CSPs."

One day after going to office, I heard that Khuda Buksh sir was looking for me. I went to his chamber immediately. He said, "You have secured the policy of a doctorate amounting to taka three lacs. I myself visited his Bakshi Bazar residence and handed him policy documents. I have also given a forwarding letter. Have you got a copy of the letter?" I said, "No." He at once called the dispatch clerk and said to him, "If you don't know S.R. Khan, go downstairs, and you need not do the job any more." Being very perturbed, I said, "Sir, I have come running to you, and so I haven't got time to see today's letters. The dispatch clerk is not to blame." A line of his letter was as follows, "Dear Dr. Khan, my able colleague S.R. Khan secured a valuable policy on your life."

Maybe more things cram my mind. So far, I can remember the year was 1973 or 1974. Khuda Buksh sir asked me about my maternal uncle. He said, "Is T. Hossain Sahib your maternal uncle? Your own? But you haven't told me anything." T. Hossain was a bosom friend of Abdur Rahman Siddique, a top leader of Bengal's Pan Islamic Movement (he was Governor of East Bengal and Chairman of EFU). Mr. T. Hossain was a man of Bengal Civil Service. I am to some extent shy from the very beginning of my life. My English professor Dr. M.R. Hillah once said, "Your shyness will pay you in long run. You won't be shameless. People will trust you. Insurance business is a business of trust." I said to my sir, "Your word will remain in my mind as an asset."

I can recall another event. I knew a professor cum business magnet who was a super tax payer. Very possible the year was 1967. I made an appointment with him to take Khuda Buksh sir to him. The professor gladly accepted the proposal and, it being the month of Ramadan, invited us to ifter. I actually got into a trouble. It was because I had not yet informed K.B. of the invitation. I came to his office and told him everything. He told me to go to his residence at 6 p.m. The time of ifter was perhaps 7 p.m. I reached his residence in time. I found him surrounded by a large group of people. I reminded him. K.B. said, "I can't eat much. Let us take ifter at my residence and then set out for the house. You give him a ring and intimate him." I did so. I also thought that there was little probability of an insurance. It will only create an atmosphere of botheration. Though we were not held up by a traffic jam (it was rare then), it was already 8:30 p.m. by the time we got there in old Dhaka from Dhanmondi. We found that good number of guests had not yet had their meals, just waiting for us. The "iftar" party began, actually in a slow motion, and continued for a pretty long time. It was already 11:30 p.m., but not a single uttering about insurance. The subject of discussion was Ayub Khan, Justice Ibrahim and so on. I was thinking what would be the benefit of the toilsome visit. I had not a telephone at my residence then. And mobile was only a dream. I was thinking about the anxiety the members of my family will feel because of the unusual delay. I had a son and a daughter at that time. And I was unaccustomed to staying out of home for long.

After 11:30 p.m., Khuda Buksh sir all of a sudden told the professor, "Show me your matric certificate." And at the same time he told me, "You write a good hand, so copy it." Photocopy was not in vogue then. I don't think my handwriting is very good. Incidentally, I can say that Khuda Buksh's handwriting was very nice, matchless. I was copying, and in the meantime, Khuda Buksh took a proposal form from me. On the blank space above, he wrote about two plans, one short term and one long term, five lacs [$105,000] each. He also wrote about half yearly premium, put his signature on it, and handed over the form to me for assessment. I did so. He then told the professor to write a crossed check in the name of EFU. The professor took out the check from the party drawer. It appeared to me that he was hypnotized or mesmerized. I returned home with a mixed feeling of anxiety and pleasure.

It must be mentioned here that insurance was Khuda Buksh's profession, as well as dedication. He used to take me to many places, and this enriched my practical experience. He took me to many places and told me to have a cup of tea. He would tell me later on that he understood whether the potential buyer was a diabetic patient by observing his mode of taking sugar with tea, without his having to test his blood. An insured senior advocate told me about Khuda Buksh's early days. The story goes thus: A gentleman always denied his presence at his residence (though he was present). He also told his children to declare that he (the gentleman) was out of house. One day, Khuda Buksh was waiting patiently outside the gentleman's residence. At the sight of K.B., the gentleman hid in a corner of the third floor. And K.B. was extremely tenacious; he, too, got up to the third floor, looking for the guy. The guy was heavily enraged and told K.B., "I will throw you out of the floor. Why do you disturb me?" K.B. replied instantly, "It won't be a bad idea to hug you as I fall. I have an insurance policy. You too have big business, no doubt. Possibly you have taken a big loan. But do you have insurance policy that has cash value?" And such words of K.B. weakened the guy considerably. He entertained K.B. heavily and later bought an insurance policy. In fact, a few words of sympathy can create a psychological moment, which tall talks can't.

I also have experienced a lot of things like that, but to mention those here will be superfluous. Actually, K.B. was K.B.; he could be compared only with himself and nobody else. Even the hard facts about him will appear to you like a story because truth is stranger than fiction. K.B. was not a man to sit idle. He took rest aboard a plane, and he would sell insurance even on the plane. I, in my effort to follow him, tried to sell insurance even if it was a token. And I have done so in London, Washington D.C., New York, Miami, Paris, Frankfurt, Tokyo, Osaka, Kathmandu, Bombay, New Delhi, Kolkata, Singapore, and Hong Kong. Am I not telling my own story while trying to tell about K.B. sir? Maybe, but I don't care. The first chairman of Bangladesh Public Service Commission, Professor Doctor A.Q.M.B. Karim, rang up the first governor of Bangladesh Bank, Mr. Hamidullah, from his 1 Minto Road residence and said, "K.B. Sahib's disciple S.R. Khan will see you." He, too, bought an insurance policy from me and also did me a favor by supplying me with foreign currency at the time of my going abroad.

Just a few days ago, I had a conversation with my honorable elder brother, former justice of Bangladesh High Court and Vice Chancellor of BGC Trust University, Mr. Habibur Rahman Khan. Incidentally, we started to talk about K.B. He was highly pleased to learn that a memoir is being published on the life and ideals of K.B. sir. He called me in my nickname and said, "Kachi, I had the opportunity of coming in touch with K.B. once. It was the year 1961. EFU's development officer and a man of Barisal Anwar Hossain Sahib once took me to K.B. Sahib. I was then an advocate of Dhaka district court. K.B. Sahib was very pleased to see me. I also took an insurance policy. During our talks, I quoted a reputed insurance personality (so far I can remember, S. Shamser Ali), "Life insurance is necessary for those who live long and also for those who die early." K.B. Sahib was amazed to hear the quotation from me and said, thanking me, "Your knowledge about insurance is deeper than mine, I see." I was enchanted with K.B.'s modesty.

Another quality of K.B. sir that has inspired me was that he often arranged grand dinner parties in big hotels. He was once the president of Dhaka Club. Some parties were named "Ladies' Night" – a real chance to have women's flavor. He often said, "Without women's cooperation, it is quite difficult to survive in such an unpopular occupation, let alone make a headway."

At the end of his life, Khuda Buksh once said to me, "The Bengalis realize the importance of a person after his death, not when he is alive." He also said, "If anyone among Bengalis makes name and fame, others will be all set to pull him down, by the leg if necessary." All these he said in great sorrow.

I still think if we measure with a balance between life insurance and Khuda Buksh, it will be extremely difficult to measure which one is heavier. A wizard and a legendary stature in insurance, Khuda Buksh's achievements will enliven the spirit of the Bengalis of today and tomorrow.

The Memories of Old Days

Quazi Abdus Samad[24]

IT WOULD BE appropriate to say first that Khuda Buksh is my *Dula bhai* (brother-in-law). He joined Eastern Federal Union Insurance Company as Life Manager of East Pakistan branch on the second of July, 1952. Soon afterwards – in fact, at his insistence, I joined EFU's cash section on the first of August, 1952, just one month after his joining. I could hardly say whether my joining was accidental or not. The guy who worked at the cash section before me was dismissed on charges of embezzlement. I had a government job at the moment, but Dula bhai persuaded me in many ways to debar me from joining the government job and ultimately succeeded in his effort. He said to me, "You will continue to do the Tk 400 [$84] job and eventually you will grow old, feeble, and haggard, in fact, without any real benefit."

EFU's office was opposite Victoria Park (now Bahadur Shah Park). Only eight employees constituted the office staff. Although there were only few staff members, Dula bhai was very particular about maintaining office discipline and keeping the office trim and tidy. He also maintained an attendance register. If anyone was a latecomer, he would not put any previous marking on the register. He would put a late marking on the register before him after his arrival. He would usually say, "You are ten minutes late." Such straightforward actions decreased the number of unwanted late arrivals.

He would usually go home for lunch. Excluding the lunch period, he would spend the rest of the time in his office. Although office hour was up to 5 p.m., he on most days would stay up to 7 or 8 p.m. He prepared replies to official letters coming from various places and was meeting different persons. What he could do today, he

---

[24]Former Chief Accountant, Eastern Federal Union Insurance Company Ltd.

did not put off till tomorrow. His everyday habit was to accomplish the day's work within the day. It should be borne in mind that in those days, you could not avail yourself of the opportunity of the fax or e-mail as comfortably as you can today. Letters would have to be written by hand or with the help of a typewriter.

Not only did he do his works in time, but also closely watched the activities of the other office workers. If someone was in a relaxing mood owing to a shortage of works, he would instantaneously send him to any busy section so that he could extend a helping hand there. He disliked the staff sitting idle for lack of work. The rule he started kept everyone busy. As a result, staff attention to works would not be marred, and office works would not lie pending. We cannot even conceive of such things in today's situations.

I still remember a story which Dula bhai told me about how he achieved the position of the Inspector in Oriental Life Insurance Company in Kilkatta. Dula bhai saw an advertisement in the newspaper for the position of inspector, to be appointed by OGSLA management. Dula bhai applied for that position along with other applicants. He was the only Muslim applicant among all the applicants. All the applicants had to appear for a written examination for the selection. Dula bhai stood first in the examination, but management declined to offer him the position. Their rationale was that he was too short to be selected for this position. (Khuda Buksh's height: 5 feet 1 inch). Perhaps Dula bhai was discriminated against religion by denying the selection. Dula bhai vigorously protested the management's decision and told them that job performance had nothing to do with physical height. After his protest, management caved in and appointed him provisionally. Management informed him that the position would be made permanent, provided he fulfill the business targets within a set time period. Dula bahi fulfilled those targets in a very short period of time, and the position was made permanent

When Dula bhai joined EFU's East Pakistan branch as Life manager, general manager was then Mr. K.F. Haider. So far as my knowledge goes, he was given a task of fulfilling a target within three months. He proved his worth by fulfilling the target within a month. After that, he never had to look back. He did not merely confine himself within the four walls of his office, at the same time; he continued to increase individual and social contact with people from all walks of life, with a view to extending business. Thus, EFU gradually made headway in business. As the business progressed, so did increase the number of office people and field workers. In such a moment, a small scale office building of the Victoria park areas was abandoned, and the main office was shifted to Dienfa *Bhaban* (building) at Gulistan.

In the event of promoting an officer to a higher rank, he never failed to make a proper evaluation of the performance of the related person. He never gave promotion to an inefficient worker. He had a significant consideration for the concerned person's integrity and dexterity. Though I was his brother-in-law, he never favored me. This extraordinary quality was inherent in his nature. To me, it seems that he may have deprived me from my due. Why did he do that? So that people cannot say that he has favored his brother-in-law. He severely scolded a worker who neglected his duty.

Once, I was traveling with him in his car. Dula bhai stopped near Sutrapur police station, Dhaka. He told me to accompany him, watch, and listen, and not to talk. We went inside the office. He introduced himself and started friendly talk with the police station chief. The way he was talking, it seemed that he knew that person for a long time, although it was his first meeting. Khuda Buksh wanted to know about his family, children, and other stuff. Interestingly, he convinced the police chief in half an hour to buy a life insurance policy. It happened just like magic. There are lots of stories like this.

A.R. Chowdhury was a branch manager in Chittagong. He used to take Dula bhai there sometimes to do business. I heard a story how Dula bhai managed to seal a policy.

One time a man, who was very rich, would not buy a policy from Chowdhury Sahib. When Dula bahi was on a business trip to Chittagong, Chowdhury Sahib took him to the man's home. When the man saw Chowdhury Sahib, he became very angry.

"You don't have to do insurance, I'm coming from outside Chittagong. I will take a cup of tea and have some friendly conversation," Dula bhai told the man.

The man's expression then changed, and he calmed down.

They talked and talked and talked. Eventually, insurance came into the conversation. Dula bhai left, selling the man an insurance policy of Tk. 2 lakhs [$42,000]. He was a wizard in insurance. He had such a unique way of convincing people; it's very difficult to say how he did it. It's amazing.

He always remembered any favor done to him by anybody, and he tried heart and soul to repay it. Incidentally, mention may be made of Ainuddn Ahmed, superintendent of Damodya High School and a teacher of his school life. Dula bhai not only sent him a monthly honorarium, Mr. Ainuddin himself would personally come to his residence every year and would stay there for over a month. Many of Mr. Ainuddin students worked all over the country. If informed, most of his student would come to see him. Many of them are today established in the society, some are passing a life of retirement, and a few are deceased. Dula bhai arranged the marriage of one of his daughters. Even after the death of Dula bhai, as long Ainuddin Ahmed was alive, he would come and stay at Dula bhai's residence whenever he would come to Dhaka. Even Dula bhai's children would send him regular monthly honorarium.

Many of his office staff were not in a position to read write or speak English correctly. Dula bhai got the help of this teacher in helping the staff brush up their English. When the teacher came to Dhaka, he would take classes after 5 p.m. in the afternoon.

His memory was extraordinary sharp. I can remember one incident. When Dula Bhai went to Kathipara (Khulna) for the second time, I was a high school student.

I gave him some money and said," Please buy me a bicycle with this." He said, "All right". But no bicycle was in sight. I assumed that he has spent up the money. Two years passed. In 1952, when he was life manager of EFU East Pakistan, he called me one day, gave some money and said, "buy up a bicycle!"

I retired from Eastern Federal and later joined Federal Life as head cashier. Federal Life company was progressing well, and there was about Tk. 56 lakhs [$1.18 million] in fixed deposit. There were shares, also, and bonuses were about to be declared. However, Bangladesh emerged as a new nation, and the government acquired the company after nationalization.

Honesty was ingrained in Dula bhai's character. He earned a lot but had little fascination for saving something against a rainy day. He was reluctant to buy land. He was persuaded to buy the plot of land at Dhanmondi where his wife and children reside today. He bought the one *bigha* (0.33 acre approx.) plot for Tk. 4,500 [$940]. A house was erected here, with a loan received from House Building Finance Corporation. Who knew then that one day, at the insistence and inspiration of his wife and children, Khuda Buksh Memorial Trust and Foundation would be established at this very house?

Insurance was his Day and Night Dream

Sardar Mohiuddin[25]

AT THE BEGINNING of his career, Khuda Buksh started as a worker at the Oriental Government Security Life Assurance, Calcutta. During his stay here, he deeply noticed that those who were earning barely enough money to keep body and soul together were actually earning a lot by becoming insurance agents. Mr. Atahar Ali of Barisal was then engaged in the act of selling life insurance policies in Kolkata. It was he who motivated Khuda Buksh to sell insurance policies. Khuda Buksh expressed his deep interest in this field to the Oriental's administrative officers. They gladly gave their consent. I heard these stories from Khuda Buksh himself.

This was how Khuda Buksh set his foot on the grounds of insurance. He had an inherent ability to make friends with or to attract someone effortlessly. So, he did not have to face any difficulty in achieving success in the field of selling insurance policies. He worked hard for this. Oriental's officers also found in him the advent of a rising salesman. Oriental's authorities were really pleased with Khuda Buksh's continuous success, and as such they did not hesitate to promote him to the position of an inspector in 1946. He always retained the highest position in the field of selling *bimapatra* (insurance policies).

Before the division of India in 1947, considerable qualitative change took place in the politics of the subcontinent. What worried people among them was the Hindu-Muslim communal riot of '46. During this riot, Khuda Buksh Sahib had an attack of appendicitis, and he got admitted into Calcutta Medical

---

[25]Former Assistant Manager, Jiban Bima Corporation, Dhaka, Bangladesh.

College for surgery. No one could go and see him due to the riot. On the third day, the company's general manager, D.K. Dastur, went to see him and was concerned about Khuda Buksh's physical weakness. Khuda Buksh mentioned to Mr. Dastur that he would start working as soon as he recovered. Mr. Dastur paid no heed to this and advised Khuda Buksh to apply for a leave and have complete rest. In accordance with this, Khuda Buksh, along with his wife and three sons, went to Modhupur of Mymensingh for rest. Khuda Buksh did not stay there for a long time, and after two days, he returned to his work. This incident clearly reveals how deeply he bounded himself with insurance. He always thought about life insurance. So, he did not think about having a rest, even at the time of need.

Three years after the division of India in 1947, he was thinking of returning to his motherland. At one stage, K.F. Haider called D.K. Dastur to know more about Khuda Buksh Sahib. Daster said, "I have a good man, if you take him your insurance business will be successful."

In 1952, Khuda Buksh returned to East Bengal as life manager of Eastern Federal Insurance Company's East Pakistan branch. When he began working here, many things started to change quickly. During this period he and his organization steered the people towards buying life insurance. Those who once hated the two words "life insurance," changed their views towards life insurance. They began to say "yes" the life insurance was a business of the gentlemen, and that anyone could honestly earn a lot of money through insurance business. One had to pay Tk. 10 [$2] as a license fee for taking insurance agency at that time.

Not only did Khuda Buksh work singly for the betterment of insurance, but he also cooperated with others in order that they could make a considerable progression in this field. He had undying eagerness for having an insurance business. He visited the house of every field agent. He wanted to know from them whether they had financial or any other problems. We have seen many cases of how he helped the field force. In one case, he appointed a man as inspector who couldn't secure business. In that case, Khuda Buksh himself accompanied the inspector and went to the people and brought the business. That business was in the name of that inspector. The inspector was very much encouraged. In this way, many inspectors became wealthy and bought houses and cars. In general, he helped all the agents, inspectors, and field managers. He did not take any credit for this. After a while, people called him, "Wizard of Insurance."

Khuda Buksh always advised the agents or the related people to maintain the work ethics. He recapitulated the fact that punctuality was really important. He himself would come to the office very early. After office hours, he would stay longer in the office, and it was his habit. Actually, life insurance was his life; it was his day and night's dream.

As I have already stated, people disliked buying policies in those days. But Khuda Buksh Shahib was able to bring about a change in the minds of the people who gradually realized its fruitfulness and became interested in buying policies, bit by bit. But this change of mind did not take overnight. Khuda Buksh shahib and his field workers had toiled day and night for this. People were made to understand that a policy could be bought with a small amount of money. If the policy holder died all of a sudden, or if he fulfilled the policy term, his family would get a big lump sum, at a time which would come to the use of the retired person or be a great use to the rest of the family in case of the death of the policy holder. At least, the family would not have to be totally eliminated.

If someone died, Khuda Buksh himself handed over the check to the wife or other member of his family. This not only benefitted the family financially, but his action helped to spread the usefulness of the insurance policy to reach everyone.

Nowadays, people learn a lot about insurance by reading books and booklets. Such books were virtually non-existent before, so people relied on verbal assurances. Insurance workers had to spend a lot of time in this difficult task. But I have never found Khuda Buksh tired on this job. To him, insurance was a devotion. Before, people hated the word "insurance." He was the only man in the insurance business who organized it in such a way that people said, "No, it is a noble business." There is no denying the fact that Khuda Buksh Sahib contributed greatly to the development of insurance, and his contribution brought life insurance to today's height.

When he was the life manager of the company, K.F. Haider Sahib once came to Dhaka. He visited Khuda Buksh's Eskaton residence. I heard of their discussions from Kazi Abdus Samand, his brother-in law. I can still vividly remember what he said.

Haider Sahib asked Khuda Buksh, "Have you got any property in East Pakistan?" Khuda Buksh replied, "I have one bigha land in Dhanmondi." Then he stopped for few seconds and said, "I also bought two bighas land in Dilkusha Commercial Area, in the name of EFU."

The seller of the land was a friend of Khuda Buksh's, and he had offered a reduced price for the property if Khuda Buksh would buy it for himself. Khuda Buksh, however, informed his friend that he was interested in buying the land for EFU only. In this way, he made many sacrifices in his life. The foundation stone for the EFU building was laid here, but Eastern Federal building was not built in the Pakistan period. Bangladesh got independence in 1971. The building was built on the soil of the free country and on the land bought by Khuda Buksh.

I can recollect another incident which happened in Kolkata. I heard this from Khuda Buksh Sahib. An insurance agent came to the magistrate while canvassing for life insurance. The agent visited the magistrate several times in his office with no success. One day, the magistrate became very angry and told the agent, "I will dash you down the stairs if you come again with the talk of insurance." The agent got nervous and was disappointed. He was not sure what else he could do. He went back to his inspector, Khuda Buksh, and told him about the incident. After a while, Khuda Buksh met the magistrate in his office and introduced himself. With due respect, Khuda Buksh asked the magistrate, "If you don't mind, sir, how much is your salary?"

The magistrate replied, "Rs. 800 per month."

"How much is your bank balance?" Khuda Buksh asked.

"Nil."

"What will happen to your wife and child if you die today?"

The magistrate was stunned and was silent for a moment, but he thought the matter over in his head and finally said, "Yes, yes, Mr. Khuda Buksh, you are right." The magistrate promptly took out a policy of Rs. 20,000. He was transferred to East Pakistan after partition of India. His insurance policy matured in this country. Salesmanship of insurance at that time was very hard; people did not like it.

Khuda Buksh Sahib is no more today. But the motto which he took up to convey the benefits of insurance at every house has not failed. People today are being benefitted through insurance. This is really rewarding.

He had considerable generosity, but he hardly paid any heed to anything other than insurance. If anyone of us wanted to have his opinion about anything else, he simply said, "I don't understand anything other than insurance." And it was in this way that he dedicated his life for the development of insurance.

May his soul rest in peace!

Khuda Buksh:
The Vacuum has not Been Filled

Majibur Rahman[26]

I FIRST MET KHUDA Buksh at his office in 1961. The late M.A. Rashid, development manager, introduced me to him.

Khuda Buksh's lifestyle was quite simple. His dedication to work and his integrity fascinated me. The way in which he extended the insurance business and attracted the clients bears testimony to his enterprising expertise. In harmony with the wishes of Khuda Buksh, I've always gotten in touch with different official projects and tried my very best to implement them. He was a workaholic, active and honest. I also tried to follow his footsteps in my field of activity, and I was successful. He always advised me to how to bring dynamism to my works. Almost every night, he called me over the telephone and wanted to know regarding the progress of my work. This greatly fascinated me.

Khuda Buksh had an uncommon power to influence people from all walks of life. I can remember many things relating to this. In the event of any altercation or conflict of opinion between two persons of his acquaintance, he quickly took the matter in this and defused the situation. He also helped solve some of my personal problems. I can recall once – I resigned. He knew this and came to my residence. He persuaded me and my wife to withdraw my resignation. He was such a personality.

These superb qualities of motivating people were rightly befitting for a man like Khuda Buksh. I think it was this honesty and confidence that enabled him to earn these qualities of a true leader.

---

[26]Former Deputy General Manager, Jiban Bima Corporation. For details, see Appendix L.

The technical expertise that he earned for running an insurance company was by dint of his own qualities. He carefully heard the saying of his opponents. He himself was a good speaker. He inspired his agents through his fascinating speech to bring in more business, more success. With a view to encouraging agents, he personally sent them letters of applause and even arranged for meetings for giving the rewards.

Khuda Buksh did everything possible for the good of East Pakistan, but the authorities in West Pakistan tactfully opposed this. It is my personal assumption that some people secretly gave wrong information about Khuda Buksh to the authorities in West Pakistan and thus fulfilled their evil motive. So far as I know, some officials in East Pakistan were actively opposed to Khuda Buksh and poisoned the mind of Roshan Ali Bhimjee. The truth is that Khuda Buksh invested all his efforts and energy for the commercial success of the company. After his resignation, he took initiative to set up a new company, and it really gladdened me.

After Khuda Buksh's resignation, Eastern Federal's business had a catastrophic downturn, and the field works came to a virtual halt. We could not even imagine that he could ever depart from the company. He was an ideal insurance personality and a symbol of the insurance industry. After his death, none could fill up the vacuum.

Life Insurance and Khuda Buksh

A.R. Ansari[27]

THOSE GREAT LEADING personalities who speeded up the development and progress in our national life with their intelligence, hard work, dedication, guidance and patience – the late Khuda Buksh was one of them. Today Bangladesh is an independent, sovereign, and developing nation. We have to compete with the rest of the modern world in the march towards progress in fields of knowledge and science, education and culture, business and industry, banking and insurance. We inherited a lot of it from the past – the rest we are carrying on in the same tradition.

Today insurance business is an integral and indispensable economic arrangement for providing social security in our lives. The most part of our social existence, knowingly or unknowingly, is made secure under the cover of insurance. Mr. Khuda Buksh is the helmsman of the entire insurance industry. He started his career as an insurance agent in 1935. It is really amazing how much dedication to work, self-confidence, strength of character, and determination is needed to grow into the insurance tycoon that he turned into.

About sixty years back, he realized how ignorance of a good financial system can deprive ordinary people from its tremendous benefits. At that time in undivided India, the "system of insurance" wasn't clear to the people of Bengal in undivided India. Besides, due to improper presentation strategies of acceptable ideas on "insurance," people often turn their backs to insurance agents. Young and intelligent Khuda Buksh easily realized these facts. He knew, "If people didn't entertain the agents without knowing what it was all about, the latter would have to make room for themselves in order to bring it home to the people. Once people understand,

---

[27]Former Development Officer Eastern Federal Union Insurance Co. and Federal Life, London, U.K.

they would offer the workers a seat and listen." For this reason in those days, we always found him carrying a small folding chair in his hand wherever he went. In the course of time, Khuda Buksh was able to establish himself as the undisputed hero of the insurance industry, first in undivided India, later in undivided Pakistan, and ultimately in Bangladesh.

He felt gratified if any of his requests and recommendations benefited anyone. His well-wishers had jokingly named his ever-busy, crowded living room "the hall of requests." It is difficult to estimate how many near and dear ones used to approach with such a variety of pleas and requests. He never disappointed anyone. With his unassuming nature, he used to fathom the importance of things and attempted wholeheartedly to find a solution to the problems. His empathy towards people was unparalleled.

Fortunately, I have a beautiful relation with the family of this great man. Even in his private life, as head of the family, he was responsible and affectionate towards everyone. He was extremely mindful about social responsibilities and fellow feeling. The love and hospitality towards his friends, emanating from his wide heart, is still vibrant in everyone's heart.

Above all, his far-reaching contribution towards the expansion of insurance industry and its influence on national life is beyond all words. He is the one who taught us so nicely that "insurance is a service," and that the profession of insurance is a noble service-oriented profession – in which the manifestation of skill facilitates one to ascend the ladder of success up to the sky. Where unemployment is sitting like an immovable rock on the top of our nation, insurance system points at a bright potential out of it. There are no proper safety rules and regulations for social security in our country. Hence, it's only insurance which can be projected there as a dependable solution. There is no comparable field for one's overall development, except through human service rendered by wide contact with people and creation of public awareness. By becoming a member of this noble and active environment, the insurance workers should feel honored. It was only Mr. Khuda Buksh who, through his thoughtful and noble service and the untiring, practical, life-long experience, made us aware of the alternate, colorful aspect of life.

With the working skill of his entire life, he proved that insurance policies are not just a business, but they are a service as well. Lots of people can weave dreams of future security from disasters; lots of young men can build their future for themselves and their families through their ability, intelligence, and hard work in a respectable and progressive profession.

I met this great personality for the first time in London in 1967. He was then the main driving force of the Life Section of Eastern Federal Union Insurance Company. From the first introduction and meeting, he impressed me so much that my relation with his family even after his death has continued uninterrupted. When he started a new insurance company by the name of Federal Life Assurance Company, I obtained the responsibility of its European Representative. From the moment of our first acquaintance, I became enchanted by this ever smiling, ever friendly, charming, generous, and attractive personality. Many of the ideals of the life of this extraordinary man – his continuous dedication and concentration, his infinite inspiration and enthusiasm for work, his motivation and determination to fulfill his objectives – still provide inspiration to me.

A simple and unassuming man lurked behind the stern exterior of Mr. Khuda Buksh. He was born in a simple, tree-covered, river village surrounded by agricultural fields in Madaripur. He was educated and had come out victorious in struggles of life. He was adjusted to the behavior and ways of the civilized world and was a skillful and talented man with progressive taste. When the speed of the progressive world and the emotion of green and colorful nature integrate in a man's life, human being invariably comes through him.

He had unwavering faith in honesty, integrity, self-esteem, idealism, and patriotism. Hence, we witnessed that this man, with a sparkling personality in following his conscience and honesty, did not hesitate in the least to put an end to his long career in Eastern Federal, which had been founded with the efforts of his own hands. In every field of his life, he kept himself vigilant and bounded by his duties and responsibilities like a soldier. He was always eager to offer appropriate cooperation to every client of insurance in distressful situations. His motto in life was to serve humanity. He has proved how easy it is to improve any industry though an expansion of human service; or to put it otherwise, human service is one of the ways or promises for the development of any industry.

A Man Who Never Bowed His Head to Unjust Demands

Abdul Awal Mojnu[28]

TRADE UNIONISTS HAD been active in different insurance companies long before the establishment of Jiban Bima Corporation (JBC) in 1973. Those trade unions were extremely powerful. After the formation of JBC, union leaders from various companies had a get-together, and after long consultation, they reached an agreement to form a trade union at JBC. Its registration number was 1138. It was Eastern Federal Union (EFU) Insurance Company's registration number. In 1973, the prime role of the union at JBC was played by employees of the defunct EFU. Subsequently, the union of the JBC was transformed into a very powerful bargaining organization.

To form a trade union is one of the fundamental rights of every organization. Since each company had a separate union, union leaders played a key role. No outside power or group was involved in the formation of the trade union. The then field officers association, however, actively participated in the formation of the same.

The employees of the companies which merged with the JBC in 1973 were involved in the formation of the trade union. Then there were no directly employed workers of Jiban Bima. The company workers assimilated with Jiban Bima took part in the process.

The crux of the question was that the government took the companies and included them with Jiban Bima. The new employees of JBC were actually the workers of different old companies. So, the old company workers (now JBC employees) were

---

[28] Former Deputy Manager, Jiban Bima Corporation, Dhaka, Bangladesh.

all set to retain the facilities such as high level salary and benefits, increasing house rents, education allowance, transportation allowance, entertainment allowance, house building loan, obtaining one's whole pension at once, assurance of corporation jobs for the employee's children and dependants, car loan, washing allowance, and residential facilities for the employees.

Their main demand was to double the salary they got when they were company employees. They also demanded a higher rank. These were two remarkable demands of the old employees. Political parties did not give any active support of the activities of these employees, but evidently they provided moral support, I think.

After the establishment of JBC, the government appointed Mr. Khuda Buksh the chief executive – that is, the first managing director. As he was the general manager of EFU, the largest insurance organization of that time, and successfully conducted the operation of the company even in the teeth of formidable union leaders, he was quite aware of the trend of the times. And the union leaders of the JBC knew very well that it would be next to impossible to get any undue and unreasonable demand fulfilled from an indomitably strong managing director like Khuda Buksh. Khuda Buksh did not bow his head to these unjust demands. And that was exactly why the union leaders and the field officers association leaders came in confrontation with him, simply on false grounds, and tried to remove him. Consequently, he was released from the JBC.

It is true that union activities disrupted the normal functioning of the JBC. But since the union plays a vital role in getting the reasonable demands of the employees fulfilled, the Jiban Bima has so far complied with the same, without demonstrating tangible opposition.

(Reprinted with permission from KBMT&F)

Khuda Buksh (Inspector) along with Insurance officers of Oriental Government Security Life Assurance Company, Kolkata. D. K Dastur, managing director (Center, front row), 1946.

(Reprinted with permission from KBMT&F)

Khuda Buksh with senior managers of Eastern Federal.
Standing (L-R) M.A. Qasem (Sr. Regional Manager), Muzafferuddin Ahmed (Regional Manager), the young man is unidenfied, M.A. Rashid (Development Manager)
Sitting: Ahmed Ali (Sr. Regional Manager)

(Reprinted with permission from KBMT&F)
A group photo of Dhaka Rotary Club members.

(Reprinted with permission from W.W. Karnowski)

Khuda Buksh welcoming Mr. E.C. Iven at Dacca Airport for EFU's Second Convention Feb 1967, seen also Ahmed Ali (left) and Dr. Tajuddin Manji (right).

(Photo source: EFU Field Force, Sept 1966)
Khuda Bukah and Roshan Ali Bhimjee speaking at an Agency meeting of the Dhaka – Narayanganj, East Pakistan.

Khuda Buksh being received at Dhaka airport by family members, members of the EFU management and field force after being promoted to General Manager at Karachi (January 1966).

Khuda Buksh awarding prize to M.A. Mowjee (Chief Development Officer) at a prize distribution ceremony.

(Photo credit: Asif Zaman.)

Khuda Buksh awarding prize to M.A. Zaman (Superintendent of agencies) at a prize distribution ceremony.

(Reprinted with permission from KBMT&F)
Khuda Buksh with S.M. Morshed (Chief Justice, East Pakistan).
Also seen in the picture
Muzafferuddin Ahmed (Regional Manager, EFU) and Mir Mosharraf Hossain.

(Reprinted with permission from KBMT&F)
Khuda Buksh and Sheikh Mujibur Rahman (Father of Bangladesh)
at a marriage ceremony.

PART II

Pakistan Insurance Personnel Interviews and Memoirs

Khuda Buksh : Fair, Loving, Trusted and Respected Leader

Rizwan Ahmed Farid[29]

I STARTED MY INSURANCE career in the American Life Insurance Company (ALICO) in 1962. Mr. S.A.A. Hasanie, the then-regional manager of EFU, introduced me to the late Khuda Buksh, who asked me to join EFU in 1964. I was reluctant to switch from ALICO to EFU and work under Mr. Hasanie and, as such, declined the offer. Thereafter, in 1965, Mr. S. G. Jeelani, the then-regional manager of EFU, also approached me with an attractive package from EFU; again, I was formally introduced to Khuda Buksh for the finalization of my appointment with EFU. After approving my appointment, Khuda Buksh told Mr. Jeelani that Mr. Hasanie originally introduced Mr. Rizwan Farid to EFU. The late Jeelani got the hint and asked the administration that I be placed under the supervision of Mr. Hasanie. I should add that the recruitment of marketing personnel in the life insurance business is an extremely tedious and difficult job; in Pakistan, the sales force retention rate over five years is less than one percent, as compared to worldwide rate of 20 percent; nevertheless, this type of recruitment is the most rewarding because the recruiter receives a substantial commission for the sales force working under him.

Soon after joining EFU in 1965 India attacked Pakistan. An immediate agency (marketing and sales persons) meeting was called and it was announced that the field workers should fully participate in defending the homeland; and they should not worry about at all. All the commitments made to them would be honored by

---

[29]Executive Director, Alchemy, Karachi, Pakistan. For details, see Appendix K.

EFU, irrespective of the flow of new business. Fortunately the war was ended in seventeen days.

In January 1966 or 1967, Mr. Hasanie invited about a hundred insurance industry people to his residence for dinner in honor of the son and daughter-in-law of Khuda Buksh, who were then recently married. When the late Khuda Buksh arrived with his family, he observed that the reception was in a *shamiana* (canopy); in response to the grandeur, he said, "Hasanie, it seems as if it is your own son's marriage reception!"

These memories show the quality of Khuda Buksh's leadership and how fair, loving, trusted and respected he was. I know many people who worked with the late Khuda Buksh. Mirza Faiz Ahmed and Mr. M. A. Idris both suggested that I interview some of the old associates of the late Khuda Buksh to trace his contributions to the early development of life insurance in Pakistan as well as the part he played in inducting the leaders of the insurance industry. I was confident those who worked with the late Khuda Buksh would agree to be interviewed and share their memories.

[From Rizwan Ahmed Farid's email to Muhammad Obaidur Rahim, 18 Jan 2003, Karachi, Pakistan. Rizwan provided extensive support to the Khuda Buksh Memorial Trust and Foundation by taking interviews of colleagues and associates of the late Khuda Buksh in Karachi, Pakistan from 6 March to 30 April 2003. Rizwan's interview questionnaire appears under "A dialogue about the late Khuda Buksh" in Appendix B. The responses to the questionnaire formed a framework of the articles presented in the book. However, the articles did not follow the interview order but were edited for clarity.]

"Where's the Business?"

Michael Joseph Pereira[30]

I OFFICIALLY MET MR. Khuda Buksh in 1967, but unofficially I knew and had heard about him from before because he was from the then East Pakistan. I also happened to reside in Chittagong and we had met there when Mr. Walajahi visited Chittagong. Besides, my father was there at the Agrabad Hotel, and I knew Mr. Khuda Buksh from that. But formerly, I was introduced to him when I came for the selection process in Eastern Federal, which consisted of a series of interviews and other things. I do not recall Mr. Khuda Buksh being on the interview committee, because these were all prominent citizens; but everybody told me that he was there on that floor. So, my association – if that's the word, because he was very senior and I was a new recruit – with Khuda Buksh lasted from March 1967 till his departure from Eastern Federal; I think it was in mid-1969. Subsequently, I did have some contact with him in Dhaka when he created the Federal Life Assurance Company in the old Dienfa building where EFU used to be once, and I visited him there once or twice.

Mr. A.J Dias was my immediate boss in those days, and my immediate superintendent or assistant manager was the late Iqbal Anjum, who was the late stalwart of the industry. Mr. Dias and Mr. Khuda Buksh were quite close, particularly since Iqbal Anjum was an underwriter and Khuda Buksh was the business generator. So, there was always this sort of closeness between the underwriter and the business generator: not necessarily a good closeness, because sometimes the underwriters don't like the business which the business

---

[30]Former Executive Director, State Life Insurance Corporation in Pakistan. For details, see Appendix K.

generator brings. But, I must say that Khuda Buksh's business was good business and he knew how to get life business in those very difficult days.

I remember Mr. D. M Qureshi, the divisional manager, once recruited a new agent, who brought a reasonably large amount of premium on a new policy and had to be garlanded. It was really amazing! A simple field agent being garlanded by the office people – by the executives, officers, and staff members, and Khuda Buksh, the leader, was also present there to garland the achievement of the new agent!

I found Mr. Khuda Buksh very simple, quite unassuming... At that stage, with a fresh MBA or a fresh business school training, to see this very unassuming person as the head of such a large life department. My impression: there are only two types of people, those people who work and those people who get work done. The interesting thing about Khuda Buksh was that he defeated that maxim in that he could do work himself *and* he could get work done. And he did it in a very unassuming way. His accent was slightly Bangladeshi or Bengali. He'd hand us the proposal or the case and say, "We understand that was an important... policyholder or an important matter." So he was that type, and I would like to repeat: My impression of him is that he could work himself and, more importantly, he could get work done by others. To a certain extent also – which was also business-oriented – he had this knack or ability to find people who could do business. How he did it how he found people like... how they were put together... how they were made to work... only he could do that.

His unassuming nature, his very direct approach, his simplicity inspired me. I am told that he was, at times, hot-tempered. He could shout sometimes, but I've never had the *opportunity*, if that's the word, of being shouted at by him. He would use Mr. A. J. Dias who was very close to him to do the shouting at me. Dias respected Khuda Buksh extremely, and Khuda Buksh couldn't do without Dias. I am very close to Mr. Dias, because one of my relatives is married into his family. He was an accountant by training and basically joined Eastern Federal as an accountant. He was deputy chief accountant, but he was very close on the life side with Mr. Khuda Buksh. Indirectly, because I was close to Dias, I would get some feedback about Khuda Buksh. Besides being unassuming, Khuda Buksh was very straightforward, very dynamic as far as business was concerned. I had no occasion to be able to say anything about his management skills or his office administration skills. I've never had any opportunity to judge that. But, as far as promotion of life insurance business in Pakistan was concerned, I think – especially in the 50's and 60's – Mr. Khuda Buksh's role was undoubtedly the greatest.

"Where is the business?" As far as I recall, he would come to every EFU department, walk in, and say, "Where's the business?" I remember he would always talk about business, business, and business.[31]

---

[31]Response to question: What were the most common words that the late Khuda Buksh used to use in his daily business conversations?

I don't know about his direct intervention, if that's the word . . . but I think he would use Dias, if I recall, I think his conflict management would be in tandem with Mr. Dias.

He was very precise, straightforward. The insurance agents basically live on their commission, and there's a practice – I don't want to justify the practice or want to be critical of it – it's a practice of the industry that agents used to take advances against the premium even before the processing; they got the commission against the premium. Mr. Khuda Buksh would accept that, tolerate that, if I could say, and even agree to that, but if anybody took undue advantage of that system, then he would be very tough. I understand, though at times I was very critical because I was very junior and I had to pass the voucher and make the checks. I was in the field development department. He'd walk in our corridor and he said, "Joseph, you call me. Joseph, don't give that man any more advance commission." That was the kind of ability he had to control financial actions. He did give some concessions in the cause of business. If the practice aided in promoting business and that agent was really down-to-earth and he had no money in his pocket, then he would do this. In those days, agency commission wasn't too much because the premiums were not very large. A lot of the field-force's wives or children would visit Mr. Khuda Buksh and come to point out "My husband is working for you. But he doesn't get enough money for us to live comfortably." One such lady called on Khuda Buksh and informed him that there was nothing in the house or kitchen for the children to eat. Khuda Buksh became concerned for the family. The husband of the lady was a sales officer of the company, who was spending lot of money on smoking and gambling. At that point, I was in the agency section of the field development department of the company. Khuda Buksh called me and scribed on a piece of paper to advance Rs 50 [$10.50] to the concerned sales officer, and asked me to see the account's supervisor to make the advance voucher and attach Khuda Buksh's slip with the voucher and get the cash. He further instructed me to buy with that money sugar, wheat, flour, and some other food items and deliver the ration at the house of the concerned officer, and hand over the balance amount, if any, to the lady.

In those days, Rs 50 had value and, with that amount, one could buy foodstuff for the family kitchen for a week or so. For two or three months I, along with Mr. Hamid Rashid Siddiqui, used to deliver the ration to the family of the concerned officer at his residence, which was next to Lal Masjid, in PECHS [a posh locality of Karachi]. Then, the interesting thing was not that the continuation of the thing stopped, because Khuda Buksh used a very good psychological ploy: The sales officer himself became embarrassed and ultimately corrected himself by lowering the quality of cigarettes. At one point, Khuda Buksh told me, "I have no official right to do that," but he realized after meeting the wife that this man is not giving much of his commission to run the family.

He built his credibility and trust by straightforwardness, sometimes bluntness and he was a man of his word. It went against him many times. As we know – this is a negative aspect; I don't know whether one should mention it – that at the time of nationalization, the agents' balances that the people in the field borrowed from the company were too much. But, somewhere along the line, I think Mr. Khuda Buksh's honesty or straightforwardness was taken advantage of. His intentions were good, but people took advantage.

He never mentioned that he was a technical, skillful fellow. He always told me, "I am measured by the amount of business." I still remember, because he would still say *business* in that East Pakistan – Bengali accent. He never said he was technically trained; I never remember him mentioning that.

Mr. Khuda Buksh would be very personally involved in the welfare and the personal interest of each field worker. As I mentioned, that story – about how he asked me to send half of the commission as rations rather than give all the cash to the agent – that shows one of his characteristics: that he would motivate people in different ways. But, mainly, he would be involved, he would inquire, he would ask, he would advise, he would make one sit down and talk and try to make him understand. He had this ability of being closely involved in the person who is doing the business, in his welfare, in his interest. In this way, he inspired the workers to be dedicated to the company. So, he would have that sort of godfather or father image. I would see that in the insurance people of those days, the stalwarts: They may have gone against him, for whatever reason, but they would look up to him like an uncle or a father – if not a father, at least an uncle or a good old man who'd look after us, who'd be interested in us, who'd care for us. Subsequently, I guess he must've had little pressures and troubles because, if I recall correctly, Mr. Dias would be delegated these works more and more to keep them all going and motivated.

I can't say – for three reasons [How Khuda Buksh delegated his authority?] One is, we were at the lowest level of the hierarchy . . . right at the bottom. So, we did not have any occasion to see how he administered, how he delegated, how he checked responsibility, how he sponsored. But, as I mentioned, he must have done a lot of delegation to Mr. Dias and to Mr. Zulfikar. How he did it, I'm afraid I can't say, because I never had occasion to be present.

Khuda Buksh treated his junior staff or field workers very comfortably. He never made one feel uncomfortable.

It is a difficult question to respond. I never had the occasion to view all these aspects of him but, from secondhand hearing, we used to hear that he would not accept criticism too willingly. He would listen if it were constructive. I recall Hamid Rashid once had some problem with him; I never had any. If you were constructive, basically if you were positive in your observations about the field or their behavior or their approach . . . because he was a field-oriented person . . . we were in the office, so there was a rift . . . so he would cut you short.[32]

---

[32]Response to question: If Khuda Buksh was a willing listener, accepted feedback and criticism?

In 1966, I was 25. I met three people – Mr. Zulfiqar, Mr. Dias, and Mr. Khuda Buksh – in the first few days of my joining Eastern Federal. Mr. Khuda Buksh and Mr. Dias were instrumental in my continuing in the life insurance industry. A lot of people have been critical of our education background and more importantly, apart from myself, everyone in my family including my sister, brother and father are seasoned bankers. In spite of that, I continued with life insurance. When my father retired, he was holding the number two or three position with Eastern Mercantile Bank in Dhaka. When my sister retired, she was general manager of Pubali Bank, Dhaka. My brother was, before his departure for America, a senior officer in another leading bank in Dhaka. So, I was the only one who was a non-banker, and I was in Karachi and my parents were in Chittagong. But, those of us at EFU who were recruited (Under Officer's training Scheme) would get a subsidized ticket to go on vacation . . . and, on every occasion, my father would say, "What are you doing in insurance?" I would either ask Mr. Khuda Buksh (I think he did it twice) and more often Mr. Walajahi, to tell my father that a career in insurance is not as bad as people make it out to be. No doubt, if we remember, in those days in the late 60s, early 70s, with the creation of all these banks, the banking sector was the most dynamic and attractive sector to a 25-year-old person. Immediately after I got my MBA degree, I applied for a position in EFU under the officer-training scheme. I never planned for a post late in my life. I didn't even apply for any position after that, even though my father said, "Why don't you try in UBL [United Bank Limited], or why don't you try in Pakistan Tobacco?" But I just stayed on. One reason was Mr. Khuda Buksh because, whenever my father would hint, "what are you doing in insurance – I am a banker." . . . But I continued with life insurance. So I credit a large part of continuing in life insurance till my retirement to Mr. Khuda Buksh. I found that the life insurance industry is directly business oriented and if one is working in the field side and have some management and communication skills, he can rise. There were two tiers: the officer training and the field side. On the office side, there were enough examinations, so there was always an incentive to rise or to grow both academically and in our job. The other thing that was attractive, apart from banks – which I never joined, much to my father's regret in his earlier days – is the fact that insurance is a universal subject. If one was capable and had taken any of the examinations or courses, he could stand at par with the rest of the world. I think the banking industry and the insurance industry have these qualifications or courses or scope for development, which are universal.

I spent my entire life in the life insurance industry. There's not much in my life that is not linked in some way with the life insurance industry. Now, I have gained a lot socially because, you know, the life insurance agent – because of his field worker as well as the employees in the office – [he has] to be a social human being; they have to interact with human beings because they have to develop business and business relationships. I have to be honest, the life insurance sector is a very confined sector, but I was able to travel, thanks to life operations. With EFU, I visited Lahore, I visited Dhaka again, and I visited Peshawar. I visited Qatar apart from Karachi and for a newcomer who had spent his entire life in three cities – Karachi, Dhaka, and Chittagong – this was quite an education, to see how the country lives. Lahore was impressive in those days . . .

I appeared for the officer-training exam in 1966, and my date of probation was March 1 or March 2, 1967. We had to attend a three-month course of training. The officer-training scheme of Eastern Federal was an interesting scheme. It was a replication of the CSP [Civil Service of Pakistan]. They tried to remove some of the bureaucratic aspects of the Civil Service of Pakistan scheme by making it more socially oriented and business oriented through Mr. U. Karamat, Vice Chancellor, Punjab University. He was brought in to make the scheme more socially linked toward business and not bureaucratic; but basically it was the same.

Now, the scheme was interesting. Eventually, we had no interface with Eastern Federal. We were brought from Dhaka, Chittagong, Lahore, and many other places to Karachi. Even if one stayed in Karachi, he still had to live in Sarag Villa Road in Bothrabad. We were all taken there straight away by Mrs. Summit, who was our training officer. So, we had no exposure – initial exposure – to Eastern, apart from meeting Mr. Bhimjee . . . Khuda Buksh . . . just shaking hands and introducing us to potential officers whose careers were going to be a part of this organization. I believe that the idea was to equip us with complete academic training about insurance from the training institute before we were thrown into the swimming pool of Eastern Federal. Now, as I said, lectures at the training institute were conducted by employees of the company, so we got in touch with Khuda Buksh, C.M Rahman, and Walajahi.

Khuda Buksh was purely business-oriented, so we got some exposure to Mr. Khuda Buksh's style, his style of speaking, and his style of motivation. As I have said before, he could do two things. He could get work done as well as work hard himself. He was a hard worker, his body, didn't show how hard he worked, but he worked hard. He was a great motivator: He had a story or a motivational point for every occasion, that sort of thing. How much of it was correct, how much he produced – but he produced it so quickly that one believed it. So, Mr. Khuda Buksh was quite instrumental in making the scheme a success on the practical side. Although we are talking about Khuda Buksh, there was a general stream also, but then we went into two different streams. How they selected who opted for life and who opted for general, we don't know.

Insurance was not very popular in Pakistan; there are probably religious reasons for that. Of course, in the earlier days, in the 60s, it was basically lack of savings or poverty. Now, we do business with Rs 3 lacs [$5,000] or Rs 4 lacs [$7,000] premiums. In those days, if you brought a 300-rupee [$63] premium or a 1,000-rupee [$210] premium, it was considered a huge success. I remember I did one case with my own sister-in-law; she was a teacher in some school in Karachi. I brought a 300-rupee premium, which was the annual premium. Mr. Dias actually took a photograph of me giving the check. Mr. Khuda Buksh was very instrumental in the growth of EFU, particularly its life branch.

Assistant manager, field development department: obviously, the initial interface . . . of a field officer or a field worker is with the new business, but that is a very short interface. His longer interface is with the field development department, because it is on the basis of the field development department's clearance that a field worker got his commission, and that his business was recorded in the business statistics. So, until we recognized the business, it didn't come to us. The field worker, especially the sales officer and sales manager, would go to all the big people, but the junior sales officers and sales managers would come to us. I recall some very good sales officers and sales managers. The late M. A. Rahman would visit me twice a day every day, and Khuda Buksh noted that. I think Zulfiqar pointed it out.[33]

I recall that East Pakistan business (policies, records) was recorded, maintained in East Pakistan. Then, suddenly, they decided to have it brought to Karachi. In that project, we got to know Mr. Khuda Buksh more closely. There was a hands-on, direct, daily interface with Mr. Khuda Buksh. Now I understand why, because this was his business, so to say, from East Pakistan, so, he was very careful in ensuring that it was all recorded correctly here. So, in that period, Mr. Iqbal Anzum, Mr. C. M. Rahman, Mr. Ahmed Rashid, and Siddiqui were involved with this project of getting all the records transferred into Karachi and maintaining that first premium register and all the registers. Khuda Buksh would come every little while – and definitely in the evening before going – to check how the work was going and if there were any problems. He was much older, wiser than us, and he realized when you do such a lot of jobs at one time under deadline pressure. If someone's performance were poor or very immature, Mr. Khuda Buksh would know easily. He would understand that these boys are young and they are getting fed up with these jobs, and so he would come frequently. That was one occasion when we had a close association on some sort of job or task or project, as we call it, with Mr. Khuda Buksh. Since I sat in the same room as Mr. Iqbal Anjum, I remember that Mr. Khuda Buksh would frequently visit him on his way up or down the stairs. And on many occasions, he would stop and ask how I was and all that.

I must say that Mr. Khuda Buksh was very progressive, very good in marketing and sales development, a very good motivator, but I don't think he was much impressed by modern technology. As a matter of fact, we still had to write in the ledgers by hand. There was no such thing as typing.

I think the business in East Pakistan, as far as number of policies was considered, may be new business in those days (1965 to 1970, whatever that period I remember) was that the number of policies may have been the same as in West Pakistan. I don't exactly remember the figures, but the ratio was something like two to three

---

[33]Response to question: Can you shed some light on Khuda Buksh's business dealings?

in West Pakistan and one to three in East Pakistan. But the number of new policies was almost equal.

In those days, as far as West Pakistan was concerned, it was concentrated business. It was in Karachi because of Abul Mahmood, S.G. Jeelani, and E.A. Jaffery. It was in Lahore because of M. Zulqarnain. It was in Rawalpindi because of Alvi. So, these were – if you pardon my saying so, these were my observations as a young man – this was personality-generated businesses. That personality was given by Mr. Bhimjee or Mr. Khuda Buksh.

In East Pakistan, Khuda Buksh may have used a different approach because, in East Pakistan – the business was bad throughout East Pakistan. In East Pakistan, business was more widespread; in West Pakistan, it was concentrated around personalities and big towns. Because of that, business in East Pakistan was small business – lower middle-class business – and spread out to small towns. At the time of natiionalization also, it became obvious that the business in East Pakistan was, by number of policies, not disproportionate but by volume, amount of premium, renewal first, it was very small. But, on the plus side, there was this fact that the business in East Pakistan, although small, was more wide spread equitably among the whole country, the whole province in those days, while, in West Pakistan, the business was basically in four or five cities. I don't think we did much business in Faisalabad or Multan. Eastern Federal's business was from Karachi, Lahore, Peshawar, Rawalpindi, because Mr. Khuda Buksh's approach or personality or thinking was that he wanted the business to be more widespread. But, this leads me to a very interesting point, because this happened in State Life also: There is always this battle between those people who want large business and concentrated business because of the volume: They wanted more income. And on the other side, we have a certain section of the field or the management who would like the business to grow and spread. So, in a way, I think that Eastern Federal – I may be wrong and I hope I'm wrong – in a way Eastern Federal may have developed business in East Pakistan more at the grass-roots level rather than the concentrated upper-class level in West Pakistan.

In those days, business was generated with the tax-saving orientation. People got a tax refund and/or tax investment allowance. Because of this linkage between insurance and tax saving, there was this income tax team. So the team was created with all these (in the initial stages, because I was in it) different departments and I remember all these people, because they had to fill the agency form and I had to sign and countersign it. Mr. Khuda Buksh was very interested in seeing that this worked, that it was a success. So this was one team he personally created and nurtured along with Abul Mahmood. Another team I saw developed by Mr. Khuda Buksh was Mr. M. A. Rahman. M. A. Rahman was a very simple worker, a straightforward worker, not very dynamic, very boring sometimes, very soft-spoken. (He died in 1973.) Mr. Khuda Buksh would constantly be inviting, if that's the word, Mr. M. A. Rahman to go to visit him, to sit with him. I think Mr. Khuda Buksh understood there were two types of field workers. One is the rash, dynamic type that's always doing business, good, bad, or indifferent: *Business comes first*. And then there was the meticulous, precise, very slow, calculative type of person, like M. A. Rahman. So, I think somewhere along the line, though Mr. Khuda Buksh may have been more fond of or impressed by people like M.A. Rahman – because they produced greater or more business – may be in his heart of hearts he also liked people like Mr. M. A. Rahman, who produced the stability and general business.

Khuda Buksh created a unique motivation system: instant reward, instant recognition, photographs and so on. This is a convention in the insurance industry, but he would give the rewards quickly and that made all the difference. The top producer or sales officer of the month would have his photograph stuck on the wall. He took a photo of the first big check, and he put it on the wall in a frame. This sort of things I recall, if one did good business from income tax, Khuda Buksh would invite him for a cup of tea. So, he had a system of instant recognition. He would not postpone for an extra day: He used to come and inquire right away. He would know which business was coming, because people would tell him. Then he'd come to the commission section or to Zulfiqar or to me or may be Nazeem Zaidi and say, "Has that premium come?" I'd say, "The premium has come." "Is it check or cash?" We'd say some was an adjustment. "How much is check? Okay, tell so-and-so to come have tea with me." So, he would instantly give one some sort of pat on the back or recognition, which was informal.

It was a very sad day for me, especially as a young 28-year-old, to find him depart suddenly. I think for us, in the very lower level, at the junior level . . . his departure was sudden, but it was a very surprising and sudden departure. I don't think I shook his had before he departed. I myself was surprised, and I don't even think we had any occasion or opportunity to wish him farewell, so I don't know the background behind his resignation. And, since I was too junior, we were not kept involved in the affair, but it was unfortunate, his departure. He left in March, and then he tried to compensate for that, I think, by creating Federal Life. I remember hearing about early retirement . . . this was second, third hand information.

I joined Eastern Federal in 1965. I was in the marketing side. I observed that there was no traditional farewell. About 15-20 people were invited, and most of them received a telephone call warned not to come . . . [34]

His resignation must have been shock and surprise, I don't know, but at our level, we were surprised. On the business it may have an effect, but really I don't remember the statistics, but may be it did affect the growth of EFU.

I don't have any comment on that. I really don't know if anybody have – because when we joined in 1967 and 'til he left in 1969, all of us were made aware that life business is Khuda Buksh. We don't remember anybody else.[35]

---

[34]Comment by Rizwan Ahmed Farid, the interviewer.

[35]Response to question: If Khuda Buksh ever felt that the phenomenal progress achieved by Eastern Federal during the decades of the 60's was wrongly attributed to some personalities other than Khuda Buksh?

Mr. Khuda Buksh, as I mentioned earlier, was a worker. I don't think he made any pretense of being a thinker or any assumption of being a thinker, in that broad sense as a thinker. Mr. Bhimjee had more vision. Mr. Bhimjee had the skill of looking at the broad picture. He knew exactly where he was going himself. We see where Mr. Bhimjee was in the 50s and where he rose, so he had a clear vision for himself and, more importantly, for the company. As a matter of fact, when he joined the Eastern Federal scheme, we were told that the scheme was a part of this broader vision of these gentlemen – Abbas Khaleeli, Roshen Ali Bhimjee, Abdur Rahman – who were the team of EFU: that until and unless a parallel educated group of people was inducted in the industry who could look after the technical sides, the administrative side, the underwriting, the claims, the actuarial side, the industry could not just grow on just business. It needed a support and infrastructure in the office, so the officer-training scheme of Eastern Federal was a part of that vision. So basically, in one word, I would say Mr. Khuda Buksh was a worker who knew how to get things done. But I must be honest: I don't think he attributed to himself a broad philosophical or visionary image or role. As a matter of fact, Mr. Bhimjee always thought about himself as a visionary and a forward thinker.

If you recall, in those days, we still have that culture, but it has reduced and perhaps it was because of the political history behind the creation of Pakistan. We had a very strong attachment with personalities, perhaps because of the Muslim culture or the history behind the creation of Pakistan. So, the insurance industry had its personalities, and Mr. Khuda Buksh was one of them. Now, I am not clear about the reason for it, but I think in the 1950s, when Mr. Bhimjee was in Bombay Life and Mr. Khuda Buksh and Mr. Abbas Khaleeli and the other group got together, the life insurance industry was at a disadvantage. Life insurance business was more in the hands of Indian-based and non-Pakistan-based insurance companies. Strictly speaking, I don't think there were any composite companies; but they were doing general business rather than life business. It would not be wrong to say that life insurance grew in Pakistan with Eastern Federal's growth and that is to the credit of the forward-looking approach of Mr. Khuda Buksh, Mr. Bhimjee, probably led by Mr. Abbas Khaleeli.

As I was telling, somewhere along the line we got more matured and developed. The personality cult that was initially there did not stay on. One reason may be the bureaucratic setup in State Life. In general insurance – if you see – now there are personalities equivalent to Khuda Buksh; even from Bangladesh, there is Mr. Choudhury and there are equivalents to Khuda Buksh in general insurance in other companies. But you may have noted that in the life insurance industry, there is no fresh or new Khuda Buksh at the present time. May be this is a consequence of natiionalization of the life insurance industry and the bureaucratic baggage that comes with it. Because of the monopoly situation that persisted up to the 90's till insurance was privatized, there was no need for personalities; in fact, there was the need to create teams. So, if you remember you are associated with State Life of the Eastern

Federal there were no real, large-scale personalities like Khuda Buksh or Roshen Ali Bhimjee in the State Life period. You could see all around, in all the different sectors of the insurance field; but there was nobody of the same class and of the same skills as Mr. Khuda Buksh. In the general insurance industry there are some personalities still with us; one, of course, is Mr. Choudhury and the Subjalli Ali brothers.

A Boss Without Bossing

Naimuddin Khan[36]

INSURANCE IS A noble profession. It is not only a means of earning one's living; it also creates the scope for undertaking some community work. I was allowed to work simultaneously in the office and in the field at Eastern Federal. I was very satisfied with my job.

Mr. Khuda Buksh was my boss. At the time, I worked in Karachi and he was in Dhaka. Since I was head of the general department of Eastern Federal in Karachi, I used to contact him through letters. Traveling was difficult; but still I think Khuda Buksh used to come to Karachi, three or four times in a year. When we met in Karachi for the first time, he embraced me. I was very much impressed. He was a man of dynamic personality. He was always smiling.

He was helpful to every one, irrespective of whether he was from the field or from the office. He was honest. He used to help the field workers in claiming the cases. He also assisted them in financial crises. In meetings, he used to help the field workers in securing more business. He used to give examples of the great leaders of life insurance. He often spoke of how he had risen in life by selling policies. Whenever he made a promise, he fulfilled it. He never made any false promises. But he never made any claims about his technical ability. He strongly believed in teamwork. In my opinion, Khuda Buksh was a good listener.

Before Mr. Khuda Buksh joined Eastern Federal, Mr. Wisaluddin was heading the Life department of Eastern Federal in the head office in Karachi. I remember his younger brother, Mr. Jamaluddin, who died of pneumonia, sometime in the third week of October 1951. He was an honest man and a very dedicated worker. Mr. Jamaluddin was looking after the business in Karachi. In 1949 or 1950, Mr. Jamal was

---

[36]Former Assistant General Manager, State Life Corporation, Karachi, Pakistan.

sent to East Pakistan. The business was not very good before he went to Dhaka. After he assumed charge in Dhaka, the business surged and Eastern Federal did well.

I can think of no other example. I have not seen any person like Khuda Buksh. After the late Khuda Buksh's resignation, Eastern Federal suffered a setback. He was straightforward in his dealings. Although he was my boss, he never behaved or gave me orders like a boss. I was very much impressed with him.

A Man Thinking of Insurance, Dreaming of Insurance, and Sleeping with Insurance in His Conscience

Sharafat Ali Quershi[37]

INSURANCE IS A very interesting profession. It depends on how you take it. If you take it as a profession, it is a very good profession. It gives you both money and satisfaction; satisfaction, where you pay the claim to the widow. The satisfaction you get is far more than the money reward that you get from the commission. So it's satisfying in both ways.

I joined Eastern Federal in 1964, upon the persuasion of Late Mr. Jeelani. It was then that I first met Mr. Khuda Buksh. Believe me I was shocked to see a man holding the post of the general manager could be so simple and humble. Later on, I found Mr. Khuda Buksh was really nice and humble to the field workers.

At that time EFU was like a family and the credit goes to Khuda Buksh. He created such an environment in the company that it felt like family. We used to take care of each and every worker and used to feel that everybody was a family member, and the credit goes to Khuda Buksh. Whenever he used to come from Dhaka, almost everybody went to receive him at the airport and when he used to

---

[37]Former District Manager, Eastern Federal Union Insurance Company, Karachi, Pakistan.

go back to Dhaka almost everybody used to go to see him off. Khuda Buksh created this atmosphere, by his actions and act.

His devotion towards the profession inspired me the most. It was, in itself, an inspiration for everybody. He was more a salesman than an office executive. He always did what he said. I always saw more field workers in his room, rather than office executives. Office work was always secondary to him. He would give time to the field workers and solve their problems first, and then turn to the office people. By his action, he created trust in people. He was straightforward and polite. He never used to interfere with his subordinates' work. He only kept an eye on them, to ensure that they were working and not creating problems. He used to boost the morale of the field workers by quoting the examples of those people who were doing well [in business].

He led a very simple life. He was very fond of taking tea and would occasionally visit Shehzan on Victoria Rd. Whenever he saw any field worker sitting there, Khuda Buksh would pay his bill. He would never think that this is a field officer or a sales officer and I am the general manager. He was a very friendly person. He treated his junior staff or field workers just like his children.

He used to make a team and then convert it into a family, by interacting with each individual and discussing, not only their professional, but also their personal issues. He used to say *Kam karo!, Kam karo!, kam karo!* [work, work and work!]. If you don't work you will be in trouble. If you have a problem let me know.

Whenever he visited Karachi, (usually once or twice a month), he used to ask about every field worker. He tried to find out each individual's good and bad sides; if he came across someone who was not working or not coming to the office, he used to visit his residence accompanied by his manager. In a very polite manner, he would tell the family members: "*Bahen dekho, aap ka bhai ham say naaraz ho gaya hai. Aap hamara sifarish kar do. Is nay ham logo ko chhor diaa hai. Ham usko lay nay aye hai.* [Sister, your brother has become angry with us. Please plead on our behalf. He has left us. We have come to take him back]. A man of such high capacity (General Manager of EFU) used to talk like this to the unmarried field worker. To Mr. Khuda Buksh, every worker was equal, regardless of his position within the company.

Once, when Khuda Buksh visited Karachi, I was in some difficulty. My car loan was pending, and I told him, "Sir, I don't have a car." He said, "Take my car, and when you fix the loan, bring the car back." It was really something for me – a general manager could offer me his car. And then within couple of days I got my loan and bought a new car. But I still remember that he offered me his car.

His dedication to the profession, coupled with his humble, straightforward nature, was sufficient in motivating those who worked with him. He used to say, "Think of insurance, dream of insurance, and sleep with insurance [in your conscience.] Devote your time to insurance. Work hard. It will give you many things – it will allow you to earn money and a comfortable life." He would tell them that there was no limit as to how much you can earn, sky is the limit for you. You can write your own salary check. If one worked hard enough, he could earn as much as he wanted, and basically he was right. We ended up making as much money as we wanted.

I was working as district manager in 1969 when Khuda Buksh left Eastern Federal. I think he left the company because he was very badly hurt. He was a very loving person. I don't think I've ever come across such a dynamic person with whom I will work again. He was an extraordinary leader and an unbeatable legend of insurance. We will never forget him.

If Your Man has Committed the Wrong Thing to a Client . . . you Have to Fulfill that Promise

Syed Kaiser Abbas[38]

I'M VERY HAPPY to tell something about Khuda Buksh. I joined Eastern Federal Union Insurance Company in 1956, as an agent. In 1958, I became an organizer. I continued working over there, under the guidance of Jaffery, Jeelani, and Hasanie. Then, in 1960, Mr. Khuda Buksh came to West Pakistan.

I met him for the first time in 1960. He took over the charge of both East Pakistan and West Pakistan. Reysatullah was actually retired. He was given the position of chief manager and was working from home. When Mr. Khuda Buksh came to Karachi, there were a lot of problems, and there were differences of opinion. There were so many crises . . . but as soon as Mr. Khuda Buksh took charge, everybody was happy.

Eastern Federal was the leading insurance company after I joined. When Mr. Wisaluddin left Eastern Federal, it was going down. After Mr. Khuda Buksh joined, it started going up and reached the top of the life insurance industry. It became the leader after his joining Eastern Federal. He was actually the general manager . . . He never thought he was a big boss; he was constantly busy improving the team and he always provided us with guidelines for achieving success. He was very interested in increasing the business, particularly in East Pakistan.

---

[38]Deputy General Manager, Adamjee Insurance Company Limited., Karachi, Pakistan.

He was an extremely straightforward man. He never made any claims about his technical ability. Actually, that was his greatness, that he himself did not say anything. But other people said he was a great man, technically very sound. He was a very simple man and he always said that everybody should be treated equally.

He was a team builder . . . Then their organizer, who is building, doing the work of a team . . . if he resigns, [he] can't take all the men with him, it will hurt the entire team . . . He was a good orator. Actually, as an orator, in Eastern Federal, I would rate him No. 2. Roshen Ali Bhimjee was a very, very good orator.

He was a really a great man. He was actually a strategist, like a minister. He was a very good man, and not just in the insurance industry. In the government also he was a much respected person. He was so familiar with the workers. He was interested in knowing about the workers' personal lives as well, and he always inquired whether there were any problems in the family. He was so nice actually. He not only took care of the business, but also took care of the workers and tried to solve their personal problems. That was the most interesting thing about him.

One time, some differences arose between me and Hasani. At that time, Mr. Khuda Buksh was not in West Pakistan. I discussed that problem with Mr. Jeelani and Mr. Jaffery, and said I don't like so and so, I don't want to work with him. But the problem was not resolved and on that point I resigned suddenly. On the same night that I resigned, Mr. Khuda Buksh reached Karachi.

At the airport, Mr. Dias or Mr. Wasif Ali told Khuda Buksh, "Mr. Kaiser has resigned today." "But why?" asked Mr. Khuda Buksh. "Because there is some difference, some discontent, Mr. Jaffery would not solve . . ." Suddenly, he asked, "Who knows his house?"

He took Mr. Wasif Ali and Dias and he told Mr. Dias, "You come with me, I'm going directly to see Kaiser Abbas." I still remember it was 11:30 or quarter to 12 when he reached my home. I was going to sleep, when he knocked at my door.

I was shocked. I said, "Sir, how did you come?" I didn't say "Why."

Mr. Khuda Buksh said, "OK, if you don't like it, I'll go to my home? Then, I'm going back."

I said, "No, I like," and opened the door.

He said, "Mr. Kaiser, look, actually I don't know the way to the homes of my team mates in West Pakistan. West Pakistan is difficult for me. In East Pakistan, I know their homes and visit most of the field workers irrespective of their status in the company."

I said, "But at this time, you are coming straight from the airport."

He said, "I have come because you have abused me."

I thought somebody had told him something wrong and was angry with me. So I said, "No, sir, I haven't said anything."

Khuda Buksh said, "You resigned . . . you discussed your problem with Jaffrey and Jillani. But you didn't feel the need to discuss it with me?"

I said to Khuda Buksh, "I am a small worker."

Actually, Mr. Khuda Buksh's visit was a great honor for me because at that time I was really a small worker. Up to 12:30 he was sitting in my house. He asked what I wanted. I told him I had money problems. Khuda Buksh said that he was very sorry Eastern Federal hadn't been able to keep me. He said, "But you must come to the office. Forget that you resigned."

I met him again after a long time. He was looking old and he was very disturbed.

I asked him, "What's the matter with you?"

He said, "My son died."

"No," I said, "the eldest son?"

He replied, "No, no, no, a son is a son, whether the eldest or the youngest. Actually, I don't know whether Mr. Hasani or Mr. Walajahi is elder. They are all my sons. All the workers are my sons. So don't say you are like the small one because I like you too much. I love you more than Hasani . . . That's all."

My friend, Mr. Akbar, was from East Pakistan. One day, Mr. Walajahi and I were sitting with Khuda Buksh. Mr. Walajahi said, "Khuda Buksh, there is someone standing outside Eastern Federal." He mentioned someone's name who had borrowed money. After discussing Akbar's financial situation . . . he paid all the amount [and] told him to start working . . . that was a great thing, actually. He was capable of solving problems.

I have an example of a leader like late Khuda Buksh in the insurance industry – Mr. Mohammed Choudhury. He is quite like Khuda Buksh. He's still working at Adamjee Insurance Company. He joined in 1977.

I attended the Eastern Federal's Dhaka Convention for the Field force in 1967. Mr. Khuda Buksh had decided that the juniors (life insurance agents) would stay at Hotel Continental (5-star) and the senior people, from regional manager to the directors, would stay in a four star hotel. All of Dhaka is filled with shopping centers. I felt it was much too busy. But the arrangements were good.

The late Khuda Buksh left Eastern Federal in 1969. I left in 1968. I was then the district manager. He was a very honest man . . . there was only one thing he resigned . . . Mr. Roshen Ali Bhimjee was not happy. There is a big difference, Roshen Ali Bhimjee was thinking actually that Mr. Khuda Buksh was the only man . . . Roshen Ali Bhimjee actually left this company. I feel that Roshen Ali Bhimjee was taking the credit, that was actually the reason he (Khuda Buksh) resigned. I think, I feel like that . . .

Actually, Khuda Buksh was the one to increase the growth of the business. In another sense, he was not the politician. He was very straightforward. Mr. Roshen Ali Bhimjee was the politician, but he was very fair. Khuda Buksh developed the life insurance business. As soon as Mr. Khuda Buksh resigned, the company started going down.

He constantly kept saying one thing, "If you work hard, then you will get the reward." He was a good man and he was constantly busy discussing life insurance.

He was so nice, and so curious. He used to say, "When you have to pay something to someone, you should do it immediately. Before insuring, you should ensure whether the deal is safe." As far as the bank affiliate was concerned, he was anxious to pay as soon as possible so that the business could progress. He would say, "The main thing is the claim in the life insurance, but try to settle the claim as soon as possible."

He told me and other people that if your man has committed the wrong thing to a client, and he is working under you, then you have to fulfill that promise.

There Was no Team Leader Better than Him in All of Pakistan . . .

Abul Mahmood[39]

I CAME TO KNOW Mr. Khuda Buksh and his family since he was posted, at that time, in Karachi, West Pakistan. I was appointed deputy manager of Life. I became very close to him, and I really appreciated his effort. But I was not very much impressed with Mr. Khuda Buksh's features and appearance, the way he used to talk and all. But he had the ability to get accepted by people very quickly. He took care of me . . . during the field side first.

I was doing my business in those days, and he appreciated me and wrote good letters to me, until his death. He, along with his entire family, took me as their family member. They called me *Chacha* (uncle). When I went to Dhaka, I always visited Mrs. Khuda Buksh and I was well entertained.

He used to work like anything, even at the cost of his family. He would forget his family and live this side, that is in West Pakistan, only with the help of a servant who used to cook for him. Sometimes, his family came to visit him and went back after a few days. In one way, Mrs. Khuda Buksh helped him reach success by allowing him to run about places here for the sake of his business.

He did not give much importance to the officers and the field side became his friend. The business he used to be associated, was both East Pakistan and West Pakistan, and he became very famous. His lifestyle was very simple. He wanted his field officers to get good cars and didn't mind if he himself had to use an ordinary

---

[39]Former Senior Executive, State Life Insurance Corporation, Karachi, Pakistan. For details, see appendix K. Interview date: 25 March 2003)

car. In those days, Fiat and other cars were there. And slowly, he earned Mr. Bhimjee get him cars, Mercedes, and other thing.

He, himself, earned his status through his personality – he was such a good man. If anybody were sick, Mr. Khuda Buksh would go to his house right from the airport and ask "Why are you sick?" If the concerned worker said that he had not been well for the last few days and had therefore not been able to come to office, Mr. Khuda Buksh would immediately arrange for monetary assistance, and with that help, the worker would be able to resume his job. In this way, Mr. Khuda Buksh kept the workers mobile and the business was benefited.

There was one more thing about Mr. Khuda Buksh – he was very punctual. He would come to the office at 9 0'clock and every day, he would be very well dressed, in suit tie and all, even if it was very hot.

Mr. Khuda Buksh never took advantage of his position in the life insurance business. In fact, he never indulged his family members to come into insurance. He was a very honest and kind-hearted man, and he was also very successful. He never instituted any policy himself; he always used to depend on organization. There was no team leader better than him in all of Pakistan. His leadership skills surpassed even those of the leaders in foreign countries. He brought people from other companies to Eastern Federal. He treated his junior staff or field workers very justly and in a friendly manner. Anybody could come and see him. He never made any claims about his technical ability. He depended on people like Mr. Walajahi in those days.

I attended the Eastern Federal's Dhaka Convention for the Field force in 1967. The courtesy and hospitality extended by the hosts there were very good. They put us up in a hotel and they were very welcoming. Mr. Bhimjee gave the finest speech that I have ever heard in my life. When Khuda Buksh used to give a speech, it was partly in English, partly in Bengali and partly in Urdu. But both the Urdu speaking and non Urdu-speaking people accepted him.

When I went to Dhaka, (it was not Bangladesh yet) I went to Mr. Khuda Buksh's office and then people came to meet me, and they said, "Oh, Mr. Mahmood, you can sell some insurance in Karachi, but not in Dhaka." I sold three insurance policies, each of 5 lacs [$105,000] and telephoned Khuda Buksh and said "Please send the medical man here. I'm sitting here." He says, "No EFU." I said, "Look, you have to take this policy because I have come here." When I came to Karachi, everybody was very happy. That was the first time I sold policy in East Pakistan.

In West Pakistan Mr. Bhimjee was the main man who guided Mr. Khuda Buksh and the success here is due to Mr. Khuda Buksh. In East Pakistan Mr. Khuda Buksh used to work by himself and that is how the feeling was there.

When he gave resignation, he had not yet reached the retirement age. But after the death of his mother he became very much disinterested about his life and everything fell apart. She died one year before his retirement. After Mr. Khuda Buksh retired from EFU, he formed some company in East Pakistan – Federal Life Insurance Company. When I heard the news that late Khuda Buksh had launched his own company in the eastern wing of the country I appreciated it very much, because Khuda Buksh at that age, had great love for the life insurance business.

He offered me directorship. I told him that the political parties of East Pakistan would throw me out. Besides, my clients, my property – everything was in West Pakistan, and I could not really leave Eastern Federal. Other companies also tried to take me. I told them, "I will never join any other company. I have joined Eastern Federal to stay. My dead body will be carried by Eastern Federal people and not by anyone else." I am still with Eastern Federal and people still respect me. But I must say that Mr. Khuda Buksh was the backbone of life insurance at Eastern Federal and he gave me much encouragement.

If Bangladesh had not Come into Existence . . .

M. A. Chishti[40]

I MET MR. KHUDA Buksh for the first time in a convention, organized by the Insurance Association of Pakistan. I was introduced to him by a friend of mine. I don't remember the exact date, but when I met him I found him very straightforward. He was a very lean and thin person. But he was a very good conversationalist. I was always working in general insurance and he was with life insurance. At the time, I thought, he is the person who can deliver goods and to be very frank, later on, I came to know that the person introduced to me was Khuda Buksh, the man who had done his best to create a name for EFU in East Pakistan. Previous to that, Muslim Insurance was Muslim Insurance and Ideal Life, which was previously Indian Life. They were very active in East Pakistan. I also found him to be a very humble person.

Thereafter, I remember having met him at a certain convention that was held in a Beach Luxury hotel. It was organized by Roshen Ali Bhimjee, and since we knew each other, I was also invited there as an outsider, as a guest. I recall that by that time, I had the understanding that Khuda Buksh had done wonders for EFU.

I'm also in insurance profession. Insurance is the most difficult profession in the world because it is very difficult to sell insurance policies. This is a universal fact. A person who is in insurance knows how to persuade people. He knows how to sell insurance policy. Unless you are convinced about your own profession, about the product, which you are going to sell in the market, you cannot achieve success.

---

[40]Former Managing Director, Prime Insurance Company, Karachi, Pakistan. For details, see Appendix K.

Once you are 100 percent convinced that this is a very good thing, it will bring some benefit to the person who is going to buy this product, you can succeed because 50 percent convincing has come from your heart. When a person has that kind of conviction it also becomes very easy to convince his subordinates or those people working under him. If you consider what attributes a good manager or leader should possess, the most important thing that comes to mind is that he should know how to manage people. Once you know how to manage people, you can easily train them, you can easily convince them about those things, which you want them to do. Mr. Khuda Buksh had a strong conviction about his profession. He had no problems in convincing anybody or training them since his integrity was exemplary. So everybody trusted him, and when a person trusts you it becomes very easy for you to convince him or to launch something in the market.

So, as far as his character is concerned, it was exemplary. His integrity was wonderful. Of course, to be very frank, he was a self-made man.

He was down-to-earth and very humble. He never took airs. EFU was, at that time, the largest insurance company in Pakistan. And the entire trust of Roshen Ali Bhimjee was on life side, not on general side. And despite being the No. 1 person on the life side, Khuda Buksh did not have any airs. He was absolutely humble. He never behaved as if he was the chief of the Life Department, of the largest company of the state. If you ask me if he accepted criticism, I would say that a man who is humble is usually prepared to accept criticism. Besides, as I said, he was straightforward and honest, and if a man is straightforward and honest he will welcome that somebody is pointing out his shortcomings and then start from scratch.

When people met him, they instantly liked him. That was his quality. When for the first time I met him, I don't know why I started liking him because he was selling Life Insurance and I was selling non life insurance.

He was a very good leader, and this was apparent from the fact that he could train not one, but hundreds, and thousands of people. All his subordinates were just like his children. They were loyal to him. They would have sacrificed their lives for his sake. To be very frank, I heard that when Bangladesh came into existence two years after his resignation, the people who were working with him in EFU were prepared to resign and join his new company. That shows he was a leader, he was a team builder and he was a manager in the truest sense of the word. EFU was not popular, not well received in East Pakistan at that time. But when he joined EFU, he started progressing by leaps and bounds.

I think one can build his credibility if he is sincere and straightforward with himself as well as his subordinates. He must be prepared to help them, educationally, morally, physically, financially, then he can gain their loyalty. Secondly, he should be prepared to sacrifice his time and his energy for subordinates, then he can gain their confidence as well as credibility. Late Khuda Buksh had all these qualities, and that is how he gained the credibility and trust of his subordinates.

He was a very good speaker, he had his own style. He was always very convincing, no matter what he was saying. The proof lies in the fact that he could not have been such a successful salesman if he were not a good conversationalist, or if he was unable to deliver his ideas or express them properly. I think he was the only person who could match Wisaluddin on life side.

As far as the salesmanship is concerned, Wisaluddin was No. 1. Wisaluddin's way of working was completely different. After Wisalaluddin if there was any other person, it was Khuda Buksh. Wisaluddin was a very good speaker and a very good salesman. But his father and his younger brother, Jamaluddin, were also in insurance. In contrast, Khuda Buksh came from a poor family [Not true – Editor]. He was a person who was self-made.

He was not a politician. So when he joined EFU, the Field Marshall wanted to have a very good commerce minister, so somebody suggested the name of Mr. Khuda Buksh. And he was called by Field Marshall Ayub Khan and he said "No, I'm not a politician." This episode is to be interpreted in another context. If he had been after money, or if he had been a greedy person, he would've joined. But because he was honest and straightforward, he decided to stay in his own profession instead of joining the cabinet of Field Marshall Ayub Khan.

Khuda Buksh joined in 1952; Bhimjee came in 1960 as general manager of EFU. The main contribution to the success of EFU came from Khuda Buksh. To be very frank, the credit goes to Khuda Buksh, not to Roshen Ali Bhimjee. But the method of Roshen Ali Bhimjee was absolutely different. His method and the method of Abbas Khaleeli was the same. They were employing very good people, the best people from the market, and they were taking the entire credit to themselves. The differences arose when Roshen Ali Bhimjee tried to take the entire credit instead of giving the due credit to Khuda Buksh. In a company, there are always some people who are very honest and who say whatever is right. But there are other people who are flatterers and who are after their own promotion. So, these people created the differences between Khuda Buksh and Mr. Roshen Ali Bhimjee. So Mr. Roshen Ali Bhimjee was thinking to have some excuse, or something due to which he may . . .

Mr. Khuda Buksh was certainly very humble, very accommodating. But he was very, very stubborn. He was stubborn not without any rhyme or reason, but he was stubborn with regard to his principles. When he saw his principles being threatened, he would take his position without caring whether he would stay in the organization or not. I don't remember exactly, but my recollection is that the main reason behind his resignation from EFU was related to some property or land, which he purchased in East Pakistan . . .

Mr. Khuda Buksh's departure left a huge dent on EFU. Because at that time, on account of Mr. Muhammad Ishaq Khan, Muslim Insurance had become very very active in East Pakistan. Their business was coming from East Pakistan, and lot of business was from West Pakistan. And then, initially they were including American Life . . . But the dent was very severe. That is my assessment.

To be very frank, if Khuda Buksh had stayed in EFU and Bangladesh had not come into existence, then I'm sure Khuda Buksh would have become No. 1 in insurance industry in Pakistan.

If I Would Have the Opportunity to Work Again with Mr. Khuda Buksh!

Ahkam Siddiqui[41]

I MIGRATED FROM INDIA and stopped at Lahore while coming to Karachi. At Lahore I was staying with my uncle. Aga Nasir, a friend of my uncle happened to be there. Aga Nasir found that I was coming from India and was interested in joining some insurance company. Mr. Aga Nasir took me and introduced me to Mr. Roshen Ali Bhimjee, who was visiting the Lahore office. Mr. Bhimjee took a detailed interview and he inquired where I would like to settle. I mentioned about Hyderabad and then he gave me two names, Mr. Alam and Mr. Khuda Buksh. He advised me to meet them. I went to Mr. Khuda Buksh. That physically small person had a big brain and heart for this insurance field.

When I met him I was very much impressed with the way he was interviewing me. I introduced myself to him in reference to Mr. Bhimjee. We talked and then he sent me to late Mr. Alam in Karachi. I think he was number two of Mr. Khuda Buksh. I went back to Hyderabad and started the business.

I joined Eastern Federal in October 1963. I started as organization officer. Mr. Khuda Buksh gave me the choice of Hyderabad. Mr. Fakhruddin Siddique was there who was my senior. He was dealing with Eastern Federal and we had a very small team there, consisting of myself, Mr. Fakhruddin, Mr. Rizwanul Haque, Mr.

---

[41]Former Deputy General Manager, Southern Zone of State Life Insurance Corporation, Pakistan.

Abul Hassan Siddique and few other people. Mr. Khuda Buksh always gave me a personal touch, for which I was in need at that time because we had migrated from our native land. We had, of course, come over at our own wish. But we were still disturbed at having left our country and everything there.

When I joined Eastern Federal in Hyderabad there was a small office. It was a combined office of Eastern Federal General and Eastern Federal Life. Mr. Fakhruddin was in charge of the Life section and Mr. Rahim was in charge of the General business. I also left the job there. But Mr. Khuda Buksh encouraged me very much. He was a man of great character.

As soon as I joined Eastern Federal, I wanted money because I had great responsibilities of my own. In the last quarter of 1963 – 5th October to 31st December – I personally produced Rs. 46,000 [$9,600] of premium. Since then we could not provide any approach to any person to beat us. Of course, this miracle was not only my achievement. Behind the curtain was Mr. Khuda Buksh, who helped us and encouraged us in the field. That was actually his effectual interest on the profession of insurance. Once he was talking about the importance of a salesman. He was saying that people feel shy in selling, but it is not like that. Khuda Buksh had started business in Calcutta. He said that whenever he traveled by bus, he kept his business card to display his dealing with the insurance industry. So, that was the cause of his success, when he joined Eastern Federal himself as the life manager in Karachi and also when he was in charge of the business in Dhaka. He was in charge of both wings of Pakistan.

His lifestyle was very encouraging. Whenever we happened to be here in Karachi we used to go to his residence. We discussed the business and progress in Hyderabad. In the office he invited people for dinner and lunch. He was always very active. One never felt bored in his company. He was determined and motivating. He was a life soldier. He was ready always. He was very homely, very loving, and always busy in interacting with the field personnel and talking about insurance. The main characteristic of Mr. Khuda Buksh was that he was the personal fan of every field worker. He was always asking about their family members, their worries, and if there was anything they wanted for the family. He was always helpful to other people. That was one of the best years – our business was always increasing and the other companies were losing business. Eastern Federal's profit was increasing every year. Ultimately, we were the top insurance company in the country and the credit goes to late Khuda Buksh.

He was in the hearts of the people. He grasped everything about them – what their needs were, how much they should be earning and so on. Then he dictated the things to the person. That was the secret of his success.

He was personally involved with the people and we could feel it. He would talk to people just like an elder brother. He was always talking about the benefits of the other side – about the concerned person. He could act like the common man and he was very friendly. I can say this because he was involved in my personal matters.

I purchased almost a brand new car in 1964. Unfortunately it was not working. In the morning, it wouldn't start. In the Eastern Federal parking lot at about 6 p.m., my driver, the *chowkidar* (guard), and I were trying to push it. It was not starting. Fortunately, Mr. Khuda Buksh came down from his office and inquired, "Ahkam, what happened!" I said that the car was creating problems for me. Khuda Buksh said, "That's really sad! You should dispose of it! Leave it here, and come to my office tomorrow, and you will have another car, a Volkswagon!" Next morning I came early and went to Khuda Buksh's office. Mr. Jeelani and Mr. Hasanie were there. Khuda Buksh told them, "He's having some trouble; he has this car from Mr. Salim. He will take another car – you go and give him another car from the lot."

He was a very sincere person. He was sincere with the workers. He always wanted that the people should progress in the industry and then the industry could progress as well. He had the capacity to talk to one like a best friend.

In my opinion, he was a big team builder. He talked to people and they always retained what he said. The basic characteristic of Mr. Khuda Buksh was that he was a very personal observer. He touched the heart of a person and that was the main thing. He never made a claim that he was very knowledgeable but his worked proved it. He was a good listener and that was the secret of his success. He always appreciated the job done by everyone. He was a very big admirer of the field workers. When they did a good job or an extraordinary job he always showed his appreciation by writing letters to them. He had the charge of both wings – East and West. He was doing a nice job and everybody was appreciating his efforts and his success. The people respected him highly.

Khuda Buksh was always helpful to people who were in trouble. He believed that if anyone was suffering, he deserved to be treated rightly and justly. He was always helpful – he would always give his decision in favor of the client.

I attended the Eastern Federal's Dhaka Convention for the field force in 1967. It was quite good, in every aspect. That was the first time I visited Dhaka. It is a known fact that Mr. Khuda Buksh was a very good host. He served everyone like anything. He said, "You are in my own town." We fully enjoyed the weather there. Everyone enjoyed it, and remembered it always.

I did not ever feel that the phenomenal progress achieved by Eastern Federal during the decade of the 60s was wrongly attributed to some personalities other than late Khuda Buksh. But at Dhaka Convention we could feel that there were some things between Bhimjee and Khuda Buksh. We felt it . . . it was something, which was started there, it came to light that there was something fishy between the two persons. And we knew the result of course. In my opinion, both Late Roshen Ali Bhimjee and Khuda Buksh had their own positive and negative sides. But when we compare the two personalities I have a feeling that Mr. Khuda Buksh was a very simple and fair person, whereas the other was a businessman and he always thought like that. This is my personal feeling; I don't know whether it's correct. In my opinion, Syed Jeelani was the person in the insurance industry who followed in the footsteps of the late Khuda Buksh.

I was working as the division manager when Khuda Buksh left Eastern Federal. When Khuda Buksh left us, I was compelled to leave Eastern Federal. The disappearance of Mr. Khuda Buksh from Eastern Federal was a shock to all, mostly to the field workers. It had a bad effect on the insurance business of this wing. People worried for the sake of their earnings and they had to earn the money. There was a gap left by the absence of Mr. Khuda Buksh. But the fact that late Khuda Buksh had launched his own company in the Eastern wing of the country came to us as good news. I personally wondered if I would have the opportunity to work again with Mr. Khuda Buksh. It was very difficult, but I felt like being with him. Before my retirement in July 1999, I was heading the southern zone as the deputy general manager.

"Even Today, my inspiration is Khuda Buksh... It is Almost 30 Years!"

Iftekhar A. Hanfi[42]

IT WAS WAY back in April 1960 when I met Mr. Khuda Buksh and that was in a hotel. Now it is Frederick's Cafeteria; formerly, it was Ampies, near Metropol Hotel. I had gone there with a friend of mine who was working for Eastern Federal and Mr. Khuda Buksh came in there and I was introduced to him. Then Mr. Khuda Buksh invited me to see him in his office, and I went after two days. My friend's name was Mr. Majed, a class fellow of mine. Ampies was a very popular place for insurance people and a lot of insurance people used to sit there in the evening. When Mr. Khuda Buksh was in Karachi, he used to buy bakery products from there. Whenever he visited that café, he would find some people from life insurance sitting there. He would quietly go to the counter, take his things from there, and then tell the counter man that the bills of all the insurance people should be sent to him the next morning. It was understood, that the next day's bill would be paid by Khuda Buksh.

My first impression was that Mr. Khuda Buksh was a Bengali. He used to talk in Urdu, and the manner in which he pronounced words in English and in Urdu interested me. He appeared to me to be a very cheerful person. And I must say, I was impressed by Mr. Khuda Buksh because of his simplicity and his sincerity, which was reflected in the conversation.

---

[42]Former Manager Development, State Life Insurance Corporation, Pakistan. For details, see Appendix K.

I joined Eastern Federal, as I said, in April '60, and until Mr. Khuda Buksh left, in 1969, I was with that company. Whenever Mr. Khuda Buksh was here in Karachi (his family used to live in East Pakistan), I used to see him almost everyday in the afternoon when he would come back from the office or late at night, say around 9 o'clock or 10 o'clock. If any day I didn't come, he would call me, "Hanfi, what happened? You didn't come." I would say, "Sir, I am coming." Whether it was 10 o'clock or 10:30, I would reach Mr. Khuda Buksh, despite the distance, which was there between my residence and his.

He was a very simple person. His lifestyle was very simple and he had set principles. He would come to the office 10 minutes earlier. And he would leave the office after 5, 5:30. At lunchtime he used to go home and take very simple lunch. There was only one person, who acted as his cook. He would prepare a simple dinner and Mr. Khuda Buksh would invite people – me, Mr. Jeelani, Mr. Abul Mahmood – anyone at all. He was not interested in any expensive dresses, in any expensive car, or in any expensive hobbies. All the time, his concern was his company, his business, and his people. He never boasted about anything or said the like of – "I have done this, I have done that, and I am such a great person". He was very humble, simple, down-to-earth and straightforward. As far as we are concerned, if he promised anything, he fulfilled it. He would never go back on his word.

He used to love his people like a father would love his children. From Chittagong to Peshawar, he knew the name of each and every field worker, whether he was an agent, a manager or a regional manager. He personally knew the name and family circumstances of a person, irrespective of his designation. He used to call so many people . . . "Last time I came to your city, you told me about your difficulties in getting admission . . . did you get it?" "No, sir I didn't." "OK, give me the name of the school and I'll talk to the education authorities." He used to talk to the government people and the influential people, and help us that way. His simplicity, his love for his people . . .

Luckily, I was very near to him. I joined in 1960. In 1968, after eight years of association with Eastern Federal, I became Regional Manager. That was only because of the motivation, which came to me through Mr. Khuda Buksh. I told you that I used to go to his house almost every day when he was in Karachi and he used talk to me, "You are a young man, you have to do this, you have to do this, you have to do this." I also got married in 1960 and after 2-3 years, when my children were very young, he used to tell me, "You have to get your children educated in that school, in that school, in that school, and if you ever feel any difficulty, tell me. I will be able to talk to the education secretary. I will be able to talk that minister, I will be able to talk to this and that . . ." And he did all that for me. So, I was very, very close to him. I can still tell you that whatever I became in life insurance was because of Mr. Khuda Buksh. No one contributed as much to my progress as Mr. Khuda Buksh.

He would never say he was a great man in life insurance. He used to say that in order to be successful, one had to follow great people, read about them, know them and then one would get inspired with the achievements of those people. He would tell us stories about the days when he was selling life insurance. He told stories about so many people, with whom he had come into contact, and who were engaged in selling life insurance in his days. He would tell us motivational stories about these people – how they started their businesses, how they resolved the problems that came their way and continued their journey toward progress. He gave us real stories about real people.

He was a team builder. He would not sleep if he got the disturbing news that somebody was leaving the company. He was always so concerned about these people and he often helped them without letting anyone else know. He was a man who never liked to have all the power. He used to authorize other people. He used to share. Whenever he would delegate some job to someone, he would do it with all sorts of faith in him. He never gave responsibility and power to people, only to question them later, "How have you done this?" He would delegate responsibility to other officers, but with full confidence, that he would do the right thing. He never used to doubt his people.

He used to treat his field workers like his own children. He had respect for each and every person, even for the peon in his office. He would visit his house. He was forthright, but with discretion. He was businesslike. At times he was diplomatic also. He had all the plus points, which a senior executive needs. He meant each and every word he said. He was also receptive to criticism. I think he would listen, and then he would either give his explanation or agree, saying, "You are right". He was a very good orator. He used to talk to people for hours and he would never get tired. He was not only a good orator, but also an effective one.

Eastern Federal had become a household name in those days. Everyone used to know Eastern Federal, and any officer you talked to, would mention Mr. Khuda Buksh. He was such a popular man. But he would always give credit to others, saying, "Mr. Roshen Bhai has done this . . ." He would never take credit. Whenever there was a meeting, and Mr. Bhimjee was present, he would give all the credit to Mr. Bhimjee, then to Mr. Alam, then to Mr. Jeelani and so many other people.

Khuda Buksh was not a Ph.D in life insurance. He had practical experience. But the great thing about him was that he was a sincere person. He would never tell lies and he meant every word he spoke. He used to help people in their bad times, and if you were sincere to yourself, your friends and your institution, you could always build that kind of respect with Mr. Khuda Buksh.

I remember many incidents [related to Mr. Khuda Buksh].

In 1964, there were some linguistic problems in Karachi. And in those incidents, some people were killed also. Eventually, curfew was imposed. As a result, Federal

B area, where I used to live, came under curfew. And many of our Eastern Federal workers were living in that area. Soon after that, Mr. Khuda Buksh rang me up and told me: "Because of this curfew, you and many of our friends would not be able to come to the office. So I have obtained two curfew passes – one for you and one for my driver. And I'm sending my car to you. In the boot [trunk] of the car, there are packets of flour, ghee, rice, and cereals packets, et cetrea. And in addition, the driver has Rs. 8,000 [$1,680] in cash. I have asked the driver to go to your house. You will go to all our people who are residing in those areas and see if anyone needs anything. All the things, which are usually needed, are there in the car. You give these things to them. Cash is there and can be paid to them. If there is any real difficulty, if someone is sick and needs help, collect these information and come down to my office, and then we can send the doctor or any other help which is required by those people. We will immediately arrange that because I cannot ignore my people who are working for my company or for me. I cannot leave them unattended; I cannot leave them alone, so you have to do this."

So I went to each person's house, and provided him with whatever he needed. And there was a gentleman, he was also from East Pakistan, Mr. Muhammad Ali Akbar, whose child was sick, and there was no medicine available because of the curfew. I informed Mr. Khuda Buksh about this. He arranged for another pass and for a doctor. The doctor examined the child and the medicine was provided. He was such a fantastic man and was so concerned about his people. He used to love his people so much that not even for a moment, he would forget about them. He was always concerned about their welfare, about their health and about their families. Mr. Khuda Buksh used to tell me that when a person joins a life insurance company, it is not a contract that you will give us this much premium and we will give you this much commission. He used to tell me that introducing a person into the sales side of life insurance is a comprehensive and total arrangement. "You have to motivate him for doing business. You have to be concerned about his family circumstances. You are responsible also for their admission into schools and colleges, and whatever they need . . . because it is a complete contract. It is not just a business contract."

Akbar, one of our field workers, was producing a very meager amount of life insurance. He resigned and joined another insurance company. One of the days, while talking to Mr. Khuda Buksh, I told him that Akbar had left Eastern Federal and sent in his resignation. He asked me, "Do you know his residential address?" "I do," I replied. Those were winter days, and around 1 0'clock in the night, I received a telephone call from Mr. Khuda Buksh. He told me, "Can we talk?" I said, "Why not? If you want, I can come down to your place." He said, "Where does Akbar live?" I gave his address. Then he told me, "I'm coming to your house." My house was eight miles away from Mr. Khuda Buksh's. I said, "Alright." So he came and told me, "You told me that Akbar has resigned, and I was unable to sleep. Then I thought that I am going to visit him, and you are the one who can guide me. So come, let us go." But I said, "It's past 1 o'clock. I can bring Mr. Akbar to your office tomorrow morning." He said, "Don't say all these things. I'm not general manager; he's not a small worker." So I took him to Mr. Akbar's house, and everyone there was asleep. There were no chairs; they were all sleeping on the floor. So, when I told Mr. Akbar that Mr. Khuda Buksh had come and wanted to see him, Akbar started crying, and said, "Why has Mr. Khuda Buksh come? I could have come to his house," Mr. Khuda Buksh came out and he asked only one question, "Akbar, why did you leave? Why didn't you say you were having difficulties?" Akbar was still weeping. He said, "Sir, I'm not leaving Eastern Federal. I will stay with Eastern Federal until I die." Akbar was a Bengali also. Then, after 1971, all those people who came from East Pakistan were allowed to go to the Eastern Wing. But Akbar refused and he told me: "I had told Mr. Khuda Buksh that I would work for Eastern Federal until I die." And in 1973, Mr. Akbar died. He was a great person.

I once had a dispute with the chief, Mr. Roshen Ali Bhimjee. But there was no mediation from Mr. Khuda Buksh. He advised me to pay the utmost respect to Mr. Roshen Bhai and said, "This is a very small matter when you think about it. But you have to respect your seniors." Once, I had gone to Hyderabad. I wrote a proposal worth Rs 10,000 and the gentleman gave me the agreement of that proposal. I stayed in Hyderabad for two days and after two days I came to Karachi and submitted the proposal and the premium. But after two days I came to know that the person who had signed that proposal had died the same night in an automobile accident.

The information came to Mr. Alam and he called me and said 'You collected the premium and you did not deposit it and this is a criminal activity.'

I said, "I had gone to Hyderabad two days back, then I wrote this proposal, collected the premium, and since there was no office in Hyderabad, I could not deposit the premium. But when I came back to Karachi after two days, obviously the first thing I did was deposit the premium." So, I told Mr. Alam that since everything appeared to be absolutely in order and complete, I felt he would have to pay the claim.

Mr. Alam became furious and was very annoyed. "You did not deposit the premium during the lifetime of the person and now you are saying the company will pay the claim."

I said, "How could I deposit the premium during the lifetime of the person? I collected the premium and the proposal in the evening. The same night the person died. Even if I was in Karachi, I couldn't have deposited the premium in the office because the office was not open. But I, as a responsible person, had collected the papers."

He said, "We cannot pay the premium and this is something very bad and I'm going to take action against you."

Then I went to Mr. Khuda Buksh and told him the entire story. Then, Mr. Khuda Buksh said, "You are right. It wasn't possible for you to deposit because the office had already been closed and you were not there. But Hanfi, I tell you it will be very difficult to pay the claim because we had not received the papers and the premium. At the most, we can refund the premium deposited."

Later on, I consulted some people and went to court of law. And the claim was paid. But, that was on the advice of Khuda Buksh and he said that insurance is all about trust.

One day I left the office around 5. Mr. Khuda Buksh was still in his office. I came to the parking lot. I had an Opal car, hardly 2 years old. But the engine wouldn't start and I asked the *chowkidar* [guard] to push the car. So when the chowkidar started pushing the car, suddenly Mr. Khuda Buksh also appeared there. Then he told me in Urdu, in typical Bengali accent, "*Nai nai hum bhi dhakka lagayega, hum bhi dhakka lagayega.*" [I will also help push the car].

I came down and said, "Please sir, don't do this."

He replied again, "*Nai nai hum bhi dhakka lagayega, hum bhi dhakka lagayega.*"

I said, "There's some little problem with the battery. I will go to the shop and have it fixed up."

And after a great deal of difficulties, we managed to convince him to sit in his own car and go. Anyway, next day when I came to the office, our Deputy General Manager of Accounts, Mr. A.J. Dias, called me. He said, "Mr. Khuda Buksh has asked for you two, three times. You go and see him."

I said, "What is it all about?"

He said, "I don't know. But the first thing he did was to call me and ask, 'Where is Hanfi?'"

When I went to the office of Khuda Buksh, he was reading some papers on his desk. He looked at me and asked, "Hanfi, do you have your car?"

I said, "Yes."

"Give me the keys," he said.

So I took it out from my pocket and gave it to him. Then he asked for a cup of coffee, and when we finished the coffee, he said, "I need your car. Go and see Dias."

Then, I again visited A.J. Dias and narrated to him what had happened in the office of Mr. Khuda Buksh, and asked, "What do you have to say?"

He said, "You have to go to Munoo Motors, because they are the dealers of Toyota cars, and you choose whatever color you want. Mr. Khuda Buksh wants you to go to Munoo Motors. He has already talked to them. And meanwhile, we're keeping your Opal and we'll sell it out."

So, that's the kind of boss I had in Mr. Khuda Buksh.

I remember having attended the Dhaka Convention. He looked after hundreds of people from West Pakistan at that convention. He would inquire about each and every person – what his needs were, how he was feeling and whether he was comfortable. He used to come to our hotel. In my case, towards the end of the convention, I became sick, I was running high temperature. I stayed at Mr. Khuda Buksh's house in Dhanmondi for seven days. I was looked after.

Mr. Khuda Buksh, for me, was a role model. He was my idol. Even till today, I have never seen a better person in the insurance profession. I used to enjoy every moment of his company. He wouldn't talk much; he would say one word, and then he would sit, and ask questions, and suddenly come back to my family . . . These were the things, which he used to ask when I went to him for professional guidance. He would never say that this man is working with Eastern Federal. He would always say that man is working with me, that man is working with my company. He would not say Eastern Federal. Whenever he introduced a worker, he would say "my man."

He would recognize people. His methods of recognizing people were altogether different. If I had done a wonderful job, first of all, he would send a telegram to my wife and he would write in that telegram: "I wish to congratulate you, that your husband has done this, this, this, and we value his contribution." And when the wife told her husband that Mr. Khuda Buksh had talked to her, he would naturally feel very proud of the company and Mr. Khuda Buksh and the people. That was the first thing he would do. Then, most of the time in those days, ornaments, saris and household items were given as prizes. He would say, "I want these prizes to go to your house because if your wife is wearing this ornament, she will always cherish and remember the institution. And if EFU presents you a dinner set, every time there is some function in the house, you will tell your people that the company has given you this beautiful set." He wanted that the institution should always be with a person, whether he was in his house or elsewhere.

His strategy for resolving the disputes and conflicts among the parties was very interesting. He would call both the parties, ask for a cup of coffee, and then sit silently doing his job. He wouldn't talk to either party. They would sit there for one hour, two hours, or even three hours in the office. Then he would say, "Do you still have some differences?" People were so tired of sitting there, they would say, "No sir, there is no dispute."

I felt that Mr. Khuda Buksh's departure from Eastern Federal was the worst thing that could have happened to Eastern Federal, or for that matter, to any institution. That was most unfortunate. Probably, there was some sort of personality clash between the higher ups. Since Mr. Bhimjee was No. 1. and Mr. Khuda Buksh was only heading the life department, so obviously Mr. Bhimjee had too many cronies and flatterers around him. When they felt that the boss was not happy with Mr. Khuda Buksh, they all started ignoring Mr. Khuda Buksh. But in reality, as far as the company is concerned, the late Mr. Khuda Buksh was by far the most important person.

The way he left that company was very painful. But the corporate politics, as you might call it, or clash of personalities, was probably responsible for it. Mr. Bhimjee was perhaps afraid of Khuda Buksh's popularity. For instance, whenever the news came that he was coming from Dhaka, hundreds of people would welcome him at the airport and garland him. He was not a very tall man, so at times you would not be able to see where Mr. Khuda Buksh had gone. He was drowned in those flowers. So that was the extent of his popularity. I had once said to Mr. Khuda Buksh, "You have to see from this angle also, that you are becoming very popular. In fact, you are in our hearts."

Apparently the show might have hurt Mr. Bhimjee and he might have felt threatened. And that is exactly what happened. So, they were unhappy with the kind of popularity Mr. Khuda Buksh had and they developed some kind of fear, although that was perhaps not real. But still, that was the cause. He was such a great man, but his departure from Eastern Federal was disgraceful.

I was very depressed. I was absolutely disturbed. The circumstances in which he left Eastern Federal were puzzling to me. Because when he sent his resignation, he probably had some difference of opinion with the higher ups. I wouldn't mind naming the person, perhaps, besides Mr. Bhimjee, Mr. Alam was also to some extent involved in it – in tarnishing the image of Mr. Khuda Buksh. The way he left Eastern Federal was so painful, that none of the people even invited him for lunch or a cup of tea, which can be termed as a meeting just to say farewell . . . Myself and late Mr. Wasif Ali . . . the two of us arranged dinner for Khuda Buksh, and invited around 14 persons, 14 friends from Eastern Federal to join us. But no one came. And instead I got a message, that the high officials would not be very happy with us. There were 16 tables, but there were only 3 persons there having dinner.

He again came back to Karachi and when I heard this, I went to see him. He was alone and he was sick, probably he was running a high fever and no one had come to him. So I took him to the doctor.

Roshen Ali Bhimjee and Khuda Buksh, both of them are not here. I have great respect for Mr. Bhimjee also. But these chief executives, they have their own roles to play and there is some amount of corporate politics inside the offices. But I can only tell you one thing: Mr. Khuda Buksh was a great man and I have not yet seen a person who is like him.

I was very happy when I heard the news that late Khuda Buksh had launched his own company in the eastern wing of the country. I had decided to join his company as soon as a branch opened in Karachi, and in fact I told Mr. Khuda Buksh of this wish. He said, "No, you have a set career with Eastern Federal. Don't do this." I said, "I'm not with Eastern Federal. I'm with Khuda Buksh."

I have only one thing to say. In the business of life insurance, I have never seen a person as great as Mr. Khuda Buksh. I can say safely that Mr. Jeelani, Mr. Wasif Ali and Mr. Alvi followed Mr. Khuda Buksh. And even today, my inspiration is Khuda Buksh. My role model is Khuda Buksh and my teacher is Khuda Buksh. It is almost 30 years, but he is still my professional guide.

Even After so Many Years I Still Remember Him. That is his Greatness

M. Fasihuddin [43]

I JOINED EFU IN 1964 as a junior officer and I was recruited on an all-Pakistan basis from a competitive examination. This was the first batch of young officers which Eastern Federal decided to induct into the company. The first batch was comprised of four young officers – two from East Pakistan and two from West Pakistan. After our recruitment we were given the option of joining the life department or general department. This arrangement was that one person from East Pakistan and one from West Pakistan should be on the general side and similarly one officer from East Pakistan and one from West Pakistan should be on the life side. So in this way, four officers were assigned. I opted for the general department, and with me was a Bengali gentleman named Kamal Ibn Yusuf, and on the life side there were two gentlemen, Mr. Rezaul Hakim, from East Pakistan, who rose to become the managing director of National Insurance Company of Bangladesh, and Mr. Afsar Akhtar Hossain, from West Pakistan, who remained with EFU on the life side and after natiionalization joined Credit & Commerce Insurance Company (UAE), which Mr. Bhminjee started. I am the only surviving person of the first batch who is still in EFU.

---

[43] Advisor, EFU- Life, Karachi, Pakistan. For more details, see appendix K.

My association with Mr. Khuda Buksh was very short – of about 4 or 5 years. But at that time, we had a lot of functions in EFU and there I had occasion to meet him because he was very kind to young officers. Whenever he saw us he would call us and ask how we were doing, whether we were facing any difficulties and if there was anything he could do. Also, I was not on the Life side, but even then he would call and ask what I was doing, what I was doing about the exams of chartered insurance institute and how much I was learning from it.

When we were recruited, Mr. Roshen Ali Bhimjee who was the managing director of Eastern Federal at that time called all the senior officers in the boardroom and introduced the four of us. I still remember – there was a galaxy of senior officers and we, newly recruited officers, were sitting on the other side. Mr. Bhimjee was conducting the program. Mr. Khuda Buksh was sitting on his right side and on his left side, was Mr. S.M. Moinuddin, who was the general manager of the general department. Mr. Khuda Buksh was the general manager of the life department. The other officers of the life and general department were also present. In that meeting, Mr. Bhimjee asked the officers to say something. Mr. Khuda Buksh complimented us on the selection because it was the first time in the history of Pakistan that any company had recruited young officers through a competitive examination, and great care had been taken to make the selection board as impartial as possible. The people who headed the board had interviewed us and we had had to sit for a 3-hour exam. There was a written paper. Mr. Khuda Buksh said that such a selection system had been devised by Eastern Federal where recruitment was being done on pure merit. This applies to me because I applied, I had no support, and I come from a middle class family. So he appreciated this. I think it was not the brainchild of any one person in Eastern Federal, but a decision taken by Mr. Bhimjee in consultation with two great men – Mr. Khuda Buksh and Mr. S.M. Moinuddin, that the selection board should be such. He made sure that no one from Eastern Federal should sit on the boards such that no one could influence the decisions of the board. Mr. Khuda Buksh congratulated us and assured us that we would have a good future in Eastern Federal. I was much impressed by the way he talked.

He was such a kind-hearted, learned and caring person, that I was very much impressed by him. Later on whenever I met him, I found him to be a person having the finest human qualities. As a leader, Mr. Khuda Buksh was excellent. Whenever he came to East Pakistan, which was quite frequently, people used to go to the airport to receive him in large numbers. I really used to wonder why so many people were going all the way there to receive him. At times, there used to be 30, 40 people receiving him at the airport. And they would always make a beeline when Mr. Khuda Buksh was in his office, and Mr. Khuda Buksh would patiently hear everybody. I used to see him moving about very frequently to various departments, and there used to be at least 4 or 5 senior officers all moving with him from department to department. You could see the love and affection, which Mr. Khuda Buksh generated from the faces of even the smallest person, the peon, I mean. It was not because of his position; it was because of his personality, his very fine human qualities. He genuinely cared for people.

I can narrate an example, which was related to me. We had language problems after '62, and there were curfews in Karachi for 2, 3 days. It was narrated to me that when this curfew period was relaxed, Mr. Khuda Buksh would send envelopes containing money to those areas where field workers and officers of Eastern Federal Life department were living. Each and every officer was visited and handed an envelope because the curfew made it impossible for them to draw money. And at that time 300 rupees or 400 rupees [$63 or $84] was given to each officer to buy necessities. He was so caring about his staff and field workers. I can say that on the General side, this thing was not done, but on the Life side because of Mr. Khuda Buksh this was done and this was a great motivating factor in whatever the EFU on the Life side could achieve as the number one company in the country. Mr. Khuda Buksh could motivate people to work and give their best to the company because of these small, small things. If you care about people they really pay you back in terms of their love, hard work, devotion and gratitude. And this was the quality of leadership I found in Mr. Khuda Buksh. Mr. Tarique Muktar – used to work for life department and then left for Dubai and is now working with a local company there since about 14 or 15 years. He narrated this incident to me because he himself was a recipient of one of the envelopes. He was living in north Nazarbar and at that time the curfew was spread throughout.

He always encouraged me. He said that I had a great future because in insurance industry very few companies were bringing in new blood. EFU was the first company to do it, and he said that I had a very great future. He would always encourage me. Whenever he saw me he would call me by name. He would say, "Fashi, how are you doing? I am sure you're happy and comfortable."

He was a very simple person, full of humility, and had no airs. If you met him, you would not be able to say that he was the chief of Eastern Federal Life department. He was such an outstanding person. He would meet you in a very humble manner – that was a great quality of his. Once, when he was taking rounds of the department, he saw a broom lying on the floor. He picked it up himself, instead of asking somebody, and put it in the right place. This was a great quality in him. Being the general manager he could have ordered somebody or he could have become angry about why the broom was lying there in the wrong place. But he himself picked it up and placed it in the right place. I still remember that. The picture is very vivid in my mind. And he would help a lot of people secretly. This quality I found in a lot of great people. People didn't know what a large number of people were being helped by him. When they passed away, you came to know that he was the source of constant financial help to many widows, orphans and students from middle class families, who could not afford the fees. God always appreciates this quality in a man and this makes a man a great person. Mr. Khuda Buksh was one such great person.

I had very little interaction with him in business dealings because I was on the general side. I had no touch with the Life department. But I'm sure you cannot succeed in life unless you are fair in your business dealings.

He was a great team builder also. I mean I have just told you whenever he came back from East Pakistan or Lahore, so many people used to go to him. Even after he left Eastern Federal, most of the people used to visit him at his house. Normally, in our culture, if a person has left or has retired, people forget him. People could have stayed away from Mr. Khuda Buksh under the circumstances in which he left Eastern Federal. But I know, this is my personal knowledge that people used to visit him. That was the secret of his team building. He used to care for people and when you care for people you can make a team.

I think the key to his success was that he was available and accessible to everyone. Anyone could walk into his office and there were no restrictions. He had an open door policy. There is another aspect. No one can build credibility and trust if he is not honest. Credibility and trust are built if a man remains true to his commitments. Whenever Mr. Khuda Buksh made a commitment, whenever he said something or made a promise, he would fulfill it. That was the secret of his credibility.

Mr. Khuda Buksh was a willing listener; he accepted feedback and criticism. I mean this is the quality of all great people, and I consider Mr. Khuda Buksh to be a great personality. They listen to everyone very patiently and with full concentration when someone is talking to them. When someone visited Mr. Khuda Buksh, he would make that person feel as if that were the only thing he was doing at that time. He would give him full attention, with no distractions at all, and this really gave one confidence. Despite being the chief of Life department, he would listen attentively to the problems of a junior officer and would not get angry even if he were making some critical comment. Mr. Khuda Buksh never got angry, he would listen to problems and see to it that they were rectified.

I don't have any details as to why Mr. Khuda Buksh resigned, because I was then only a junior officer. But I think that at that time, in 1968-69, there was some disagreement on policy matters, about how the company should be run. And Khuda Buksh gave resignation from Eastern Federal. This is what I heard from other people.

In my opinion, the late Roshen Ali Bhimjee and Khuda Buksh were the most important players of a successful, dynamic and winning team – The Eastern Federal Union Insurance Company. Mr. Bhimjee, if I remember correctly, joined Eastern Federal in '60 or '61. And Mr. Khuda Buksh joined in 1952. Now we have to make a comparison, how Eastern Federal was doing before '60, '61 – Mr. Khuda Buksh was there all the time, since '52. And Mr. Bhimjee came at a very crucial and critical period because of some losses on the general department side. Mr. Bhimjee salvaged the company. And so far as the progress of the Life department is concerned I am not very familiar it. But if we take the figures before Mr. Bhimjee – how Eastern Federal was performing on the Life or General side – then later on 10 years after he joined – we'll be able to get an assessment of our own. Both of them were very good team builders – they had great qualities of head and heart. Both of them were very outstanding people. I think it was a combined effort.

I never had any occasion to talk to the late Khuda Buksh on this subject.[44] My own feelings are that any kind of success is achieved through teamwork. Any great achievement in any field is a result of a good team. If you have a good team in which various people are performing their jobs, success cannot be attributed to any individual. Because if somebody is saying this, I think it is wrong. But you can always say that the lion's share of what is being achieved is due to a certain person, because of his personality, his dynamism.

Under the rules, the retirement age of Eastern Federal was – 59 years – but it was not strictly followed. The officers whom the company needed were given extensions on a contract basis. Everybody has to retire but I was one of those persons whom the company considered could still serve them. They were even prepared to renew my contract as Deputy Managing Director but I decided that now young people should come up. So, I said that I would remain with the company in a different capacity, as adviser, such that the main line remained available for the young people to rise.

After the late Khuda Buksh's resignation, initially, I think there was a lot of gloom, because he was there with Eastern Federal for a long time. But since I was not very closely associated with the Life department, I am not able to say how the people on the Life department and the field force really felt. But there was a lot of gloom, a lot of questions were being asked as to why this had happened, because it came so suddenly.

There is a particular incident that I would like to relate. I had applied for a job in Pakistan Insurance Corporation (PIC). Mr. Khuda Buksh was the director of PIC and the board of directors was taking the final interview. And the chairman of PIC said, "Mr. Khuda Buksh said that I know this gentleman." He said I was very capable . . . But jokingly he said, "Mr. Khuda Buksh, since you have left Eastern Federal, your vote will not count in the selection." This was after he had left, of course, but even then he spoke so well of me and the board of directors listened to him. And they had a lot of respect for him. He commanded lot of respect in government circles. Wherever he went, everyone from the common man to the top man regarded him highly.

After resignation, Khuda Buksh launched his own company in the eastern wing of the country. My thoughts were that he would make it a great company just like he had made Eastern Federal, because he possessed great leadership qualities. Had

---

[44]Response to interview question: Did Khuda Buksh ever feel that the phenomenal progress achieved by Eastern Federal during the decade of the 60s was wrongly attributed to some personalities other than Khuda Buksh?

he been given time by God I think he would have made it as big a company as Eastern Federal.

I think Khuda Buksh has influenced a lot of people. I mean those who worked with Mr. Khuda Buksh, they imbibed a lot of his qualities, they tried to emulate him, they tried to follow his accomplishments. He set standards of how to motivate people, how to get the maximum out of them. I think the whole insurance industry owes a lot to Mr. Khuda Buksh. He was a great person, a great personality. Even after so many years I still remember him. That is his greatness.

Khuda Buksh: Who Treated me as his Own Son, his Child

M.B. Qadri[45]

IN AUGUST 1966 I first met Mr. Khuda Buksh in one of the functions of Eastern Federal. At that time I was with Mr. S. A. Walajahi and Late Mr. Roshen Ali Bhimjee, and they introduced me to general manager Mr. Khuda Buksh. On that first meeting, I was not actually impressed by his personality. However, many people came to meet me since I was in the library department, and from them, I gradually learned about his personality, and his understanding of life insurance and the development of life insurance.

As I said, when a person has interactions with another person, he gets to know him more deeply. So, after a while, I actually became an admirer of Mr. Khuda Buksh. He was a man with great heart and soul and his understanding of life insurance was outstanding. One of my very first interactions with him was at the closing time of EFU – around 6:30 p.m. He was walking in the Building # 7 and I observed that he was very much curious about the life insurance business and he was giving instructions to these other fellows about the business and he was encouraging people. Thereafter, I met him on various other occasions.

He was a simple man, and was not at all showy. He was a man of commitment. He was a great motivator to others. He was of the opinion that business should come by fair means and he was encouraging new business for EFU. Actually he was a very hard worker. I think that was his main quality, along with the fact that he was very

---

[45]Chief, Staff-training department, State Life Corporation. For details, see appendix K. (interview date: 12 March 2003).

soft-spoken. He never insulted anybody; rather he was always motivating people. And whenever I met him he shook hands with me, smilingly and very cheerfully.

I was in the research department looking after the library and he was not a very regular visitor but he was a casual visitor. He was interested in getting books and he also instructed me to get books on life insurance in Bengali language so that people could read them as well. And he gave me tips on purchasing them. I was a very young man at that time, about 25. He treated me as his own son, his child. He never scolded me or talked to me in a rough manner. He treated me with love and affection. And he used the same manner with all the junior staff.

There was one sales officer at that time, Mr. D.M Qureshi. Mr. Khuda Buksh inspired him to work hard and told him that he should get everyone who came his way insured, whether it was a policy worth Rs. 2,000 or 5,000 [$420 or $1.050]. His vision was to spread the message of life insurance. He was always talking about bringing more people into the life insurance business and working for the cause of life insurance. In this way, he made a good team for the insurance business. Whenever he promised to promote a person on the accomplishment of a certain task, he always fulfilled it, regardless of what other people thought. That is how he built his credibility and trust.

He was a good motivator. Whenever any of the field workers had done good business, had bought a policy, say worth Rs.2000, Mr. Khuda Buksh would arrange a function for him and garland him. That was the extent to which he would go in order to motivate the staff.

He was not a technical person, I think. He was a salesman, and he proved that selling is all about meeting and knowing people. But he never made any claims about his technical ability.

It is my observation that Mr. Roshen Ali Bhimjee had a very loud [opinionated] thinking about insurance and about people, and in that loud thinking Mr. Khuda Buksh is not to be compared with him in my opinion. He was a far better loud thinker of life insurance and about the people of Pakistan at that time than Mr. Khuda Buksh. I think that there should not be a separation of East and West Pakistan, [that Bhimjee] should have [been a] better man for EFU, and EFU should have done wonderful business with Mr. Bhimjee.

I may be wrong, but I think that when it came to a choice between East Pakistan and West Pakistan, Mr. Khuda Buksh was favoring some of the East Pakistani leaders. Bhimjee was managing director at that time and he probably did not honor Khuda Buksh's words in that matter.

But I don't think that Mr. Khuda Buksh felt that the phenomenal progress achieved by Eastern Federal during the decade of the 60s was wrongly attributed to some personalities other than him. He was a good friend of Mr. Bhimjee, he honored him, and he never claimed that "I did this, or I did that."

There was a setback in the business after the late Khuda Buksh's resignation because he was a popular general manager and a popular man in EFU, and after his departure people felt that the business had suffered a major drawback. When I heard the news that late Khuda Buksh had launched his own company in the eastern wing of the country, I thought that he was a man of insurance and he had taken the right step in establishing a company.

What I Remember of Khuda Buksh

Mohammed Choudhury[46]

I KNEW KHUDA BUKSH from the 50's since I was also in Eastern Federal in Calcutta in 1948 and '49. So I was the oldest associate of anyone in EFU. Khuda Buksh was a very fine man and I feel that he was not fairly treated. The way he was treated when he left and set up his own Life Company was not fair on the part of his employers. I think it was called Federal Life. There was a time when he was associated with Pakistan of today. After that he lived in Dhaka where he tried to promote his own company, Federal Life. But he didn't live very long. I think he passed away soon after the separation of Bangladesh from Pakistan. In my memoir, I shall try to give you a true picture of the man, without either praising or condemning him. I will not be able to say much about his working abilities. But I can certainly say that the man was capable of doing much more than he was allowed to do. That is the sad part.

* * *

It was in the month of September that I had the most interesting encounter with Mr. Khuda Buksh in London. The year was 1967. Mr. Khuda Buksh and I were staying at the Mount Royal Hotel on Oxford Street, but we did not know that we were both there at the same time. It was only per chance that we met each other outside the Hotel. Mr. Khuda Buksh was wearing a dark blue coat. The gentleman was short with a small built but he had a very powerful personality. He was a Bengali

---

[46]Managing Director and Chief Executive Officer, Adamjee Insurance Company Limited, Karachi, Pakistan. For details, see Appendix K.

on all accounts. Both he and I have always been proud of our origin, except that I always pulled his leg by saying that he was too short to compete with me!

Brilliant as he was, when I asked him where he found that coat, as obviously it was not from Dhaka, he whispered in my ears that it was from the Petticoat Lane in London, a place famous for defective clothes or cheap or rejected ones. Yet the place was enormously popular because every Sunday there was a market for the sale of things, mostly clothes and other apparel. With his expert Bengali eye he had selected that coat which was without any defect except that the inner buttons were in the wrong place and the big stores had rejected it. Thus it had landed in the Petticoat Lane for Khuda Buksh to buy.

His keen sense of economy was ideally suited for a Life Insurance man. He had to consider economy because he did not travel to London often and the coat would not have any value in Dhaka, it being a virtual tropical rain forest. Consequently he had to economize. He further added, in his exceptional sense of humour, that not being a *chaprasi* (an office attendent) he could not claim this from the Company, because only chaprasis were provided uniforms. He did not want to spend more of his hard earned money on the coat than he had planned.

Khuda Buksh had displayed exceptional calibre as a life insurance man in EFU. He was extremely successful as a business planner, sales man, sales executive and life insurance underwriter. The business volume of EFU in Life had reached such a level that the company could advertise that every second person having life insurance policy was insured with EFU. It was no mean success, in my view, and the credit goes almost entirely to Khuda Buksh. It was however sad that he was not appreciated as much by the higher management of his Company. This was perhaps out of jealousy and shortcoming in other life insurance executives within and outside the Company at that time. His success was not confined to the people of his own type but was all over Pakistan – at that time East and West Pakistan.

His visit to London was with a view to set up EFU in London – a soft beginning essentially with Pakistani population. Khuda Buksh was aiming to insure the Bangladeshi restaurant operators throughout London and their number was considerable. The gentleman was able to muster support mostly from his own people from Bengal, in London, but that was a good start in the field of life insurance for EFU in London.

Brilliant man that he was, EFU lost him because of the indifferent attitude demonstrated by the higher management. One day some years later we got the news that Khuda Buksh had left EFU. A man of his age, perhaps at that time he was in his 50s, could not sit idle and he decided to set up an insurance company in Dhaka and he did. I have not followed him since then but I expect that he had established that company with considerable success.

Since he was mostly in East Pakistan at that time, I lost contact because I was in Karachi and this continued. In my view, Khuda Buksh died relatively early and deprived Bengal of his immense value as a life insurance man. The man was a genius.

[Ed. The first paragraph was tape recorded by Rizwan Ahmed Farid when he met Mohammed Choudhury in March 2003. The second part was written by Mr. Mohammed Choudhury on 28 April, 2003.]

I Wouldn't Compare Anybody with Khuda Buksh

Vazir Ali F. Mohammad[47]

MY FIRST ASSIGNMENT was zonal accountant of the Central Zone based in Karachi. When I was auditing Eastern Federal, their life business was growing fast. There were a lot of field workers. Eastern Federal was a big company and there used to be a lot of hustle and bustle going around. At the time, I had not met Mr. Khuda Buksh because he was based in East Pakistan. But I had been hearing about him from the field staff. Mr. Khuda Buksh was the main name in EFU. The people were motivated by his personality. There used to be messages from him and newsletters, and I read those. It was through these that I came to know about the late Mr. Khuda Buksh. One day, after joining Eastern Federal in Sept. 1967, I was in my office . . . [office was on the ground floor]. One day, a gentleman walked in, in a completely unassuming manner (he had a garland around his neck and there were couple of people following him) and introduced himself as Mr. Khuda Buksh. So this is how I met Mr. Khuda Buksh and it was a very impressive way of meeting him. The way he came and met me, it seemed as if we had known each other for years, although it was our first meeting. So as you say, the first impression is the last impression, and this is how I got impressed with Mr. Khuda Buksh's personality from the very first meeting.

Mr. Khuda Buksh was a great man. I had about two year's association with him. Although he was based in East Pakistan, he regularly visited West Pakistan. And

---

[47]Executive Director, HASHOO group of companies, Karachi, Pakistan. For details, see appendix K. (Interview date: 30 March 2003).

every time he came to the Karachi office, I was the first person he visited since my office was situated very close to the staircase leading to the first floor. Every time, he would first walk into my office, wish me and then go upstairs.

He was punctual and regular in his office. The main thing about late Mr. Khuda Buksh was his personality. I would say he was a down-to-earth person. Though physically he was a short man, I think he had a very large heart. He was a large-hearted and a very kind man. I never saw him getting angry or annoyed or losing his temper. He was a very friendly, very amiable gentleman, and this is how I think he won the hearts of his friends and the people. And this is how he motivated his field force and the people around him. When I recall those days, I think people almost worshipped him because of his personality and his kindness and his amiable nature.

There were many facets of his personality. He was kind-natured, he was a good listener, and he never lost his temper. I think he would listen to anybody. He was not shy in meeting anybody, regardless of whether the person was a top officer or a peon. He would meet both these people in the same manner. So he was not discriminatory. People knew he was easily accessible. One could talk to him. The other thing was that he had a very friendly nature. One did not have to take an appointment to see him or knock on his door to enter his office. Anybody could walk into his office, and even if he were busy, he would never lose his temper or turn one out. He knew how to treat a person, and his methodology of handling people attracted others to him. I think people really loved him and because of his love, and his friendly nature, he was very successful in motivating the field force. He always had new ideas for promoting the field force.

One of the ways he motivated his field force was by delegating them authority. He gave them guidance, but he did not act like he was the master. He invited their suggestions and then he gave his counter-suggestions. Afterward, he would give them authority to act on those suggestions and those decisions. So, he was a person who loved to delegate, and he knew that by delegating he was promoting or motivating the field staff. I think one of the reasons why Eastern Federal had a highly motivated field force was Mr. Khuda Buksh's personality. It was the field force that brought EFU life.

I was not in the field, but sometimes I used to see him or listen to him talking to the field force in the corridors or some of the meetings. He used to talk in an unassuming way, not like a boss, but like a friend. Just like Mr. Roshen Ali Bhimjee. I think they had something in common – their personalities, their way of talking to people, and their interpersonal relationship. He was a very good speaker, and obviously a friendly speaker.

I think his idea of teamwork was to bring people together. It was not to divide and rule, but to work as a team, and as I said, he would meet everybody in the same manner, whether the person was a sales officer, a sales manager, a chief manager or a simple agent. My impression was that he met people in an equal manner. He gave equal footing to every person, and this is how he built up his team. Even an agent could access him, in the same way as a chief manager.

He built his credibility and trust in a practical way, through his own actions and his character. The way he met people, the way he talked to them was very impressive. He attracted other people with his own behavior and the way he conducted himself. I remember I used to hear his speeches, in which he addressed the field force. I don't recall anytime [when] he blew his own trumpet. He presented himself as a down to earth person, a very humble man and this was another important facet of his personality.

The main reward that he used was to call a person from East Pakistan and congratulate him. "You've done such and such thing, I've heard about such and such thing." He was aware of what was going on, what each field officer was doing, and what his achievements were, regardless of whether he was an agent, a sales manager or a chief manager. The personal touch he added in his dealings with people was most effective. I remember that even if he was in East Pakistan and somebody achieved something here, he used to get a call from Mr. Khuda Buksh, either a telephone call or a complementary letter. So, he was very close to the people. He used to react timely, and this was his method of motivating and rewarding people. I think rewarding by way of personal words is more attractive and motivating than certificates.

I observed that there was a significant difference in the enthusiasm of both field and office staff in the public sector, as compared to the private sector. The field force was not as motivated as it used to be when life insurance was in the private sector. Similarly, the office staff was also not that motivated or enthusiastic. I'm sure we all became lethargic – the staff – our efficiency went down – I'm including myself. I feel that the enthusiasm and the interest that were there in the private sector were missing after nationalization. It did affect the morale of the people, and their efficiency went down.

I knew Mr. Khuda Buksh for about two years. I really love this man because of his personality. He talked less and listened more. I remember he used to use one Urdu word, which I'm trying to recollect. He had his own dialect of speaking Urdu because of his mother tongue being Bengali. I never heard him criticizing anybody. In fact, I always heard him praising people.

He always invited criticism and never tried to avoid it. He accepted criticism, even if it was not well founded and he never showed any sign of displeasure. I think he was a very good listener, and a person who could accept criticism and respond to it. I didn't think Khuda Buksh ever felt that the phenomenal progress achieved by Eastern Federal during the decade of the 60s was wrongly attributed to some personalities other than him. I think most of the credit rightly went to Mr. Khuda Buksh. He played a very big role in what EFU achieved during that decade. He built a very sound foundation for life insurance business as far as EFU is concerned. He contributed not only to EFU but I think, to the whole country. He not only promoted life insurance for EFU but he had promoted life insurance in Pakistan.

I really don't know why he had to leave Eastern Federal when he had taken it to such a height. There may be some other reasons, relating to the management. But I remember I really felt very hurt about it. He was a great man. It was apparent from the reaction of the field force that they were depressed and perhaps some of them were de-motivated. It took some time before the field force again picked up but then, you know, natiionalization came into the way and there were some problems going on between East Pakistan and West Pakistan, so all these things were happening at the same time. But I was happy when I heard the news that Khuda Buksh had launched his own company in the eastern wing of the country. The fact that he was forming his own company was also a credit to EFU.

I don't think there is any person like Mr. Khuda Buksh. There have been other people, but none have the same stature as him. Mr. Khuda Buksh worked for the promotion of life insurance in a very difficult time and other people entered the field after some ground had already been built. I think Late Roshen Ali Bhimjee and Khuda Buksh strongly complemented each other. They had a lot in common. Each played his role in his own way. They worked very closely, and shared a very friendly relationship. It's very difficult to make any distinction. But I wouldn't compare anybody with Mr. Khuda Buksh. I really love this man because of his personality.

How are you, Babu?

Waris Ali Khan[48]

AFTER I JOINED EFU, I heard Mr. Khuda Buksh's name being mentioned almost every day by people who knew him. This showed how apt he was in procuring business for EFU and I was strongly impressed. I met Mr. Khuda Buksh in 1966. Mr. Hussain introduced us. When we first met, I didn't realize that he was such a big leader. He was a very simple and levelheaded person. His manner of talking reflected kindness and dignity.

He was a very straightforward man. But from a marketing point of view, I can say that he inspired the field personnel so deeply, that people wanted to work with him and under his leadership. His subordinates saw him as a father figure. Mr. Khuda Buksh has done so much for us.

He was an exceptional leader. Whenever he came from East Pakistan to Karachi, we used to receive him at the airport. I was not the only one; there were many people who went to welcome him. I don't think this was done for any other person. His love and affection forced us go to him. He was really an honest person and everybody trusted him. He was never doubted. Whenever his juniors performed well, he used to honor them. He knew how to respect his juniors. He always stood up for their rights. I believe that it was this inherent ability of Mr. Khuda Buksh, to appreciate the efforts of others that made him such a great leader.

He used to speak very well. We really enjoyed his speaking in Urdu rather than English. So whatever words he spoke, we used to enjoy it. He spoke respectfully towards everyone.

---

[48]Former district manager, EFU. Interview date: 17 March 2003.

Actually, he had a unique way of motivating people. He used to look after our families, and was genuinely concerned for our welfare. That was the prime factor, which encouraged us to do business wholeheartedly.

I don't know what was the cause of Late Khuda Buksh's abrupt resignation in 1969 when he was truly the doyen of life business, not only in Eastern Federal, but all over Pakistan. I might be right or wrong; but we heard that some differences had started arising between Mr. Khuda Buksh and Roshen Ali Bhimjee. I must say, Mr. Bhimjee was jealous of Mr. Khuda Buksh's popularity and intimacy with the field force. Late Khuda Buksh's resignation from Eastern Federal was a shocking news for all of us. We had lost a very good leader. It was really shocking for some time.

Late Roshen Ali Bhimjee and Khuda Buksh were the most important players of a successful, dynamic and winning team of Eastern Federal Union Insurance Company. Definitely both of them are very great leaders. Mr. Bhimjee excelled in managerial and administrative work. But Mr. Khuda Buksh was very popular among the field workers, and within EFU, he was seen as a leader par excellence. I can't think of anyone in the insurance industry who can be compared to Mr. Khuda Buksh.

I remember so many incidents related to him. Once, a friend of ours took some loan from a pathan. Incidentally, Mr. Khuda Buksh witnessed a discussion and struggle between the two. Upon learning what the matter was, he asked our friend, 'Why did you take loan from a Pathan? Am I dead? Why didn't you ask me for help? And how many loans do you have?' After this Khuda Buksh gave our friend the amount of money he owed and asked him to repay his creditors. Then Khuda Buksh said, "From tomorrow onwards, I want to see you in the field. I want you to do business and nothing else." That was a very good inspiration for all of us and our friend started doing very good business after that.

Khuda Buksh was the only person, who would go out of the way to help others, even to the extent of ensuring that we had groceries at home. That is why everyone loved him. He was a Bengali. I can still hear his polite Bengali voice, asking, "How are you, *Babu*? (address a young person affectionately). Is everything OK?"

Khuda Buksh (Life Manager) speaking at the first EFU Conference at Karachi, 1963.

Khuda Buksh receiving Gold Medal from Central Commerce Minister M. Wahiduzzaman, Roshen Ali Bhimjee (General Manager) is on right (March 1963).

Khuda Buksh addressing EFU management meeting at the lawns of Beach Luxary Hotel, Clifton, Karachi, 1963.

Khuda Buksh being received at the Karachi Airport by EFU managemt.

Khuda Buksh at his Karachi residence discussing life insurance development strategies with S.F. Alam (Manager), A.J. Dias (Deputy Manager) at right.

(Reprinted with permision from W.W Karnowski.)

S.F. Alam (Zonal Manager), Dr. Sayeed Khan (Chief Medical Officer) and Khuda Buksh (Feb 1967).

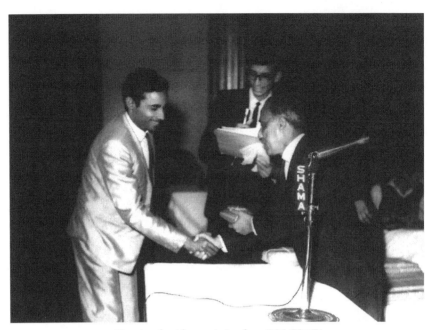

(Reprinted with permission from KBMT&F.)
Amin Ullah Salman (Development Officer) receiving a prize from Khuda Buksh. Iftekher Hanfi conducting the prize distribution function, Karachi, West Pakistan.

Khuda Buksh being received at the Karachi Airport by field force, regional managers and senior managers of EFU, Karachi, West Pakistan.

(Photo credit: Rizwan A. Farid.)
A group photo of EFU Senior management, Karachi, Pakistan (1968).
(Standing from left): Rizwan Ahmed Farid, not identified, not identified, Salim Tariq, Noor Uddin Farooqi; (sitting from left): Syed Kaiser Abbas, E.A. Jaffery, Khuda Buksh, R.A. Bhimjee, A.A. Hasanie.

(Photo Source: Beema, Vol, No.1, May 1968.)
Khuda Buksh addressing the zonal conference at Lahore, West Pakistan, March,1968. Sitting from left: M. Zulqarnain (Zonal Manager, Lahore) and R.A. Bhimjee (Managing Director).

PART III

Interviews and Memoirs of Friends, Associates and Family Members

A Respected Person

Qazi Anwar Hossain[49]

I HAD HEARD ABOUT him a lot, but I met him only three times in my life. The first time was at the Eastern Federal Union Insurance Company during Pakistan times. He was probably a general manger or so at that time. I can't recollect the year – probably it was 1966 or '67. Reputed late T. Ahmad used to work in that office. He forced me to take an insurance policy for Tk. *one lac* [$21,000]. When I came out into the corridor after completing my medical tests and signing all documents, I saw a thin-looking gentleman of a medium height wearing a gray suit come out from another room. T. Ahmad introduced me to the gentleman, saying, "This gentleman today has taken an insurance policy for one lac."

When he heard that my father was Dr. Qazi Motahar Hossain, he remembered him and surveyed me from top to bottom. Then he tapped my forehead a couple of times, smiled pleasantly and commented, "Intelligent forehead!" He uttered just these two words and then quickly went down the stairs.

I enquired from Mr. T. Ahmad who he was and came to know that he was the famous Mr. Khuda Buksh, who had created a legend in the insurance world. I must admit that those two words from his mouth really left an impact on my mind.

Later in 1972, I saw an advertisement for the sale of a Volkswagon car and reached the address after a long search. I had to wait for five minutes before the master of the house entered the lounge. Then, lo and behold! My surprise knew no bounds to find the famous Mr. Khuda Buksh in front of me. He immediately recognized me. He had the capacity to strike an intimacy with people. The car was very old (probably a 1953 model or so) and left-hand drive, but he convinced me why I should purchase it by showing me a basketful of parts, which he had changed

---

[49]Founder, Publishing House Sheba Prokashoni, Dhaka, Bangladesh. For details, see Appendix K.

in the car to transform it into almost a new one. It was then that I realized why he was regarded as such a great salesman. After completing the payment, I told him that I would take the car later, as I had traveled there in another car.

But he rejected my proposal to do that. It seemed he needed to get his garage vacated. He replied, "You needn't worry about that. My driver will drive this car and follow you all the way to your house."

I met him for the last time in Dhaka Medical College Hospital. I am not good at remembering dates – probably it was the beginning of 1972 or '73. I had gone to visit my very revered professor of psychotherapy, M.U. Ahmed, who I heard had fallen ill. The professor said he had no serious ailment except severe pain in his hands and feet. When I offered to massage his body, he consented. While I was eagerly engaged in this act, the insurance giant Mr. Khuda Buksh suddenly entered the room.

I greeted him. He acknowledged it with a nod in such a way that it looked as if he didn't recognize me. He shifted his attention from me to look frowningly at the professor. Then he hollered, "Are you pretending or fussing? Nothing is wrong with you, I know. Come on, get up. Why are you behaving like a lord and getting him to massage you?"

Though initially shocked, I guessed from the smile on the professor's lips that they were either friends or relatives. He talked for a while and then quickly left the hospital cabin.

It's my opinion that in spite of all his preoccupations, if Khuda Buksh ever heard about the indisposition of any of his acquaintances, he would invariably appear by their bedside, try to understand the patient in his intimate manner, and comfort him with encouraging and hopeful words for their quick recovery.

There is no doubt Khuda Buksh was a great personality. I am grateful to have this opportunity to say a few words in the reminiscences collected by his near and dear people.

One - Day Memoir

Belal Mohammad[50]

IN ABOUT THE middle of 1972, my acquaintance with him was immediate and lasted only a day – as far as I can remember, it was on the second floor of Dienfa Building, opposite Gulistan Cinema Hall. He was then the MD [managing director] of Jiban Bima Corporation. I had visited his office with Mushtari Shaffi, the editor of the currently extinct monthly journal Bandhobi from Chittagong. In spite of the wide age gap, by right of relationship, Mushtari Shaffi addressed him as *dulabhai* (brother-in-law).

On 26 March 1972, I had started my escapade from "Mushtari Lodge," the Enayet Bazar house of Dr. Mohammad Shaffi, towards Kalurghat. This is that house which was later termed by littérateur Monoj Bosu from Kolkata as the "Cradle of Independent Bangla Radio Station." Mr. Shaffi never returned home after the Pakistan invaders arrested him on 7 April. Begum Mushtari Shaffi left the Shaffi home with seven minor children and joined the War of Liberation. When she returned to the country in January 1972, she found her second floor room devastated and unsuitable for living. With the urgency to undertake the minimal repair work for the house, she came from Chittagong to Dhaka in order to arrange the withdrawal of the amount from her husband's paid up insurance policy and went with me to beseech dulabhai Khuda Buksh for his help.

During a maximum of forty-five minutes' discussion, I was impressed by the way this experienced, elderly person could so easily overcome the difference in age and establish friendship with those of his children's age group. A signature was needed from a first class magistrate on some form. He suggested, "Will it do if I sign? I may not be a magistrate, but I hope my signature will be accepted. Where

---

[50]Writer and former Freedom fighter, Liberation of Bangladesh.

are you going to look for a magistrate?" The form was accepted at the right place at the right time.

The honorable Mr. Khuda Buksh is called "the father of insurance." He said, "Do you know that we were taught the Carnegie method during our first training period? This teaches how to win friends and influence people. After training in that method, I was rebuked indiscriminately by an elderly pedestrian. That was a long time ago; Mirpur Road had then just been constructed. There wasn't much of a crowd in that area. As an insurance worker, I drive around in a car. One day, I noticed an elderly man walking on Mirpur Road with two heavy bags in his two hands. His fair complexion had turned red with sweat. I stopped the car next to him and enquired, 'Uncle, if you don't mind, I would like to offer you a ride in my car to wherever your destination is. Please get in my car.' The man replied scornfully, 'Get lost and mind your own business. There is no need to show off the possession of a car.'

"It must be mentioned that hijacking or robbery were not prevalent in those days as they are today. So, there was no reason to mistrust even a stranger like me." The elderly pedestrian had taken offence at the offer of help from the young Khuda Buksh. On this, the honorable Mr. Khuda Buksh commented, "The Carnegie method then seemed ineffective to me in our country, though not fully so. Because even otherwise, any behavioral practice varies from person to person and with time and place. Hence, we can say, 'One man's meat is another man's poison.'"

Mr. Khuda Buksh expired around the middle of 1974. He had witnessed the framing of the constitution of Bangladesh, based on four fundamental morals. Besides, he had also seen the nationalization of his insurance company along with a few other business organizations, with the founding of the government office of the Controller of Insurance. But he didn't live to witness the outcome of this ineffective nationalization of merely a few financial organizations without nationalizing the manpower of the country, as a result of which many institutions had to return to individual ownership in the face of bankruptcy.

The brief discussion with a knowledgeable personality like Mr. Khuda Buksh just for a day has been a tremendous learning experience and left an indelible mark on my mind, even after so many years.

Brother Khuda Buksh: To Whose Incomparable Nobility I am Indebted

Mushtari Shaffi[51]

I RECEIVED A LETTER from Gonoshastho Kendro in Savar, written by Belal Mohammad. On opening the envelope, another letter in unfamiliar handwriting suddenly fell like a stone on the surface of the sea of my memory, on whose trembling water appeared a face. It was the face of a legendary person in the history of insurance in Bangladesh. This man was called "the father of insurance" – my immensely respected brother, Khuda Buksh.

After finishing the letter, I thought that in this unfortunate country, a great man is rarely if ever appreciated, and that is also done very late. He expired in 1974. At last, after twenty-seven long years, his memorial collection is going to be published through the initiative of his worthy sons. With the publication of the book, people of this generation will not only come to know him but will also learn a lot of things.

The very experience of my first meeting with him is very amusing. Even now, I derive immense pleasure remembering it. I used to hear about him from others long before my acquaintance with him. The reason is that at that time, there weren't so many insurance companies as there are now. Prominent among the few that existed was Eastern Federal Union Insurance Company.

---

[51]Former Editor, extinct monthly journal, *Bandhabi,* Chittagong, Bangladesh.

I met brother Khuda Buksh for the first time nearly forty-five years ago. Although I was the mother of one child, I was very young and immature. As I was married in my teens, my mind was full of some childlike superstitions. My husband, Dr. Shaffi, is a physician by profession. People from different classes and professions used to come to him. Shaffi's friendly behavior turned many of his patients into close friends. I also enjoyed their affection and closeness. I came to know and learn many things. During difficult situations in life, I received selfless help and cooperation from some of them.

Such a person was brother Khuda Buksh, who has established an everlasting, permanent place in my memory. Brother Khuda Buksh used to visit Chittagong occasionally in connection with his work. On one such trip, he came to Dr. Shaffi's chamber as a patient. And he did what usually people of insurance companies do. That is, he proposed to Dr. Shaffi to take an insurance policy. When I heard about it, I got very upset and prevented Shaffi from doing so. I told him, "You must promise never to take an insurance policy."

Shaffi was surprised and wanted to know the reason.

I replied very seriously, "No one lives after taking an insurance policy – he dies immediately."

At these words, Dr. Shaffi laughed heartily and said, "You are still a child. This is your childish superstition. Death is an inevitable fact. A man will meet death wherever and whenever he is destined to; it has no connection with insurance. You have a totally wrong assumption."

I had told him that it was not my misconception, and then cited an incident about one of my relatives who had made an insurance policy and had died in a road accident the day after he had paid his first premium. Besides, I had heard from many other people of similar misfortunes. Therefore, I knew insurance only brought bad luck.

Shaffi then answered in a dejected tone, "I realize it's not possible for me to convince you. One day I'll introduce you to him and he will explain this to you."

At this I almost cried and replied, "No, no, I don't want to understand anything. I just don't want you to have an insurance. That's all."

It was summer time – perhaps it was May or June, and our house was Dr. Shaffi's "chamber cum residence." One evening, Dr. Shaffi returned from his chamber and informed me that Mr. Khuda Buksh of Eastern Federal Union Insurance Company had come with another sick patient. He was a relative of Mr. Khuda Buksh and was S.D.O. of Chittagong. They wanted some water to drink. Shaffi told me to send some snacks along with water. There was watermelon in the house. Instead of water, I took some juice out of watermelon and sent it for them. After a short while, Shaffi returned smiling and said, "Now, let's go and meet him."

I asked, "Where? To obtain knowledge about that insurance of yours? No, no, I don't need that knowledge."

Shaffi continued to smile and replied, "No, no, not for that. It's because you have stirred the name of your paternal land in the sugar of the drink."

I asked in surprise, "What do you mean?"

Shaffi was still smiling and said, "The moment they had a sip of the drink, they knew that the maker of the drink is from Faridpur. Immediately, they wanted to know where you hailed from. When I told them you were from Faridpur, they started interrogating me about your sub-division, police station, village, and parentage. How can I provide them all these details? I only mentioned Gerda as the name of your village. At this both of them expressed, 'Hmmm! We got it right. Who can, other than a girl from Gerda family, make such delicious watermelon drink? Can you introduce us to your wife?' I replied, 'Certainly.' Come on, then, save me by meeting them. My patients are crowding up."

Having no other option, I was compelled to face them. On seeing me, both of them stood up and enthusiastically welcomed me. "Please come in. Your watermelon drink has revealed that you probably don't just hail from Faridpur, but may also be related to us." I was then overcome with shame and fear.

The two brown-skinned, thin, and short people were extremely jovial and expert conversationalists. In responding to their queries, it was revealed that Mr. Khuda Buksh is a distant cousin of mine and Mr. Zohurul Haque, a brother-in-law. After that, through light-hearted talks, they removed my hesitation in a short time; and that same day the distant relationship also disappeared, and they both turned into my very near and dear people.

In this I got acquainted with the institution named Khuda Buksh, and I had the good fortune to receive his affection and nearness. I termed him an "institution" because if a person really dedicates himself to the welfare of others and develops an institution by his lifelong devotion, undiverted service, and merit, then he himself also turns into an institution.

Late brother Khuda Buksh was such a benevolent person – he had devoted his entire life to build a welfare organization, Eastern Federal Union Insurance Company. In doing that, it cannot be enumerated how many unfavorable situations he had to overcome and how many storms he had to withstand like a banyan tree. He used narrate those tales whenever he met us. He was an unassuming, pleasant and open-hearted person. He used to tell us, "Are you aware that I started my career simply on a monthly salary of 50 taka only? I have reached this stage through sheer hard work, honesty, and dedication."

Needless to say, the affectionate and skillful conversation of brother Khuda Buksh very soon, before long, removed my superstitious apprehensions regarding insurance, and Dr. Shaffi took out an insurance policy for one lac taka (100,000) from Eastern Federal Union Insurance Company.

When my monthly journal *Bandhobi* started coming out from Chittagong, he supported it by signing a one-year contract for a full page advertisement for his institution. He provided further support by procuring advertisements for *Bandhobi* from other commercial institutions of his friends and associates. Brother Khuda Buksh had such affection for me that he never turned down my request if ever I asked him for employment for anyone. In this way, with the help of brother Khuda Buksh, I obtained employment in his company for quite a few poor boys and girls known to me. My head bows in respectful gratitude even when I remember those matters. He has also left his marks as a real patriotic Bengali.

All officials – senior and junior – in his organization, Eastern Federal Union Insurance Company, were Bangladeshi nationals. Among those, the majority were from Faridpur district. Once, when questioned about this, he replied, "One can't love the whole country unless one loves the people of his own area. The country is made of people, isn't it? Yes, it's true, people from Faridpur are in a majority in my institution, but have you noted that there is not a single non – Bengali in it?"

I had asked, "Why not?"

"India was divided on the basis of religion, and Bangladesh was named 'East Pakistan,' but did this land thereby really turn into Pakistan? If it that were so, there would have been no problem – so many boys would not have lost their lives for their language. There would have been one state language, and that would have been Urdu – we are Bengalis, rice-and-fish – eating pure Bengalis. Whatever may be the present of this land, this is indigenous Bangladesh and will remain Bangladesh forever. The name of this country will always be Bangladesh. The pasted name will fall off. Have you understood, my sister?" After saying this, he laughed heartily.

I don't hesitate to say that brother Khuda Buksh seemed to have opened a closed door of my consciousness, and since that day I consciously began to write "East Bengal" in place of "East Pakistan" in the editorial and other articles in the *Bandhobi*.

After that, many years passed in busy involvements. The tide of transformation started in the country. The "War of Liberation" came as part of that tide. In getting spontaneously involved in the war, a series of events started to take place in my life. Dr. Shaffi and my only younger brother got captured by Pakistan Army. Having no alternative, I had to run away with my minor children to take shelter in India. Even there, I continued to help the liberation war in many ways. Later, I joined the independent Bangladesh radio station as a sound fighter. I lost contact with brother Khuda Buksh. But during such political upheavals in the country, I often remembered his utterance, "Whatever its present name may be, this is indigenous Bangladesh, permanent Bangladesh, and its name will always remain 'Bangladesh.'"

After nine long months, I returned to my own country, freed from Pakistan aggressors. I found the totally plundered and devastated house, but I didn't ever find Dr. Shaffi or my younger brother again. Then started a different type of war for me – I was thoroughly lost with unlimited financial distress, uncertain future for the children, day and night filled with worry, and repairing the house to make it fit for living. During such a time, brother Khuda Buksh suddenly appeared on the scene. I was surprised to see him. How did brother Khuda Buksh know I was there? I was still gaping meaninglessly.

Reading my thoughts, he said, "I learned about your whereabouts at Karim's office." Then he added sympathetically, "Sister, I have been looking for you since I heard about your misfortune. However, whatever had to happen has happened. The country will definitely evaluate and appreciate. You can't afford to break down at this time. You will have to straighten yourself and stand up firmly, because you a long way to walk. I haven't come here only to express my sympathy. I came here to tell you about that insurance policy of Dr. Shaffi, which he had paid. I have enquired and found that there is some money in it. You should withdraw that amount as early as possible, because it can't be predicted how this brand-new, inexperienced government of this new nation may behave."

Now I remembered Dr. Shaffi, that he had bought a piece of land in Chittagong, and in order to construct a house on it, he discontinued the payment of the insurance premium. This he had told me much later. When brother Khuda Buksh was talking about it, I had asked how much money there was, and he had mentioned about ten thousand. But he had also said, "You will have to come to Dhaka along with his photograph in order to withdraw this amount. You probably don't have any related documents. I shall get them out from the office." Ten thousand taka had seemed equivalent to 10 lacs (one million) to me at that time.

With great difficulty, I went to Dhaka by myself and visited the office of brother Khuda Buksh with brother Belal. But I didn't have to run around anywhere else for this money. Beginning with dictating my application, he took care of all necessary formalities with the responsibility of an elder brother. That's why I didn't have to wait too long to receive the amount.

When I got the check in my hand, I saw that instead of ten thousand, it was for an amount of twelve thousand four hundred and fifty-four rupees. That time, this amount seemed like a huge protection for me. While handing me the check, he said with great affection, "Sister, I shall be very happy to be able to help you in any way. If you let me know without hesitation whatever and whenever you need anything, I'll know that you really consider me as your own brother." I had replied, "I'll definitely let you know if I need anything. What you have done for me today, is that anything small? I shall never be able to repay this debt of your affection in my entire life. Now I want you just to give me your blessings that I can bring up the children left by my husband successfully." Then he affectionately placed his hand on my head . . . and assured me, "Yes, sister, I'm sure you will."

This was our brother Khuda Buksh, who with his peerless magnanimity drew close to him not only me, but many others. Hence, he remains unparallel in his own example.

A Good Man's Memoir

Husna Banu Khanam[52]

I WAS A WEE school girl when I first met Khuda Buksh. He was then living in Kolkata. He being a friend of my father, Abu Lohani, Khuda Buksh frequently visited our residence. We were three children in the family. I was the only sister in between two brothers, Fateh Lohani and Fazle Lohani. At a later period, my brothers got a considerable reputation in film and electronic media. For some years, my father worked as the editor of *Rangoon Times* (Rangoon, Mynamar). After returning to Kolkata, he connected himself with literature and also worked as co-editor of *The Mussalman* and the *Khadem*. He was appointed editor of the *Daily Sultan* a few months before his death.

When Father died of a heart attack in Kolkata Medical College in August 1929, Fazle Lohani was then only six months old. No memory of my father is alive in me now. I've only seen his beautiful picture. After his eternal departure, his colleagues and journalists frequently came to our house, took care of us. Though Mother taught in a school in Kolkata, we did not have any relatives there. Our relatives from our village home, Sirajganj, Pabna, and Shahjadpur visited our Kolkata house all the year round. They observed our "fatherless" condition and advised us to go back to our village home. Our mother did not agree to this. She said, "I'll maintain them here. Please help them here if you can."

Though many journalist friends of my father visited us after Father's departure, our closest person was Mr. Nasiruddin, editor of the *Sawgat*. He cared for us as affectionately as my father. Father also worked in the *Sawgat*. I could not say how

---

[52]Former Professor, Home Economic College, Dhaka, Bangladesh. For details, see Appendix K. The interview was taken by Lutfor Rahman, deputy agency director, American Life Insurance Company, Dhaka, Bangladesh.

Father was acquainted with Khuda Buksh, but surely there was a connection. I have also heard that Khuda Buksh visited Mr. Nasiruddin's office. Here, mention may be made of the fact that in the second decade of the twentieth century, the Bengali Muslims assembled in Kolkata on 4 September 1911 and formed the "*Bongyo Muslim Sahittya Samity,*" with a view to developing awareness about history, tradition, and culture and take tangible steps for their preservation. One of the leading organizers of the same was Abu Lohani. Abu Lohani had friendly ties with Kazi Nazrul Islam. Abu Lohani was one of the members of the committee formed for giving reception to Kazi Nazrul Islan at Kolkata's Royal Albert Hall.

It is not impossible that Khuda Buksh got acquainted with my father at any golden moment of that renaissance of the Muslims. In keeping with that relation, he used to look after us even after my father's death and often visited our house. I have gotten fatherly affection from him throughout my life.

This was how we got acquainted with each other. A deadly riot took place in Kolkata in 1950. I was then a student of class ten at Shakhawat Memorial School. Considering the situation, I came to Dhaka from Kolkata. My brothers already left Kolkata. They were newscasters at the Dhaka Radio station. They lived in a rented house near the Lion Cinema in old Dhaka. Fazle Lohani brought out a monthly named *Agaytta*. Our familiarity with Khuda Buksh brought much benefit in our lives. We've always found him by our side at the time of need, at the time of crisis.

Khuda Buksh was very beneficial and benevolent. Some incidents of his benevolent mentality may be mentioned in this context. I got a scholarship from the Ford Foundation. I was at a loss as to how to take necessary preparations to visit America. Khuda Buksh helped me with all the necessary formalities and gave me valuable instructions. He was in Karachi at that time. In accordance with his advice, I got into his residence, and from there, I flew to America. Khuda Buksh also helped me even on my return.

I can vividly remember the dreadful days of 1971. When on the night of 25 March, the Pakistani forces were all set to crush the unarmed Bengalis, I was then living at a quarter of Home Economics College. My younger brother, Fazle Lohani, lived at a house close to Dhanmondi Road No. 32. His wife was British. Given the situation, Fazle Lohani had already abandoned his residence and moved to another house. The Pakistani army was looking for him. They came to his residence, but when they saw a British woman there, they got back.

I went to the DIT building on the twenty-fifth of March to do a program. All of a sudden, there was an announcement that curfew had been imposed. All were directed to go home immediately. I returned to my college. Owing to the imposition of the curfew, I could not come out of the house for three days. After three days, the curfew was withdrawn for an hour. In the meantime, the Pakistani army got into our college quarter and plundered all valuables, including my TV, cassette player, et cetera. Many of these things I got from America.

I sensed danger ahead, so I did not have the courage to live at the residence with my two young daughters any longer. Khuda Buksh then lived at Dhanmondi. I drove a car myself, went to his residence, and gave vent to my feelings. He told me to take courage and said, "You stay here at my place." I then got to his house with my husband and two daughters. His house was a considerably large one. Together, we formed a virtual family. How profoundly did he fondle us. This he did exactly as my father.

After a month, the situation improved, and I went to college, off and on. I faced some disadvantages coming from and going to college from Dhanmondi. So, I told him everything and with his permission got into a rented house at the China building lane at Azimpur. He looked after us even there. He said, "Do not hesitate to come to my house if you face any difficulty."

This sympathy and empathy towards people is simply very rare. He was not our relative, but he always helped us exactly as a relative. When my brother, Fazle Lohani, was compelled to abandon his house in 1971, Khuda Buksh maintained everything there. We had hardly any near and dear ones in Dhaka or Kolkata. We did not even have our father, but he did not allow us to perceive the vacuum. His wife, too, similarly cared for us.

A few years after he got acquainted with my father, Khuda Buksh took up insurance as a career. It became his be all and end all. He made us understand the advantages of taking a policy. I took a policy from him. While in Kolkata, Father also took an insurance policy from another company.

He loved music very much. I can remember, when his new house at Dhanmondi was completed, he arranged for a musical program at his house. On that day, I sang many songs with a joyous mind.

Khuda Buksh is no more today, but his memory is still unbroken. I feel good to tell about a good man. In the course of my telling about him, I have frequently remembered my father, whom I lost when I was young. While talking about Khuda Buksh, many old memories occurred in my mind. I felt good to tell his story.

Khuda Buksh:
An Enlightened Individual

Roushanara Rahman[53]

IN THE ORDINARY sense, "light" is what removes darkness. Light naturally brightens the surroundings. Moreover, it also removes fear and anxiety, and it brings to mind courage and delight. But what does somebody exactly mean when he uses the term "an enlightened man?" A person who takes away all the cruelty and petty interests and selfishness from his surroundings, who can drive away meanness and brings to mind bravery and a bit of affection, who can help forget a formidably painful past, who can inspire to hope against hope, who can rise above all meanness and stand upright like a towering mountain – is verily an enlightened man in the true sense of the term. In my brief past, I was fortunate enough to be in touch with such a man, and he was our beloved *dada* (elder brother), Khuda Buksh (K.B.).

Whenever I happen to turn over the blurred pages from the memories of the past, I find our beloved dada. All of us were his "fans" or devotees. It won't be easy to end his story in a few words. In the midst of a thousand events, the man is still vivid in our memory like a blazing flame. He was a man above his common level, and his personality was extraordinary. He was always prone to give everyone his due respect and consideration. He was ever ready to forgive and forget the frailties of others. It was his pleasure to contribute his best to the service of others.

The fact is – K.B. has left us forever. Departure is the reality of life. Everyone is bound to go one day, and K.B. was no exception. He was affectionate, efficient, and kind. His heart bled to see the sufferings of others. His heart swelled abundantly

---

[53]Former Bengali Professor Dhaka College, Dhaka, Bangladesh.

with goodwill, sympathy, and love for others. He looked upon all men as his fellow brothers, irrespective of caste, creed, and color. It pains me to think that a proper evaluation of a person like him was not done during his lifetime.

After his eternal departure, we seem to try to see and comprehend him, as if from another fringe of the sea. Perhaps this is the reality. This is more so because whenever I think of him, I painfully miss him everywhere; his absence becomes extremely conspicuous in every walk of my life. Emotion chokes my heart. I remember him today after a considerably long period of twenty-eight years. Human memory naturally becomes blurred and cloudy with the passage of time. The fear is that after so many years, some pearl-like aspects of his character will simply get lost for good.

When I was a very wee gal – the time I can no longer remember – I used to see dada at our house. I can recall, on holidays he would come to our village home in Barisal along with my Siddique dada, another brother of mine. Siddique dada studied in Calcutta and lived with Habibur Rahman, a maternal uncle of ours. It was not yet time for him to go to his village home alone. My uncle served in a foreign country. My maternal aunt, Monju bhai, and Siddique dada – all were actually guided at home by K.B. dada. As a matter of fact, he shouldered all the responsibilities alone, practically like the eldest son of the family. K.B. dada himself studied at the Calcutta Islamia College and took care of the study and proper living of Siddique dada and Monju bhai. He was extremely finicky about their dress before setting out for school. Taking them to Park Circus playground to play in the afternoon and putting them to sleep at night after studies. He shouldered all the responsibilities of the household, and everything was at his fingertips. Aunt remained ailing most of the time. K.B. called uncle "Baba Sahib" and auntie, "Ma". His real mother lived at Domodya village in Faridpur, but a second mother, who lived at 18 Park Circus Road in Calcutta, bound K.B. in the bondage of undying love and affection. It was from then that I myself, my father, mother, *fufa* (husband of father's sister) *fufu*, (sister of father) – all were bathed in the overflowing stream of his love; and the stream of his love remained flowing up to the end of the chapter.

After finishing his college study, K.B. dada tried his utmost to earn himself a living, and in 1935, he had a job at the Calcutta Oriental Insurance Company. Before that, he, for a brief period of one month, worked at the Presidency College library.

I set out for Calcutta to study at the Shakhawat Memorial Girls' school. At that period, K.B. dada also lived in Calcutta together with *bhabi* (K.B. dada's wife) After partition of the county in 1947, all the members of the family found themselves scattered in various spots. But even after that, dada was at the Oriental Government Insurance Company for about 5 years more, though he sent bhabi and children to Dhaka in 1950. He permanently returned to Dhaka in 1952, and it was then when I had the opportunity to come in touch with him once again. I was then a Dhaka University student. Dada lived at a nice house in Gandaria. Occasionally, dada took me from my university hostel to his residence at Gandaria. He had five sons then. As he did not have any daughters, he loved someone so sisterly to him, so dearly that it appeared that the affection he intended to bestow upon his own daughter, he gave to sisterly gals.

At last, he was blessed with a beautiful daughter who adorned bhabi's bosom. She was named "Kumu." I went to see her, and dada's delight was literally boundless. I went to London soon afterwards, and I heard that Kumu had breathed her last. I was deeply shocked. I was then in no position to see him agonize before my very eyes, but truly could I feel the deep, excruciating pain he had experienced at the premature death of his dearest daughter. In a later period, however, the birth of his second daughter, Ambereen Sultana (Milan), mitigated the sorrow and agony dada had.

Khuda Buksh was the pioneer of creating awareness about insurance among the people of East Pakistan. He can verily be called the father of insurance. He was the nucleus of insurance in East Pakistan.

His characteristic amiable manners, excellent style of speaking, and a surprising technique to win others' hearts were some of his inner qualities, and those were very successfully reflected in the insurance business. The people whom he got in touch with had no alternative but to be fascinated with his sweet conduct. It was not only in the field of insurance. He was always first to extend his helping hand whenever any of his acquaintances was in distress. He loved a man in the street and the big guns alike. He was the last hope for the financially distressed students.

He bore the educational expenses of an uncountable number of students and provided them with jobs. None failed to get his help. His great concern was to make everyone at ease and at home. It is why I would like to call him an enlightened man.

There was always a rush of relatives and of unknown people at his residence. Special lunches were arranged many times each month. He was very much respectful towards the superiors. His regard for the people of the teaching profession knew no bounds.

His boyhood school teacher, Aniuddin Ahmed, regularly visited his residence every year. Other relatives also would come. He looked after them. Today, everything in the society seems different. Life seems to flow in a different stream. Everyone is busy with himself. Today, ours is a money-obsessed society. Let alone distant relatives – we hardly take care of even our neighbors'. K.B. was a man with a difference. He regularly visited the houses of near and distant relatives every month, though he had a very busy life. He had hardly any respite at daytime, so sometimes, he visited a relative's house on the other side of Dhaka after 11:00 p.m. He usually found them sleeping, but he did not care. Almost speechless and always smiling, bhabi generally accompanied him most of the time. Surprised relatives with sleepy eyes asked, "What's up?" "Nothing, we have just come to see you." Thus, he spent a few minutes with them at midnight. This was how he took care of them. He had close contact with all, all the time. Not only relatives: he also had constant contact with the friend circle.

He was very much social in his personal life. His main duty was to motivate people. This characteristic of his is one of the reasons why he succeeded in the insurance business. He was a member of Dhaka Rotary Club. Every year, he got the prize for his one hundred percent presence in the club. When I, along with my husband, Masihur Rahman, returned to Dhaka from London, it was he who introduced us to Rotary people. He was also a regular member of the Dhaka Club. He never drank. He did not smoke, but he visited Dhaka Club every day. He talked with friends and asked them about their conditions. He also introduced my husband to this club, and in this way, he helped people enter the high society of the city. At the same time, the general mass was not out of his sight. Eastern Federal Union Insurance Company was then headquartered at today's Bangabandhu Avenue. A medicine store named Bham & Company was at the ground floor. He treated very amiably the people around him, big or small. This was how he won the love and respect of all.

In 1971, one of his sons joined the war of independence. We were then living at Dhanmondi. K.B. dada, too, lived in a house just in front of ours. The repressive activities of the Pakistani army were increasing day by day. Under the circumstances, all were thinking of leaving Dhanmondi, but dada had not the slightest fear in his mind. He said that he would stay here. He surrendered himself to Allah. Being frightened, his neighbors later departed from Dhanmondi and went to their respective village homes, but dada stayed there up to the last.

One day in April 1971, the Biharis, with the active support of the Pak army, started to kill Bengalis living at Mohammadpur and Shaymoli areas. Roads and drains were stained with the blood of the Bengalis. In the meantime, the *darwan* (gatekeeper) of my brother's residence at Shaymoli told me over the telephone that their lives were in danger. Being informed, Masihur Rahman, my middle brother, Siddique dada, and K.B. dada rushed to the spot in a car. We could not know what was happening there. As soon as their car reached Mirpur Road, the Biharis intercepted them and dragged them out of the car. They started to beat them. Considering the gravity of the situation, they gave up their hope of life. It was then such a critical situation that only a miracle could save them, and the very thing happened.

Quite miraculously, the non Bengali darwan of the Bham medicine store rushed to the spot. Seeing K.B. dada, he loudly said to the Biharis like an angel, "They are my own people, don't harm them." Thus, the three stars of the family and the drivers were saved from the grip of death. It appears that Allah gave his reward for his many good deeds.

He turned Eastern Federal Union into a large insurance company. He made it a more successful company of East Pakistan than it was in West Pakistan. It was our conviction that after his death, his name would be remembered as a pioneering insurance personality. It did not happen. Nevertheless, he is remembered today. He is still localized in the hearts of many, with due respect. He bound us all in the bonds of love and affection. He will not and cannot disappear from our hearts. His able children have established a trust in his name. The main objective of the trust is to assist the destitute. In the midst of this project, he will remain alive. Moreover, worldly name and fame is short-lived. For his good deeds, he will get his reward from Allah in the hereafter.

He was our Guardian, Friend and Well Wisher

Mahbubur Rahman Manju[54]

[In 1929 Khuda Buksh left his loved ones in the village, Damodya with the ambition of enlightenment and set his foot into the total unfamiliarity of Kolkata. He got himself admitted in Islamia College and returned to Damodya to prepare for college. An unexpected incident removed any doubts he had and solved the problem of finding a place to live in the city. Habibur Rahman and his wife gave him shelter and facilitated his learning and were like parents to him while he was away from home. Habibur Rahman, originally from Faridpur, lived at 18, Park Circus Row in Kolkata with his wife, and their son, Mahbubur Rahman (Monzu as he was affectionately called) and his nephew Siddique. Habibur Rahman was the captain of a commercial ocean liner and he had to travel different seaports of the world. He used to visit his family for a week at best before he had to go on tour again. How Khuda Buksh got acquainted with this family, how he took the responsibility and became guardian of two children are reflected from the interview of Mahbubur Rahman. Mahbub's sister Lutfu Nessa Rashid helped in this interview – Editor]

My mother was ill and she was bed-ridden most of the time. Under the circumstances, it was difficult for my mother to manage the household and look after us. My father was searching for a solution to help my mother while providing me and Siddique with much needed guidance. In this situation my maternal uncle *Mahi Mama* (uncle) came forward with solution:

---

[54]Eldest son of the late Habibur Rahman.

Mohi Mama was like a vagrant, with no fixed aim in life. He had a propensity to travel to villages extensively. After admission into Islamia Collage, *Dada* (Khuda Buksh) was staying at Damodya. Mohi Mama also, reached Damodya at one stage of his journey. Though a vagabond type, Mohi Mama was fairly communicative and persuasive and he could easily make friends with people, and in the course of conversation with the local school superintendent, he related the problems of our family. Superintendent Sahib told about Khuda Buksh, citing an earlier acquaintance. He also heard of Khuda Buksh's deep interest in higher studies. Mohi Mama then related how he met Dada at Damodya and requested him to live at the house of Habibur Rahman and to take the responsibility of teaching the two boys there. Dada thought about the matter with some seriousness and judging the pros and cons of it, consented to live at our Kolkata residence with his father's approval.

Early in 1930, Mohi mama accompanied Dada to Kolkata and introduced him to my parents. Dada stayed with us as a family member, began his studies at Islamia College and shouldered the heavy responsibility of the looking after us. We used to call him Dada (elder brother). Dada was responsible for sending us to school, helping with our studies and taking us to park. Dada did those like a family member. He became our guardian, friend and well wisher. My mother provided Dada with his college educational expenses. Dada regarded the parents as surrogate parents and called my father "Baba Sahib" and my mother "Ma."

He did the Right Thing by Employing People from his Own District

Abdur Razzak[55]

THOUGH KHUDA BUKSH was my maternal uncle, my scope to see him closely was limited. This was because I lived in the village, and he lived in the city. He spent his early life in the city of Kolkata, and later he came to Dhaka. I, too, came to Dhaka after passing the matriculation examination, and I had a fair chance to meet and talk to him. And it was then that a suitable moment was created for me to know him better.

Coming to Dhaka, I started to dwell in his residence. His residence was then at Eskaton Garden Road. I had an elaborate conversations with him about my studies and future plans. He asked me what I wanted to study. I replied that I wanted to study law and would be happy to be able to become a barrister. I was there at his residence for eight to ten days, and I noticed his extreme restlessness because of his being under the heavy pressure of work. In spite of that, he could make time to discuss family matters, and he was all attention during talks regarding my studies.

I did not see what he did at his office. But immediately after his office hours, he started to contact people from all walks of life, simply to expand EFU's business. And whenever necessity arose, he visited people and places alike, practically like a

---

[55]Politician and member of Parliament Bangladesh. For details, see Appendix K.

shuttlecock, with the very purpose of business expansion. In fact, the full responsibility of the insurance activities of East Pakistan was virtually bestowed upon him then.

In the past, life insurance was in practice in foreign countries. But there is no denying the fact that it was by his untiring efforts and under his dynamic guidance that the insurance business made a tangible progress in a backward country like ours. It was he who popularized insurance among the masses and made them aware of the necessity of the financial support later in life. He was able to make them realize that insurance was an urgency for the overall security of a family. He gave insurance the shape of a social movement.

He was called the "giant" of insurance, because he was literally dedicated to the insurance business. Many of his time hated this profession. But he was in a position to establish it in the country as a respectable occupation. In his characteristic manner, he would mix with people of every section of the society. He was closely related to the big guns and their children, in order that they continue to realize the importance of insurance from generation to generation. He also tried to make the older people realize that it would be wise to save something through insurance against a rainy day. And he was close to the middle class, too, because it was they who were the major insurance clients. All the steps he took in this regard were in fact enterprising and challenging. Such bold initiatives by him have taken insurance in Bangladesh to the current state. I would like to say that Khuda Buksh bears testimony to the significant role a single man can play in the overall development of insurance.

Today, people are on the increase, and so are the resources. And now is the time to make an assessment of whether the growth of insurance in the country is compatible with that of others. I think that the insurance business is now in a state of decline. This is my personal assumption: that if he were alive today, this would not happen. In fact, the social movement he introduced should have flourished considerably by now. I think that for the security of every conscious citizen, for the security of every family, insurance is a necessity.

I visited his residence every now and then. He had a magnetic personality and extraordinary charisma to get deeply in touch with people. This was why he invited high-ranking people to tea parties or dinner, sometimes twice a month. I don't know whether anyone does this nowadays. And to do this, he would spend money even from his own salary. He frequented various functions, mainly with these ends in view. He also took part in multipurpose social gatherings. I have also seen him invite people from all walks of life, particularly the journalists, every year on the first day of Bengali New Year. He was equally intimate with all the people of his office, from top to toe. He was very accessible; his door was open to all.

And so I have noticed people's reaction after his death. I was astonished to find the depth of sorrow felt by people close to him. He was friendly towards everyone, whatever his occupation. He knew very well that public relations was a marvelous weapon for the steady growth of the insurance business. He tried his utmost to make everyone's family his own. And so he had little time to take care of his family. In spite of heavy pressure at work, he managed to spend a little time with his children and wife.

He made himself a true member of the society. He was quite aware of the fact that in the great task of the building of the society, everyone should come forward with his active help. We, as relatives, had considerable advantage to freely mix with him. He had a progressive mentality; whoever came in touch with him, talked to him, worked with him, had the experience that he was quite easy to access but impossible to forget.

He took up insurance not as a job – frankly speaking, he took up insurance as a motto. This was why he was called the "giant" of the insurance industry. None except him has as yet got the name. None ever came close to him.

And if anyone could take his place, it would have been better. He himself was a self-made man, and he helped prepare others, but none had the greatness to take his place. Because the place was his only and not others. He was unique, without an equal.

He gave away a portion of his income to the poor and destitute. He actively participated in the management of a school and a *maktab* (school) in his village home, Damodya. He also bore the expenditure of many boys and girls and helped them in many other ways.

I am highly glad to find that an initiative is under way to keep him in memory. And this will certainly act as a memento. I am also disgruntled at the same time. He sacrificed his whole life for the economic emancipation of the general masses, for the betterment of the men in the streets, for the uplifting of the society. Nevertheless, the people seem listless. And family-based efforts are being made to commemorate him. In our national life, we have already failed to show due respect for too many such persons or events; and as a nation, such listlessness is inglorious for us. It will certainly traumatize and dismember our national character. Most people of East Pakistan's EFU office were from Faridpur. Some take it negatively. But I think he was 100 percent right in appointing them. If he did not do so, many families of our country would be totally eliminated. So, I think he was quite right in giving them the last chance to survive.

My Beloved Father

Md. Ataur Rahim[56]

MY EARLIEST MEMORY of my father was in Calcutta. I was only four or five years old then. The sun barely up, I would run a few blocks on Park Circus Street and get the morning newspaper for him.

When I was five, my three brothers and I would sit in a circle before school began. Our father would sit with us and discuss important issues of life like honesty, sincerity, truthfulness, and hard work. The meanings of other words of wisdom like knowledge, education, love, affection, and caring were explained to us in great detail. I was too young then to realize the importance of those explanations, but over time, I recalled those valuable lessons and the parts they played in my life.

My father bought his first car when we were in Calcutta. I learned from my mother that he was able to buy that car because of my luck.

I was seven or eight years old when we moved to Dhaka. Every morning around 5:00 a.m., my father would drive us four boys from Ganderia to Ramna Park, then a vast open field equal to four or five football fields which included a horse-racing track. There, he would lay out a bed sheet and sit with my mother to have a cup of tea while he told us to run around the race course as fast as we could. These runs eventually paid off for my younger brother, Nannu (Muhammad Rahim), who became a champion sportsman in the junior section among all the schools in East Pakistan.

My father, a loving and caring man, showed us that health is wealth and knowledge is power. His philosophy was simple: You do what you think is best for you. But whatever you do, educate yourself and be a caring, loving person.

---

[56]Second son of Khuda Buksh, Former Marketing Manager, Toronto Dominion Bank, Calgary, Canada.

After high school, I studied at Notre Dame College and then at Rajshahi University, where I graduated with honors in history. He was very supportive when I decided to go to Rajshahi University in Rajshahi, Bangladesh, and when my other brothers, Nannu and Dalu, went to Lahore and Chittagong, respectively, to study.

My father's dream was for me to become a civil servant, but I had other ideas. After I completed my master's degree, I traveled to Europe for a year and did all kinds of voluntary work. He was a little disappointed, but he told me, "Son, this is your life. You have to do what you are comfortable with."

After I returned from Europe, I wanted to work at an oil company. He was very supportive, and thereby, I joined Imperial Oil (formerly known as ESSO and now called Jamama Oil Company).

After independence, I was totally disillusioned with the corruption of the ruling party. At that time, I decided to leave to seek my fortune somewhere in Europe or North America. When I told my father my decision, he again supported me. He said, "Son, this is your life. You've got to do what is best for you."

In July of 1972, when I left Bangladesh, he personally came to the tarmac to see me off. He hugged me and said, "Son, I wish you all the best in your adventure. This will be my last visit with you." I was astounded and totally shaken by that remark. "What are you saying!" I exclaimed. He did not reply. He just hugged me again, and I went up the stairs into the plane. Unfortunately, his remarks were true. He passed away in May 1974. I immigrated to Canada that same year and became a successful banker from a very humble beginning. I was not able to see my father again. I still experience a deep wound inside of me, that I could not share my success with my beloved father. I succeeded in life only because of his childhood teachings of simple values such as sincerity, honesty, and hard work. He was such an admirable man, and I miss him every day of my life.

Glancing Beyond the Picture

Tanisha Bukth[57]

TO ME, THE word 'Dada' had always been associated with a picture hanging on the wall of my grandmother's house. It is a portrait done in somber colors, depicting a stately gentleman in a black suit and tie. When I was young, my parents would point at that picture and tell me, "That's Dada". Over the years, that picture got etched in my mind such that whenever I heard about Dada, I found myself thinking back to it. When this book was being compiled, I was given the responsibility to edit a small portion of it. Small, but deeply revealing, it contained the views of Dada's associates and contemporaries and I found myself coming much closer to knowing him than I had ever before.

"There was no street in Kolkata, which Khuda Buksh had not traversed in his quest to sell insurance." This is something my family had told me countless times and when I read the memoirs, I knew that this was no exaggeration. Dada's love for insurance and his sedulity, of which I had only heard till then, assumed a tangible quality. It amazed me to know that whenever someone resigned from Eastern Federal, Dada would turn up at his house to find out the reason behind his resignation and persuade him to rejoin the company. The sheer humility and warmth that shines through such an act filled me with respect for Dada. In his indefatigable spirit for his profession, Dada touched the lives of so many people and I felt a glow of pride at the fact that such a person is my grandfather.

Dada's generosity was not limited to those with whom he was associated professionally. His family, too, no matter how distant knew that they would never return empty-handed from his threshold. Whenever one of his or my grandmother's

---

[57]Tanisha is senior Business Administration major at the Institute of Business Administration, University of Dhaka, Bangladesh.

relatives expressed a wish to study, Dada took on their full responsibility and treated them with the same love and affection with which he treated his own children. Arranging marriages was another thing Dada loved and I have heard that he did it with an ardent enthusiasm. My admiration, in these respects, extends to my grandmother as well, because without her support Dada's efforts could never have been complete. Dada, too, hardly let his dedication to his profession and the numerous obligations he had, undermine his responsibility towards his own family. In fact, I have often heard my grandmother mentioning that after returning from work, he would take her out even if it was as late as ten in the night. The admiration, which still shines through my grandmother's voice when she talks about Dada, testifies more strongly than any words that he was indeed a good husband and father.

The image of Dada in my mind is still instinctively attached with that portrait. But now the portrait has begun to gain dimension and has become much more alive, because what I read has familiarized me with the person in that portrait. My parents had always told me that Dada loved girl-children more and if he had been alive, he would have pampered me beyond limit. Now I can perhaps guess how much he would have loved and pampered me, because through the memoirs, Dada came across to me as a person, whose very nature was to love and care for people.

That Large-Hearted Man

M. Faizur Razzaque[58]

AMONG THE GREAT personalities whom I have known during my busy career, the late Khuda Buksh is one of them. He happened to be related to me by marriage – his eldest son Mohammed Zubaidur Rahim was married to my younger sister Noor Afza. But even before knowing him as a relative, I used to hear about the great reputation of this giant personality of the life insurance arena. When I came to know him from close, I had no problem realizing the appropriateness of the title "father of insurance" by which he was known in this part of the world. The people of what was then West Pakistan used to refer to him with this title.

"People live for people" was the motto of his life. He implemented this ideal not only in his working world, but he never, ever deviated from it even in his social and family life. It is [not] rare to find examples of the way the late Khuda Buksh extended his benevolent hand towards people. He was always ready to extend his helping hand not only to his relatives and friends, but to immediate acquaintances as well. In this connection, I can recall two worthy incidents from my own life.

The first incident took place in 1969. At that time, in spite of his multifarious preoccupations, he was not only acting as the go-between in arranging my marriage, but was constantly keeping in touch with my late father and father-in-law, helping them in every possible way. It looked as if his own son was getting married. My parents-in-law were initially introduced to me and talked with me in his Dhanmondi residence.

The second incident is about buying my first car. In 1972, I got transferred from Mymensingh to Dhaka Secretariat. I needed a car very badly. Uncle sold one Austin

---

[58]Former secretary, Ministry of Power, Energy and Mineral Resources, Government of Bangladesh. For details, see Appendix K.

Mini to me for just Tk. 8,000 [$1,680]. Though the car was a 1952 model, it was in very good condition. Besides shuttling between home and office, the car was very useful to me. I still remember what genuine pleasure uncle used to derive when I narrated these to him. It makes me emotional when I think about it.

In the '60s and '70s, his income was sufficiently large. But the way he used to give away a good portion from it in order to help others as well as entertaining friends and important people, I sometimes wondered if he had left enough for himself and his family. But I never found him worried over that. Frankly, he was never anxious to amass wealth and money. He sincerely enjoyed helping people and entertaining friends. I realized much later that by entertaining acquaintances and friends, he also cultivated a fine brand of public relations. It is without a doubt that he was a consummate public relations person. His circle of friends and contacts was so large that sometimes I would wonder as to how he was able to keep track of them. It extended all over Pakistan and not confined only to Dhaka and Chittagong. He would throw lavish parties and dinner for his friends not only in these cities but also in Karachi, Lahore, and other cities of former West Pakistan. One such very well-attended and colorful party – at that I remember, he had organized at the then Karachi Boat Club in 1967 for a total of forty-five newly recruited Civil Service of Pakistan (CSP) and Pakistan Foreign Service (PFS) officers, including the senior officers of Lahore Civil Service Academy and Karachi Civil Service Administration, was a dinner which was talked about not only for its very tasty food but also for quality of participation. His matchless acumen in public relationships during this dinner earned him the goodwill of the new CSP and PFS officers and also later, I heard appreciative words for him in this connection. As far as I know, he was the first "East Pakistani" (now Bangladesh) whose offer to invite the CSP and PFS officers to the dinner was accepted by the Federal Government of Pakistan at Islamabad.

I had seen how much Bengali he was at heart. On the first day of Bengali New Year, he used to invite the dignitaries of the newspaper world to lunch at his place. The lunch menu was limited to only items of Bengali cuisine. The ceremony used to turn into a meeting fair of members of the newspaper world in Bangladesh. He continued with this tradition until he fell ill on 12 April 1974.

Side by side with the involvements of his career, he was actively involved in various national and international organizations. In spite of his busy schedule, he always found time to devote to his family. He was a friend to his children and discussed different aspects of life with them, guided and advised them. His advice and guidance inspired them to grow up and live as better and honest human beings in society. This role with his children definitely portrays his image as that of an ideal father and guide. This gave him both the love and respect from his children.

I remember the last day of the late Khuda Buksh in the hospital. When he was oscillating between life and death, the doctor on duty prescribed such a medicine, which was unavailable not only in the hospital itself, but in any other shops outside. By the time his eldest son, Zubaidur Rahim, obtained the medicine after a long search, uncle had already departed from this mortal world. After completing the formalities of the hospital, the dead body had already been brought to their Dhanmondi residence. It was after another hour that Zubaid returned home there, heartbroken and with the medicine bottle in his hand after making a round of the hospital. He had fulfilled his last duty to his father, but his father did not live to see it – this memory pained and haunted Zubaidur Rahim a lot in his later life. Now when I am reminiscing about uncle, Zubaidur Rahim has also reached far beyond all mortal pains.

Our Beloved Uncle: Khuda Buksh

Dr. Mizanur Rahman[59]

TRYING TO SELL insurance is a lot like digging for gold. But in 60's lot of people bought insurance by trusting Mr. Khuda Buksh. I met my uncle, Khuda Buksh, only a few times. However, I remember vividly every occasion. From very young age I knew that he ran the most successful insurance business in the country and was famous, influential and rich. He was not only a very successful insuranceman; he was also a man of great vision. His generosity and kindness made many people successful. I am one of Khuda Buksh's nephews who received his blessings, help and became a reality of his vision.

In early 60's my father used to have a professional job in a small town named Kustia. His income was nearly enough to provide a living for his wife and eight children. Unfortunately, after three years of his service the reorganization of the sugar mill made him redundant. He had no choice but to return to his small house in Dhaka.

Soon, his financial resources started to dry up. Until today the Bangladesh government can't afford a social security welfare system for the unemployed, and in my father's days the opportunities for a job were far more slimmer than today. When my father did not have a job, it was happiness for us to have a plate of rice with meat or fish. Often we had none of those luxuries. My desire for going to school was stronger than getting a plate of a happy meal but to afford my school uniform was not an easy task for my parents. Life was very tough for us. My mother

---

[59]Nephew of Late Khuda Buksh, currently resides in Sydney, Australia.

approached Khuda Buksh for a job for my father. Consequently, the EFU insurance company temporarily employed him. As my father found a new permanent job in a daily newspaper office, the salary started to come on a regular basis. However, it was not enough to give us proper food and education, but with Khuda Buksh's assistance we were given some sense of security.

First my elder sister, Hirun, was accommodated together with Khuda Buksh's daughter in his house. As my elder sister was sheltered, she was also dressed, fed and sent to a good college. Then my elder brother was given free boarding in his house. Khuda Buksh took some of the burden of financial difficulties from our family, however the size of our family continued to increase with the arrival of new children. At the end we became twelve siblings. In those days there was not much recognition for birth control education. People were very shy to talk about it. As the number of children in our family increased, the heat of financial discomfort started to be almost unbearable.

Although Khuda Buksh's involvement with the insurance business led him to a higher status and busier lifestyle, he was never a distant person to his poor relatives. His children were raised with good manners and always very nice to us. They often presented us their own clothes and shoes. Especially in late 60's, his 13 years old daughter, Milan's loving and caring relationship connected us very strongly. We were treated as if we were real brothers and sisters.

Khuda Buksh decided to support other families of his relatives. In mid 60's, he started to accommodate and educate more nieces and nephews together with his own children in his house. On the one hand he was building the family infrastructure by educating the young, on the other hand he continued to support a number of families of relatives by providing food, clothes and other financial expenses.

It was 1967, the first time I saw a Mercedes Benz car. As the car stopped in front of our small house, a driver dressed in white got out from the car; I ran inside the house and loudly informed others that the uncle and auntie arrived to visit us. Them I returned back to watch the car. When Khuda Buksh got out and stood at the rear of car, The driver opened the boot [trunk]. I noticed it was packed with rice, sugar and other stuff, which was bought for us by this busy, high official businessman Khuda Buksh. A man who was passionate in caring for people.

In Bangladesh the tradition and culture are in favor of arranged marriages. Outside of this tradition, there is almost no scope for women to get married or fall in love. Most young women are not allowed any romantic engagement with young men before the marriage. Therefore, when a daughter reaches the age of 20, the parents normally look for a husband is costly, frustrating and almost an agony for people in financial turmoil. As my elder sister exceeded the traditional marriage age my parents were very concerned about her future. As our experience of finding a groom proved that people didn't like to build a relationship with a large family in need, so my sister's chances of getting married were under the clouds. I guess my parents often begged God for a leadership. Luckily, all the responsibilities for my sister's marriage were taken care of. My sister got a life. My parents were relieved. A leader was within the family – it was Khuda Buksh.

According to my secondary school results, I had the opportunity to get an admission to a top college in the country. But for my father the college admission fee was very expensive and simply unaffordable. So, one early morning my father and I went to see Khuda Buksh in his house and asked him to pay my admission fee. He hugged and congratulated me on my school results and gladly paid not only the admission fee, but also gave me some money for the books. The new chapter of my life started. As I finished my college, I received a scholarship to study overseas. Hopes for our family survival started to rejuvenate. While studying overseas, deep down in my mind, I had always known that I would follow the Khuda Buksh's example and help my sisters and brothers to succeed in life. I was fully charged with determination and was able to help my family. So did my other brothers and sisters. Because of combined efforts of our family, we were unbreakable and till today we are no longer unwanted people. It would be impossible without the help of Khuda Buksh. Therefore I believe that our survival and success are the legacy of his vision.

[Australia, 15th January, 2002]

A Man in Action

Hasan Nawaz[60]

MR. KHUDA BUKSH is more than Jiban Bima. He is an icon, a Bengali business and community leader as Bangladesh was emerging as a nation in the 1960s. There was often a negative connotation of salesman in Bangladesh. Mr. Khuda Buksh exemplified salesmanship and became a great entrepreneur.

I never saw Mr. Khuda Buksh hug his own kids or kiss them. I did not see him play football or cricket with them, either. I did not see him read any books of fairy tales to his children, but I saw different things that seemed a lot more important to me at that time and even now.

Mr. Khuda Buksh had earned a nickname from us, friends of his son. He was simply known to us as K.B. I also heard his own son calling him K.B., which was very novel at that time. If any of his children's friends happened to be in the house during lunch or dinner time, they would always be asked to join in his family dining table to share the meal with them.

He was a man in action. He would do things that would normally seem to be very ordinary, but they carried a far-reaching effect on those who came into contact with him.

There were always a few extra young men around the house, whether they were from his village or his less fortunate relatives. He would take care of them, give them shelter, and send them to school or college for education. All these young people just melted into one big family. I am sure there were inconveniences to his family. But I guess he was also educating his own family to share their fortunes with the less fortunate.

---

[60]Hasan Nawaz, currently resides in Wilmington, Delaware, USA is a childhood friend of Muhammad Rahim.

I remember him as an invisible organizer. We would go out on field trips or excursions back in the '60s. His car would be available in the early morning to take us to the Dhaka Railway Station (now Fulbaria Train Station). When we went to Chittagong, there was a clean room ready for us at the top of the EFU building. He was not with us, but he made sure that we were well taken care of.

Mr. Khuda Buksh: Someone we can Never Forget

Hubert Arun Rozario[61]

THE LATE KHUDA Buksh, former general manager of the Eastern Federal Insurance Company, was a great Bengali executive with vision and strong faith. I knew him from my childhood, as I am a class friend of his third son, engineer Muhammad Rahim. That dear friendship is still in bloom for the past 50 years. I am greatly honored and happy to have become a family friend of Mr. Khuda Buksh's family. The late Khuda Buksh loved us. He had a great capacity to love many, with his simple and affectionate way. He was a man of small structure with a towering personality. I have noticed him mingling with all kinds of people. He loved each human being as the loving creation of God, and respected all with compassion. He handled human beings with care.

The late Khuda Buksh wanted to help the people of the country by improving their economy. He introduced insurance to the masses, advocating savings for families for future rainy days. Through his forty years of hard labor, he was able to fulfill his mission to popularize insurance and generate savings, and provided salvation from financial hardship to many families. Through his able leadership, he found employment for thousands of young educated people of our country. He proved that with conviction and purpose and vision and hard work, any person could reach his goal. The late Khuda Buksh was deeply concerned about East Bengal's economic stagnation and social inequity. He lived and worked hard for bringing change and

---

[61]Former Special Assistant to the US Ambassador in Bangladesh on Protocol Affairs (1980 to 1995). Currently resides in Virginia, USA.

for a just, more egalitarian social order in the country. He served humanity in his humble way.

The late Khuda Buksh was an affluent person but lived very simply. He had strong faith in Almighty Allah. He was a quiet man, but his silence spoke much louder than words many a times. I have seen him talking to his chauffeur as if talking to a relative from his village, respecting everyone. Being such a big name in the country, we were amazed to see his humility and simplicity. All his children are highly educated and are reared-up in strong faith and compassion. His greatest quality was his faith in Allah and his raising a true Islamic family. The late Khuda Buksh brought in many honors for all Bengalis, and we are all thankful to him.

Bangladesh became poorer at his demise. I am thankful to God for having the high privilege of having known him. His strength of character was such that never did he stumble in his effort to achieve decency and fairness. All Bangladeshis must attempt to carry on the tradition that he has left behind.

A Pleasure Seeking Palmist

Dr. Zillur Rahim[62]

MANY PEOPLE BELIEVE in palmistry, and many people do not. Whether palmistry is a science or not is yet to be established. Still, I will mention two incidents regarding palmistry that occurred in my father's life. The first incident was relayed by our aunt (the second daughter of Mr. Habibur Rahman – Mrs. Kazi Latifunnesa Rashid). One day, while talking to my aunt, my father studied her palm and casually declared that she was going to live till 80 years of age. My aunt surprisingly asked my father whether he knows palmistry. My father replied by saying that he used to practice palmistry a long time ago but now had given it up. He also told my aunt the reason. It should be mentioned that, in spite of a cerebral attack 18 years ago and multiple operations, our aunt is still alive and well above 70.

My father was residing in Kolkata. His *Akth* (a ceremony of marriage) was over. He used to study the palms of his friends and foretell the future. During this time, a very close friend of my father got married. One day he went to the friend's house and met the wife for the first time. After introductions, during the ensuing conversation, that friend requested my father to study the palm of his wife. It was immaterial what my father predicted but one comment, that there was a mole below the navel of the bride, created the entire problem.

Though this person was a close friend of my father, he could never take this comment as a matter – of – fact. After this incident this particular friend avoided my father. He started drinking and returning home late. The relationship with his wife worsened into a very bad marriage. My father was still ignorant of these matters. One day, he again visited his friend. His friend was absent at that time but the friend's wife broke into tears and confided in my father the serious nature of the problem.

---

[62]Fifth son of Khuda Buksh, Pediatrician, presently rsides in Ames, Iowa

He immediately understood that the comment 'there is a mole below the navel' had made his friend suspicious of the integrity of his wife's character. My father somehow consoled the disturbed wife of his friend and left.

After searching for a few days, Father finally came across his friend on the road. He tried very hard to make his friend understand that whatever he had predicted was by studying the wife's palm, but the friend refused to believe any of this. Then, my father agreed to a test that he would point out any birthmark or abnormality in any person that is not apparently visible. This proposal worked. It was decided that the friend would bring a person completely unknown to my father at his place and subject him/her to the test. Before that, it would be ensured that the person had a birthmark on his/her body.

My father arrived at the friend's place accordingly. His friend produced a boy about 7 or 8 years old before my father. My father started studying his palm and finally declared that the boy had a birthmark on his back. And he was proved to be absolutely right. The friend apologized profusely to my father for misunderstanding him and embraced him. Peace was restored once again in the couple's conjugal life. After this, my father decided to give up palmistry altogether because certain truths can destroy lives, and he was about to lose a close friend and almost destroy the married life of that friend

The following incidence was relayed by our mother and also happened in Calcutta. One day, a friend of my father dropped by and during the conversation casually requested my father to study his palm. Remembering the above mentioned incident, my father hesitated for some time but finally changed his mind. He studied his friend's palm for some time and then with a somber look refused to say anything. Father's friend was surprised by this lack of any prediction and wanted to know what the future held for him. Father replied, "Nothing". Hearing this, the friend was even more surprised. Actually, my father was very disturbed upon studying the palm of this friend. He could distinctly foresee his imminent death. But he obviously could not say this to his friend. The friend also refrained himself from asking further and bade good bye.

Two days later my father received the news of his friend's death. This disheartened him so much that from that very day he gave up this hobby of palmistry altogether.

Helping Anyone was a Part of His Life

Ambereen Islam[63]

DAD ACCOMPLISHED MUCH in his life as a dynamic insurance sales leader but he also accomplished much by setting an example as an individual. In family life, he would never do anything that may hurt someone. In his own way, he elevated the standard of living of many less-fortunate relatives, acquaintances, and strangers, having a significant impact not only on their lives but also on those of their children (generations to come). Despite his position in society, he treated everyone like an equal and helped everyone as best he could. Whether it was a roof over their heads, a meal, or a job, my dad's habit of helping anyone became a part of his life that started early with his parents, a mother and father who never seemed to be let down by their son. I heard lot of the stories from my mum and brothers.

    Dad had immense respect for his father, Shonabuddin and mother, Arjuta. After dad started working and earning a steady salary at Oriental Insurance Comapny, he did not allow his father to work any longer. Dad knew that his father worked very hard all his life to maintain the family. And he was worried about his father's health. Dad told his father, "You have worked all your life for us. You don't have to work now. Take rest, I will bear all your expenses." It may be mentioned that there was no social security benefit available to the old people in the country. Often dad would send somebody in Damodya to bring his parents so that they could stay with us. They would come to Kolkata or Dhaka, spend an enjoyable, relaxing time with

---

[63]Daughter of Khuda Buksh, presently resides in Davenport, Iowa.

their grandchildren and return to Damodya. Unfortunately, my grand dad died in 1959 before he had the chance to witness my dad's glorious days.

In 1961, we lived as tenants in the residence of the late Lulu Bilkis Banu at Eskaton Garden Road. Banu was the headmistress of Viqurunessa Girls' School. There was a vacant plot of land measuring about half a bigha (0.33 acre approx) opposite the Ladies Club, which was located near our house. The owner of this particular piece of land had proposed that Dad buy it from him at a relatively cheap price. Dad could have afforded it, but he declined because situated right behind that plot was the residence of Mr. Shamsul Haque – the former principal of the Dacca University and the ex-minister of external affairs during the Ziur Rahman regime. He had a nice and friendly relation with my dad. Dad disclosed to my mum, "If we build a house on that particular plot, the house of Mr. Shamsul Haque would be totally obstructed and that might offend him." Despite informing the landowner of the reasons for not buying that land, the landowner repeatedly asked dad to buy, who however declined the offers modestly every time.

Azizul Haque of Damodya was one of the students who received dad's help to complete his higher education. Haque had no relationship with us. He was referred by Ainuddin Ahmed, my dad's teacher. Aziz stayed at our home as a member of the family for six years and completed his M.A. in Philosophy from Dhaka University. Haque later became a successful Professor of Philosophy at Brahmanbaria College. He was contacted for this memoir, but he was unable to share his thoughts as he had passed away during the writing.

In the process of helping people, a tragedy once took place. Khalilur Rahman, a nephew of my dad, came to Dhaka to pursue a college education. He resided with us at Eskaton Garden Road and got himself admitted in Dhaka College. Unfortunately, Khalil was contracted with small pox. He was admitted to Dhaka Medical Hospital and died within a week. This incident did not stop my dad from extending his helping hand towards other needy people.

One day, in 1963, on his way home from the office, dad brought with him a young boy named Humayun Kabir. Dad said to my mum, "It is another son of yours. He will stay here and pursue his studies in the university." It was known later that Kabir had been pursuing a B.A. (Hons) in Economics, but because of financial problems he was compelled to give up his studies to look for a job. He sat for an interview at the Eastern Federal where he met my dad. Kabir got a job at Eastern Federal, but after a few days dad learned more details about Kabir's financial situation. He convinced Kabir to give up the job and brought him home. Dad said to him, "Stay here as you stayed in your own house." Kabir stayed with us as a family member for a few years and received an M.A. in Economics from Dhaka University. He later joined a government service and is now passing into his retirement. He used to call my mother *Amma* (mother).

Dad went to Damodya, his village home, after the death of my grandmother. This was his last visit there. During this visit, one of the villagers came to see him with an injured leg. Some insect bit him in the leg while he was fishing in the river. The untrained doctors and poor supplies of medicine in the village aggravated his condition. The man's leg was inflamed and swollen with infection. His condition was so bad that the stink from the leg repelled everyone around him. Dad was severely shaken by this condition. He instructed the man to visit his residence at Dhaka. He even handed him transportation fare. A few days after, the man turned up one morning to our residence. Dad was getting ready to go to office. The servants were troubled by the foul smell emanating from the man's leg but Dad told them that the man could hardly survive if he lost his leg. Dad persuaded them to allow the man to stay at our home. He also told them that after two days he would get him admitted into the hospital. He got the man admitted into the hospital, and the man returned home, fully cured after proper treatment. Fortunately, his leg was not amputated. Dad bore all the hospital expenditures.

In 1972, dad bought a Toyota for his personal use and did some repairing too, when required. It was almost a new car, but what was in his mind, only God knows; he decided to sell the car and buy another one. He had spoken with a certain gentleman regarding the sale of the vehicle. It was finally decided that the gentleman would buy it. In the meantime, another gentleman wished to buy the car. He said that he was prepared to pay taka 5,000 in excess of what was settled earlier. Dad refused, saying, "I am not a car dealer. I have given my word to someone, I can't break my promise." The second gentleman, nonetheless, made urgent requests to my father, all in vain. Dad had already given his word, and so he sold the car to the first gentleman.

In June of 1972, shortly after Bangladesh gained its independence, a rickshaw puller was found lying senseless near our gate at our Dhanmondi residence. When he was informed, my dad called the servants and with their help, brought the man inside and let him lie at the porch. My younger brother, Zillur Rahim, a medical student, was at home that day. Dad told him to examine the man. Water was poured on his head. After about ten minutes, the man regained his consciousness. He said he had been pulling the rickshaw in extreme hunger, and so had fallen unconscious. He was given food and a glass of milk. After getting somewhat well, the rickshaw puller wanted to return home. Another rickshaw puller was called. dad said to him, "Go home in that rickshaw and keep your rickshaw in my house. Come tomorrow to take back your rickshaw." But the rickshaw puller did not comply, fearing that the *mahajan* (owner of the rickshaw) would disagree. Dad gave him the rickshaw fare and, being perturbed by his crying, gave him his due. This was because he could not earn mahajan's due till then.

Dad was vehemently averse to publicity regarding the help and cooperation he extended towards the poor. He regularly bore the educational expenditures of many poor students but hardly did he let this be known to anyone. He did not disclose it even to his wife. After the death of my dad, a number of poor students came to mum and asked for help. It was only then that she could discover a new horizon of the altruistic mentality of her husband. Mum could only say to the help-seeking boys, "My dear sons, you see my former days of prosperity are gone. Had I been in my former state, I could certainly help you."

An Ethical Will of Action

Sara Rahim[64]

AS WE GO through life there are people we read about, hear about or meet, who set an example for us to emulate. Those people inspire us and their lives educate us in how we can be more giving, compassionate and successful. While I wasn't fortunate enough to know him while he was alive, my grandfather, Khuda Buksh, was one of those people. Over the course of the last several years, what he did and who he was in his lifetime have come alive through the efforts of my father, Muhammad Rahim and my uncle, Bazlur Rahim, as they set out to write a biography on Khuda Buksh's life and his impact on the insurance industry. To them he was "larger than life" and because of their hard work he now is to me as well.

Throughout the planning and writing of the book, I learned a great deal about my grandfather as I transcribed interviews given by his associates and colleagues from Karachi, Pakistan. Time after time, every person stated characteristics about Khuda Buksh that made him so dynamic. He was a "willing listener, a great motivator, a big team builder, devoted to his profession, had a humble, straightforward nature, and was a man of commitment. He was an extraordinary leader and an unbeatable legend of insurance."

I have often heard the phrase 'ethical will', which, to some degree, is a way of leaving behind something more meaningful than material goods when one passes away. Generally, an ethical will can take the form of a letter in which the writer tries to state certain values or morals they wished to pass on or be remembered by. While I've never seen a formal ethical will written by my grandfather, it has become obvious that he left behind an ethical will in the form of actions rather than words.

---

[64]Granddaughter of Khuda Buksh. She is Production Scientist II, Integrated DNA Technologies, Inc., San Diego, California, USA.

The work that he did revolutionized the life insurance industry, and in turn, countless numbers of people's families benefited from the product he and the people he trained sold. However, what was most elemental in his personality was his kindness.

More than anything else, Khuda Buksh's ethical will of actions shows us that if you have the ability to do so, then you should help a person in distress. Khuda Buksh constantly lived his life out of concern for others. It never mattered to him whether a person was a friend or critic. Whether they were family members, employees, colleagues, clients or someone he had just met off the street, he always gave them the consideration of his attention and kindness, and the examples of his generosity are endless. Having lived through two of the most defining and violent periods in history on the Indian subcontinent – the end of British rule in India combined with the partition of the country, and the independence of Bangladesh from Pakistan – Khuda Buksh faithfully took care of those around him, regardless of their class or loyalties.

For example, when the country was in the midst of an independence war with West Pakistan and 24-hour curfews were in effect, the moment the curfews were relaxed for a few hours on March 27th, 1971 Khuda Buksh went out in his car to meet with acquaintances and friends and make sure they were okay. Before the curfew resumed he returned home with two people. They had just resigned from Khuda Buksh's newly established insurance company, Federal Life Assurance, on personal grounds. Even so, he went to their home and when he came to know that they had no food to eat, he brought them back to his house and gave them food from his own kitchen and garden.

Another time, in the summer of 1972, when he found a rickshaw puller who had fainted from hunger near the gate of his home, he brought the man in and gave him food and milk. When the rickshaw puller regained consciousness Khuda Buksh called another rickshaw to take him home. He gave him enough money to cover the fare of the rickshaw ride and enough to pay off the rickshaw puller's financier.

Over the years, Khuda Buksh provided for the education of countless nieces, nephews, cousins, and people who he took a liking to. Often, they stayed at his house while they commenced their education at nearby schools and universities. His generosity knew no bounds between family member and villager and because he had the money he used it to help whoever he could. And when he didn't have the money, he gave them what he could from his own possessions.

Everyone has critics and it is inevitable that Khuda Buksh did as well. However, whether they were former business partners or friends who had an argument with him, he never held a grudge and went out of is way to be compassionate even if he was the injured party.

His life sets a great example to everyone, and I hope he knew what an important part he played in people's lives that came in contact with him. I have often wondered what he might think of his family today. Although his untimely death prevented him from seeing it fully, out of his example his sons became successful businessmen, bankers, an engineer, doctor, and writer each with families of their own. Perhaps he never realized the influence he had on each of their lives, but as each strived to build a career, provide for their families and help others, they remember him and his remarkable life.

In the end, Khuda Buksh's ethical will of actions illustrated a number of values for his sons and daughter and their children to follow: an enthusiasm for life, a sense of responsibility and concern for others and sensitivity for their situations, and above all, a closeness and regard for one another. Although there's a void in my life from never meeting my grandfather, the legacy he left behind of his generosity, integrity and compassion inspire me in ways that cannot ever be expressed. All I can hope is that he would have been proud of what we've have and will accomplish in our lifetime.

As Dolly Parton, a famous American country singer and songwriter, once said, "If your actions create a legacy that inspires others to dream more, learn more, do more, and become more, then you are an excellent leader." If that's the case, then Khuda Buksh was an excellent leader, and we can only hope to follow the example he set appropriately.

An Icon of Life Insurance: A Personal Reminiscence

Muhammad Rahim[65]

THE IDEA FOR this book was conceived thirty-four years ago when my father died in 1974 in Bangladesh. I was a graduate student at the Indian School of Mines in Dhanbad, India when my father passed away. When I reached Dhaka, all the funeral arrangements were completed. It was a very tragic event in my life. While I was in Dhaka, I had a discussion with my younger brother, Bazlur Rahim, about writing a book about our father. At that time we were young, in school, and working to make our own way in the world. As the years passed by, my siblings and I married, got jobs, and created our own lives. Now, I have two brothers in Bangladesh and two brothers and a sister in the United States.

In 2000, the idea for a book, spearheaded by conversations with our mother who was visiting the United States, reawakened our mission to tell the story of our father's life. I discussed the project with Bazlur in Bangladesh, and we decided to launch the project.

The challenge and enormity of writing a book soon became apparent. We realized that we had very little information to start with, in addition to having to deal with the global distance between Bazlur and myself. Subsequently, we started collecting memoirs and interviews of colleagues, associates, and acquaintances of my father.

As I started my work on the project, I found through Internet research that Wolfram Karnowski, a retired senior executive of Munich Reinsurance Company and

---

[65]Third son of Khuda Buksh. For details, see Appendix K.

former Director and Advisor of Eastern Federal Union Insurance Company (EFU), had published two books – *The EFU Saga* and a biography, *Roshan Ali Bhimjee: Between tears and laughter* in Pakistan. I came to know that there is a chapter on my father in *The EFU Saga*. *The EFU Saga* opened the door to numerous contacts in Pakistan, where my father worked every six months from 1960 to 1969 for the development of life insurance. Rizwan Ahmed Farid, a marketing professional in Karachi, came forward and extended his helping hand, offering to interview my father's colleagues in Karachi, Pakistan. Without Rizwan Ahmed Farid's help, a lot of stories would have been unknown to us.

My father meant more to me than anyone else in the world. From childhood, I noticed that my father stressed three things to his children – education, extra-curricular activities, and meeting people. He used to say that "I would like to see that all my children have an M.A." Due to my father's encouragement in school life, I joined scouting and participated in track and field events. I vividly remember my father was overjoyed when I earned the junior championship in Inter-School and Inter-District sports in track and field. During that time, he told me about his school days: how much he enjoyed playing soccer and how he earned a lot of trophies for the team. When I decided to study Mining Engineering at Lahore, he provided his wholehearted support. He was thrilled when I earned a fellowship for postgraduate studies at Indian School of Mines, Dhanbad, India.

I noticed from childhood that Father used to treat and help people, known or unknown, just like a family member. I remember a person who was meeting Father at our residence in the early 1960s. After the person introduced himself, Father started talking to him. The way Father was talking to him, it seemed to me that he had known that person for a long time, although it was the first meeting between the two.

Father used to say, "Try to adjust your life to everything. You don't know what situation you may encounter." He was a very caring and loving father. I remember many events with my father that helped me to shape my life.

Father was a positive-minded person. He never worried about small problems in the family. He easily solved those problems with his positive attitude. One day in 1962, there was a heated discussion between my mother and her cousin-sister. The discussions led to severe arguments between the two. I do not exactly remember the topic of the arguments or who was involved. It was between my mother and one of my aunts, either the late Mrs. Alimullah Khan or the late Mrs. Anwara Monsur. (The sisters were identical twins.) Mrs. Anawara Monsur is the wife of the late Professor Kazi Abul Monsur, a microbiologist of international repute who developed the world's best known culture media for cholera known as "Monsur Media." At a peak moment of argument, my father returned from the office for lunch. As soon as my aunt saw my father, she told him, "*Dula Bhai* [brother-in-law], I will never come to your house again." Father, without asking the reason, calmly said to her, "You may not come to my house, but I will always go to your house." This response had an immediate impact in the room. There was a pin-drop silence. My aunt quietly left the house. Everything returned to normal after that incident, and there was no break in the family relationship.

When Father helped a person, it was against his principles to receive anything in return. I can recollect such an event when I was in high school. Father helped one gentleman get a job for himself or one of his relatives. The gentleman was so happy that he badly wanted to give something in return. I was sitting on the verandah, reading the newspaper, when the gentleman entered our house with a cake in a box. The cake seemed to be of large size. Father received the gentleman in the living room. The next thing I remember was Father talking and smiling with the gentleman, but he declining the cake. I vividly remember him saying, "Please treat your children with the cake." Then Father followed the gentleman with the cake in his hand until the person was in his car. I was a bit upset when Father returned the cake but I realized its significance much later in my life.

Father started his career at a time when people were hostile to life insurance and only a handful of Muslims took this profession. In spite of all the criticism and controversies, Father took this profession, as he decided to serve humanity. He started his professional career by knocking at people's doors. During that time many houses had signs on doors reading, "Beware of Dogs and Insurance Agents."[66] Selling life insurance is a difficult job, and I realize his determination when he used to carry a folding chair for his work because well-off families were reluctant to offer seats. He did not see insurance as a job but as a motto in life. He had the least fascination for money or material possessions. The lion's share of his income was spent on the entertainment of his acquaintances and on helping the poor. All his life he tried to raise people's standard of living. He used to help people, sometimes in public, sometimes secretly. He never had recourse to any excuse for this. He was vehemently averse to publicity and was never interested in any reward. Perhaps he received his rewards as the blessings of many orphans and widows, as many of them were saved from imminent danger with the money obtained from insurance.

I believe Father carried out the mission of life insurance through his passion, obsession, dedication, devotion, and continued public relations. He earned a reputation as the country's "most magnetic and dynamic sales executive" and "wizard of life insurance."

After working for thirty years in the insurance industry, he felt happy with what he accomplished when he said, "I think that nowadays, no insurance worker is to carry with him a folding chair like me when I first started my career. Rather, in the present day society, an insurance worker is the most honorable and welcome guest to a family . . ." According to Walter A. Friedman, author of *Birth of Salesman*, "All countries throughout time have had charismatic individuals who possessed the

---

[66]Rahman, M. Lutfar, *Firay Dekha Sei Sab Din* [Looking back into those days] (Bangladesh: Fah-Ra Printing & Publications, 2008, pp 83-84).

ability to charm and persuade." May be my father was one of the individuals who fall into this category.

While Father might have had the opportunity to amass a great fortune, his money went where his heart was. He went beyond the responsibility of just providing for his own family and provided for extended family, friends, colleagues, and strangers. In the end, he put his heart, soul, and money into the development of insurance. As a result, it was his own life insurance that ultimately kept his family financially afloat after his death.

Twenty-five years ago, I became a naturalized citizen of the U.S. After the oath of citizenship, a small ceremony was held in Chicago's downtown area, sponsored by a church in Chicago. During the ceremony, the president of the sponsor told the new citizens: Do not forget your past, your country, and your tradition.

I did not.

Life insurance is on the path of progress in Bangladesh and Pakistan. However, I want readers to remember that the foundation of the life insurance industry in Bangladesh and Pakistan was truly established in the 1950s and 1960s by thousands of field agents, field officers, inspectors, managers, office staff, administrators, and executives of all insurance companies. My father was one of them. However, like many people, my father has faded into the pages of history. I believe the deeds of my father left an indelible impact and may serve as a reminder of his vision on life insurance in Bangladesh. His life's work has passed to the next generation.

I made a brief visit to Bangladesh in May 2003, to collect some information and conduct some interviews for this book. During that time, one evening there was a quiz program on Bangladesh television. One of the questions on the program was: Who is known as the "Father of Insurance?" The answer was Khuda Buksh.

That was the first time I heard my father formally referred to in this way. I can proudly say that my father loved people without any prejudices of color, race, nation, or creed. There is no doubt in my mind that he sacrificed his whole life for the economic emancipation of people through his insurance awareness movement.

Many years ago, I read an article from a story in which a mother said to her son, "You embrace what defines you." My father embraced life insurance, and it truly defined his life – *An Icon of Life Insurance*.

A Granddaughter's Perspective

Shuva Rahim[67]

LIKE MOST OF Khuda Buksh's grandchildren, I did not get to know the man our parents did. But chances are, he was not the same man our grandmother knew, nor the same man many in the insurance world in India, Pakistan and Bangladesh came to know.

Regardless, Khuda Buksh did live to be a grandfather for a short time before his death in 1974. The rest of my cousins, my sister and I, unfortunately, missed out on having him in our lives. However, I am sure he was and would have been a different man as a grandfather than as a life insurance icon.

I was born in 1976, two years after his death. Throughout my life everything I learned about Khuda Buksh was from old photographs, stories from my grandmother, interviews from numerous friends and former colleagues, as well as the detailed chapters in this book.

It has been a fascinating history lesson to say the least. Not many kids learn about their grandfather this way. But still, none of it can replace his being a real presence in my life.

What would Khuda Buksh have been like as a grandfather to me?

What words of wisdom would he have shared after my graduating from high school and college?

What would he think of the stories I wrote as a journalist for six years?

How would he have reacted to his oldest granddaughter going into the Peace Corps in South America for two years?

What would he think of my interest in documentary photography? Sea turtles? My role in this book?

---

[67]Granddaughter of Khuda Buksh. She is a Journalist and freelance photographer.

There are a million more questions that will remain unanswered. And while one can always speculate what Khuda Buksh would say and how he would react, I have my own personal thoughts.

In the meantime, this biography – more than a generation after Khuda Buksh's passing – is here to serve as a legacy to him as well as the life-insurance era during which my grandfather was a huge part. It is also a timeless journey of spirit and lessons learned for my contemporaries and future generations.

My Father's Memoir

Bazlur Rahim[68]

WHEN EVENING SETS in, a man returns to his homestead after a day's hard work. His near and dear ones like father, mother, wife, or children eagerly wait for his early arrival. There was a time when we, too, waited for our father, who would return from his office. We had a very rare chance to have our busy dad in our midst because of the heavy pressure of his work. His fascinating personality, affection for children, his tough but meticulous management of family affairs, and his indignation combined with his extraordinary charisma made him extremely dear to us. As we feared him, so was our eagerness to be in his nestling company. He performed his duties as a father in a very meticulous way. He kept himself aloof from us for a big portion of his life, yet he kept us closely tied in a bond of fathomless affection and love. We have spent our childhood and boyhood days in an admixture of his love and admonition.

As his job demanded, he had to stay in West Pakistan for almost half of the year; nevertheless, we felt his warm presence in our hearts. So lively was his company that in spite of his being away from us, an avid desire to have him in our midst always encircled us. We learned from him to be truthful in any circumstances, to have empathy for the people around us, not to be engaged in any wrongdoing, to encourage games and sports, to be attentive to studies, and to be steadfast, guided by the light of self confidence. He used to tell us to lead an honest life, and to extend helping hands to the poverty-stricken; and he advised us not to be angry with anyone – which he himself maintained all through his life.

---

[68]Fourth son of Khuda Buksh. Editor, monthly *Gonoshasthaya* (socio-health) magazine. For details, see Appendix K.

My mother (she is now ninety-two) always distanced herself from the scene of activities. She was soft spoken, slow, steady, practical and worldly. But in thinking of the family's future, she had more advanced foresightedness than her husband. Her husband's life was focused on life insurance as he dreamt of the future of the people around him, but she had a vision about his family. She thought of buying a piece of land for building a decent house. Father was, however, reluctant to buy land; but as a result of repeated reminders from Mother, he was compelled to buy one *bigha* (0.33 acre approximately) plot at Dhanmondi in 1954 for taka 4,500.

But he was not involved in the buying process. A one-story house was built on it in 1956 and was later rented to the first secretary, British High Commission. We lived in another rented house. After independence, due to inflation, house rent went up along with other things. House owners were fairly in an advantageous position. But Father took the same rent from him [tenant]. In 1973, the first secretary once asked jokingly, "Every house owner is increasing the house rent, why aren't you?" Father simply replied, "Because I am not a businessman." He never raised the house rent in his lifetime. The incident probably surprised the secretary, but surely he observed with a respectful heart the sterling character of my father.

As a matter of fact, Father had not the least fascination for money or material possessions. And it was why he did not show an iota of eagerness when the president of Pakistan, Ayub Khan, offered him the post of commerce minister. And what is more, he was bold enough to call it a "part-time" job. The lion's share of his income would be spent on the entertainment of his acquaintances and in helping the poor. The man who dedicated his whole life for insurance passed away on 13 May 1974. So, this is not surprising that at the time of his eternal departure, his savings were virtually zero except for the one-story Dhanmondi house and a bank deposit of Tk. 50,000 set aside for the wedding of his only daughter.

After his death, there was no bank balance, and there was no regular income except my eldest brother's income. In such a predicament, we decided to leave our rented house and move to the house built by Father. Soon after we disclosed our intention to the honorable secretary, he hurriedly vacated the house in that month. We believe that the secretary had a vivid memory of the past (i.e. no increase in house rent) and did not delay in leaving the house on short notice.

Another incident related to house rent may be pointed out here. He lived in a rented house at Pakistan Employees Cooperative Housing Society (PECHS) residential area in Karachi. He had a mind to leave the first house and was looking for a better house. In the meantime, a house owner himself met him and said, "I have heard that no problem arises regarding house rent." Father rented that very house. The owner even employed a gardener at his own cost for taking care of the garden.

We lost our father and came to his house, where Father himself did not live. Our eldest brother, Zubaidur Rahim, was working at Industrial Development Bank, and the next brother, Ataur Rahim, was in the process of immigrating to Canada. The remaining four brothers and one sister were students. My eldest brother's single income was hardly enough to make both ends meet in a big family like ours. We had also two relatives in our home attending university, who fully depended on us. In such a situation, we newly started our life. But even in the midst of all these obstacles and hindrances, we did not succumb to despondency, and despair hardly touched our lives. We were still guided by the light of optimism. Father always inspired and said, "Adjust yourself in everything in life, you don't know what situation you may encounter." Actually, he raised us in such a way that we can face any unfavorable or formidable situation in life.

We never found my father interested in worldly possessions or wealth. Insurance was his be all and end all throughout his life. So, I have seen that though he has visited foreign countries several times, he never bought any show piece or decorative item for his living room. He used to lead such a simple, down-to-earth life. He rather bought us pens, view cards, or instructive books. He wrote us most of the letters in view cards. A view card was attractive to us, no doubt, but to us, more delightful was to get Father's handwritten letter.

I can remember an acquaintance of Father who was a sojourner in London. I cannot recall his name. He once wrote to my father, "Many of my friends write me to purchase items for them, but you've never told me so. I want to bring something for you." He also requested my father to send him a list of items to bring from London.

For twenty-five years, Father remained very close to me. He is no longer with us in reality, yet I perceive his lively presence throughout my life. Though I got Father for a period of twenty-five years, more than half of the time, I remained deprived of his affection owing to his being in West Pakistan or elsewhere for call of duty. So, Father's short-time presence or company was really a source of boundless pleasure for us.

My first memory with my father started in Kolkata. Father used to go to his office in a black Austin car. Our Park Circus residence was in a narrow lane, and it was why the car would have to kept in a roadside garage. On his way to the office, he used to give me a lift for a short while and then let me get down at the lane-crossing. I no longer remember a good many things about my living in Kolkata, but bits and pieces of some memories are still untarnished in the deepest corner of my heart. Park Street tram plying, collecting long tram tickets, a failed venture to climb a guava tree in the courtyard, playing with our tenants' daughter Jolly at the downstairs – such memories are still vivid in my mind. But most illuminating of all memories is the short drive with my father.

My father had a deep pain in his life. It was the premature death of my younger sister, Kumu. After five brothers, my first sister was Kumu. She left us when she was only one and a half years old. I, too, was too little to properly understand what death was. The day before her departure, she got diarrhea. I saw a doctor pushing an injection in her buttock in the evening. I got up from the bed in the morning and went to my father and mother. But I did not find Kumu with them. I asked father, "Where is Kumu?" Father gave no reply. He only pointed his finger at the sky and said, "She's gone to Allah." I also noticed that Mother was crying. I still didn't realize that Kumu would no more return to us. I learned later that Kumu had had cholera. However, in 1954, the birth of my second sister, Milan (Ambereen Islam), followed by another brother, Timu (Javed Bukth), in 1956 mitigated my father's sorrow and agony.

Kumu's premature death left a deep stain in my father's mind. He never forgot the shock. By 1962 or 1963, we three brothers and sister (second sister Milan) went to visit Cox's Bazar with my parents. One day, Father took us to Ramu to see Pagoda. After going to Ramu, Father found a hawker selling open food. Flies were flying over and sitting on the food. Father instantly went to the seller, told him about the bad effects of selling open food, and advised him to keep the food duly covered.

His every workday started with the spread of the morning light. He was in the habit of taking bed-tea. He would take with it banana, salted biscuit, or grapefruit. Grapefruit was his favorite. When he lived in old Dhaka (Gandaria), he occasionally had *Bakarkhani* (special bread). He glanced at the newspapers during his breakfast. He would keep two newspapers at home up to 1965. One was the *Statesman* of Kolkata and the *Morning News* of Dhaka. After the Pak-Indo War in 1965, the government banned the *Statesman* from Kolkata. He then started reading the *Pakistan Observer*, *Ittefaq*, and *Morning News*. I have noticed that side by side with newspapers, he would eagerly read the news of the "Appointment and Transfers" of government employees. Whenever he read about any promotion and transfers of anyone among his acquaintances, he would instantly congratulate him over telephone. It is my assumption that if anyone would get any promotion or be transferred, he would invariably have the first congratulation from my father. This is my understanding today, that these were unique and unfailing strategies to augment public relations and spread out his range of acquaintances. I am astonished to think even today that he knew a good many people and could remember their destinations.

After finishing reading newspapers, he talked to a few people over the telephone for a while. Then he used to shave with his favorite Seven O'Clock blade. He used all along Bathgates oil, manufactured by a Kolkata company. He, however, faced difficulty in getting the oil after the Indo-Pak War in 1965. The oil was later produced by Kohinoor Chemical Company of West Pakistan. Perhaps the item's popularity was in his mind.

Before having his bath, Father occasionally went downstairs and strolled along the verandah. Here, he took pleasure in gossiping with Abdul Aziz, office chauffeur, who would be found washing his car. He had keen vision and took particular care of the car. He would be dissatisfied even in the case of a tiny stain on the car. Incidentally, Abdul Aziz was a World War II veteran. During World War II, he served as a truck driver of the Allied Forces, and he was actively engaged in several areas, including

Mesopotamia. He got several medals as a recognition for his participation in the war. He wore those medals only on special occasions.

My father's usual office dress was a full sleeve white cotton shirt and suit. I have never seen him wearing fashionable or colorful shirts. The buttonhole of his coat was usually garnished with the coat pin of the Rotary Club. His time companion for twenty-five years was a CYMA wristwatch, fitted with a black belt. He also wore glasses with black frames for writing or signing documents. He never used any brand of pen other than a Parker or Shaeffer.

Father would normally leave home for the office by 8:00 a.m. Among his favorite dishes were double-poached egg, bread, cheese, and coffee. He also liked half-poached egg. In the winter, these were combined with cabbage or cauliflower. He favored eating his lunch at home. But when he first joined Eastern Federal, his lunch would be sent to his office by a tiffin box. Those days of the '50s were very important in establishing a company like EFU; the fruition of his efforts came later. After he started his office at the Dienfa building on the former Jinnah Avenue, he used to have his lunch at his residence. Occasionally, he would be accompanied by some buddies or visitors. However, he would call home and let my mother know about it. The fact was that whenever someone from Kolkata or elsewhere would come to visit Dhaka, Father would usually invite them to lunch. This was his habit, and my mother knew too well how deep was her husband's friendliness.

After lunch, he would lie in his easy chair for a while, closing his eyes in something like day-drowsiness. By 3:00 p.m., he would leave for the office again, before which he would drink a glass of creamless milk. By 6:00 p.m., he would return home for tea. He was never addicted to smoking or any drink. But during my visit to Karachi, I found him drinking a soft drink called Canada Dry for a few days. It was very likely that Abbas Khaleeli, chairman of EFU, presented him a box of drink as a gift from one of his commercial enterprises.

During Father's stay in Dhaka, the afternoon would be very delightful to us. He would sit on the cane chair placed on the lawn. He would take tea there, and Mother would come from inside the house; my father would stand up and say to us, "When a lady comes, it is customary to stand up." Mother showed false resentment. I have also seen Father sing *Chithi* (Letter) for Mother. Chithi is a famous song by the immortal singer Jagan Moy Mitra. Mother's wardrobe was full of letters bound with red tape. When they were away from each other after marriage, these letters were written to Mother from Kolkata. Some were also written from Karachi or London. Perhaps it was why Chithi was so dear to him. My father bought a gramophone on the occasion of the wedding of his brother-in-law. He bought a good number of gramophone records, and he did not forget to buy Chithi.

But this afternoon meeting was not an everyday happening. On most days, someone would come from the office with Father, and they discussed various official problems and matters for long periods of time. Mother also had to be busy as a bee at that time to entertain the guests. After evening, Father talked to people for almost an hour. His telephone conversations once again proved his uncommon sharpness of memory. I have seen him dialing and talking to a large number of people, without using any telephone guide. He seldom used such a guide.

Dinner would be served by 9:30 p.m. It was customary to sit at the dining table and eat together. My father showed much resentment if he didn't find everybody at the dining table. As he discussed various family matters at the dining table, he expected the presence of everyone. Father's dinner was somewhat different. Occasionally, he preferred soup, handmade bread, boiled vegetables, fish or chicken cutlet. Among other preferred items were *Kaliza* (goat liver) and fried cattle brains. He also preferred sugarless pudding or milk. If any acquaintance or friend was present at that time, he, too, had to appear at the dining table. This turned into an unwritten rule. On weekdays after dinner, my father would talk with somebody on the phone for a while before he went to bed by 11:00 p.m.

Father imparted to us moral teachings through his various behaviors. He also taught us to speak the truth and keep a promise. I remember such an incident that took place at Dhaka New Market in 1962, that could very well be cited as a conspicuous example of a truthful relationship between two people. I accompanied my father to Dhaka New Market to do some shopping. Having finished his own shopping, Father decided to buy two shirts for me from a garment shop. But when it came time to pay the shopkeeper, Father found that the money he had with him fell short of the required amount. Father wanted to return the shirts to the shopkeeper, but the shopkeeper did not comply and urged Father to take the shirts and pay him the rest any day later. However, Father, in his characteristic manner, wanted to give him his business card. This, too, was vehemently refused by the shopkeeper, who, holding his hands, told my dad that he was doing the transaction with full confidence in him. Father thanked the shopkeeper and took leave of him. The next day was the weekly market holiday. On the third day, Father did not forget to send me to the shopkeeper at New Market with the rest of the money.

This may be an insignificant incident, but in it we find the images of an insurance buyer and a seller in a different light. On this occasion, one thing that carries weight is the buyer's satisfaction; another is to be trusting toward him. Similarly, business is a kind of social service, too. It takes one by surprise to think how faith and morality can be considered strong forces and also objects of pleasure. People usually forget such trifling things, but if we analyze them deeply, we will find that such things have a lasting impression upon our minds.

My father always motivated us to read story books, instructional books, biographies of renowned people. He gave us money to buy books every month, and he himself took us to Warsi Book Center (now abolished) at Jinnah Avenue (now Bangabadhu Avenue). He was also sufficiently aware of his children's recreation. During the summer vacation, he would take all family members to Cox's Bazar (a coastal town in the South of Bangladesh) or Karachi. Once, my grandmother accompanied us to Karachi.

The sixth of March, 1966 was a day of unforgettable delight in our lives. On this auspicious day, the wedding reception of my eldest brother, Zubaidur Rahim, was solemnized with Nur Afza Begum, daughter of Abdur Razzaque, former additional deputy secretary, Ministry of Finance. How greatly my father's public relations network had spread during his professional life, and how profound, comprehensive, and wide-ranging his intimacy with the big guns of the society of his time, were all quite evident at the wedding ceremony. A considerable number of high-ranking government officials attended the marriage ceremony and *Bou Bhat* (marriage feat in honor of bride). Hanif Adamjee, M.M. Ispahani, and all the members of the Rotary Club were invited. The editors and journalists from various newspapers attended, bringing glory and honor to the celebration. My father himself felt extremely pleased and honored at the spontaneous arrival of the company officials from West Pakistan. Father also arranged for lunch for those who came from different districts of the country and for guests from West Pakistan, with a view to cutting their hotel bills.

Father would always say, "One of your sacred duties will be to help the distressed people." And he helped the helpless people all through his life. He used to help people sometimes in public, sometimes secretly. He never had recourse to any excuse for this. He was vehemently averse to publicity.

Though most of my father's time would be spent on insurance activities, he took care of the progress of the learning of his children. When he heard of good results of our or other peoples' examinations, he would be highly delighted. In such case, it was his usual propensity to embrace the person, saying, *Mubarak! Mubarak!* (Congratulations!) in a loud voice. It was his unique way of congratulating and encouraging us. He used to say, "I want my children to be master's degree holders." It was because of Father's keen interest and encouragement that two daughter-in-laws got admitted into MA classes in the University of Dhaka and successfully passed. This achievement in higher education helped them to succeed in their careers.

The habit of socializing was inherent in my father. He preferred to visit his acquaintances and near relatives at night; he had little time in the day because of the heavy pressures of work. After having his meal at night, he used to come out of the house, usually along with his wife; and in this nocturnal venture he released his driver, and he would be at the wheel. On many occasions, he would find that those whom he visited were in deep sleep or were preparing to go to bed. Characteristically, after going to a house, he would raise a hue and cry and awaken everyone.

Father's relation with Eastern Federal started to become strained soon after the all-Pakistan EFU convention in Dhaka in 1967. Little did I know what was actually happening inside. At one point, he totally stopped going to the office. This was very unusual to me. How could a man – who attends the office regularly, whose lifeblood is the office – spend his days at home? One day, I asked Mother directly about it. She replied:

A new building is going to be built for Eastern Federal. Bhimjee told your father that engineers and materials for the EFU building should come from West

Pakistan. But your father is opposed to this. Your father wants this building to be constructed with East Pakistani engineers and the materials available in East Pakistan. Your father has stopped going to office because of the conflict that has arisen out of this.

Doing good to others was the ornament of his character, and he disliked any publicity or taking any credit. My father would be profoundly gratified if he could do any good to others. His altruistic mentality was not only limited to the people of his homeland; it extended to unknown people and even to a man in the street – equally. An incident relating to his magnanimity may be cited here.

In February 1972, a sexagenarian named Subodh Chandra Chatterjee came from Kolkata to Dhaka (Bangladesh). He could verily be classified as an indigent person. The mission of his coming was to verify the news of his sister's husband's death during the war of independence. He worked in an ordnance factory under the government of West Bengal, India. The only sister and her two children lived with this unmarried gentleman. He knew practically nothing about Dhaka, but the name Sheikh Mujib (Father of Bangladesh) was familiar to him. He turned up at Sheikh Mujib's Dhanmondi residence and told him about his problems. It was a Saturday, and the next day being the weekly holiday, Sheikh Shahib told him to meet him at a later date. Subodh Babu told him about his problems of lodging and financial constraints. Sheikh Mujib told Tajuddin Ahmed to take the man to his residence. My father was present there at that time, and he, at his own accord, took the man to his house.

From our residence, Subodh Babu went to Chittagong and verified the death news of his sister's husband. During his stay at our house, he lived like a member of our family and took food at the dining table with the rest of the family. At the time of his departure, my elder brother Muhammad Rahim took him in his car to Narayanganj for his onward catching of the Rocket Steamer. Inter-district road communications was then not as good as it is today. Having returned to Kolkata, Subodh Babu wrote this letter to me:

> I can't express in this puny letter how greatly benefited I was under your cordial shelter. Your father virtually picked me up from the street and showed me respect as a near and dear one for which I remain grateful to him forever. Not only that, it is still my expectation that I'll get help from him in any moment of crisis. Never before have I come across a man of so great character.
>
> Your parents are really great and by dint of that virtue you, all brothers and sister are so magnanimous and hospitable. May all others have your ideals.

The Last Two Days

Our sweetest songs are those that tell of saddest thoughts
— *P.B. Shelly*

My father was admitted to the Dhaka Medical College hospital in the middle of April 1974. On 12 May 1974, my father received special permission from his hospital doctors-to return home, as if he knew that he would never be able to come back to his Dhanmondi residence to meet those who were nearest and dearest to him. After his admission into the hospital, it was only that very day when he talked to us a fairly long period of time, but owing to his physical weakness, he had to take frequent breaks in his talking.

After eating rice at noon, he said to me, "Milu [my nickname], I would like to lie on your bed for a while." My small ground floor room was adjacent to the dining room. I quickly nodded and said, "Yeah!"

He slept for a while at my room, then went upstairs agonizingly, holding my sister Milan's hand, disregarding everyone's protests that he stay in my room. He rested in his own bed for a little while, with Mother beside him. Did he realize that he would no longer be able to lie on the bed he had been using since his marriage in 1939?

He lay on my room, again in the afternoon. At dusk, he sat on the sofa. Later, my father took the time to attend to some financial matters of his own. Money needed to be drawn from the bank to pay bills. He took the pen in his hand to put a signature on the check. His hands were then shivering. His signature seemed unfamiliar to him. He said to himself, "My signature will not correspond to the former one." Observing the shivering hand, he understood that he could not sign the check. The telephone desk was just at the right side of where he was seated. He took from there a brown envelope and tried to put his signature on it, twice. But it, too, had no resemblance to his actual signature. He could not sign the check before his final departure.

It was evening, and the time to return to the hospital came to close. Before departure, he told me to get admitted myself admitted to an MA class. After some time, he got into the car along with my mother. He raised his hands up to his forehead and went back to the hospital.

It was 13 May 1974, eight o'clock in the evening. The telephone rang in our residence. We were informed to rush to the hospital. At about 8:30 p.m., we entered the hospital cabin and heard a sound of crying. He was still laying on the bed where he had lain for the last month of his life. His body was covered with a white sheet. A half-empty saline bag was hanging above his head. A fan was still running. It was as if life came to a halt.

A death certificate was issued, and his family returned home with his breathless body. Who knew that the man who had come the day before, remained there the whole day, talked with his children – would return in the form of an unmoving body?

Perhaps he knew that he would never return among his near and dear ones, so he had come back to his residence, disregarding everybody's advice so that he could spend one last day with his family.

My father's still body was kept laying on an iron cot in the living room. The man who ceaselessly worked for thirty-eight years for the wellbeing of the people, who restlessly ran after work, to whom rest was an elusive dream, was today lying in his eternal sleep, on a simple iron cot. And there is a small event behind this iron cot. Thinking of future advantages, my father left Habibur Rahman's Kolkata residence at Park Circus Road and took a rented flat at 84 Jhawtala Road. He bought a small iron cot for taka 10. After the partition of India, he took a job at EFU and left Kolkata for Dhaka. At that time, he brought the iron cot along with other household articles. Who knew that father would sleep his last sleep on that 10 taka iron cot?

Our father's memory and his ideals are still a motivating factor behind our drive. When greed, the politics of taking possessions, conflicts, and corruption poison us from all side, our family seems a bit different. We can hardly mingle ourselves with such a different world – we haven't had much learning from our father. Father himself was strict in his principles; we have only tried to follow his footsteps. The more we see utmost moral degradation all around, the more we come across the memory of our father. I think by myself, where have all principled people gone?

We have initiated a project to keep alive the memory of this morally untarnished, greedless, top to bottom Bengali, benefactor, and social server. The project has been named "Khuda Buksh Memorial Trust and Foundation." Vigorous works are in progress to build up the foundation. We wish to be enlightened people. The expedition of Bangladeshi people towards the path of enlightenment will certainly provide them the clue to a happier life – and we hope for those bright days to come in the near future.

A Great Soul Indeed!

M. Rahman Mahbub[69]

*What a piece of work is a man! How noble in reason!
how infinite in faculty! in form and moving how
express and admirable!*

HAMLET 2ii
– William Shakespeare

I FIRST HEARD THE name of the late Mr. Khuda Buksh from a very respected and senior person, and from him, I have come to learn that he was not only the pioneer of life insurance in Bangladesh but also greatly contributed to the growth of this industry. I then happened to see the cover page of this book in Bengali, which displays a portrait drawn by Qayyum Chowdhury of - Khuda Buksh, depicting a stately gentleman in a suit and tie. Finally, when that book was compiled, I had the opportunity to read the English portion of the book that contained the views of his associates, relatives and contemporaries; as a result, I found myself coming very close to knowing his great personality. I became acquainted with a true human being who is not in this world yet was revealed as a man with distinction in my mind because of his positive characteristics. His works, intellect, honesty, integrity, and courage, not only fascinate, but also provide inspiration to others to follow a path of nobility. When I was invited to write about him, I felt very insignificant as I dared to write anything about him. I was confused as to how much I could reflect the true nature of this great soul. I felt so unable that my poor pen stood still for

---

[69]Lecturer, Department of English, Gano University, Savar, Dhaka, Bangladesh. For details, see Appendix K.

many days without producing a single word. I simply contemplated how and from where to start. According to Dr. Lutfor Rahman:

> In this material world, people are very much occupied and wide awaken about their own happiness. When will people realize that showing sympathy and rendering help to other people is the most beautiful thing and noble deed – when will they understand? Where is true happiness? Is there any true happiness in enjoying mirth that deprives others? Material happiness is not as important as the happiness of our soul. Only when people will receive pleasure from making people happy can people enjoy true life.[70]

The greatness of making people happy was an innate characteristic of Khuda Buksh. He always donated a portion of his income for the well-being of poor people. He contributed money to schools, colleges and *Madrasha* on a regular basis. In addition to that, he helped many people secretly. Other people do not realize what a large number of people were helped through his efforts. He was the source of constant financial help to many widows, orphans and students from middle-class families who could not afford school fees. There were always a few extra young men in his house, including residents of his own village and less fortunate relatives. He would give them not only shelter but also bear the costs of their education. He treated his junior staff and field workers just like his children, that is, as members of one big family. To Mr. Khuda Buksh, everyone, whether s/he was a worker or executive, was equal, regardless of her/his position in the company. Khuda Buksh was truly a great person, and it was obvious that his mission was to make people's lives blissful.

Not every individual can be noble, as we neither have the right type of mind nor are ready to sacrifice our self-indulgence. Khuda Buksh could become noble because he was a human being, a human in the true sense. Only human beings can claim to be a king. Ignoring sorrow, grief, pain, and ignorance, only human beings can raise themselves to a higher level.

> What a world of light, which is full of delight – what an enlightened path before human beings. Why should mankind forget their glory and walk through the path of darkness and death? They have to become noble. Because s/he must prove that how great s/he is even
> undergoing grief, pain, illusion and greed. How enormous s/he is – so s/he must not show any kind of weaknesses, if not, it will be insulting to her/his sense of self. Nature summons us to be great – vast sky, dawn,

---

[70] *Mahot jiban* (Noble life), Dr. Lutfur Rahman, *Bishaya Shahitya Kendra* (World Literature Center), Dhaka, 1990

the symphony of the flute, the melodious song, and the tears of destitution are calling human beings to be great.[71]

Khuda Buksh heard the calling of nature. That is why he remained and will remain ever alive in the hearts of human beings. He used to tell his children, "If we have capacity, we must help others." Why did he believe this? It was the deep-rooted belief that there is no glory in enjoying the riches of the world alone; there is no divine pleasure in such ventures, as God has created this world for everyone, and so we have to share everything with everyone to attain heavenly pleasures. Khuda Buksh possessed that kind of lofty mind, which enabled him to give shelter to a villager whose feet were rotten and produced an awful odor. Even his servants were annoyed about the odor, yet Mr. Khuda Buksh took care of him, provided medication and cured him. He was deeply concerned about human beings and always wanted to help people. His generosity knew no bounds, whether it was with regard to a member of the family or merely a member of the public. Since he had substantial wealth, he used to help whomever he could. He treated Aziz, his driver, as a member of his family. He never differentiated between men, whether they were a servant, refugee, guest or offspring; they all took from the same dish. Nowadays, this kind of humanity and fraternity is very rare in our selfish society.

* * *

> Be not afraid of greatness. Some are born great, some achieve greatness, and some have greatness thrust upon 'em.
> TWELFTH NIGHT 2v
> – William Shakespeare

The nobility of Khuda Buksh rested in his instincts. Nothing could separate him from these natural feelings. That is why during our war of liberation, when 24-hour curfews were in effect, he did not idle away his time at home. Rather, the moment the curfews were relaxed for a few hours on March 27, 1971, Khuda Buksh went out to his car to meet with acquaintances and friends to ensure their well-being. Before the curfew resumed, he returned home with two men who had just resigned from his newly established insurance company, Federal life Assurance, on personal grounds. Yet unlike us, he went to their home, and when he found out that they had no food to eat, he brought them back to his house and gave them food from his own kitchen and garden for their wives and children. This sort of love and care for humankind is rare and exceptional indeed;

---

[71]ibid

the word "humanity" cannot express everything about him. It is simply beyond our understanding.

This feeling of fellowship, this desire to do good for others was not restricted to people to whom he took a liking, but also to unknown foreigners. That's why when Sheikh Mujibur Rahman (Bangabandhu) asked Mr. Tajuddin to provide shelter for a poor man who came to Bangladesh from Kolkata in search of a relative of his, Khuda Buksh willingly took responsibility rather than Mr. Tajuddin. He treated Mr. Rahman as his respected guest. Khuda Buksh constantly lived his life doing good for others. It never mattered to him whether a person was a friend or someone whom he had just met by chance; he always gave them his consideration, attention and kindness.

He never differentiated a man from another man, and he taught this principle to his children through his actions. His actions taught his offspring that "If you have the ability to do so, then you should help a human being in distress." This quality is reflected in his children. I know Mr. Bazlur Rahim, the fourth son of Khuda Buksh, and, to be honest, I have never seen such an amiable, contented, benevolent and devoted gentleman in my life. Regarding his dedication to others, he is second to none. Here I quote from a letter written to Mr. Bazlur Rahim by Mr. Rahman from Kolkata: "I haven't seen such a noble person [Khuda Buksh] in my life so far – your parents are great indeed, and as a result of their virtue, all of your brothers and sisters have become very noble minded and hospitable. If only everybody would become as noble as you guys are."

It seems that this is the influence of father upon offspring, with the offspring mirroring the true image of the father. Now even a rickshaw puller could escape from Khuda Buksh's attention and generosity. On one occasion, during the summer of 1972, he found a rickshaw puller who had fainted from hunger near his house, and he brought the man in and gave him food and milk. He gave him enough money to pay off his financier as well.

Throughout his life, Khuda Buksh was devoted to uplifting other people's lives. His efforts were spontaneous, like water springing out from a cascade. Whenever he helped a person, either directly or indirectly, he refused to accept anything in return or to even expect anything from anyone else. If anybody wanted to offer something in return, he declined it humbly and smilingly. His devotion toward the profession is a source of inspiration to others. He was the guide who helped field workers and office executives to achieve their goals. Nowadays, it is rare to find a boss like him whose attitude is friendly rather than bossy. He always tried to sow the seed of hope in people's heart, and this was his mission.

> "True hope is swift and flies with
> swallow's wings;
> kings it makes gods, and meaner
> creatures kings."
> *Richard the Third* 5ii,
>
> – William Shakespeare

In this regard, I quote Sharafat Ali Quershi, former District Manager of the Eastern Federal Union Insurance Company; he said Khuda Buksh was an inspiration for everybody. From him, we come to learn that Khuda Buksh used to say that "work, work and work . . . work hard. It will give you many things. It will allow you to earn money and a comfortable life . . . there is no limit as to how much you can earn; sky's the limit for you. You can write your own salary check. If one works hard enough, he can earn as much as he wants."

This type of inspiration helps bring prosperity to people's lives. Life Insurance was his mission and vision. He took this profession as a challenge. He worked hard all his life. He started his profession life by knocking on people's doors. At that time, selling life insurance was a difficult job. He never considered this to be an economic proposition or a mere means to earn money. He believed that by doing his job, he was rendering a social service to his country. He deeply cared for human beings and wanted people to have security in their lives. By dint of his work, he earned fame as the country's "most magnetic and dynamic sales executive," a "wizard of life insurance" and now the "father of insurance." He raised himself to an unparalleled position in his field, and he achieved this unique fame through his competence and integrity.

* * *

> What's in a name? That which we call a rose
> By any other name would smell as sweet.
>
> *Romeo and Juliet 2ii*
>
> – William Shakespeare

Whoever came to close to him could not help but feel the warmth of his compassion and the radiance of his enormous personality. Indeed, it was impossible not to be attracted to him. In this regard, it is worth mentioning his associate Mr. Wolfrom W. Kamowski, who described him as "very much a Bengali, with a small body and a big heart for almost everyone . . . and whose simplicity and sincerity made him look much bigger than his body." Another colleague, Sharafat Ali Quershi, said, "Believe me I was shocked to see that a man holding the post of the General Manager could be so simple and humble . . . At that time, EFU was like a family, and the credit goes to Khuda Buksh. He created such an environment in the company that it felt like family ... Whenever he used to come from Dhaka, almost everybody went to receive him at the airport, and when he used to go back to Dhaka, almost everybody used to go to see him off. Khuda Buksh created this atmosphere, by his actions and act."

By dint of his perseverance, merit and expertise, he achieved for himself a very big name in the field of life insurance. He even attracted the attention of President Ayub Khan. But his courage, determination and sincerity made him a unique person, as he was free from avarice and not thirsty for political power. His name had become so well known in the whole country that he became a candidate for an important government post. When Ayub Khan began looking for a suitable candidate for the highly prestigious position of Federal Minister of Commerce, Khuda Buksh's name was proposed. Khuda Buksh never wanted to be a politician. So this brave heart went to Islamabad, met Ayub Khan and told him humbly yet in a straightforward manner, "Sir, this is no job for me. I am not a politician. And, if you don't mind, sir, this is only a temporary job, something I hated to do all my life."

Whenever he made a promise, he fulfilled it. He was very positive and liberal in granting the claims of policyholders. He always urged that "you must grant the claim – with this you won't lose anything, while the widow or other members of the family will benefit. Don't harass." He exercised this good sense for all.

From Michael Joseph Pereira, we learn about the method of his work. He said, "there are only two types of people, those people who work and those people who get work done. The interesting thing about Khuda Buksh was that he defeated that maxim in that he could do work himself, and he could get work done."

Another colleague of Karachi Mr. Syed Kaiser Abbas said, "when Mr. Khuda Buksh came to Karachi, there were a lot of problems, and there were differences of opinion. There were so many crises ... but as soon as Mr. Khuda Buksh took charge, everybody was happy ... and as soon as Mr. Khuda Buksh resigned, the company started going down."

His devotion to duty and contribution to the field was so impressive that Hubert Arun Rozario admitted, "he was a man of small structure with a towering personality .... He introduced insurance to the masses, advocating savings for families for future rainy days. Through his forty years of hard labor, he was able to fulfill his mission to popularize insurance and generate savings and provided salvation from financial hardship to many families." One could see the love and affection that Mr. Khuda Buksh generated in the faces of even the smallest person. It was not because of his position; it was because of his personality and his very fine human qualities. He genuinely cared for people. His lifestyle was very simple, and he had set principles. He never held a grudge and went out of his way to be compassionate, even if he was the injured party. It never mattered to him whether a person was a friend or critic or whether they were family members, employees, colleagues, clients or someone he had just met off the street. In short, he was a "willing listener, a great motivator, a big team builder, devoted to his profession, had a humble, straight forward nature, and was a man of commitment. He was an extraordinary leader and an unbeatable legend of insurance." He loved and cared for each human being as the loving creation of God and respected all with compassion; his "very nature was to love and care for people."

Sharing my views with Sara Rahim, I also declare that "Khuda Buksh left behind an ethical will in the form of actions rather than words." He was a man who had zealously devoted himself to the service of humanity and earned an undying fame for the glorious deeds that he accomplished. More than anything else, Khuda Buksh's ethical actions show us that if one has the ability to do so, then one should help a person in distress.

The American industrialist Henry Ford once said, "an idealist is such a person who works for the development of humankind." Khuda Buksh was a person who worked and devoted his life to the uplifting of human beings. Following his life, our next generation can learn many things.

> How many goodly creatures are there
> here!
> How beauteous mankind is! O brave
> new world
> That has such people in't!

The Tempest 5i

– William Shakespeare

If our world would fill with such great man like Khuda Buksh.

> O sleep, O gentle sleep,
> Nature's soft nurse, how have I
> frightened thee,
> That thou no more will weigh my
> eyelids down,
> And sleep my senses in forgetfulness?

Henry the Fourth – Part Two 3i

– William Shakespeare

On May 13, 1974 Khuda Buksh fell asleep for the final time, but his ideals, principles, virtues, humane qualities remain ever present in this world. Following these aspects, the human race as well as individual lives could be enlightened. As the American poet Carl Sandburg has said, "I am an idealist. I don't know where I am going. But I am on my path." Khuda Buksh also remained firm in his own path. His sense of responsibility, generosity and integrity made him a complete human being. He is a representative of a true human being in this egocentric world.

My Untold Stories

Zobeda Khatun[72]

I WAS BORN AT Kathipara, a remote village in the district of Khulna. The exact date of my birth is not known. In the semiliterate village society of those days, people simply tended not to record their children's dates of birth. Yet the year of my birth did not get lost forever. I've heard from my father that Bangladesh saw a violent storm in 1926. I was only three at that time. Thus I can say that I was born in 1923.

As was the trend of the village, my education began with the learning of Arabic letters. When I got older, I got myself admitted into a school not far from my house. I was born in a conservative family; my being a girl child did not allow me to study much. The school was only a three-minute walk from my house. In those days, people did not like their daughters to obtain higher education. My father, though, obviously wanted me to study further, but to say or do something against popular mentality was damn hard. The true intent of my father was unknown to me. When I was around 17, my father sent me to my uncle Kazi Abdur Razzak's Kolkata house; I was there for 18 months. My uncle and auntie lived at Bowbazar Street in Kolkata with their six children – Manu, Ranu, Jui, Tulu, Mintu, and Rafique. I, became seamlessly integrated with their family. My elder brother also stayed there and pursued his studies.

My three younger sisters studied in schools. In the afternoon they would read with a private tutor named Ponku Sikdar. I, too, was included in this group of young learners over the course of time.

Ponku Sikdar hailed from Damodya village of Faridpur. My mother-in-law's cousin was his maternal uncle. When Ponku Sikdar visited his village home or when

---

[72]Wife of Khuda Buksh.

he remained absent, Khuda Buksh came to teach us. This, took place with my uncle's permission. Our teacher taught us Bengali and arithmetic. When we read with the teacher, we never wore burkha (veil). On the teacher's arrival, we would sit at the reading table, then went into the living room after finishing our study. We never dared to look at his face. How greatly has society changed today!

After living in Kolkata for about a year, my uncle was transferred by the Government to Chittagong. His family, however, remained in Kolkata. My elder brother, Nur Muhammad, was a familiar face in my uncle's house in Kolkata. Khuda Buksh and Nur had deep, friendly relations. They often strolled around whenever they had any time to do so. They visited cinema halls. Bengali cinema was a special favorite of theirs. During this time my mother had taken ill, and so my father came to Kolkata and took me back to Kathipara.

During Ponku Sikdar's absence, Khuda Buksh came one day to teach us after a long time. As Khuda Buksh didn't see me, he asked Nur Mohammad about my absence. This query did not escape the attention of my brother. I didn't even imagine that he had remembered me.

At that time, it was customary for girls to be married off at a tender age. Nur Muhammad knew Khuda Buksh and his family well through his friendly relations with him. He wrote a letter to my father in Khulna, describing everything about Khuda Buksh. On receipt of the letter, my father consulted my mother and my elder sister Zohura (I was the second daughter). Considering the pros and cons of the matter, they thought Khuda Buksh could be a prospective bridegroom, but when they discovered that Khuda Buksh worked in an insurance company, they were somewhat discouraged. Nevertheless, my father and my elder sister decided to see Khuda Buksh.

Khuda Buksh was surprised to hear everything from Nur Muhammad, but still he agreed to go to Kathipara, Khulna. At Kathipara, Khuda Buksh had long and elaborate talks with my father, Quazi Nawabuddin, my mother, Kulsum-un-nessa and elder sister Zohura, and they were highly pleased with Khuda Buksh. This young chap's magic with words helped dispel the wrong notion and controversies about his job at an insurance company. But the incident did not come to an end there. Since my mother was ailing, she opined that the "*Aqd*"[73] should be performed immediately. But this sudden decision put Khuda Buksh in a dilemma. He was conflicted about whether it would be appropriate to get married without informing his father. Besides, there was almost no time to write a letter to his father and have his consent. Under the circumstances, he thought about everything seriously, and at last he decided to get married. We had our Aqd on the 29th of December, 1939. Perhaps his instantaneous compliance with the Aqd had to do with the fact that my mother and elder sister Zohura were both physically unwell; their eagerness was the

---

[73]The ceremony of a marriage

main reason why the marriage took place without delay. My mother left this world within two weeks of this marriage.

I knew later that his marriage was finalized with his maternal cousin but he let them know that he was not going to marry her (cousin) planned by his parents.

After the Aqd, Khuda Buksh returned to Kolkata. He sent my father-in-law Shonabuddin Ahmed a letter in which he expounded everything in detail about the wedding.

Though not highly educated, my father-in-law was actually a progressive-minded person. He was not at all disconcerted at the news, and he had consultation with his near and dear ones about the matter. Later, he sent a group of four delegates from Damodya to Kathipara to see me and to know other related things. The group included Moqbul Munshi, Iqtajul Hazi, Sirajuddin Ahmed, and my husband's younger brother Fazlur Rahman. None of them are alive today.

On arrival at Kathipara, they virtually received a royal reception. My father Kazi Nawabuddin was a well-to-do land owner. He had sufficient landed properties. Despite ailments, my elder sister Zohura took great care of the distinguished guests and entertained them excellently. The guests stayed at Kathipara for three days. They saw me before their departure, and after returning to Damodya they gave the happy news to Shonabuddin. My sister Zohura remained alive as if to perform her last duty. Within a year of my marriage, she, too, left us and went to my mother.

After marriage, I was at my uncle Kazi Abdur Razzak's Narinda residence near Joy Kali Mondir for about a year. My uncle had then come to Dhaka permanently. On the other hand, Khuda Buksh was then living at his 84 Jhawtola Road residence in Kolkata.

Writing letters was then our only means of communication. My mother and elder sister had already left the world. There was no one to put me at my husband's hands. At least, at the end of 1940, my father-in-law took me from Narinda to his village home at Damodya. Everyone at my father-in-law's house had their bath in the pond. But I never bathed in the pond. At my father's house we used to bring water to the bathroom for bathing.

When I went to my father-in-law's house, my husbad had a bathroom made for me. I remained at my father-in-law's house for a week. Then my husband came to Damodya and took me to Kolkata. On the day of our wedding ceremony, he had given me a lot of ornaments. Those included bracelets, earrings, and a long necklace weighing 3 *bhori*.[74] The price of my wedding sari was 25 taka. My father-in-law had nothing to give me.

When my husband was at Oriental Insurance Company, he sent 25 taka from his salary to my father-in-law. The rest would be spent for the maintaining of our

---

[74] Unit of measure for gold equal to 189 grains;

family. A *mound*[75] of rice could then be bought at Tk. 8, mutton was 1.5 taka per *seer*,[76] one *bhori* gold cost Tk. 15, a bedcover for a double bed cost 12 annas.

Our 84 Jhawtola Road house was a two-storied building. The ground floor of the building was where I started my new life. But the house was very small, and after three months we shifted to another house at 66/D Park Street. It, too, was a two-storied house, but here there was open space around us. There was a cemetery to the west. Crossing a narrow lane from the main road led to the entrance of our house. We could go upstairs where there was a big verandah with railings. My three elder sons were born at this house. My fourth son, Milu, was born at our village house, Damodya. My first four children spent their childhood at that two-storied Park Street house.

I may recall a small incident that happened just one year after the beginning of my family life here. The incident is as follows:

One of my husband's friend often visited him at his residence. My husband also visited his friend's house frequently and thus he grew very intimate with the family. But for some reason the relation between the two got somewhat strained. I heard their altercations but did not understand what caused them. The friend stopped coming to our Park Street residence after that.

A few days after this there came the news that his friend's sister was going to be married. Though he did not get a formal invitation from his friend, he decided to attend the marriage ceremony, and he decided to go alone. We had some financial crises at that time, so he took with him a gift that we had received for our wedding. The friend was taken by surprise to see him at the ceremony. Khuda Buksh asked him, "Why haven't you invited me on such a happy occasion?" The friend was a bit embarrassed and he said, "I forgot."

Khuda Buksh did not pay heed to it and said, "I don't think you forgot. You have willingly avoided me because of the altercation. But see, I have forgotten all that, and this is why I have come to bless your sister and her husband on this day of happiness." The friend became very ashamed and came to realize what a forgiving mind Khuda Buksh had.

I can remember very well the days of famine in 1943. My eldest son Khoka was born in 1941. He was only two at the time of the famine. My son Baby was then in womb. In such a moment there was a food crisis in Kolkata. It was during the time of the Second World War. The people were in constant fear of a Japanese bomb attack. All traders started black marketing foodstuffs with the idea of making money. Many essential foods disappeared from the market within a matter of days. Ordinary people were having great difficulty.

To increase the weight of rice, traders started mixing small stones with rice. We had to suffer much at that time. It was really tough and a matter of patience to sort

---

[75] A measure of unit, equivalent to 82 pounds.

[76] One seer is equivalent to 2.05 pounds

out the rice from the tiny stones. We used to soak the rice on coconut shells for this sorting. We found it difficult to swallow such stony rice. My father sent bags full of good quality rice from Khulna.

After cooking the rice I would not throw out the gruel. I put the gruel in an earthen container and kept it somewhere near the door. A group of beggars came by turns and took their share of the gruel.

Time passed in this way. After a week I consulted Khoka's father and came to the village home at Damodya along with my father-in-law. I stayed there for a long period of time. As the situation started to improve, I returned to the Kolkata Park Street house.

However, it cannot be said that the situation of the village was satisfactory. The ill effects of the Second World War infected the whole world. Moreover, owing to the evil deeds of the profit-monger traders, prices of essential commodities, particularly rice, went up exorbitantly. The death toll at that time in the greater Faridpur area, including Sariatpur, because of the famine and epidemic, rose to almost 150,000.

During his days at Oriental, my husband worked very hard. He often sold insurance policies to tram passengers. I still remember, every two or three months, he went out for four, five, or six days on official tour. He visited Kolkata's surrounding districts like Mednipore, Kharagpur, Durgapur, and other places. He disliked eating out, so he took a box containing cooking utensils. A cook also followed him wherever he went. That very box is still lying at my house.

A number of students lived at our Kolkata residence to carry on their studies. Among them Hafzullah, M.A. Rahim, Moti, Bahadur and his sister, and Sirajuddin from Shariatpur also came occasionally and stayed at our place. During the month of Ramadan, Sirajuddin was not in the habit of fasting, but at the time of *iftari*[77], he would make ablutions and wear a cap as if he had fasted. Khuda Buksh knew everything very well. Whenever he saw Sirajuddin at the iftari table he asked him, "Did you fast, Sirajuddin?"

After iftari he would go to Kolkata's Tara Masjid to say *tarabi*[78] *prayer*. *Firni* (a sort of a pudding of ground rice and mix) would be sold there in a *khora* (earthen container). After saying prayers he returned home with the firni. He would not eat rice at night. He kept his fasting with that firni at the time of *sehri* (a food taken a little before dawn during the fastong month of Ramadan). There was a time when he said prayers five times a day.

He was gourmet, but not a glutton. On Sundays he went to Kolkata New Market and brought beef, particularly "*kuj*" meat. He said, "Prepare a '*bhuna*' item and cook hodge podge." Occasionally, friends came in the afternoon and took light snacks.

After the birth of India and Pakistan, communal riots took place. At one point, while riots raged through Kolkata, my husband fell ill and needed to have an

---

[77] The snacks and drink with which fasting of a day terminates.

[78] A special prayer prescribed for the month of Ramadan which is said after the night prayer.

appendicitis operation. Because of the situation on the streets, no one could get to the hospital to see him for two days. When the violence calmed for a period, D.K. Dastur, general manager of Oriental Insurance Company went to see him in the hospital.

After his release from the hospital, Oriental provided two month paid leave for recuperation. I, my husband, my three children and M.A.Rahim went to Modhupur for a change in weather. After a week my husband left Modhupur for his business. He rarely took any rest during this time. His mind was always in insurance.

After a few years, by 1950, we came to Dhaka, but he stayed in Kolkata for a few years more. At the beginning of his service life at Oriental, he did not put on pants and a shirt. After my marriage, I saw that he wore *pump-shoes* (kind of shoe), *dhuti* (loin-cloth) and *Punjabi* (kind of loose shirt). After the birth of our second child, he began to wear pants and a shirt. It was then that he brought his first car, an Austin.

We came to Dhaka but he did not quit his Kolkata job. He remained there alone, but this did not cause any inconvenience in his eating. Wahab Ali, a cook from Damodya, did all of his cooking. He got our children admitted into schools in Dhaka. I purchased from a Hindu gentleman a one-storied house on 10 *kathas* (7,200 sq feet) of land for Tk. 7,000. It was at Gandaria. I started living there with my five sons. He would come to Dhaka almost every month. When the children's schools were closed, I also visited Kolkata off and on.

Our first daughter, Kumu, was born at 12 Shashibhushan Road, Gandaria. On the occasion of our daughter's birth, he hosted a lunch for all the employees of his Kolkata office. Most of the employees at Oriental were Hindus. They said, "If someone among us has a male child, he invites friends to celebrate it. But you have had a female child!"

After putting 17 years in at Oriental Insurance Company in Kolkata, Haidar Sahib of Murshidabad took Khuda Buksh to Dhaka as Life Manager of Eastern Federal in East Pakistan. My daughter was then 9 months and 10 days old. He fondled his daughter more dearly than his sons. After her birth, he started to call me, *Kumur Ma* (mother of Kumu)." He loved his daughter very much, but she died of diarrhea on 20 June, 1950, when she was only one and a half years old. Treatment of diarrhea was then not as easy and simple as it is today. She was buried at Azimpur graveyard. After her death, he broke down, so much so that he could not even go to the graveyard. I did not know that one could be so sorrowful at the death of one's child. After our daughter's death, he no longer called me Kumur Ma. Another daughter, however, came to our bosom later.

After coming to Dhaka in 1952 permanently, he dedicated much more time to Eastern Federal. He did not return home immediately after office time; rather, he spent a considerable amount of time in the office. He could very well invigorate social gatherings, just with a view to collecting insurance customers. I often found cash memos of Myrada Restaurant in his trouser pocket. The restaurant was at the ground floor of Mukul cinema hall. Myranda was renowed restaurant of old Dhaka at that time. Under cover of gathering and light refreshment he used to encourage people to buy insurance policies. This was his nature and he followed this all through his life. Whenever he took a new residence, he would try his utmost to get familiar with the people around him.

His 17 years' experience at Oriental and his zeal to build up the new company began to bear fruit. The company's business spread. By 1956, we left Gandaria and shifted to New Eskaton Garden Road. By that time, Eastern Federal had discarded the small office of Victoria Park and had taken a new, bigger office in the Gulistan area.

He thought deeply about life insurance and a man's future, but he seemed listless about the future of his own family. Actually, he did not have time to do so; but I had a dream regarding the coming days of my children: to buy a plot of land in the city of Dhaka. One day I called Mintu, my brother, and said, "You buy land for people. Please buy us a plot of land." He replied, "What will you do with a plot?!" I said, "I need it for our children." He said, smilingly, "You give them education, build them up as men. A time will surely come when they will be able to buy land for themselves." In spite of that comment, I kept asking him to buy us a piece of land. At last, my brother went to my husband's office and said to him, "*Dulabhai,* (brother-in-law) give me Tk. 50." He said, "What will you do with the money?" My brother said, "First, you give me the money, and then I will tell you."

My brother took the money and left. He applied for a piece of land in Dhanmondi and arranged all papers. After some time, my brother visited my husband's office said to him, "I have bought a plot for you at Dhanmondi Road no. 21."

One day we went together to see that land. There were no houses around. Open land and rice fields were everywhere. One bigha of land there cost Tk. 4,500. But we could not pay the amount at the time. We had to pay it in two to three installments. Seeing the open fields all around, I commented, "I don't think people will ever build houses there!" My brother replied, "People will surely build houses here one day." My father-in-law came to Dhaka. He saw the plot. He liked it very much.

A house was built on the land, but he never lived there. This house was rented to a British who worked for the British High Commission for 14 years. We, too, lived in a rented house.

Our children hardly found him at home. He always remained busy at his office. Moreover, he had to visit various places on official duty. Besides visiting different districts of East Pakistan, he had to travel extensively through Karachi, Rawalpindi, Lahore, Peshawar and other places of West Pakistan.

I also visited many places with him. I visited London with him. During school vacations, I took the children to Karachi and lived there. I noticed that he always bore traveling expenditures himself wherever he went; he never spent office money.

He usually took his lunch at home. Occasionally, he was a bit late returning home. I got him on the phone and he said, "You take your lunch. My hands are now full. I will be delayed." Occasionally, when I called him on the phone he said, "Make arrangements for lunch. I am coming with a host of guests." During his stay at Eastern Federal, Mr. Bhimjee and other officers would come. Since Bhimjee was a Pakistani, I had to arrange various items for him. There was hardly a day when I did not have to prepare 50 cups of tea.

The company's business spread, and at the same time, its name and fame also spread. Thus up to 1969, he devotedly worked for Eastern Federal, virtually betting his life. He was promoted several times for his extraordinary performance and got the post of general manager. He never expected any reward for what he had done for Eastern Federal. He did not want anything from the company, even for himself. It was beyond his imagination that ultimately he would have to quit the company.

A time came when his relationship with Mr. Bhimjee became strained, and one day, all of a sudden, he stopped going to the office. After staying at home for a month, he one day traveled to Karachi. On his arrival in Karachi, he would usually call me on the phone, but his time he did not call me.

I got restless and called one of his acquaintances. His wife let me know that Khuda Buksh was okay, and told me not to be worried. I knew later that he had gone to Karachi to discuss with Bhimjee his decision to quit Eastern Federal. On his return to Dhaka, I said to him, "How can you bear the educational expenses of your children if you quit your job?" He said, "It is I who will think about that."

After he left his job, the money from his provident fund was delayed. Then it was given to him installment by installment. I am not sure whether he was given the full amount. He would not tell me anything that would jar my mind. This was at a time when my children were off studying in different places.

He founded a company named Federal Life with the provident fund money that he had. I heard that after the establishment of the company he did not draw any salary from it. He also did not tell me anything about this. He never told me anything that would trouble my mind. Occasionally, he would be delayed coming back from the office. When I called him, he said, "You have your meal. My hands are full right now. My return will be delayed."

Insurance workers only talk to other people in their field. They totally forget their families. He did not take much care of our family. He just handed me an amount of money at the beginning of the month. I would say, "How can I manage the family with such a small amount of money?" He replied, "Manage for the time being and I'll give you more later."

I would always make a list of my purchases and show it to him. Once the money was gone, he would give me more. He paid little heed to family matters. When he gave me the money, he said, "It's up to you to look after the family affairs."

The country became independent in 1971. Sheikh Sahib nationalized big mills, factories, and insurance companies. My husband was very upset then. He was also physically unwell.

He had good relations with Sheikh Mujib. Once Sheikh Sahib had to go to jail in the Pakistan period for political reasons. After his release, one day he said to me, "Let us go to see Sheikh Mujib. I've heard that he is ill." I said to him, "I am not going. It's better if you go." However, both of us ended up going to see him. After we arrived, Sheikh Mujib's wife said, "Brother, he had a bad headache, so he is lying down." He said to me, "Let us go inside." I, followed him hesitatingly.

After independence, Sheikh Mujib said to him, "You have so many boys and girls. What can I do for you?" He said, "You won't have to do anything for me. That is my concern."

Later, Jiban Bima Corporation came into being. He was made the first managing director, but he couldn't work properly because of the opposition of some people there. They treated him very rudely. It was because of them that he had to leave Jiban Bima in the end. It was a sorrowful event for him to leave the institution he had built by himself.

At the end of 1972, I visited London to send my grandson to live with my son, Baby (Ataur Rahim). I returned to Dhaka after staying in London for a month. He was then at Jiban Bima. He was admitted to P.G. Hospital for his illness. The people at his office, with a view to having their various demands fulfilled, 'gheraoed' (act of surrounding/besieging) him even in the hospital. Again, in 1974, when he was virtually on his death bed at the Dhaka Medical College Hospital, those very people went there and begged his pardon.

In April 1974, he had again taken ill. He was at home. Even in this ailing state of health, he said on the 12th of April, "I shall go out. Someone has died. I'll go to his burial." I said to him, "You are not in sound health. Can't you do without going?" He said, "No, I must go."

He went to bury him in that state of health. After the burial, he came back and said, "I need to go out again." I begged him not to go out him from going out, but he did not pay any heed to my entreaty. He was seriously ailing then. He got extremely emaciated. He was panting. I took off his trousers and shirt. I gave him everything and went to the bathroom for ablution. Coming back, I found him lying down with his clothes on. He was then feeling extremely unwell. After a while, he lost consciousness. Our son Dalu (Dr. Zillur Rahim) was then reading. I told my daughter to call Dalu. Dalu came and, after assessing the situation, called in a doctor. The doctor said, "The patient is to be taken to the hospital. Nothing can be done here." It was evening. He remained unconscious the whole night. He regained consciousness at the time of 'Asr' prayer the next day. He was taken to the hospital on the 12th of April.

I stayed with him at the hospital. On the day he died, he got up from bed at six o'clock in the evening. The doctor was not in the hospital then. Finding no doctor nearby, we went to a hospital to look for a niece of ours who was studying medicine. The doctor came and took his blood. As the blood congealed, he took blood a second time for reexamination. But Khuda Buksh had died in the midst of all this. It was May 13, 1974.

On the day before his eternal departure, he told me, "I am not going to live for much longer. After my death, leave the rented house and settle in our own house". Following his advice, I moved over to our own house forty days later with the children. Strangely enough, after the land in Dhanmondi was bought, I had expressed doubt about whether a house would ever be built there. But in reality, the house did get built. My father-in-law was also very happy about this. Sometimes I feel that the people who had wanted this house the most are no longer here. All that remains is their love and their memory. That is why I sometimes become sad and wistful. But I am very grateful to Allah that my children are leading their lives in accordance with their father's ideals. Today, that house does not exist. But a foundation in his memory has been established on this very land. It is a tribute by our children to their father, who had always worked for the welfare of others. I will always cherish this gesture as the most beautiful gift I ever received from my children.

Khuda Buksh: The Pioneer of Life Insurance in Bangladesh

Shafique Khan[79]

BENGAL WAS CAUGHT in a looming, vile air of xenophobic discomfort, which plagued the race during the fateful 1960's. Pakistan, at that point in time, was governed by an autocratic despot named Gen. Ayub Khan who was in cahoots with the various militant hardliners who were bent on bringing travesty to Bengal. Bengal was the cynosure of their collective chagrin and hatred because apart from a few quislings and turncoat brokers the common Bengali rejected their advances and did not acknowledge him as their primary patriarch. The erstwhile administrators of Bengal hatched a potent conspiracy against the socially mobile class of Bengali government officials, to defame them, and in the process, attack the integrity of Bengali culture and ethos. This was echoed in the vile designs of Ayub Khan, who, after countless failed attempts at defaming and demonizing Bengal, issued an ultimatum – "Don't force our arsenal to speak". Needless to say, this rather ludicrous declaration won him no followers, and ironically, this despot was overthrown by none other than General Yahya Khan, an autocrat equally condemned by history.

During these turbulent 60's, an article was published in the *Pakistan Observer*, authored by Mr. Khuda Buksh. I was a young reader then, and was completely alien to the influence and recognition that Mr. Khuda Buksh had on the contemporary Bengali literati. However, it must be accepted that at the time I had come across this article, my young mind was more impressed with the words industry, philosophy, and the imaginative possibilities that they entailed rather than any deeper understanding of

---

[79]Executive Director, Ganoshasthaya (Peoples Health Center), Savar, Dhaka, Bangladesh.

the concepts. Even though I had crossed the rose-tinted romantic teenage years, I was still in my early adulthood and concepts of theory, philosophy, and the development of industrialization were not only beyond my level of understanding, they also scared me with their complications, and I dreaded such discussions. So I always thought that it was most prudent to avoid all debates that concerned themselves with profound and complicated reflections on the morals and ethics of industry, philosophies, and the pros and cons of a certain theory. However, whenever I came across a piece of writing that seemed to have sprouted from political ideas or had close associations with politics, my young mind was instantly drawn to it. When I read this paper by Mr. Khuda Buksh I liked it immensely because it seemed to be more than a mere bland discussion on theory. I read and re-read the work a number of times, spell bound, and was most keen on meeting the author. I have no qualms in accepting that one of the major reasons I was drawn to the article was because of its incomparable style that enamored and enthralled my youthful mind. His powerful message and philosophy never fail to rejuvenate my worldview, even to this very day.

It must have been destiny that three years later I actually got an opportunity to meet the author, Mr. Khuda Buksh. The interview was pre-planned but the session held an astonishing charm for me. Mr. Khuda Buksh had been invited by a few of people of renowned social standing for an informal chat. The environment was homely. I was amongst the people anticipating his arrival with more eagerness than the others. He arrived right on time in a grand car that looked very expensive.

At first glance, he seemed like a quiet and reserved kind of a person. From the few words that he spoke while greeting the people present and his dress and demeanor, he seemed to be the epitome of what we call a refined gentleman. There was nothing in the excess either in his words or in how he carried himself that could be vaguely interpreted as vulgar. His clothes looked imported, his eyes reflected an intelligent bearing, and overall he seemed confident and genial, eager to meet anyone who would talk to him. He was not haughty or arrogant.

He was tired from the long journey, so he rested a bit. After our chief guest was refreshed we headed to the dinner that was arranged for us. That done, we all sat down in the living room for the much awaited chat session. Surrounded by the choicest people, who had organized the discussion, our chief guest started interacting with the people present, opened the debate, and slowly began talking. The topics that were being discussed, though not too complicated, were not shallow either and carried much weight. The contemporary socio-political situation was reflected upon, as was the present condition of the economy. It was also decided that bringing democracy to the land was a top priority and that the first step to forming a republic was self-reliance and for that, it was necessary that Bengalis lose their dependence on Western rulers and develop means for solving their own problems. There were few dissenting, and some complicated comments and questions as well. Mr. Khuda Buksh explained everything in few words only, never raising his voice or losing patience but at the same time with a fervor that struck me. He explained in easy language all the complicated propositions, however with a certain command. He even found his way out of all the hostile situations quite like a general with years of experience in combat. All that he spoke was rooted in reality; his propositions were never impractical or unrealistic. All were enamored by his words and watched him, awe struck, as he calmly mouthed powerful words impregnated with the depth of his feelings. I was particularly impressed with the amount of knowledge that he had. Towards the end of the discussion he sped hastily to round up the talks. Suddenly he stood up and with an expression that betrayed nothing but humility he slowly said, "I cannot claim to be anyone of extreme importance but sometimes it happens that I have some important work to do, like the engagement I have at present. So my friends, I beg your leave today."

This was the first and the last time that I ever met him. He had gone over from one subject to another in the course of the discussion and imparted invaluable advice, all with an air of lightness that stopped his words from seeming didactic. He had none the less provided us with precious sentences that summed up the way one should interpret the current socio-political and economic situation. From all that we saw and heard, I realized that this was an individual dedicated to the cause of not only his country but that of humanity as a whole. To me, he had seemed like a skilled musician who through his sheer expertise had sung the most delightful music. To this day I remember and cherish that interview with Mr. Khuda Buksh.

And I could not discard that article, that remarkable piece of work in the pile of old newspapers; instead I saved the piece carefully. I felt such a closeness to him, and his thoughts, writings, humanity, and compassion ever remained in my heart and forever inspired me.

Mr. Khuda Buksh was born on 1st February 1912 in a middle class family of East Bengal. His father, Moulvi Shonabuddin Howlader, and mother, Arzuta Khatun, had five sons and one daughter. Among them Mr. Khuda Buksh was the eldest.

Shonabuddin was an open hearted, academically enthusiastic person. In the village courts and conventions he used to be the center of attraction. During the British regime, he worked in a jute company in Chandpur. In later years, he became the owner of a small jute mill through his high intelligence, hard labor, and honesty. He could easily form bonds with others through his excellent manners. However it was the extremely competent and intelligent wife of Shonabuddin who contributed actively in various aspects of life, from the education of the family's children to the establishment of the Shonabuddin family as a reputable and economically solvent family in the society. Almost a hundred years ago, this lady succeeded in creating a wonderful and charming ambience in her family. Throughout their life, and even in their old age, the children of the family reminisced about the golden and compassionate nature of their mother.

Even in his old age, the elder son, Mr. Khuda Buksh, commented while remembering her mother:

> From my childhood, I was very friendly. I always used to have a gang of friends with me. I used to bring them home without any previous intimation. And then I used to ask my mother to give food to all my friends. She used to indulge my demands with a smiling face. Never ever I have seen her being embarrassed or disappointed. On the other hand she was happy.

She used to treat all my friends as her own children and fed them.

Though in his childhood Mr. Khuda Buksh spent a lot of time with his friends and was involved in various sports, he was extremely sincere and respectful when it came to obeying religious instructions. From his teens he never missed his *Namaz* (prayer) and felt a deep affinity for the teachings of the Quran.

Throughout his entire life Mr. Khuda Buksh showed extreme respect towards elders and teachers of all spheres, and this was an exemplary trait of his character. Beginning in childhood, he had a uniqueness to his thought process that surprised everybody. Once, the very young Mr. Khuda Buksh was going to Chandpur (Bangladesh) with his father. He could not keep pace with his father and was running behind him. In the process, he did not realize that he had lost one of his shoes. He was unable to answer his father's query about the shoe on one of his feet and the absence of it on the other. His father immediately anticipated what had happened. However, when his father did not say anything, young Mr. Khuda Buksh immediately took off the remaining shoe from his other foot and threw it out of the train window. This he did assuming that the person who would pick up the first shoe would not be able to use it in any way but he might find the second shoe and hence use the pair. From his childhood, Mr. Khuda Buksh had such individuality in his character that made him different from children his age.

Mr. Khuda Buksh received his primary education in the village school. From the very beginning he was recognized as a meritorious student. He took it upon himself to help his schoolmates who were poor and in distress. It is to be mentioned that in those days students who attended schools were mostly from poor families. They earned their living and educational expenses by taking refuge in well-off families and teaching the children of those families, or by performing the Imamhood during the *Azan* (muezzin's call to congregational prayers) or Namaz sessions. However, it was impossible for them to buy books and other accessories necessary for school. Young Mr. Khuda Buksh used to help his schoolmates who, in spite of all their problems, showed interest in education, by them lending his own books. For this reason his father was compelled to buy more than one set of text books but never showed irritation towards his son's display of compassion towards his friends.

This was the pre-independence era, when India was still undivided. The opportunities for higher education in East Bengal were not very bright. Since the scope of higher education was not possible in erstwhile East-Bengal, children from solvent families were compelled to travel to Kolkata. Young Mr. Khuda Buksh was also sent to Kolkata for higher education.

Mr. Khuda Buksh was enrolled in Islamia College, one of the most renowned colleges in Kolkata. Within a short time after his arrival he started acquainting and introducing himself with other students. However, the young man was most disturbed by the living conditions and general lifestyle of his fellows and mates who, like he, had come from East Bengal to study. He was pained by the poverty and was very much perturbed with the poor state of the Muslim community. As a result, instead of yielding himself to the beckoning and temptation of the luxurious life of the dream-city of the Bengalis, Kolkata, Mr. Khuda Buksh was desperate to analyze the reason behind the poor plight of the Muslim community as a whole in East-Bengal. To understand Mr. Khuda Buksh's concern about the Bengali Muslim community in erstwhile East-Bengal, we have to retrace our steps in history a bit.

According to the recorded history, the British East India Company and a few other conspirators from the ruling regime overthrew the Nawab of Bengal, Bihar and Orissa, Nawab Siraj-ud-Daulah, in the prefabricated "Battle of Plassey" on the 23rd of June, 1757. Within a short period of time the British businessmen expelled the "puppet" Nawab Mirzafar Ali Khan and assumed power of Bengal indirectly. However, they were still feeling insecure. Despite the "unfair victory", the apprehensive British started expelling all the Muslims indiscriminately from the various government administrative posts and jobs established during the Nawab Regime. The first blow was the disbanding of the Nawab's army which created a job vacuum amongst 80,000 Muslims. Later on, the decision to disband the entire army of the Nawab regime, excepting a few bodyguards for the existent Nawab, resulted in joblessness amongst thousands more Muslims. Finally, when Lord Cornwallis started making amendments to the law-and-order division and declared English as the national language, hundreds of educated Persian Muslims became jobless. So intense was the Muslim eradication policy of the British that they even compelled the Muslim weavers to quit their profession in order to market the England-made clothes in Bengal.

Finally, there came a stage when the top officials of the East India Company were expelling Muslims from the various posts on the one hand and continued filling the vacancies by appointing Hindus on the other, especially in high ranking posts, in exchange for bribes.

Because of this diplomatic policy of English businessmen, the minority Hindu community was being established in the various important administrative posts, whereas the Muslims, despite comprising the majority in Bengal, slowly succumbed to unemployment. As a result of this one sided policy of the British, the symptoms of a crack became evident in the age-old peaceful coexistence and brotherhood of the Hindus and Muslims. We have witnessed the horrible and inhuman consequences of this policy in the ensuing communal riots. In this way, as all the means of income were cut off, the huge unemployed Muslim community left their lands and shifted to the south-east of the erstwhile East-Bengal. They cleaned up the land there and engaged themselves in farming. Even during those bad times, the English did not spare the Muslims from further harassment. This time, the target was the respected and highly placed Persian literate Muslims of the ruling regime. In almost no time, they were reduced to beggars living on the streets. Because of the serial conspiracy of the unscrupulous officials of the East India Company towards the Muslims, the glorious and grand history of the Muslim community was transformed into a history of deprivation and oppression in just four decades.

Observing the history of the Bengali Muslims very minutely, Mr. Khuda Buksh was convinced that the reason behind the gradual and fatal decay of today's Muslims was deep-rooted. The other important factors were the incompetence of the previous Muslim rulers, ignorance towards proper mass-literacy, un-enterprising attitude, inactivity in regaining independence, and wasting valuable time like their ancestors, among other factors, also contributed in the degradation of the Muslim community.

The above stated particulars are evidence for the fact that the English businessmen considered the one and only crime of the Muslims to be that the Muslim rulers of Bengal, Bihar, and Orissa dared to resist the insolence and the indecent monopoly of the British in anything and everything. For this reason alone the British rulers inflicted severe torture and harassment on the Bengali Muslims for over 200 years.

Additionally, the British rulers literally destroyed the social life of the Muslims by rendering them financially handicapped and socially humiliated. The other deep rooted conspired trap was to engage the Hindus in higher administrative posts. The imperialist British succeeded in making a rift in the age-old brotherhood between two main communities, the Hindus and the Muslims, in this region. Later, the British rulers induced a sense of contempt between various religious communities and destroyed the integrity and peaceful coexistence, especially between the Hindus and the Muslims. Needless to say, such actions were entirely against humanism. But the irony was that the British people proclaimed themselves to be "civilized" even though they were engaged in such inhuman activities as apartheid.

In this respect, it is to be observed that British patronization and privileges granted to the Hindus made them remarkably successful in economic and educational spheres amongst all other communities. As a result, the Hindus got inspired by the consciousness of nationalism and thus began the era of the freedom movement. But even at the advent of the movement for independence, the Muslims did not join hands with the Hindus. Instead, complacent with the titles received from the British, they wasted time in daydreams. However, in the early 1920s the major Hindu leaders unified under the National Congress, whose main agenda was the complete independence of India. Additionally, secret armed revolutionary groups were terrorizing the British with random guerilla killings. It was sad, but the fact was that the Muslims still failed to participate in the nationwide movement for independence against the British. The unscrupulous English businessmen at first conspired against the Muslims in India and assumed the power to overthrow the legal Muslim rulers. The British tortured ruthlessly, looted, and converted India almost into a land of the dead. They reduced the great Muslim community from rulers to beggars on the streets by mauling the world famous Muslim tradition and culture. Mr. Khuda Buksh was so disconcerted by the utter distress of the Muslim community that he was desperate to find the way out of this sorry state of affairs. How is it possible to eliminate this state of affairs? In order to find an answer to this problem, he dedicated his whole professional life for the betterment of people.

Mr. Khuda Buksh started his career in uncertain times, the '30s of the past century, in an insurance company. In spite of all the criticism and controversy, he became famous and admired because of his vital contributions to the insurance industry. He became more and more confident in the solution to the unemployment of the young Bengali Muslim community of India.

The extremely enterprising Mr. Khuda Buksh had understood clearly that it was possible to succeed in the insurance industry by giving honest advice and modest behavior even if one did not have high education or a substantial capital. He realized that there were enough possibilities for the hapless Bengali Muslims to earn adequate money respectfully and re-establish themselves if a proper client base could be ensured. Though the Muslims were lagging behind the British and the Bengali communities in politics, they had certain distinctive features in their characters owing to their upbringing in Persian culture. This ability to form bonds with people easily was a tested, indispensable, and effective quality for performance in the insurance industry.

Mr. Khuda Buksh had a firm belief that the new light of the insurance industry would bring about the solvency and economic emancipation of the Muslim community of Bengal. To realize this dream, Mr. Khuda Buksh dedicated his whole life to the insurance industry. He did not pay any heed to the criticisms and sarcasms that he had to face in this process.

Even in the midlife of his career, in spite of being extremely busy, he mingled with people of the general middle and lower classes to spread awareness of saving and changing the course of their lives through hard work. On the other hand, he was an expert when it came to convincing economically solvent people who were disinterested in insurance to opt for one. He in fact accumulated a vast army of trainees and taught them the art of insurance salesmanship. After three decades in the independent Bangladesh, it was under the leadership of these disciples of Mr. Khuda Buksh that his dream was finally realized. He also fiercely protected the interests of the insured people. So in the last century, every person associated with the insurance industry at every level praised unconditionally Mr. Khuda Buksh's expertise in this industry, his honesty and his immense contribution towards this industry. No wonder that everybody was so respectful towards this silent dreamer for his tremendous contribution towards the development of the nation, namely Bangladesh, and the Muslim nationals of that nation.

His extreme hard work and tremendous expertise had mobilized the nation's economy, even if infinitesimally. Without a doubt, he had trained, advised and motivated a huge segment of the unemployed, ambition-less Muslim youths of the erstwhile East Bengal to become successful in life. To them, Mr. Khuda Buksh was a respected leader, a close friend, and finally, a philanthropic colleague. He still dwells in their sweetest memories. It goes without saying that his well-thought futuristic steps taken more than half a century ago were the first mappings of the nationwide awakening.

Deshabandhu Chittaranjan Das (C. R. Das) was an indispensable political personality in solving the crises between the Hindu and Muslim communities created by the various ruling powers of undivided India. At this stage, Mr. Khuda Buksh's principles were somewhat influenced by this great personality. Though Mr. Khuda Buksh's field of work was never as vast as that of C. R. Das, it can be safely commented that the resemblance was undeniable.

It is quite surprising to see that in contrast to his popular image of 'The Dreamer', as the Pakistanis call Muhammad Allama Iqbal, the great poet-philosopher raised his voice in favor of humanistic revolution:

> "Rise and rouse the poor of my world.
> Strike and shake the palaces of the rich.
> A field that does not give bread to the
> farmer should be burnt completely."

It can be said without hesitation that the stern voice of the poet Iqbal fell flat to the deaf ears of the erstwhile Pakistani ruling powers. If they had understood, they would not have embarked upon a vicious and inhuman game involving the fate of seven and a half crore (750 million) Bengalis.

At last, in the year 1966, the Bengalis finally lost their patience and started a movement for freedom from the dictatorship of the Pakistani regime. They made a Six-Point Program as the constitutional solution of East Pakistan's problems in relation to West Pakistan. The declaration comprised demands like fundamental rights and sovereignty, amongst others. However, the Pakistani despots discarded these demand without any sympathy and threatened to use the language of weapons. The intrepid Bengalis did not pay any heed to such threats and continued unabated towards their goal of freedom. It was an era of the rise of the indomitable Bengalis.

It is to be mentioned here that after the establishment of the Pakistani regime, the Pakistanis declared the Bengalis as worthless and unfit for national security or any other constructive work.

The Bengalis vehemently opposed this biased and conspiratory propaganda of the Pakistanis. In 1960s.In the annual report of EFU it was declared that of the total business revenue of Tk.98.50 crores [$205.9 million] of the 27 insurance companies in Pakistan, EFU alone earned Tk. 35 crores [$73.5 million]. This turnover was the realization of the nationalistic awareness and principles followed by Mr. Khuda Buksh from the dawn of his career.

The Pakistanis were very much moved by the staggering success of the EFU. This also proved beyond a reasonable doubt that the Bengalis were capable of handling a vast workforce, quite contrary to the popular belief of the Pakistanis. The tremendous force behind this success was a Bengali who was a pioneer of the insurance industry.

This article describes in detail the career of Mr. Khuda Buksh, starting from his entry in the insurance company with respect to the political, social and economic scenarios of the erstwhile East Bengal. It should be mentioned here that Mr. Khuda Buksh had a definite dream and a roadmap behind his choice of taking a job in the insurance industry. However, when he was halfway to realizing his dreams, the Second World War broke out resulting in tremendous destruction – huge loss of human lives due to famine, a new political turmoil in the British regime, communal riot between the Hindus and the Muslims – and a new chapter of death and destruction in recent history. Finally, the imperialist British government left this country after dividing it into two different nations, in effect creating three different nations under the rule of two different ones.

It is again to be mentioned here that soon after the British left India, the Bengali Language Movement of the Bengalis became a much discussed topic of the Pakistanis and the ensuing violence and carnage during the movement disillusioned the Bengalis of the nation that had been formed on the basis of religion.

Under these circumstances, Mr. Khuda Buksh resigned from his previous job and arrived in erstwhile East Bengal in 1952. The same year, he joined in a high and respectable position the Eastern Federal Insurance Company of Pakistan.

After coming to erstwhile East Bengal, the humanist Mr. Khuda Buksh dedicated himself to the uplifting of the Bengali Muslim community in various realms such as education and economic condition, in other words, a total rehabilitation of the Bengali Muslim community.

After coming to Pakistan, Mr. Khuda Buksh found a way to realize his dreams. He started EFU with only a handful of officers and slowly advanced towards his goal.

No Bengali Muslim was ever accredited as an expert in any field or post in the entire East and West Pakistan. There was no hesitation, no fear, only the constant drive to work from a healthy competitive mentality. The chief of the office was giving hands-on training to all the employees, starting from the officers to the general workers and so everybody was performing voluntarily without any formal orders. The office head used to work from dawn to dusk. Any employee coming to the office in the late evening was always asked, "Had your dinner?." "Serving dinner in the office in the evenings is against the office policy," came the unhesitant reply. Then, the superior Mr. Khuda Buksh used to say, "From now on you can have your dinner from the restaurant downstairs when you are working late in the office. No need to tell anybody anything. Just submit the bill to me."

Mr. Khuda Buksh was the manager, colleague, teacher, and close friend, all rolled into one. After a long time, Mr. Khuda Buksh, a leader of the national awakening, got whatever he wanted. The lower middle class youths obeyed him unconditionally. He was a teacher even in small ways, for example in how to converse in the office, how to write official letters, how to process files, and even how a ranking official should dress while going to a conference; he took care of it all. The colleagues were literally an extended family. When somebody was absent in the office, Mr. Khuda Buksh made it a point to visit that person's home after the workday was over to enquire of that person's well-being. He would look after his employees in every possible way, which sometimes involved even their personal lives and home fronts. He helped them financially, giving them loans for everything if need be, even car loans. When somebody turned out to be sincere, honest, and hardworking, he was made a member of the EFU team with a proper salary. When somebody was in debt, Mr. Khuda Buksh would call up the cashier and instruct him to give a check to the indebted person so that he could clear his dues. The entire process was like a dream to the concerned person. If somebody was lacking an office space, Mr. Khuda Buksh would offer his own to operate from. His dream of financially rehabilitating the Bengali Muslims and ending their curse of unemployment finally came true. He always aimed at making the Bengali Muslim youth community properly employed, which in turn would promote their competitive spirit and interest in education. They would be keen to prove their qualities. This would also improve social interaction amongst them and in this way they would overcome their mental blocks. Competitive spirits in education and the urge to prove themselves in life keeping pace with the changing times would finally dissipate the financial darkness. Whatever decisions he took at the beginning of his career, throughout his life Mr. Khuda Buksh followed them unannounced and undeterred – a victory unparalleled in its nature.

The prospects of the insurance industry were becoming brighter day by day. In fact, the insurance industry was able to cross the darkness of religious superstitions in just a decade. General people, ranging from solvent businessmen to lower-middle class people, came out of the general belief that insurance was only associated with death and started showing an interest in insurance. They slowly became aware of its benefits. The population was increasing and so were the expectations of the general masses. People were looking forward to a healthier and more organized lifestyle. The general people, who once avoided insurance agents, voluntarily came forward with the intention of making insurance policies and planning out how to save properly to pay the insurance premiums. Insurance companies devised new schemes for all classes of people. One step ahead were the field workers of the insurance industry. They held unhesitating discussions with the locals and the policy holders. As a result, the number of policy holders increased, thereby increasing the revenues of the insurance industry and hence the capital and investment opportunities.

This success was the realization of the nationalistic awareness and principles followed by Mr. Khuda Buksh from the dawn of his career. This success belonged not only to the prime insurance expert of Asia but also to the Bengali Muslims.

The reforms introduced by Mr. Khuda Buksh were largely based on the experience he had gathered from the history of the past 200 years. He achieved this very carefully but fearlessly, staying outside all political arenas in the face of sheer dictatorship. First, he brought the children of numerous poverty stricken Bengali Muslim families to the insurance profession. As far as my knowledge goes, this feat performed by Mr. Khuda Buksh was a next to impossible act for anybody else during that time. A top notch official of an Industrial Bank, while answering a question on the inequality of East Pakistan, commented to a journalist in Dhaka airport that he would try to be impartial in investments made in East and West Pakistan Industrial Banks. For this reason, he was forced to retire from his post. Under such circumstances the feats performed by Mr. Khuda Buksh, like employing Bengali Muslims in insurance companies, arranging intensive training programs, purchasing land in Dhaka within two decades for the establishment of EFU head office, drawing up plans for a modernized construction with maximum budget of that time, preservation of the documents of the East Pakistani policy holders in East Pakistan itself, and using Bengali as the official language instead of English, which was conventional at that time, were truly exceptional.

The courageous, sincere, and unconditional steps taken by Mr. Khuda Buksh for the betterment of the Bengali Muslim community made him immortal, and as long as the map of Bangladesh exists, Mr. Khuda Buksh will be remembered with deep respect as the man behind the resurrection of the Bengali Muslim community.

From the little information we have unearthed about Mr. Khuda Buksh, it is evident that between the mid 1930s and the mid 1940s the insurance industry made remarkable progress in erstwhile East Bengal, Pakistan, and later, independent Bangladesh, consecutively. The person behind this phenomenal success was Mr. Khuda Buksh. However, he was more of a humanist than an industrialist, who rose above caste, creed, religion, language and geographical barriers and embraced nothing but the whole truth. All human beings are products of nature and every human being has the right to exercise his or her own religious beliefs and culture. Therefore, it would be sheer meanness to categorize them on the basis of social and cultural differences.

The necessity of the above discussion is because of the fact that, like any other person, Mr. Khuda Buksh had his empathy for his religion, culture, and country. But even in extreme moments he never slighted other cultures or was contemptuous towards other religion. However, this does not mean that he was indifferent towards his country and religion. He had only one principle throughout his working life and that was the welfare of the entire human kind. He was especially sympathetic towards the oppressed Bengali Muslims during the British regime – their crises, their education, and their superstitions. Even after the partition, he ardently fought for his country and its interests, and relentlessly pursued the fight for freedom and rights of the people in general. He did not work under any political banner or any particular religious community, nor did he have any conflict of righteous interests with any individual or community.

His indisputable logic completely curbed the unjust enthusiasm of those people who posed as 'true Pakistanis' and made fun of the Bengali Muslims. However, he never deviated from his principles. This same person never failed to enquire about the conditions of the lower class non-Bengali workers of his company in both good and bad times. Even during the 'Liberation War', as soon as the curfew imposed by the Pakistanis was over, Mr. Khuda Buksh immediately reached out to the workers of the lower echelons of his company. These poor people were deceived systematically by the Pakistanis, sometimes in the name of religion and sometimes in the name of nonexistent enemies. These harmless poor people were suffering from fear, interminable tension and restlessness during these troubled times. Mr. Khuda Buksh used to bring them to his house in his own car, give them food, and advised them to take care of themselves. They bade him goodbye with tears in their eyes – a touching scene indeed.

Once, upon the loss of a close relative, Mr. Khuda Buksh went back to his native village with the hope that the childhood memories and familiar places and people might give him some solace. A village woman, upon receiving the news of Mr. Khuda Buksh's arrival, came to visit him one morning with a very sad story. She lamented the fact that her husband was dying of gangrene and everybody refused to help because of the obnoxious smell. Mr. Khuda Buksh immediately took the sick and dying farmer to the city hospital, where he was completely cured. Mr. Khuda Buksh ultimately received his solace from this great humanitarian effort.

Mr. Khuda Buksh had a unique style of Conversation, Logic, Criticism and Protest. In this respect, one incident can be cited that happened in the last century during the regime of General Ayub, who used to pass new laws at his pleasure in the name of the regime.

Once the military regime imposed an illogical ban on everything associated with Bengali poets, Bengali literature, and all Bengali cultural activities. It was further declared that the celebration of the birth centenary of Sri Rabindranath Tagore is irrelevant to the Pakistanis. Consequently, all cultural functions were closed down and all institutions were discouraged from holding such functions. However, Mr. Khuda Buksh was strictly against the Tughlaq-like attitude of the Pakistani regime and he protested in a unique way which can be said to be completely his own.

People who knew Mr. Khuda Buksh closely would agree that he was a music lover and he often held close circuit cultural functions in his residence. To point out categorically the illogical nature of the bans of the Pakistani regime, he deliberately chose to organize cultural function with aspects and songs on which the bans were imposed.

Secondly, the celebration of the Bengali New Year is a very important cultural event of the Bengalis. Keeping with the old tradition, the Bengalis hold carnivals, musical entertainments, races, and various other programs on this particular day. People participate from all spheres of life, celebrating the occasion by meeting and exchanging food treats. Even the businessmen welcome their customers with delicious sweets. It goes without saying that imposing a ban on such an age old festive occasion was nothing but a deep rooted conspiracy to destroy the culture of the Bengali Muslims.

Adding fuel to the fire was the fact that the communal forces joined hands under the aegis of the erstwhile ruler. Normal activities of life were disrupted in every sphere including institutions and working places. Mr. Khuda Buksh, even in that trying time, rose above the common vices like selfishness and self-centeredness and dedicated his life in the uplifting of his community or mankind as a whole and in building a moral character with an iron determination. It is truly surprising to see a man traveling such a steep path littered with bottlenecks with complete generosity and perseverance.

It is a fact that only great men can dedicate themselves towards the betterment of their country and community. Only those who believe that humankind rises above caste, creed, and religion, and that revolution is the only solution to injustice, can sacrifice their own interests and even their lives for their country. They are the true pioneers of the new era. Mr. Khuda Buksh was such a highly gifted person.

Mr. Khuda Buksh, starting from his brilliant career to the end of his experience-rich life, had undoubtedly made important contributions to the insurance industry. Even when the West Pakistanis were torturing the East Pakistanis, Mr. Khuda Buksh deftly protested against the whole process. In spite of grave danger, Mr. Khuda Buksh emphasized the correct evaluation of the contribution of the East Pakistanis to the Pakistani regime without a shred of doubt or fear.

The phenomenal success of EFU as per the annual report of 1967 was a direct answer to the two-decade-old baseless propaganda of the Pakistanis that the Bengalis were an incompetent community. It would not be an exaggeration to comment that the huge success of the EFU cut through the darkness like a shaft of light and rejuvenated the slumbering Bengalis.

However, even before this phenomenal success mentioned above, Mr. Khuda Buksh had always tried to establish this credit with the Pakistanis as evident in the book – *The EFU Saga* by Wolfram Karnowski:

"Mr. Khuda Buksh always emphasized upon the fact that the huge contribution of the East Pakistanis in the total development of Pakistan needs extensive acknowledgement and his view coincided with those of the important political personas and industrialists. Mr. Khuda Buksh was vehement in his expressions which sometimes appeared to be a little unexpected to some people. He used to make this statement with severe enthusiasm and sternness. Though he was critical about his stance, he never gave it a political angle. He never mixed it up with the then-raging political issues like formation of a new nation on the basis of religion or the relationship of the government of West Pakistan with post-partitioned India."

Mr. Khuda Buksh attributed and shared his success with the uniqueness of the Bengali community, their political awareness and cultural heritage.

During his long and colorful career, Mr. Khuda Buksh became the cynosure of the eyes of his colleagues through his cooperation, sympathetic attitude, and general friendliness and as a guide. It is impossible to cover all the aspects of Mr. Khuda Buksh's life within so few pages.

Throughout his life, Mr. Khuda Buksh worked with hundreds of people but there were hardly any instance of conflict. Amidst the political upheavals of the Indian subcontinent, the life of Mr. Khuda Buksh was not a smooth sail either. Though he faced many crises during the Pakistani regime, Mr. Khuda Buksh maintained his unblemished character.

Such was the twist of fate that the man who witnessed and tolerated the despotism of the imperialist British followed by the heartless and deep-rooted conspiracies of the Pakistani regime and survived, had to part with his position silently because of the conspiracy of a group of mean-minded Bengalis at the threshold of national awakening and sovereignty. Those who had witnessed the return of this humanist, great revolutionary, and unforgettable personality can speak of the trauma and pathos of this great loss.

The great leader of the national awakening of the Bengali community, who dedicated himself to laying the foundations of the economy of Bangladesh much before the Liberation movement that the country had enjoyed hereditarily, was harassed by a group of anti-national class enemies. Is there any explanation as to why these people were never brought to justice even after the passing of three decades? It is unfortunate that we still have not been able to identify the rot in the national structure, as a result of which such incidents still occur in our country.

Parents, Khuda Buksh and Favorite Teacher.

(Reprinted with permission from KBMT&F.)
Khuda Buksh and Zobeda Khatun (1960).

(Reprinted with permission from KBMT&F.)
Sitting from Left: Latifun Nessa (wife of Q.A. Rashid), Ambereen Sultana (Daughter), Zobeda Khatun, Mrs. Zubaidur Rahim, Javed Bukth (youngest son), Standing from Left: Muhammad Rahim (3rd son), Zillur Rahim (5th son), Q.A. Rashid (Zobeda's brother), Bazlur Rahim (4th son), Khuda Buksh, Zubaidur Rahim (eldest son), Ataur Rahim (2nd son) (1966).

(Reprinted with permission from KBMT&F)
Khuda Buksh with his grandson, Kaihan Rahim (1973). Inset, Kaihan after graduation (1991).

Zobeda Khatun with her daughter-in-laws.
From left: Taniya Bukth, Shirin Farhana,
Nasreen Rahim, Selima Rahim,
Shahnaz Rahim and Nur Afza Begum (1985).

Dr. Mahbubul Islam, Zobeda Khatun and Mrs. Ambereen Islam (2006).

The next generation. Zobeda Khatun with her granddaughters,
Shuva Rahim (left) and Sara Rahim.

(Reprinted with permission from KBMT&F)
The next generation. A group photo with uncle Ataur Rahim.
From left: Asif Rahim, Muhammed Rahim, Sajidur Rahim, Tanisha Bukth, Ashiqur Rahim, and Akif Rahim (1992).

(Photo Credit: Shuva Rahim.)
The next generation. Muhammed Rahim, Adil and Rakhshanda Jabeen (2007).

The next generation. Asif Rahim and Eshita Islam (2009).

PART IV

Articles and Newsletters

by Khuda Buksh

(1960-1973)

My Memoir

Khuda Buksh

(In 1967 Khuda Buksh agreed to publish his memoirs in the magazine EFU Eastern Zone Field Force Review. He was considerably encouraged by the editor of the magazine, Mir Musharraff Hossain, who was also his secretary. The first installment of his memoir, *Introduction to Life Insurance*, was published in the 1967 June edition. The memoir mainly conveys the socio-economic situation during 17 years, between 1912 and 1929, along with a description of the author's childhood and adolescence. After the publication of the first installment of his memoir, Khuda Buksh went to Europe to expand the business interests of EFU. After his return, due to his busy schedule, he could no longer pursue recording the varied and colorful experiences of his life-editor.)

My father's name was Moulavi Shonabuddin Howlader Sahib. I am the eldest son of five brothers and one sister. Presently, four brothers are alive. Although my father was not a formally educated man he had a great deal of influence in the village. His mode of speaking attracted those around him to listen and villagers often called on him to settle disputes. He loved the social atmosphere and relished being in the limelight. A tall, robust man, my father was involved in the jute business, working in a jute company in Chandpur. He left the world in 1959.

If I take a glance backwards, the scene that unfolds before my eyes is that of a peaceful little village located in the Madaripur subdivision of the Faridpur district. The name of the village was Damodya. I was born in this village on February 1st,

1912 and spent my childhood days in here. During the rainy season I fell on the same slippery soil that had taught me to walk.

Our family was solvent, though opulence was absent. In this family of so many siblings, we never felt any inadequacy. Our father always desired a decent upbringing for us and he worked hard for our future. Our mother was always very busy with her children, being mostly involved with our demands, entertainment and general welfare. However, I do not remember ever seeing her annoyed. She used to cater to our needs with a smiling face. Being the eldest son, my needs were a little more than the rest of the siblings.

Beginning in childhood, I was always very friendly. I always had a gang of friends with me and used to bring them home without any prior warning. I would then ask my mother to serve food to all my friends, a request she would indulge with a smiling face. Never did I see her embarrassed or disappointed on these occasions. On the contrary, she was happy. She treated all my friends as her own children and fed them happily. To this day, I bring home a flock of friends without prior notice and request my wife to serve them. Every time, my wife complies with a smiling face. In my childhood I requested this from my mother, now it is my wife's turn. Both of them catered to my demands with a smiling face and they still do. My wife is well versed in this habit of mine. If any day I call her from my office and tell her, "Zobeda, today three friends will take lunch with me", she unfailingly arranges for at least six people, as she knows perfectly well that when I mention three guests I might actually come home with six. My wife has always tolerated all my demands with smiling face. I don't want to cancel this debt by simply thanking her; I would rather be indebted to her always.

Of my childhood friends, I frequently recall memories of Mujibar Rahman, Kader, Abdul Gani, Abdul Halim Buksh, and Ashok Sen (who later became the law minister of the Indian Government). These people were my childhood playmates. As a child I was very docile and despite my childlike impulses, I was never a brat.

My education formally started under the guidance of Quari Mohammad Ibrahim Sahib. He had been our family teacher for three generations. Like my father, I started my primary education under his tutelage. *Ustadjee* (Teacher) used to take Arabic classes in the morning and Bengali classes in the afternoon. Later, he supervised the primary education of my eldest son, Zubaidur Rahim. My mentor, Ustaadji Ibrahim, is long gone, but his memories, teachings and values still glow like a diamond in the core of my heart. Whenever I close my eyes, the image of Ustadjee unfolds before me. I float in the world of imagination, where my mind breaks the barriers of time and place and goes back to the dreamy childhood days when he used to take me by the hand and say, "Read Khuda Buksh – *Alif, Bay, Tae, Chey . . .*" (Alphabets of Arabic).

I still remember the day my formal education started. I was adorned in new pajamas, new shirt, and new cap and was looking very smart in that attire. On this occasion, plenty of candies were distributed amongst the children of the village. Our whole family was beaming with pleasure. Though I was a good student, I was never a bookworm. In addition to my studies, I took part in outdoor activities and games. I was a renowned soccur l player then. I was the captain of the soccer team and played the centre forward position. Our team even competed outside our subdivision and won many cups and shields. We had sumptuous food treats after the games.

I attended the Shyamacharan Edward Institution[80] in Koneshwar village about two and a half miles from our home in Damodya village. I used to go to school from our home, and even during winter I would traverse these two and a half miles on foot. During the monsoon season I traveled in boats or rafts made of banana trees. The trunks of several banana trees were tied together with ropes using bamboo sticks to support the structure of the rafts. These rafts were then floated in the water and steered using long, sleek, hard yet thin bamboo sticks as oars. I liked this mode of transport very much; I felt like Robinson Crusoe stranded on a desolate island.

Another personality who had a profound influence on my life, equal to that of Mr. Ibrahim, was Moulovi Ainuddin Ahmed. He was the superintendent of the Damodya Muslim High School. He is still alive, and whenever he comes to Dacca he spends a few months in my home. My children address him as 'grandfather'. His blessings still give me peace of mind.

As a child I used to dress simply. According to the student dress code of that time, I wore a *dhuti* (loin cloth) and a shirt. Sometimes I wore pajamas and a red fez cap. As a child I was very religious and prayed five times a day with *Ajan* (call to prayer). I could recite the Quran very well and liked listening to *Waz* (a religious sermon). At times Jounpuri Moulanas visited our village to preach the religion. I would accompany them and serve them food and drinks and fan them with a hand fan. In other words, there was no dearth of effort on my part to impress them and have their blessings.

As a child my favorite foods were *rosogollah* (a sweet and juicy drop made of curd and flour), *sandesh* (kind of dry sweetsade of posset), *luchi* (kind of soft, thin, fine saucer-shaped bread friend in melted butter), *alu dom,* and curd. I still like these but in this age of adulteration where can one possibly find pure food?

I remember that a seer of cow's milk could be bought with one *anna* (one-sixteenth of one taka), one maund of high quality *balam* (a fine variety) rice with 2.5 taka, gold with 20 taka per *tola* (=160 grains), mustard oil with four annas per seer, pure *ghee* (melted butter made from milk of cows) with one taka per seer and so on. Two hilsa fishes could be bought with one *paisa* (=0.01 taka or rupee). A shirt made of foreign cloth was worth 15 annas. A good quality *gaynji* (A-Shirt) could be purchased with three *annas.* In these days of want and scarcity the memories of those good old days still haunt my mind and I wish I could go back to them once again.

---

[80]Established in the year 1913, The Shyamacharan Edward Institution still pursues the light of education. The old dilapidated building has been replaced by a new construction.

I was very kind and soft-hearted in nature. As a youth still in grade school, I bought the book for my math class countless times, not because I kept losing it but because whenever I heard that a classmate could not afford the book I gave him my own and my father would have to buy another one for me. Father would never hesitate to spend money on educating us.

The first town I ever saw was Chandpur. I was then in the third grade. Father was working in Chandpur and I went there to meet him. While visiting Chandpur, an interesting incident took place. At that time, there was a railroad between Chandpur and Kalibari and I took it to Kalibari with my father. It was close to evening. My father was proceeding towards the station in leaps and bounds. He was tall and walked with great haste. I had to run to keep pace with him. Finally, we managed to catch the train. I was panting as I got onto the train. The train left the station. Suddenly, my father looked at my legs and said, "Hey! Khuda Buksh? Why don't I see a shoe on your right foot?" I was visibly shaken by my father's words. My father had been walking rapidly and as I had tried to keep pace with his steps I hadn't noticed that a shoe had fallen off my foot. Thinking the lost shoe was forever lost, I threw out the other shoe, hoping that whoever got the first might collect the other one also. My father bought me a pair of shoes from market the next day. I was so overjoyed at getting the new pair of shoes, I thanked God, extending two hands and saying, "Oh God, you have no limits to your kindness! Luckily I lost my shoes, otherwise how could I have gotten a new pair of shoes so soon?"

In my childhood I never even dreamt of a career in the insurance industry. It was unimaginable even for a moment that I would opt for an insurance agency for my livelihood. To be very frank, both my parents and I hoped that I would complete my formal education and gain a respectable post in the government. Joining the world of insurance was a truly surprising turn in my life and happened through a series of dramatic incidents. I will discuss this in detail in later chapters. Here, I mention that in the last seven generations of my family no one was involved in the insurance business. I was the first exception.

A Reminiscence: When I Look Back

Khuda Buksh[81]

SOME THIRTY TWO years back, I selected life insurance salesmanship as my career. Frankly speaking, I was not a bad student, although not a very brilliant one. I had also very effective backing to get a good job. Despite all these factors, when I took up insurance salesmanship as my career, my relations and after well-wishes became exceedingly surprised. They enquired of me very curiously time and again as to why I chose insurance as my means of lively hood without taking up other professions or any lucrative Government service. Whatever I said in support of insurance salesmanship could not satisfy them. Rather they were laboring under the impression that I had gone mad or else was good for nothing.

Considering the peculiar social conditions prevalent in those days, it is no use to criticize my relatives for the impression they formed about me and the professions I advocated. Because in those days, people generally had no sincere respect for insurance salesmanship. The profession itself was very much looked down upon. "Those only who are worthless worked for insurance" was the overall view of the then general public.

Now a respected profession

After the prolonged connection with the insurance industry for the last thirty two years, my heart leaps up with immense joy when I think of the tremendous

---

[81] The Pakistan Observer, 9 February, 1967.

popularity and the respect insurance salesmanship commands in the present day world. Life insurance salesmanship is no longer a ridiculous profession nor is it now looked down upon as was the case in the pre-independent period. Life insurance is now one of the most respectable profession in the world and an insurance agent is now-a-days a most welcome friend-a friend the society needs.

Though I remain always extremely busy with organizational matters yet, in my lonely moments, suddenly flash in my mind those fateful days of my career when I first started selling insurance policies. I still remember very vividly the most tragic part of my mission when people used to get frightened whenever they heard of insurance as if they had suddenly seen a snake. It is still alive in my memory that in order to avoid purchasing an insurance policy from me, people did not even offer me any seat even. The were so much afraid of insurance! But I was not a man to be easily disheartened. I had indomitable spirit. I used to carry always with me a light folding chair and if any client would not have cared to offer me a seat I used my own folding chair for the purpose.

With the passage of time, the attitude of the public has changed. Man has now been able to appreciate through his varied experience that life insurance has no substitute to protect him as well as other members of his family from all possible hazards. The Government is also fully convinced of its unique role and that is why they have taken very effective measures for the rapid progress of the insurance industry. Income-tax relief throughout life insurance is one of such measures.

Economic Security

To tell you the truth, I took up insurance salesmanship only to be able to serve the cause of humanity in my own humble way. By adapting this profession not only can one earn his livelihood in a very decent manner, but also can provide unfortunate man with fortune. He can bring to the lips of a widow a genuine smile. He can also arrange education for the children who have lost their father, and a good marriage for the orphan daughters. If the assured is alive, it is all the best. Life insurance provide an old man with monthly or yearly pension or through ready capital for investing in a business after retirement from service.

I can cite innumerable examples where an entire family faced untold miseries and hardships due to the sudden death of the bread-winner. With his demise, the whole family found itself on the verge of ruination. Even before his dead body was buried, the housekeeper knocked at the door for rent, the milkman turned up to take arrears and behind him, there was a big procession of other creditors. The helpless wife holding firmly her children in her lap cursed her destiny and appealed to God as to why the Almighty did not take her away before her husband to avoid this melancholy drama of humiliation. Because the house rent was not paid, the unfortunate widow found her way on the street from her sweet drawing room and the further education of her children had to be stopped. The role o life insurance in such perilous moments of life is indeed very commendable.

Life insurance works as a life buoy when one finds oneself in the sea of misfortune and hardship. If it as if an umbrella of fortune for a frustrated man against a rainy days of misfortune. The other day while I was working in my chamber, I received a telephone call. On the other end of the phone, spoke with me a lady who had suddenly lost her husband. She informed me with a voice choked with tears that after the sudden death of her husband, while all the creditors turned up to demand money her husband owed to them, only one gentleman came forward with a check and he was our agent. Her voice trembled out of gratitude and she became emotionally sensitive. She further informed me that she would have found her way to streets along with her children but for he insurance money of her husband. Before the lady cut off the line, she said that a portion of the insurance money was spent to meet the outstanding bills and debts and the rest were sufficient for their livelihood as well as for the prosecution of the further studies of her children. She further added that she would have to go to the doors of other persons much to her humiliation, to fetch money to purchase the articles necessary for the burial of her husband had there been no money offered by the insurance company.

I was terribly shocked at the catastrophe of the young lady. But, even in my pensive mood one thing at least made me highly consoled : The lady whom I referred to was not one of those who stood defeated and vanquished in the struggle of life. Her husband had not left her destitute. The insurance money will help children to become one day responsible citizens of the country to share their duties towards the nation with other respectable men of the society. The mother will become extremely happy that day to see her children suitably provided for in life though insurance. The widow will perhaps that day pray to Almighty Allah out of gratitude for the eternal peace of the departed soul of her husband, who did not leave her in this world helpless and homeless.

Ennobling Insurance

One becomes really noble by taking up insurance profession. An insurance agent starts his day's works imbibed and encouraged with a set of ideals. I do not claim that an insurance agent has no desire to earn money. But earning money is not the principal motto of an insurance agent, it is secondary to him unlike in other vocations.

The first and foremost object of an insurance agent it to see that any one of his neighbors or acquaintances does not fall in financial hardship nor does not any one of them die, leaving the member of his family in wretched condition. Such kind of philanthropic thinking make an insurance man noble and elevated. It is no denying the fact that noble thinking and noble thinking alone can lead a nation to the pinnacle of success. The role of the insurance workers in building up a happy and prosperous nation can, therefore, hardly be over-emphasized. The present day society has learnt to appreciate the commendable role played by insurance workers in the individual as well as collective life and as such people from different works of life are coming foreword to take up insurance as their career. Irrespective of the young and old, man and woman, rich and poor. Hindus and Muslims – everybody is now eager to select insurance as his or her career. The artists and writers, the teachers and professors, the farmers and laborers, all alike have crowded the offices of the insurance companies. They want to extend the unique benefits of insurance to the far-flung parts of the country, to the cottage of the peasant who is tilling land in the remotest corners of a district; or to the thatched house of a fisherman who is catching fish in the blue water of the Bay of Bengal, defying its terrific waves.

It gives me immense pleasure whenever I think that now-a-days no insurance worker is to carry with him a folding chair like me when I first started my career. Rather in the present day society, an insurance worker is the most honorable and welcome guest to a family. An insurance worker in modern times is not only provided with a comfortable sofa to sit on but he is even entertained with a delicious cup of tea or coffee as well This is undoubtly a gift of independence.

Service to Collective Life

Apart from extending appreciable benefits to the individual life, life insurance is also rendering real service to collective life. Everywhere one will find today rapid expansion of industry, the wheels of the mills are moving, the roads are being constructed, big buildings are seen rising higher and higher and in all these activities, life insurance has a very prominent part to play. Life insurance companies are collecting small savings from the individuals and turning them in to a huge capital. The capital is being invested for the welfare of the country and its people. Winston Churchill-one of the greatest man of the modern times remarked "Had there been ample powers in my hands, I would have written the word 'Life Insurance" on every door of the country." It is evident from this remark that the man of the century was quite conscious about the splendid role played by life insurance. Great Britain, The motherland of Churchill, is a highly developed country, its people have immense affluence. In spite of all these, Churchill could not ignore the need of insurance for the people of his country. Naturally, the importance of life insurance for a developing and newly independent country like Pakistan can hardly be over emphasized. It has got tremendous role to play.

The most fascinating part of this profession is that one's earning in it does not remain limited. Working seriously and sincerely, one's income will go up and up. There is of course no surety as to how much one will definitely earn in this profession, but for that matter his earning does not remain within a ceiling. There are many insurance workers whose income today is more than Rs. 10,000 per month.

Special Characteristic

In other professions, it has been observed that you have to spend a huge amount before you start earning. A doctor or an engineer or a lawyer, whoever you may be, you will have to invest quite a good amounts of money while you undergo training and money starts coming to your pocket latter on. But the case is otherwise with regard to insurance selling. You do not require to spend money to start your career as an insurance salesman, nor are you required to spend money while you undergo training. The day you start working, money starts coming to you. If you are functioning in a methodical way your earning will increase tremendously every day.

I do not know if you have noticed the long line of the costliest cars parked alongside Jinnah Avenue (now Bangabandhu Avenue). But I am happy to let you know that the maximum numbers of these cars are owned by the insurance workers, who started there career in a very humble way, but all of them are now decently placed in life by taking appreciable part in this service of humanity through insurance.

Unlike other parts of the world, unemployment problem is extremely acute in our country. Hundreds and thousands of young boys fresh from colleges and universities are seen moving from office to office in quest of a job. Life insurance selling can solve unemployment problem to a large extent. Any young man can change his luck by taking up this profession and working for it a bit seriously. He will not only get an avenue to live a respectable life in the society but he will also get an opportunity to serve individuals and the nation thereby. Having been associated with this profession for quite a pretty long time, I am fully convinced that energetic young and educated persons will do better in this profession than anybody else. The insurance industry of Pakistan today needs capable young man. The greater their number is the better it is for the nation.

Selling Life Insurance Successfully – A Career

Khuda Buksh[82]

THERE ARE VERY few institutions which affect so vitally the average family as Life insurance. It is a fact, that Life Insurance is the only safe method of protecting the loved ones against want and misery that may overtake them in the event of the premature death of the bread-earner. The deliberate failure to provide such protection when necessary is considered as a criminal neglect and injustice upon the dependents.

During 25 years of my service in insurance it has been felt that there is a general complaint amongst those who take to insurance that this profession does not enjoy the same prestige and honor as other professions, such medical, legal, engineering, etc., do. On analysis of the causes it has been discovered that not only the public are unnecessarily responsible for such opinion but also there are genuine causes for it.

The public judges a profession by different standards. First of all they see to what extent and degree the profession is beneficial to the society and the country as a whole. Secondly, they think whether the members of this profession come from the educated and well cultured section of the people, whether this principle is restricted only to those who qualify themselves after a thorough course of training and thirdly, they consider the prospects of the profession viz. monetary returns it can bring to its members. It has been felt that the profession, which can satisfy the above standards, can well take an honored place in the social life of any country.

---

[82]The Pakistan Observer, April 18, 1961. Paper read at the first All Pakistan Insurance Convention held in Karachi, Pakistan.

There is no difference of opinion that Life Insurance selling as a profession satisfies the social utility and service, by helping one to plan for future financial program and make provision for one's old age and for the education and future provisions for one's dependents in the event of one's premature death or sudden cessation of income. The role of Insurance Agents in the social and national service is also very great.

Young men after completion of their studies try to look for a job and the tendency has grown to find out an employment in the Government office or in a Commercial establishment with a fixed and limited income. The Employment Exchanges, it has been noticed, are registering the names of young educated males and females for employment in various Establishments in a large number. Some of them get employment immediately and other have to wait for their turn. The question of unemployment problem in the country is great and it is very difficult to find out jobs for such a huge number of unemployed persons. Since selling insurance is not looked upon as a dignified profession for some reasons or the other, it could not affect a large number of educated sections who are partly responsible for the very slow progress of the Insurance industry which is vital for the development of a country's economy. But the educated sections that have taken this profession as a career, have progressed satisfactorily and the example is not far to seek. Mr. Shamsher Ali has set up a very bright example in this respect.

A thorough education and training is a pre-requisite to the promotion of a high standard of professional ethics, without which no profession can command respect and prestige of the public. The neighboring country has made reasonable progress in popularizing Insurance by extending training facilities to their field staff. By training the members in the profession similar results may be achieved in Pakistan also. It is therefore, gratifying the Government of Pakistan have recently launched a training scheme for the Insurance Agents and have already opened three training centers in both the wings of Pakistan. They have also started publicity on a small scale and the response is very satisfactory.

Immense Scopes

Life Insurance selling has immense scopes in the development of the economy of the country. Recent preliminary Census has disclosed the alarming growth of population. The per-capita Insurance in Pakistan is very negligible. Although people living in the rural areas need Insurance protection equally as those who are living in the urban areas. On going through the statistics it has been found that a policy worth Rs 100/ – is not owned by a person out of 200 persons living in rural areas in Pakistan. The recent cyclone in East Pakistan has disclosed that practically no affected person has been benefited through Insurance protection. It is, therefore, an admitted fact that this industry has vast possibility and I doubt whether any other profession has got such immense opportunities.

Life Insurance selling from the service point of view is a noble one. It gives an opportunity to render service to the people and their families. The salesman sells money for the delivery in future when the income of any family stops or shrinks due to any hazard or death of the bread-earner. It is a fact that a person who dies needs no food, but the members of the family who are left behind need at least 2 meals a day in addition to cloth, shelter any money for education of the children. It is privilege of the Insurance salesman to provide suitably for people who, during old age, would otherwise have to starve or live on charity, in misery and humiliation.

By selling Life Insurance small savings of individuals are mobilized. These small savings when pooled together form a substantial part of national savings which can be utilized in the development of the economy of the country.

Life insurance saving has another advantage. An Insurance salesman deals with all types of people and learns the tact. He gets the opportunity to come in close touch with the various types of people can now study the human mind. He learns to be humane and can successfully learn to deal with other human beings. Thus Life Insurance Agent becomes a master of human relations. The stranger becomes friend in the course of a short time and widens his outlook and spreads brotherhood in the society. By keeping service above all he gains both materially and spiritually which is rare in other professions.

Without the help of the Agents the insurance industry cannot grow. Therefore, the scope from the viewpoint of personal advancement that Life insurance selling offers, is second to none when compared with other professions. It offers an almost unlimited scope to promising and capable young men. What an official in a clerical or supervisory job earns in his lifetime and insurance salesman can earn in ten years or in still shorter time and can be above want. He is not only serving the public by inculcating in them the habit of thrift by saving, but at the same time serving himself. Peculiarly enough, by taking this profession one can earn while he learns.

Basic Knowledge Essential

The basic knowledge for application of the effective plan is essential. It is well known that so long a man works, dreams and plans for future he will need Life insurance and those who need Life insurance will need he guidance of trained and experienced Life Insurance Agents to give them expert advice and suggest plans and programs to meet their needs in the best possible manner. Life Insurance Agents offer service and in return he gets commission, which increases with the increase of business. More the business and Agent brings the more his income increases and he get an opportunity to build up an estate in the form of renewal earnings. Insurance Act has recognized the services of the Agent and has made payment of the renewal commission hereditary. When a doctor or a lawyer dies his income out of his profession ceases. If an Agent dies after putting in a few years of service in insurance the renewal commission is payable to his dependants after his death which is rare in any other profession. Besides, if the Agent stops working after working continuously for a few years he will enjoy the renewal earnings in the shape of pension till such time his policies are in force.

Provisions For Future

Life Insurance has to look ahead and make provision for the future. This hold good for most of the people and, therefore, there is no other way to deal with the problem than through Life Insurance which involves sacrifice of some of the present day desires. The average people procrastinate. Human procrastination is one of the reasons why sale of Life Insurance is extremely different and needs the service of skilled and trained salesmen. Selling Life Insurance is now a monopoly business and the insurance policies are guaranteed by the Government.

It is an admitted fact that a blind man cannot guide another blind man. It is, therefore, essential that a salesman to make his salesmanship a success be required to learn a few essentials for successful sale of his goods. First, he should have thorough knowledge about the article of sale. Unless, a salesman knows fully about the goods he has to sell he cannot familiarize others with the special points regarding the article which is to be sold. To acquire this knowledge it is essential that he devotes some time and studies the subjects for acquiring a clear understanding. Secondly, service to his customer is also very essential. Before selling it would be advisable to place he salesman in the customer's place. He should think of the customer's interest and provide best possible service to his customer. It has been experienced that by doing so he will render the highest permanent service to himself. He will earn a good deal of reputation, which will be his assets. Since no two customers are alike he must develop adequate listening power, which normally develops with experience. Every time a salesman patiently works out solution of a difficult mental problem and he at the same time, develops and increases mental powers. For this he has to think out for himself and has to study all types of questions when only he will have the advantage of larger and fuller knowledge. An impressive personality, in my opinion, is essential to make his sale a great success. He must win the confidence of the customer in the first place. The persuasive ability in a salesman is also very essential to convince the prospective buyer. A salesman, therefore, must be able to present the merit of his article in a logical and impressive manner. Besides politeness, pleasant speech and a melodious voice in a salesman also play an important role. He has to be tactful in the arguments with his customer and persuade him to bring to his own line of thinking. He should avoid unnecessary anxieties to sell but should constantly try to win the customer with his persuasiveness and substantial good service.

It was reported recently that the neighboring country completed a New Business exceeding rupees five hundred crores in 1960 against which a New Business amounting to about rupees thirty-crores was completed in the same year in Pakistan which should have reached the neighborhood of at least hundred crores in proportion to the size and population and potentialities of the country. The services of innumerable number of Agents are necessary to reach the goal.

From the foregoing facts it is evident that Life Insurance profession has tremendous scopes for growth and expansion.

30 Progressive Years – EFU 1932 to 1962

Khuda Buksh[83]

EASTERN FEDERAL THE world's first Muslim Insurance Company came into existing in the year 1932. Its founders and promoters with their high ideals organized it in such a way that it should develop into an international institution in courage of time. The Directors and the Management later on also kept this view in the forefront. In spite of various difficulties that it had to confront the Company started making a great headway within a very short period. Owing to the cautious and prudent policy on the part of the Management "Eastern Federal" acquired a reputation for itself in unexpectedly short time and become a pre-eminent unit in the Insurance market.

Having fulfilled the objective of pioneering General Insurance business the Company directed its attention to the original idea of composite operation. In the year 1936 it started underwriting Life business thus completing its Insurance service. It was a time in which people hesitated risking their capital in the Insurance business. Many prejudices existed which made underwriting an extremely tedious job. However, the promoters had already foreseen these difficulties and these handicaps did not deter their enthusiasm to carry on their efforts for the betterment of the Company. In the year 1932 – the first year of operation of life business the company started with a small beginning of paid-for business of about Rs. 50 million. The progress in the beginning was not rapid but every year it showed an increasing trend. By the year

---

[83]Presented at First Eastern Federal Convention March 5, 1963 (Source: Pakistan Observer Supplement, Dacca, March 5, 1963).

1946 the Company had already shown an appreciable improvement in its operation and started moving ahead steadily.

The year 1947 was a year of great disturbances, the major upheaval of the century had occurred, in which Muslims all over the sub-continent sustained immense loss, both of life and property. Homes, without number, were ruined, valuable lives destroyed, people thrown out of jobs, wives were separated from husbands, children lost their parents and all this was done merely to achieve one end, and that was creation of Pakistan. Naturally, "Eastern Federal" along with almost all other insurance companies was greatly effected by the up heal. However the Board of Directors of Eastern Federal guided by the missionary zeal, of its founder Abdur Rahman Siddiqi, decided to serve Pakistan and immediately got their office registered in East Pakistan and soon shifted the Head Office to Karachi as well.

In spite of the difficulties mentioned above, the company recorded appreciable progress in the year 1947, by completing a new Life Business of 4.5 million. The results achieved during 1948, when the company transacted a total business of Rs. 139,00,000 were beyond the warmest anticipation of the management. This success would not have been possible without proper expansion of the entire field organization on scientific lines. Frankly speaking, there was hardly any organized field force worth the name in the beginning. The work of expansion of the field organization was taken in hand in the beginning of fifties and a system of training classes was introduced. This method soon started showing rich dividends and the number of Agents and Field Officers went on multiplying day by day. The company there after continued showing tremendous upward trend in its paid-for business from 25.4 million in 1953 to 42.8 million in 1957. The progress of the company from 1958 to 1962 has bee simply unprecedented. By securing a new Life Business of 132 million in 1962, the company had risen to the heights hitherto unattained in Pakistan. During the same period the premium income of the company went up from 3.3 million in 1962.

The position of business in force has successfully been maintained all-along this period. It has gone up from 6.63 million in 1953 to 32 million in 1962, which favorably reflects the quality of the business transacted Life fund have also kept pace with the year to year increase of Life Insurance Business. These funds have swelled in 1962 to 56.5 million from these of 5.92 million in 1953.

Within the last 10 years the total assets of the company have grown from 17.7 million in 1953 to 75 million in 1962. These are some of the company's major achievements for which any insurance company placed in the circumstances of our country can take legitimate pride. Various graphs shown here very well illustrate this phenomenal progress.

The Company stands for the ideal of service. It has been guided by the principle of giving absolute security to the Policyholders, who in turn repose their confidence in it. It seeks to provide the Insuring public of the most economic covers to meet their varying needs for Insurance protection. Today, Eastern Federal as the largest

Insurance Company of Pakistan is playing a leading role in building the country's economy by providing security to the growing industrial and rural population of the country, and with the present Board of Directors and the Management, which is constituted of the best brains of the country. Eastern Federal is destined to achieve yet greater eminence in the insurance world. This review, would certainly be incomplete without mentioning the greatest contribution of our Field Force, who I must say, have been mainly instrumental in achieving this astonishing success of the company.

Life Insurance Selling – A Profession

Khuda Buksh[84]

THE CHOICE OF a profession has become a great problem for educated men and women in this country. Life Insurance selling has immense scope for expansion. The educated people need not hesitate to take to this profession. The industries in Pakistan are developing very fast and they need insurance protection. Very few persons have so far availed of the opportunity to protect themselves or their families or their business from possible catastrophe. The growth of Insurance business shows that more and more men are now turning to this way of providing for contingencies. Life Insurance is playing an important part in our national and economic welfare as well as individual wellbeing. It protects family life where its existence is threatened by the death of a bread-winner. It provides ready funds to meet emergencies by way of loans against value of the Policy. It accumulates capital for investment in industry, community projects and deference of our country.

It wounds a man's pride if he and his family have to fall back upon the charity of the community. All these, therefore, create a sense of responsibility and Life Insurance as well as other types of Insurance have been invented for taking shelter against such risks. It is a way of distributing losses and eliminating uncertainty.

Life Insurance offers a plan which enables a person to join large group of people which undertakes to pay a sum of money to his family or others at the time of his death or to him if he survives till the particular date. In return, an amount of money

---

[84]Eastern Federal News Bulletin, Vol. II, No. 7, July 1965.

is invested with the Insurance Company and Life Insurance is based on careful calculations of the degree of risk applying to large number of people. In the words of Sir Winston Churchill, Insurance is bringing the magic of averages to the rescue of millions.

Life Insurance helps in mobilising savings of the individuals. The savings of the nation go to develop the country and produce more wealth thereby raising the standard of living of individauls and families.

Like other commodities, Life Insurance in this country is not purchased but sold and, therefore, manpower is essential for selling Life Insurance. The service, it offers, can be rendered to almost every citizen of the country and a very large number of salesmen will be required to take its message to every nook and corner. The per capita Insurance in Pakistan is very negligible. Under such circumstances, a person who takes up this profession earnestly, has a wonderful opportunity in building up a successful career.

Life Insurance selling offers an almost unlimited scope to ambitious and capable young men and women and also offers unlimited material rewards in proportion to the hard, honest, systematic and planned labour. It is of course an admitted fact that thorough knowledge and effective planning is necessary to make this profession a real success.

Salaried Job

Every profession has its advantages and disadvantages. It is true that in a salaried job, there is an advantage of a regular salary and there is also the great disadvantage of the inflexibility of the income. In a Life Insurance Agent's profession, we have the disadvantage of not knowing what a month's work will bring and there is also the advantage that the income may be raised if one works had enough. A salaried person's income is limited and he has to make his budget according to his income. Against this disadvantage, an Insurance Agent can, with the requisite knowledge and earnest application, increase his income to any height according to his need. Only he has to put in hard labour for increase of his income. The Insurance Agent is the master of himself and has all the independence that one could wish for. The man who earns Rs. 2000.00 a month by selling insurance is more manly, courageous and resourceful than person who earns that amount as salary.

The Pension is granted in Government or Commercial Organisations after working for a minimum period of 15, 20 or 25 years. As against this, the Agent's Renewal income is guaranteed to his family by the Insurance Act. Indeed, the potentialities are so vast and the financial reward so promising that there is hardly any other profession open to the common man which can compare with Insurance Salesmanship in respect of self reliance and bountiful reward. If today the average earning of a member of this profession is low, it is because the profession has been overcrowded more by leisure-time Agents than by genuine, active and whole-time professional Agents. The prestige of a profession cannot be high in public estimation unless proper restrictions are imposed for admission into the profession on a uniform and universal basis. I am confident an Agent's prestige will stand high in public esteem if recruitment is made on a scientific basis.

Training

It has been felt in the past that those who are not getting any job anywhere else join the Insurance profession. It is partly true that people whithout proper knoledge joined Insurance and made this profession a laughing stock. It is being increasingly realised now by all concerned, including the Government as well as Companies that Insurance salesmanship is a specialised job and proper training is necessary to make this profession a success. Training facilities have been extended by the Insurance Companies themselves and Government also are trying their utmost to train Insurance personnel to enhance the prestige of this profession. More and more training centres are being opened and with specialised training and thorough knowledge of this subject, Insurance Agents will enjoy greater prestige. People have felt that Insurance is necessary for protection of their property, business or industry as well as to protect themselves and the family.

Unfortunately, the per capita insurance in this country is still low. With proper training facilities, Insurance is bound to emerge as the best profession with unlimited earning potential. What is needed is full faith in the profession and the noble service it seeks to render, along with adequate knowledgs, to overcome the initial shyness. All this will come with training, and a trained salesman, with confidence in himself and implicit belief in his mission can reach height of success to which few other profession could have carried him.

I started my career as an Insurance Agent in an Indian Insurance Company about 30 years ago and I feel proud today that I have been able to render service to large number of people in course of my long association with the Insurance Industry. I have saved many families from possible ruination. During my association with this profession, I created a great yeam of Agents who have taken to this profession and are rendering service with good income. The balance sheet of any Insurance Company would reveal that the income of its agents is increasing from year to year. The statistics have proved that the income of an agent can be anything from Rs. 100/– to Rs. 10,000/– or as much as he likes. It is within my knowledge that an Agent of a certain Insurance Company has been able to earn a sum of Rs. 35,000/-by selling Life Insurance in a year and this agent will enjoy the benefit of renewal income till his death and thereafter the renewals will continue to be paid to his family as long as they last. Similarly, The Balance sheet of that company shows that several lakhs of rupees were paid in the shape of commission and shared by large number of Agents whose average income varied Rs. 200/ – tp Rs. 35,000/ – in the year.

By following an independent profession, one can thus earn a large amount and remain the, master of himself. Therefore, Life Insurance selling has got wonderful opportunities and people euiped with through knoowledge and the requisite dash and courage of conviction would be be able to do better by following this profession than in the salaried job.

Record Rs. 35 cr. Business in 1965 by Eastern Federal: Khuda Buksh Details Company's Activities[85]

THE EASTERN FEDERAL Union Insurance Company last year contributed Rs. 35 crores (350 million) of new life business in the country's total business of approximately Rs. 90.50 crores (900.5 million) of new business by 28 companies. This was stated by Mr. Khuda Buksh, General Manager of the Company, in course of his address of welcome at the Annual Prize Distribution Ceremony held in Dacca on June 14. He said, that the company established another record by showing an increase of 35 per cent in the paid for business in 1965 over 1964.

Mr. Khuda Buksh informed the gathering that the Company had drawn up an ambitious five-year plan of their own and hoped to complete a paid-for business of Rs. 100 crores (1 billion) by 1970, thereby substantially contributing to the country's economic advancement.

The Eastern Federal, he said, had invested a substantial amount in the industrial sectors of the country. He stated that the company's investment in East Pakistan stood at Rs. 3 crores (30 million) to date and had been increasing steadily.

---

[85] The Pakistan Observer, 14 June, 1966.

The following is the text of the address of welcome Honourable Minister, Distinguished Guests, Members of the Field Force, Ladies and Gentlemen:

It is both a proud privilege and a distinct honour for me to welcome Nr. M.N. Huda, Minister for Finance, Government of East Pakistan, and other distinguished guests to our Annual Prize Distribution Ceremony.

A renowned economist and scholar Dr. Huda enjoys the distinction of being one of those few Pakistanis whose work is known and appreciated in academic circles at home and abroad. His positive contribution for economic development and planning of the country is not only appreciable but has also enkindled great hope in the minds of our people.

Sir, your kind acceptance of our invitation to attend our humble function and to distribute the prizes has once again demonstrated how deeply you love Eastern Federal, which is, in fact an institution of the people who believe in the self-help movement. It is indeed a great occasion for us and we are really grateful to you for giving us this opportunity to meet you and talk to you personally.

I take this occasion to inform you that your Company, Eastern Federal last year contributed 35 crores of new Life business towards the country's total business of approximately 90.50 crores of new business by 28 companies. Kindly permit me to assure you on behalf of my over-energetic field force and on my own behalf that we shall spare no pain to improve the ratio of our humble contribution towards achieving the country's target of 1000 crores (I billion) of business by 1970.

Ladies and Gentlemen, you will be glad to learn that by completing a new paid-for business of Rs. 35 crores (350 million) in 1965 as against a business of Rs 25.95 crores (259.5 million) in the previous year, your Company established another record, showing an increase of 35 percent over 1964. It is also heartening to note that the total business in force of your Company at the end of 1965 amounted to Rs. 82 Crores (820 million) covering approximately one Lac (100,000) persons.

Field forces in action

We are really proud of our organization officials and other members of the Field Force who are dedicated to the mission of Life Insurance. You will definitely be glad to learn that many of these officers secured in 1965 more than one crore (10 million) of new Life Business, one of them having completed a paid-for business of nearly Rs. 3 crores (30 million) and the average productivity of our top ten Supervisory Officers is at about Rs. 1.50 crores (15 million) which incidentally is more than the total new business of many companies. You will be glad to know that our Supervising Officers, Mr. M.H. Alvi (Rawalpindi), Mr. S.G. Jeelani (Karachi), Mr. M.A. Rahim (Sialkot), Mr. S.P. Talreia (Jacobabad), Mr. M. Zulqarnain (Lahore), Mr. A.S. Khan (Lahore), Mr. Ahmed Ali (Dacca), Mr. Abdul Mahmood (Karachi), and Mr. M.A. Qasem (Dacca) are ace producers of above

Rs. 1 crore (10 million) in 1965. I would also like to mention that the Company's top ten Non-Supervisory Organization Officers produced an average and the top ten agents average is about Rs. 10 lacs (1 million) in 1965. While I congratulate all the members of the Field-force on the aforesaid results. I take this opportunity to point out the at the economic progress of a country if the best guaranteed for its defense and that is why during the War emergency, spirit did not dampen. I would urge upon every member of our Field-force to work with greater zeal and enthusiasm, both individually and collectively for the economic development of the country by diffusing the benefits of Life Insurance over a still wider area and a larger number of our countrymen.

You will surely welcome the news that under the dynamic leadership of Mr. R.A. Bhimjee, the Managing Director, the Board of Directors of your Company has drawn up an ambitious five-year plan of their own and hopes to complete a paid-for business of Rs. 100 crores (1 billion) by 1970, thereby substantially contributing to the country's economic advancement. You will also be gratified to learn that we have made necessary arrangements to impart training facilities to our Field workers in our own premises at Dacca and Karachi. We are also extending vocational guidance to our Field officers through reviews and bulletins published from all the Zonal Offices and also Centrally. For better attention and service to our valued policyholders, our members of the staff are also trained locally and for advanced training, we have arrangements at Karachi.

In this connection, I am glad to put on record the untiring attention the officers and staffs in our administration are paying to the valued clientele and the Field-force. We are working in complete harmony. I offer my heartiest congratulations to the officers and staff.

Coming to our investment programme, I may mention that funds of Insurance Companies are controlled funds as per Insurance Act and Rules. You will be pleased to know that your company has always followed a policy of careful and scrupulous investment. On principle, we believe that it is a national as well as sacred duty of all Capital-forming organizations to take active part in the economic development of the country. We at the same time continue to bear in mind very consciously the peculiar and special needs of the less developed areas, particularly in East Pakistan

> *Legally and officially, Eastern Federal is an East Pakistani company, but has preferred to be known as a Pakistani Company and meet the onslaughts of foreign companies in the field and create a prestige not only for its own but for all Pakistanis. After all, it is neither an East Pakistani company nor a West Pakistani company. It is just a Pakistani National Company and you all and supports it as your own company.*

Investment

You will be glad to hear that your company has invested a substantial amount in the industrial sectors of the country. It is gratifying to note that our investment in East :Pakistan is more Rs. 3 crores by now and has been increasing steadily every year through mortgages, approved securities and shares, land and building of our own in Chittagong and elsewhere. We have also taken a very ambitious programme for construction of multi-stories buildings in Dacca, Narayanganj, Khulna and Rajshahi. So far as our Narayanganj building is concerned we have made appreciable progress. We have also invested a considerable amount towards house building loans in this wing and have helped many a family to own a house.

Your company has also invested big amounts in the construction of three leading Cinema Halls at Dacca and also in some Jute Mills. Your company is also taking further positive steps to accelerate their investment in East Pakistan. This will not only amount to good investment but will also lead to a growth in the national economy.

War Fund

During the last September when our unscrupulous neighbor most treacherously attacked Pakistan, I appealed to my 10,000 strong Field-force to donate generously to the President's National Defense Fund or to the East Pakistan Governor's War Purposes Fund. The response was unique. I am proud to say that the members of the Field force donated within a week a sum of Rs. 48,000 to the War Fund. They spontaneously agreed to contribute minimum ten percent of their first year's commission and one percent of heir renewal commissions. The company from its own fund also paid Rs. Lacs to the President's National Defense Fund, Rs. 50,000 each to the East Pakistan Governor's War Purposes Fund, Army and Air Force and Rs. 25,000 to the Navy. Thus your company, its Field-force and the staff donated to the Defense Funds of the country more than Rs. 4 lacs (400,000).

Ladies and Gentlemen, you will be glad to learn that in almost all the important villages of the country Eastern Federal's agents are found – who preach the gospel of insurance to the rural population. Apart from the urban areas, your company is extremely popular in the mofussil areas where the man from the EFU is their best family friend.

The role played by your company, Eastern Federal in encouraging the youths of the country take up insurance salesmanship has been highly appreciated in different quarters at home and abroad. Your company has solved the unemployment problem of the country to some extent. Eastern Federal has its current role more than six hundred Organizations Officers and eleven thousand insurance agents in the country. The monthly income of some of these field officials is more than 10 thousand rupees.

Advice to field force

My dear members of the Field Force, I have now a few words to speak to you. You are all engaged in a very sacred job, which has tremendous influence on the framework of society. It is out and out a social service and its importance has increased more than ever before. There are teeming millions of people with still greater number of dependents who require protection of life insurance. In a backward country like ours, people do not generally understand the benefit of life insurance. The per capita insurance in Pakistan is painfully low and still not more than Rs. 11. The top most need of the moment is therefore, that the message of life assurance should be preached to every home in the country. It is your sacred duty to convince them of the vital role life insurance plays in individual as well as collective life.

In consideration of the increasing perils brought in by modern civilization, the responsibilities of our insurance workers have enormously widened. Never before, in recent history, the need for security was so vital as is the case today. Security for the individual, security for the family and security for the nation are the watchwords of the day, and in your hand lays the financial security of the people. Life Assurance is no longer luxury, but a necessity. The needs of modern life have thus opened up a new avenue and our field workers must cultivate it enthusiastically.

There are numerous insurance workers who are not aware of their status and position and they suffer from the 'octopus of inferiority complex'. They have a strange feeling that they are doing a mean type of work and try to be apologetic to everybody for being in such a profession. This is a wrong way of thinking. You should go about proud, dignified and sober. You are seeking neither help nor favor from anyone. You are rather doing a favor to your clients. You are arranging education for their kids; you are making provision for life income for their wives and a pension during their old age. You are giving them peace of mind, happiness and contentment. No profession under the sun has such a noble mission. In no profession can one earn such personal satisfaction and gratification, as is the case with life assurance salesmanship. So be proud of your job. Let it be written in letters of gold in the pages of your mind that it is your honourable duty as a life insurance salesmanship to mobilize and channelize the social force of life insurance in the greater interest of your community. Keep your watchful eyes ever vigilant so that no breadwinner of our area of activities dies leaving his family uncared for without insurance protection. Fight out like Hercules the colossus of uncertainty of unrest of hard times by offering life insurance protection. Attain belief in the job. Have firm conviction that life assurance is the most noble profession. Have faith that intelligent and honest endeavor never goes un-rewarded. You must develop determination and enthusiasm. Your ambition must touch the stars over your head. The moon is now being conquered why cannot a worldly object is gained?

To the proud recipients of awards and prizes in this function while extending my heartiest congratulations, I wish to advise that you will keep in mind you own records and improve on them in future and create still better records. And to do that you must work for tomorrow and do today what you planned yesterday. Make contact with as many people as you can. Spend the major portion of your time with your prospects, act courteously, be tactful in presentation and you will find that it is easier to get than to miss business.

Those who have not received the prized should not return home dejected, they should rather work with greater zeal and enthusiasm like their prize-winning friends, so that you may also get laurels in such functions.

Before I conclude, I thank again the Honourable Minister and other distinguished guests for taking the trouble of coming over here and honouring us with their august presence.

Foreword: On 2nd all Pakistan EFU Convention

Khuda Buksh[86]

I AM DELIGHTED TO learn that the Convention Number of the EASTERN ZONE FIELD-FORCE REVIEW is being published. I believe it will not only commemorate the 2nd All-Pakistan Convention, 1967, held in the historic city of Dacca but will be a vehicle to educate hundred others (who unfortunately could not attend the same) as to what a Convention means to the Company and its delegates.

I recollect with pleasure the sweet memories of the Convention days in which throughout the four days conclaves the EFU Fieldsmen assembled from Peshawar to Chittagong and Karachi to Khulna listened with mounting enthusiasm as new vistas of knowledge were opened to them. It also provided ample opportunity to the management to study the reactions of its field-force delegates to the important subjects chosen for seminar discussions.

It is indeed prudent to have a resume on the Convention and find what we achieved in the Convention.

- Throughout the Convention days the delegated moved through hectic business agenda and social activity. A fast moving, power-packed series of business sessions, plus the opportunity for plenty of fun and relaxation, – we had enjoyed both at the last Convention. Thanks to the creative imagination and enthusiasm teamwork of the members of the Convention Committee

---

[86]Eastern Zone Field-Force Review – 2nd Convention, Dhaka – 9-12 February, 1967.

synchronized with the ability of the officers of the company and the fine band of the indefatigable volunteers.

- The convention enabled us in establishing friendly union within ourselves, to imbibe a family spirit between the cadres in the field and the officers of all ranks, and brought company and its policy holders, nay, the public at large nearer and closer.

- Those who qualified to attend the Convention as delegates, did not know it advance-is it the business agenda or the social activity – what is that they were going to have in the name of the Convention. It was a fathomless joy in all hearts that right from the inauguration day to the closing session, the delegates and observers had a good time, as well as received a wealth of new ideas to make them even more successful in their chosen career.

Friends, the whole country is admiring your fine performance and you are acclaimed to be aggressive salesmen with fine spirit of salesmanship in the private sector of insurance industry of the emerging nations of the Afro-Asian countries. Our Convention, therefore, was a landmark for people engaged in our profession. Individually and collectively it is now for you to have a greater stride to reach your goal and mould and shape your destiny in this great institution.

I am confident that the EFU Field-force who reaffirmed their determination in the Convention to serve the nation best by spreading the message of Life Insurance will now galvanize their strength to write a business of Rs. 60 *Crores* (600 million) in 1967 and befittingly prepare themselves for achieving Rs. 100 *Crores* (1 billion) new business much earlier than 1970, the Company's target year for the same.

I extend my heartiest congratulations to Mr. Safiyyullah for his imaginative editing and painstaking keen interest, in publishing this special issue together with the pictorial souvenir on the Convention. I am confident these will be a source of inspiration to all members of the field-force and keep aglow the Convention spirit of dedication and service to humanity in all walks of life in the nook and corner of Pakistan.

The G.M's Visualization of a Field Officer[87]

The Field officer *is the most important ever in this establishment.*

The Field officer *is not dependent on us—we are dependent on him.*

The Field officer *is not interruption of our work—he is the purpose of it.*

The Field officer *does us a favor by bringing forth business—we are not doing him a favor by servicing him.*

The Field officer *is not an outsider to our work—he is part of it.*

The Field officer *is not a cold static—he is a flesh and blood human being with feeling and emotion with prejudices and biases, like our own.*

The Field officer *is not some one to argue or match with—nobody ever won an argument with a field officer even though he may have thought he did.*

The Field officer *who brings us his wants—it is our job to fill those wants.*

The Field officer *is deserving of the most courteous and attentive treatment we can give him.*

---

[87] EFU Eastern Zone Field Force Review, Vol. III, No. 11, December 1966 (inside cover).

The Field officer *is the life blood of this and every other operation.*

> *We salute the field officers and the members of the field organization in whose hands rests the security of thousands of our policy-holders*
>
> *and*
>
> *We greet them for the fine performance in the year just closed and wish them in the dawn of the new year prosperous, brighter and better records.*

Foreword: Symposium on Life Insurance in Pakistan

Khuda Buksh[88]

THE PAUCITY OF literature on insurance has acutely been felt in the country since long. Insurance books written by foreign authors are of course sometimes available in the market; but they are either exceedingly technical or they represent a society which depicts entirely different experience from that of our own country and as such they hardly serve the purpose. The demand for insurance literature produced by Pakistani authors based on their own experience in the light of day-to-day problems faced by a Pakistani field worker, typical and characteristic of local environments, was a long felt one. Unfortunately this side of affairs was overlooked by the insurance writers of our country and the insurance workers had to function without any basic training for want of books on insurance.

In the recent past, the role of insurance industry in the national and private economy has greatly been appreciated by all. Time is now ripe that insurance workers should function systematically, methodically and scientifically. Gone are the days when people used to work in a haphazard manner without any knowledge of the subject.

Of course, in the development of insurance in our country those who were associated with the insurance industry in the pre-partition days, played a commendable role in imparting basic knowledge and training to new-comers. But as I have already mentioned, a very negligible number of books has so far been written on insurance in this sub-continent to train our field personnel. It is the written matter

---

[88]Symposium on Life Insurance in Pakistan, June 27, 1967.

and written matter alone pertaining to insurance which can assist in increasing the ability, capacity and dexterity of an insurance worker. A serious or a research student, of course, will find a few books on insurance in the market, but most of them being of foreign origin, as I have already discussed, they are quite good on theory, but are not apparently suitable for our salesmen.

As such, when a veteran old insurance-writer Mr. A.F.M. Safiyyullah and young editor of our East Pakistan Zonal Bulletin, Musharraf approached me that I should write a foreword to the book, entitled "Symposium on Life Insurance in Pakistan", I very happily acceded to their request. This I did more happily in as much as I am associated with the development of insurance industry in the sub-continent for a period of more than 32 years. I have spent the best period of my life to extend the benefits of insurance to innumerable families of the sub-continent. I have a satisfaction of motivating countless insurance workers who are carrying the message of insurance from Peshawar to Chittagong. All along I had longed to see such a book placed in their hand guiding them how to deal with insurance problems, which are real and humane and has the indigenous colouring so that they can understand them thoroughly.

All the knowledge that can be derived through the great Alma mater of experience by those who have attained appreciable position in the art of salesmanship has been masterfully arranged in the book, by the able editors. For those who want to make a big headway in the insurance industry and hope to emerge as successful salesmen, this book, I am sure, will be of immense assistance to reach the desired goal. This book will augment knowledge of the readers and will gear them up with that indomitable spirit which is so badly required to make them better and more dashing and resourceful salesmen. This book, therefore, will go a long way in filling up the acutely felt gap.

It is really heartening to note that our Home Journals published by all our three Zones have had such a hidden treasure of valuable writings from our own men, for whom the company as well as the nation can rightly be proud. The present book is an anthology of writings published so far in our journals; and I take this occasion to congratulate the enthusiastic and imaginative editors for their yeomen's service in this behalf by compiling these educative articles for proper use by our field as well as office men for whose training the company is very keen.

Foreword: On to Ultima Thule

Khuda Buksh[89]

THERE ARE VERY few persons in the insurance industry of Pakistan who do not require any introduction. Mr. A.F.M. Safiyyullah is one of those rare personalities. I say it not because Mr. Safiyyullah is an old friend of mine, but he is a real man of head and heart whose sincere service for the cause of insurance will truly encourage the future generations. At a time when there was not a single book on Insurance in the country to impart technical as well as practical know-how of insurance salesmanship to our insurance workers, his first book "Life Insurance Salesmanship" did a pioneering good job for our salesman.

He is the first Pakistani author who wrote a book on Insurance. His experience is based not on theory alone. He does not belong to that category of authors who write books sitting on an arm-chair having no practical understanding. Mr. Safiyyullah is one of those few authors whose writings has foundation on varied experience. A staunch insurance salesman and executive from head to toe, every inch of the soil of this part of India-Pakistan Sub-Continent knows him thoroughly because he travelled upon it to carry the message of insurance to those who needed it. While working by the side of the desk as a top insurance executive, he also met with classic success. But fortunately or unfortunately, he had exhibited some short-comings while working in the office because he is rather ruled by his heart than by his head. The readers will observe the same heart in every page of his second book on insurance entitled "On to Ultima Thule." Whenever he has tried in his book to spotlight the problems faced by

---

[89]Foreword *On To Ultima Thule*, author, A.F.M. Safiyyullah, August, 1967.

an insurance worker he poured down his heart to understand them and to find out solutions for the same. "On to Ultima Thule" contains a world of writings on insurance. He has tried in his own _haracteristic style to depict all aspects of the insurance industry in Pakistan. He has not omitted to include in his book a single insurance topic of interest to Pakistani readers. The subject matters of his book are Life Insurance and Islam, Philosophy of Insurance Salesman, Problems of Life and Living, Insurance as a career, Prospecting & Life Insurance Selling, the Role of Insurance in National Economy, and Life Insurance Organization and Management. All the articles have been arranged in the book in systematic order, which will give the readers an overall and complete knowledge of Insurance Industry in Pakistan.

While our insurance workers are standing at the crossroads looking helter-skelter to find out ultimate aim of life, this book will work for them as a bacon light. When management of many insurance companies are virtually confused as to how to deal with the field-force, this book will prove to them a guide-line. There are still a good number of insurance workers who will put forth the plea that they are not is a position to sell life insurance policies, since they meet objection while canvassing for life business that Islam is opposed to insurance. Being son of an authority on Islamic concept of life, with hereditary aptitude Mr. Safiyyullah has dealt with this problem brilliantly in his book and proved after a good deal of juristic discussion that Islam approves of insurance and does not speak against it. This particular article (Life Insurance and Isalm) will greatly help our field workesr to meet such objection – alas, in the name of Islam.

"On to Ultima Thule" also incorporates an article entitled "The Role of Insurance in National Economy" which will set readers to think about the part played by insurance to augment the national economy of Pakistan. The author has discussed the matter threadbare and apart from the field-workers, the article tremendously help the general readers as well as the research students to widen their knowledge on this particular subject. In another article captioned "Life Insurance Organization and Management", Mr. Safiyyullah has dealt with a subject-matter which incidentally is his own special field of study. As an insurance advisor of Eastern Federal Union Insurance Company, he made extensive research on this particular subject and extended practical suggestion on sound planning, prospecting and programming and lastly organizational check-up, which are of immense value for the scientific functioning of workers in an insurance company.

While going through the article entitled "Insurance as a career," I observed that Mr. Safiyyullah quoted my name and an article. Frankly speaking, I feel very much embarrassed for his doing so. In the fitness of thing, he should have quoted other personalities in the insurance field. I am always an humble insurance worker and wish to be so in future and I feel very shy whenever I find that my name has been quoted.

I wish the book a great success.

Khuda Buksh
August 21, 1967

Your Duty is Onerous

Khuda Buksh[90]

LIFE ASSURANCE IS undoubtedly the noblest social service a man can think of because it is, as a matter of fact, a very benevolent piece of job for the uplift of society. It is fundamentally based on the maxim: "The greatest good to the greatest number," Life assurance should, under no circumstances, be categorised as a business or industry only, in the true sense of the term. It is more than a business or an industry only. It is rather a unique social instrument to extend humanitarian and philanthropic services to mankind.

With civilisation progressing sat an astonishing pace, mental distress, crushing worries and horrible anxieties have reached their climax. The bright moments of to-day, which are full of life and laughter, may vanish in the twinkling of an eye and become notoriously uncertain life assurance provides a solid 'China all' of security.

Life assurance is a scientific weapon for economic protection. It is an instrument for saving, a device for investment and a fortification against devastation caused by death and disease, age and accident. It is the most dependable of pecuniary assistance—a beautiful cottage for the widow, a square meal for the children, nutritions subsistence during old age, education for the sons and daughters, pension on retirement and so on and so forth. It guarantees food, clothing and shelter to the assured in difficult days and is a "precautionary against a rainy day."

---

[90]Prsented at *Symposium Life Insurance of Pakistan*, July 1967.

Insurance—A Sacred Job

All insurance workers are, therefore, engaged in a very sacred job which has tremendous influence on the frame-work of society. It is out and out a social service and its importance has increased more than ever before. There are teeming millions of people with still greater number of dependants who require protection of life assurance. In a backward country like ours, people do not generally understand the benefit of life assurance. The per capita insurance on Pakistan is painfully low and still not more than Rs. 25/-. This is due to low propensity for saving among the vast majority of our people. The top-most need of the moment is, therefore, that the message of life assurance should be preached to every home in the country. The great multitude of our people living in the rural areas have not yet been contacted with the message of insurance, the majority of them have hardly ever heard anything about the existence of insurance. Herein lies your opportunity. It is your national and sacred duty to convince them of the vital role life assurance plays in individual as well as collective life.

In consideration of the increasing perils brought in by modern civilisation, the responsibilities of our insurance workers have enormously widened. Never before in recent history the need for security was so vital as in the case to-day. Security for the individual, security for the family and security for the nation are the watchwords of the day. Life assurance is no longer a luxury but a necessity. The needs of modern life have thus opened up a new avenue and our field workers must cultivate it enthusiastically.

Be Proud of your Job

There are numerous insurance workers who are not aware of their status and position and they suffer from the "octopus of inferiority complex." They have a strange feeling that they are doing a mean type of work and try to be apologetic to everybody for being in such a profession. This is a wrong way of thinking. You should go about proud, dignified and sober. You are seeking neither help nor favor from anyone. You are rather doing a favor to your clients. You are arranging education for their kids, you are making provision for life income for their wives and a pension during their old age. You are giving them peace of mind, happiness and contentment. No profession under the sun has such a noble mission. In no profession can one earn so such personal satisfaction and gratification as is the case with life assurance salesmanship. So, be proud of our job. Let it be written in letters of gold in the pages of your mind that it is your honourable duty as a life assurance salesman to mobilize and to channelize the social force the social force of life assurance in the greater of your community. Keep your watchful eyes ever vigilant so that no bread-winner of your area of activities dies leaving his family uncared for. Fight out like Hercules the Colossus of uncertainty, of unrest, of hard times by offering life assurance protection. Attain belief in the job. Have conviction that life assurance is the most noble profession. Have faith that intelligent and honest endeavour never goes unrewarded. You must develop determination and enthusiasm. Your ambition must touch the stars over your head.

You must work diligently and persistently towards a particular objective. Plan today you work for tomorrow and do today what you planned yesterday. Make contact with as many people as you can. Spend the major portion of your time in presence of your prospects, act courteously, be tactful in presentation and you will find that it is easier to get than to miss business.

The G.M.'s Message to the EFU Field Force

Khuda Buksh[91]

MY DEAR CO-WORKERS, My friends, you are all young men of undaunted courage and determination. You are all ambitious young men. And as such I am more than sanguine that you are going to perform something miraculous this year as well. The entire insurance industry of Pakistan owes much to you and you have become leader of it. The nation is watching your activities with deep interest. It is for you to retain the LEADERSHIP IN THE INSURANCE INDUSTRY. It wants to witness that you maintain, sustain and continue your LEADERSHIP – a coveted position you have attained not by a 'magic wand' of the fairytales, but by your hard labour, sincere efforts and magic endeavours. During your functioning in for quite a good number of years in the past, you had met with many onslaughts and faced many grace challenges. But by the grace of Almighty, you had over-come all those onslaughts, challenges and crises by virtue of your high morale and indomitable courage and kept the flag of 'Eastern Federal' aloft in the insurance map of Pakistan.

What is Eastern Federal today? It is not only the largest national insurance company Pakistan; it is one of the leading insurance companies in the Afro-Asian countries. Who have built up this company? Who have brought this company to the forefront of all the companies operating in Pakistan? It is you who have achieved this glory. It is your joint efforts, united endeavours and combines spirit that brought the company to the limelight, to the front rank. Eastern Federal in today the pride

---

[91]Source: Eastern Zone Field Force Review/Annual 1967.

of the nation is boastful of you. All those credits are due to you. You are the makers of history, the architects of a bright future. Eastern Federal would not have attained what it has achieved today but for your sincerity, sagacity and dexterity. You have passed many restless nights, sacrificed many joyful Sundays, and deprived your family many times of your delightful company to bring Eastern Federal to its present coveted top position. To give Eastern Federal a respectable status in the comity of the insurance companies of the world, you have braved much inclement weather and fought many difficulties with smiling face. You could do it because you considered "Eastern Federal" as you own company, because Eastern Federal is you own dream, your own creation.

Everybody in the country knows that you are the Leader in the insurance industry. All these years, three words ring the air right from Peshawar down to Patenga and they are "You are LEADER". "You are LEADER". "LEADER", "LEADER" and "LEADER" were your watchwords. But how would you react in case your Leadership is snatched away? How would you feel in case Eastern Federal fails to continue its Leadership? How would you take it in case the business of Eastern Federal falls down?

What will be your psychological reaction in case the image that you built up for Eastern Federal is tarnished? How will you show your face to outsiders in case you are dislodged from your place of pride?

How to Win Precious Reward

Khuda Buksh[92]

THE MONTH OF June came and passed into oblivion. It is not a part of eternity. It brought message and good luck only for those who took advantage of this month and made their fortune by dint of their hard work and toil. They will enjoy the fruits of their labor for years to come. They will also enjoy the benefits of renewal income like those of pension provided they extend their continued service to their esteemed policyholders. This is not the end. The benefit of their labor would be derived by their family also even after their unfortunate demise, because payment of renewal commission has been made hereditary by the Government of Pakistan. The month of June did not bring of course any message or good luck for many of you who did not avail of the advantage of this month. It passes away silently without taking any notice of those who fell prey to lethargy and indolence – the two most vital enemies of human beings.

Time is ever fleeing. It is ever moving. Some take notice of it and others do not. Time also does not care of any one how so ever big one may be. The month of June will again come in 1969. Those of you worked hard during this month and want to continue the same enthusiasm and tempo for the subsequent months, they will surely be able to make July a better month than June. I shall tell you, how? Because you contacted large number of proponents during June but could not close business for some reasons or other. Paying frequent visits can now close the same. Those who could not derive any benefit out of June, must now have derived a lesson. You can make up the deficit by working hard and harvest rich benefit out of July and the subsequent months, which are equally important. Every day in life is important

---

[92]Eastern Federal News Bulletin, July, 1968.

provided you want to make it important as otherwise, it passes away unnoticed and unsung leaving behind its trail only repentance and frustration.

Those who will strive hard to make every day a success; precious award is stored for them both in t his world and hereafter. The figures for the month of June have not yet been compiled but I am pleased to advise you that we have been able to achieve excellent results due to your combined efforts. In the beginning of the month there was cry of depression, but thanks to your sincere efforts and hard toil, we have once again provided that our ever-enthusiastic field force can overcome any difficulty and can secure business under any circumstances.

Wishing you the best of luck.

Obligation to Nationalised Industry

Khuda Buksh[93]

DURING THE LAST 24 years of the Pakistani regime and particularly during the last nine months, we had to suffer enormously and had to shed blood profusely to achieve our liberation. The seven and a half crore Bangalees had to undergo untold sufferings, and humiliation at the hands of the barbarous occupation force and the onslaught and barbarous activities of the Pakistani hyenas have surpassed all the oppression of the history which the mankind in various parts of the world had to suffer in the past and lastly in Germany under Hitler. Not a single example could be found out to be compared with the inhuman atrocities . . . [94] They have sucked our blood, they have ravaged our economy, they have forced one crore Bangalees to leave the country and take shelter in the friendly country of India. They have molested our mothers and sisters and did whatever they could to break the backbone of the Bangalee nation.

But thanks to God, thanks to our boys, thanks to our leaders, thanks to the brevery of our people, they could not bring us to their knees rather we fought and fought with all courage and determination and last of all attained our independence, Bangladesh has thus emerged as a sovereign and independent state in the arena of world map. Once again we have proved to the world that tyrants whatever mighty they may be, the oppressors whatever powerful they may be, they must bow their heads before justice, fairplay and honest cause.

---

[93] *The Evening Post* (Insurance Supplement), Dhaka, Friday, June 23, 1972.
[94] [Ed. Parts missing]

We have no doubt achieved our goal of independence but we are to traverse ...
[Parts missing – Editor]

Today I find that our task as insurance men has greatly increased because we are now the master of our fate and no one from any part of the world will come to help us unless we help ourselves. We shall have to produce more, we shall have to increase our economic viability, industrial output increase our trade and change the fate of the people through the means selected above.

There is not any doubt that to build up our country as 'Sonar Bangla' can only be brought to reality through our hard, dedicated and sincere work but for which we would remain where we were and loud talks would go in vain. Time is now for action.

It is true that a general tendency of wait and see may occur in the minds of the people when a major change is effected in a system of national stature and it is natural people accustomed to age old ways and tradition find it difficult to adopt to the new devise. Inner resistance crop up and stand in the way to accept the new way of life whatever beneficial and good the same may be. This is the common tendency of the human beings which should not be blamed in any way. But if their inner resistance continues for long and the people delays in developing the instinct to adjust with the new system, that may cause great harm to the nation.

Our Government is promise-bound to the people to introduce socialistic economy in the country, to put an end to exploitation of man by man and reduce the gap between the haves and the have-notes. As a first step big industries including banks and insurance have been nationalised. This is a bold step to break through the much criticised system of capitalism which was rooted deeply in the society with its evils during the 24 years of Pakistan regime. This is a big challenge and no doubt an uphill task but whatever difficult and uphill the task may be, the Bangalees are equally capable of over-coming the same. They have proved it in the past and shall without any shadow of doubt rise to the occasion in the past and shall without any shadow of doubt rise to the occasion in future. Once they tought that Pakistan was established to exploit them, they fought against it and won and now once they have decided that socialism is for their salvation, they will Inshallah achieve the goal.

Now we, the insurance workers have a great role to play in our national life and that role is to put the industry in the right track. If, however, we fail in fulfilling our obligation to the nation the posperity will never forget and forgive us. We should not loose a single moment to ponder over the past rather we should go forward with new zeal, vigour and energy to make nationalised industry a success.

If we analyse the past we shall find that every year Insurance business marked tremendous increase in the face of economic depresion, floods, cyclone, war etc. and the percentage of increase in the whole Pakistan was remarkable in former East Pakistan. It was we, who worked and truly speaking were the forerunner in the industry in many ways. Of course, it is true we could not enjoy the fruits of our hard labour because taking advantage of our sincerity, the Pakistani exploiters cheated us and the major portions of the accumulated savings was invested for the benefit of former West Pakistan. But with the achievement of our independence, if we put the clock back that would be the most sad chapter of our history. I am confident that our brethern in the industry will rise to the occasion and shall devote whole heartdly ... [95]

[Incomplete]

---

[95] [Ed. Parts missing]

Nationalisation of Insurance – An Appraisal[96]

Khuda Buksh, Custodian
Federal Life and General Insurance Company Ltd.

THE EMERGENCE OF the Peoples Republic of Bangladesh as an independent and sovereign state in the world map is a symbol of hope and aspiration for the oppressed and suppressed people of the world. History repeats itself and so it has been proved once again beyond doubt that the oppression show much mighty they may be, they must bow down their heads before a just cause. Today the red and deep green flag of Bangladesh thus carries the message of victory of the oppressed people to every nook and corner of the world.

The victory which we have achieved today at the cost of such sacrifice and blood is a victory of ideals. These ideals are in a nutshell to put an end to difference between man ad man to ensure fair and equal distribution of the national wealth, to establish secularism, to end once for all the was and means of oppression and suppression. We have no doubt achieved our independence but the greater task of implementing the above ideals are now in front of us and our success in building up Sonar Bangla will largely depend on as to how rapidly and fruitfully we are able to implement the above ideals.

In order to build on a happy and prosperous country through socialistic pattern of economy, the big industries along with banks and Insurance Industries have been

---

[96]Reprinted by permission from Prof. Dr. M.A. Baqui Khalily. Source: Business Chronicle, First Issue, June 1972.

nationalised. This is not doubt a first step to reach the ultimate goal of establishing a society free from exploitation. The nationalisation of the Insurance Industry by the Peoples Republic of Bangladesh is therefore a revolutionary step and bound to bring about far-reaching consequences in the economy of the country. This decision is also a confirmation of the long standing demand of the public.

In this connection, it could be worthwhile to mention the exact condition of the Insurance Industry in the then Pakistan and also as to how the wealth accumulated through this industry in Bangladesh was taken away to Former West Pakistan by a few Capitalist and invested there for the benefit of the people there at the cost of teeming millions of Bangladesh.

In the then Pakistan, 40 companies used to do Life and General Insurance business. It is a matter of great regret that out of these companies, only ten companies had their Head Offices in Bangladesh while other companies had their head offices in former West Pakistan. Moreover, due to various difficulties and handicaps, these Bangladeshi companies could not make sufficient progress as was expected of them.

Having been in a favorable position, the Pakistani companies use to underwrite almost 80% of the insurance business and the major portion of this business used to emanate from Bangladesh. It means, every year crores and crores of rupees were taken away from this country and this huge fund was invested for building up sky scrapers and factories in Pakistan, the fruits of which were enjoyed by the exploiters. It is a hard facto that this huge fund was collected from the hard earned income of the teeming millions – agriculturists, labourers, and toiling masses of Bangladesh. Insurance Industry thus depicted a sad picture while compared with the other industries in the then Pakistan.

The supreme responsibility of economic emancipation and building up of a strong financial base which reposed upon the Insurance Industry was not fulfilled during the Pakistani regime. Due to faulty conduct of affairs, the very foundation of the insurance industry was shaken. Now that the black chapter of Pakistan Regime is over, the Insurance Industry rededicates itself for building up 'Sonar Bangla' in the truest sense of the term.

Let us now discuss as to what role the Insurance Industry can play in future in the new perspective of the country. The freedom which we have achieved after so much struggle and sacrifice is very precious and it is to be seen that this freedom does not go in vain. To achieve this end, our first and foremost task will be to ensure economic emancipation and above all to make our economy people oriented. As a first step to achieve these objectives, the big industries, banks, insurances have been nationalized. So the fruits of these institutions may not be enjoyed by a handful of industrialists only, rather benefit goes to each and every citizens of the country.

It is well-known and accepted fact that Insurance plays effective role in the economy of the country. It helps in providing with the much needed capital for industrialisation of the country by accumulating the scattered in the small savings of the people in the one hand and ensures economic emancipation in the society by eliminating insecurity and uncertainty and thus builds up a happy and prosperous society on the other hand. So at the present perspective of our country, the necessity and responsibility of the industry has increased tremendously.

Due to the various reasons and handicaps, it was not possible in the past to make concerted efforts to accumulate the scattered savings of the people. Besides, the small capital which was accumulated through Insurance could not be utilised for the greater interest of the people. But the days are not changed we expect that this industry will now be in a position to get rid of the various handicaps and thus direct wholly to attract small savings of the people and invest the same or industrialisation and greater welfare of the people under the guidance and supervision of our national government.

The greatest obstacle on the way of establishing socialism is the concentration of maximum wealth of the country in a few hands. But with the nationalisation of the big industries, the government becomes the owner of such wealth and in turn the government would ensure fair and equal distribution of the wealth for the welfare of the general masses. Moreover, under private ownership, the investment of capital was also guided by individual gains where the welfare of the general masses was secondary but this would be reversed under the government ownership because the government belong to seven and a half crore people of the country and therefore their interest would be uppermost while investing the capital and there should not be least doubt about it.

Most of our people live in the villages and these villages mostly depend on agriculture. They earn less and lead insecure life. Insurance therefore can play a vital role in the village economy by helping accumulation of the small savings of the people and offering security to the helpless family members in the event of unfortunate death of the main bread earner of the family. But previously the Insurance activities were mostly concentrated in the cities and as a result the benefit of Insurance could not be spread in the villagers as was customary in other fields of economic activities. Now in the changed circumstances of the country we are promise bound to improve the lot of hither to neglected villagers. To achieve this end I feel with the nationalisation of the Insurance Industry, it would be possible to launch a bold campaign to spread the benefit of Insurance to each and every village of the country.

Besides, in the absence of Re-insurance facilities within the then Pakistan, a large amount of foreign exchange use to go out of the country. But at the present perspective of the country, it would be possible to increase the power of the companies and make reinsurance arrangements within Bangladesh and thus lessen the outgo of precious foreign exchange.

After nationalisation of the Insurance Industry one question may arise in the minds of the people which are, of course very natural i.e. whether the clients would get prompt and efficient services as they used to get earlier. I think, the straight reply to this question lies in the very word 'Nationalisation'. The owner of the Nationalised industries is the seven and a half crore Bangalees. The independence which we have achieved at the cost of lacs and lacs of our brethren is very precious to all of us. Today, our responsibilities and duties are very much wide and free from narrow thinking of the individualism. So I am confident that imbued with patriotism, people who are associated with Insurance Industry would move prompt in rendering personalised services to the clients.

In to-day's changed circumstances, burgeous are bound to loose their hold in the society and therefore, the policyholders vis-a vis the public should not be doubtful in any way regarding maintaining which the Insurance Industry could build up in the past rather I feel, under the able guidance of the government the policy holders will enjoy more benefits. Besides, elimination of unhealthy competition, removal of individual interest, economy in management expenses and above all efficient conduct of business will surely result in earning more profit and naturally this profit would be fully enjoyed by the policyholders. We also hope, due to this reason, it would be possible to reduce the premium rates in due course, the fruits of which will ultimately be enjoyed by the policyholders.

But it should be remembered that the future of the nationalised industries will depend as to how much we are able to materialise the good points as explained above. So it is urgently felt that the industry should be reorganised on sound basis without any further delay. While reorganising, the following fundamental points are to be given due consideration for making the nationalised Insurance Industry as great success and more effective.

Firstly, healthy competition greatly helps in increasing the industrial output. So in the reorganised Insurance Industry, there should be adequate scope of healthy competition amongst the different units.

Secondly, the success of an industry largely depends on the honesty, integrity and efficiency of the person who is held at the helm of affairs. So while reorganising it should be noted with utmost care that the responsibility of running the industry is given to the hones, efficient and experienced persons in the line, as otherwise whatever may be the high opinion about the nationalisation, all will go in vain due to mismanagement.

Thirdly, service conditions of the field officers should be improved and they should be provided with more security of jobs which could not do earlier to various reasons.

To sum up, we have completed most successfully the glorious chapter of our freedom struggle, but a fresh struggle has just started and this is to build up the war ravaged economy of the country. It is the boundean duty of each and every insurance man to come forward and take his due share in nation building activities. The small and scattered savings of the people accumulated through insurance will help in placing a huge fund at the disposal of the Government which in turn would be utilised for building up a strong economic foundation for the country. This would help in building up a happy, prosperous and beautiful country in the long run and it is expected that Insurance man imbued with patriotic zeal will employ their best and take their due share in this noble aspiration of the people.

Chronology

1912 Khuda Buksh born on February 1 in Damodya, Shariatpur (Faridpur), India.

1929 Passes entrance (matriculation) examination from Shamacharan Edward Institution, Kaneshar, Shariatpur, India.

1932 Passes Intermediate Examination from Islamia College (presently Moulana Azad College), Kolkata, India.
Eastern Federal Union (EFU) Insurance Company, first Muslim insurance company is established at Kolkata, India.

1933 Enrolls in B.A. (Hons) Presidency College, Kolkata, India

1935 Joins Oriental Government Security Life Assurance Company (OGSLA) as a life insurance agent, Kolkata, India.

1939 Marries Zobeda Khatun.

1941 Zubaidur Rahim is born in Calcutta (Kolkata)

1944 Ataur Rahim is born in Calcutta (Kolkata)

1946 Promoted to Inspector at OGSLA.
Obaidur Rahim is born in Calcutta (Kolkata)

1947 British grants independence to India; Muslim Indians want separate state; to avoid conflict British divides India into India and Pakistan. Pakistan comprised of two parts, East Pakistan and West Pakistan.
EFU shifts its registered office from Kolkata to Chittagong, East Pakistan.

1948 Bazlur Rahim is born in Damodya, Faridpur (Shariatpur).

1950 EFU shifts its head office from Kolkata to Karachi, West Pakistan (Pakistan). Zillur Rahim is born in Calcutta (Kolkata), India.

1952 Khuda Buksh Leaves OGSLA and joins EFU as Life Manager, East Pakistan.

1954 Ambereen Sultana (daughter) is born in Dhaka, East Pakistan.

1956 Javed Bukth is born in Dhaka, East Pakistan.

1960 Promoted to life manager of EFU, Pakistan.

1963 Promoted to deputy general manager of EFU (Life), Pakistan.

1966 Promoted to general manager of EFU (Life), Pakistan

1967 EFU successfully hosts second All Pakistan EFU Convention in Dhaka, East Pakistan Conflicts begins between Khuda Buksh and EFU management on investment policy on East Pakistan.

1969 Khuda Buksh resigns from EFU.
Khuda Buksh establishes Federal Life and Genral Assurance Company, Dhaka, East Pakistan.

1970 Elected a member of the Advisory Committee of the Security and Exchange Authority, Pakistan Elected vice chairman, of the Insurance Association of Pakistan.
Elected director, Pakistan Insurance Corporation.

1971 East Pakistan separates from West Pakistan. Bangladesh (previously known as East Pakistan) emerges as new nation. (16 December 1971)
Khuda Buksh is selected as custodian of Federal Life Assurance Company

1972 Life insurance companies are nationalized in Bangladesh.
Khuda Buksh is selected one of the Directors of National Insurance Corporation

1972 Nominated to managing director, Jiban Bima Corporation (JBC).

1973 Conflicts with Trade Union; Government relieves Buksh from JBC.

1974 Khuda Buksh dies on 13 May. He is laid to rest in Azimpur Graveyard in Dhaka, Bangladesh.

1984 Ahmed Ali establishes Khuda Buksh Smrity Sangsad (KBSS), a memorial committee. A Milad Mahfil and discussions were held at Bangladesh Insurance Academy, Dhaka on Khuda Buksh's life on the occasion of 10th death anniversary under the auspices of KBSS.

2001 Wolfram W. Karnowski publishes *The EFU Saga* which includes "Khuda Buksh Life Insurance was his Mission" under Great Contributors in Chapter III.

2003 Daily Star publishes *Life Insurance Was His Mission – Lest we forget* written by Obaidur Rahim and Shuva Rahim.
Khuda Buksh's family establishes Khuda Buksh Memorial Trust and Foundation.

2008 Khuda Buksh Awarded Bank-Bima Award 2007 (posthumous) for his best contribution in insurance industry by Bank & Bima Magazine.
Khuda Buksh Awarded Bima Padak 2008 (posthumous) by Bangladesh Insurance Executive Club.

2009 Khuda Buksh Memorial Trust and Foundation publishes *Bimabid Khuda Buksh Smaraak Grantha Khuda Buksh Commemorative* Volume (26 February)

A Group Photograph of EFU Personnel and Guests taken on the Eve of Departure of M.S. Haque, (Ex-Branch Manager) to Karachi, July 1953.

Sitting from Left: M/s Hanif, M.Ahmed, E.M.A.Zaman, H. Rashid, K.Buksh (Life Manager), Stricklan(Guest), Major Hoda (Guest), M.S. Huque (Ex-Branch manager), G. Mowla (Guest-National Fire), Alan G. Smith (Guest-Eagle Star), E. Fartado (Guest-ALICO), M.R. Khan (Branch Sececreatry), M.A. Zaman, Q.Hoda, S.A. Ahmed

First row from left: M/s A. Quassem, Samad, R.Rahman, Nehal, Iqbal, Shafiullah, Rowhan Ali, Shafqie, A. Karim, Kamaluddin, Sharif, Nasar, Nesar. A.Hye, Delara, Reazuddin, Manzur-ul-Hasan, S. Khan, Rauf

Second Row from left: M/s M.Ahnad, Alam, Muzaffar, Momtaz, S.Haider, Aftab, A. Mabud, Mannan, Farhad, J.Murdari, Wahab, Md. Jan, Md. Asgar, Md. Razzaque, Md. Rahman, Md. Muslim, Md. A. Barak, M.Aslam

Khuda Buksh receiving P.M. Rebello at Dhaka Airport, 1963.
(P.M. Rebello of Life Insurance Corporation, Bombay, India was invited by EFU to train senior life insurance field officers in Dhaka (E. Pakistan) and Karachi (West Pakistan).

(Source: EFU news Bulletin, Oct 1966.)
A group photo of professional Insurance Agency Trainees at Dhaka EFU office with some of the officers connected to the Training Program.

(Source: EFU news Bulletin, Oct 1966.)
Hafizur Rahman handing over insurance benefit
check to Mosammat Anwara Khatun,
wife of late Md. Azizul Haque, Katnapara,
Bogra, East Pakistan (Bangladesh).

(Sketch Credit: My Da Vinci.)
Khuda Buksh handing over insurance claim
check to Begum Zahida Rahman, wife of
late Dewan Azizur Rahman, Rajshahi, East Pakistan (Bangladesh).

(Source: EFU News Bulletin Jan 1966.)
Nazmul Haq Siddiqui (Assistant Manager, Development, EFU) handing over insurance claim check to Jobeda Khatoon, wife of late Abdul Majid, Sheikherghat, Sylhet, East Pakistan (Bangladesh).

Syed Ali Ahsan, Vice Chancellor Jahangir Nagar University, Dhaka, Bangladesh receiving insurance benefit check (Rs 5,000) on behalf of late Hakim Ali Talukdar in presence of Mrs. Talukdar and her son in settlement of Group Insurance policy (6 March 1972).

(Reprinted with permission from KBMT&F)

Some of the Director's of Federal Life (1969).
Rear Left to Right: Habibur Rahman (Former Central Education Minister and Ambassador, Govt of Pakistan), Ataur Rahman Khan (Advocate Former Chief Minister, East Pakistan), M. Wahiduzzaman (Ex M.N.A. & Former Commerce Minister, Govt of Pakistan), M. Masihur Rahman[97]
Front Row Left to Right: Khuda Buksh, Ataul Haq, (Chairman Commercial Shipping), M.A. Hassan (Director, Hassan Movies Ltd), A. Raquib.

---

[97] M.Masihur Rahman was the Auditor of M/S M.M. Rahman & Co. Chartered Accountants.

(Reprinted with permission from KBMT&F)
Javed Bukth, youngest son of Khuda Buksh receiving
Bank-Bima award (Postmothous) from Feroze Ahmed, Secretary of
Commerce, Government of Bangladesh (28 Feb 2007.)

(Reprinted with permission from KBMT&F)
Ambereen Sultana Islam, daughter of Khuda Buksh
receiving Bima Padak (Insurance Award) (Postmothous)
from Feroze Ahmed, Secretary of Commerce,
Government of Bangladesh (2 June 2007).

Bazlur Rahim, son of Khuda Buksh presenting
Bimabid Khuda Buksh Smarak Grantha
Khuda Buksh Commemorative Volume
to Mr. Zillur Rahman, the President of Bangladesh (2 Nov 2009).

Appendix A

Wolfram W. Karnowski's Letter to Muhammad Rahim

Wolfram W. Karnowski

Ludwig-Behrstrasse 13
82327 TUTZING
Tel. 08158 - 8051
Fax 08158 - 8071

13th of December 2001

My dear *Mr. Mohammed Rahim,*

I was pleasantly surprised when someone from my parent company, the Munichre, phoned and informed me that one Mr. Mohammad Rahim was trying to contact me. I was even more happy when I received your very kind letter.

Eversince my two books, the biography of my close friend, late Mr. Roshen Ali Bhimjee, 'Between tears and laughter' and the EFU SAGA were in the final stage of completion I tried to contact the Khuda Buksh family in Dhaka. It was only through Abul Mahmood, my old colleague, that I received the very unexpected and sad news about the untimely demise of your elder brother. I was really shocked for I had very pleasant memories of my visit to Dhaka in 1998, - as I had written to him in my letter of 5th June of that year. I did not hear from him then and could therefore also not send the lovely photos which I had taken when my wife and I were guests at your mother's house. Abul Bhai also told me that your mother and the family of your late brother had left for the United States, - but he also had no address whatsoever.

Anyhow, - now as we have found each other let us deal with your queries:

- EFU and I, of course, have no objection to your using as much material from my two books for your publication on your late father as you wish to do.

- I am enclosing one copy each of these books for your ready reference. Once you have gone through the books you may then decide whether you really want me to prepare a special write-up on your father for I would have hardly any additional material or memories to make this a rewarding exercise. But, - I might also have second thoughts after you have digested the contents of the two books which I am sending herewith.

I would have also enclosed the photos I mentioned before, - but very unfortunately, I keep them in my Karachi office. I shall be there again in March 2002 and will definitely make it a point to have them posted to you.

Are your mother and your sister-in-law with you or can I reach them elsewhere in the USA!? If they are staying at your place, please, give them my very special salaams.

Meanwhile: 'EID MUBARAK'! May you all spend some peaceful and enjoyable holidays and have a most rewarding 2002!

I look forward to hearing from you again and remain with warmest personal regards to the entire Khuda Buksh clan

Sincerely yours

Appendix B

A Dialogue About The Late Khuda Buksh[98]

(Tape Recorded)

THE FAMILY OF the late Khuda Buksh is planning to publish two books on his life. The first book will be on his life, his contribution in the insurance industry. The second book[99] will be all interviews of the people who knew him well. A number of interviews were completed in Bangladesh. I have conducted a few interviews in Pakistan. With this series of interviews Khuda Buksh Foundation intends to fill the gap of information from Pakistan. Our dialogue will focus on the late Khuda Buksh's charismatic leadership, unique style of salesmanship, contribution to development of human resources, visible impact on Eastern Federal, foreign competition and the local insurance industry. Before we start our talk on the subject matter of the interview, I feel the readers and listeners of our dialogue will definitely appreciate it if you could introduce yourself. Please enlighten them with a few words about yourself and your accomplishments in life.

1. Where and when did you first meet the late Khuda Buksh?
2. Who introduced you to him?
3. What was your first impression? And, there after?
4. Do you have some recollections on the late Khuda Buksh?
5. Is there any particular incident or event that you remember?
6. What was his lifestyle like?
7. Can you shed some light on his business dealings?
8. What did impress you the most?
9. How did the late Khuda Buksh share his vision for your future in Eastern Federal and the industry?
10. What relationship or position did you have with Eastern Federal when the late KB left in 1969?

---

[98] *Khuda Buksh-A History, A Legend* by Rizwan Ahmed Farid (unpublished report), Jan 2004, Karachi, Pakistan, p 44-45.

[99] This book was intended as second book. But due to editorial delays it is being published as the first book.

11. What point of satisfaction have you achieved in your professional or social life?
12. What was the situation – the project, program, etc – in which you had had close interaction with the late Khuda Buksh?
13. What attributes? typical features or quality? of the late KB inspired you the most?
14. With four or five words can you describe how you felt while interacting with the late KB?
15. What were the most common words that the late KB used to use in his daily business and social conversations?
16. How did he resolve disputes and conflicts of interest? Did you have any personal experience?
17. How did the late Khuda Buksh generate the kind of enthusiasm that motivated and inspired people around him to want to perform more and more and more . . . ?
18. In your opinion, was he a team builder? How?
19. In your opinion, how did he build his credibility and trust?
20. In your opinion, did he ever claim or prove his technical ability?
21. Can you describe how did the late Khuda Buksh delegate his authority or to say empowered his associates and subordinates?
22. How did he treat his junior staff or field workers?
23. Do you have any experience of settlement of a disputed claim where you had had KB's help?
24. In your opinion, was he straightforward (outspoken, direct, candid, forthright)?
25. In your opinion, was KB a willing listener, accepted feedback and criticism?
26. In your opinion, how good was he in communicating his ideas in Agency Meetings?
27. How did you rate him as an orator?
28. What methods, techniques, ideas, or strategies did the late Khuda Buksh incorporate into his formal and informal reward processes to recognize and celebrate the achievement of extra ordinary performance by an individual or a group?
29. Can you shed some light as to what was the cause for the late Khuda Buksh's abrupt resignation in 1969 when he was truly the doyen of life business not only in Eastern Federal, but also Pakistan?
30. What were your thoughts when you heard the news that the late KB launched his own company in the eastern wing of the country?

31. In your opinion, did the late Khuda Buksh ever feel that the phenomenal progress achieved by Eastern Federal during the decade of the 60s was wrongly attributed to some personalities other than the late Khuda Buksh?
32. Did you ever feel like that too? (phenomenal progress achieved by Eastern Federal during the decade of the 60s was wrongly attributed to some personalities other than the late Khuda Buksh?)
33. The late Roshan Ali Bhimjee and Khuda Buksh were the most important players of a successful, dynamic and winning team – The Eastern Federal Union Insurance Company. Can you separately and distinctly define each one's role?
34. What immediate impact did you observe on Eastern Federal, if any, after the late Khuda Buksh's resignation?
35. Did you attend the Eastern Federal's Dhaka Convention for the Field Force in 1967?
36. How did you find the courtesy and hospitality extended by hosts there?
37. How were the arrangements, the grandeur, and the feel of Dhaka Convention?
38. Is there any interesting interaction, event or incident that you remember?
39. Can you add some other thoughts on the subject matter of our talk?
40. Do you have an example of a leader like the late KB in the insurance industry?
41. Do you know any person in the insurance industry who has/had followed the foot steps set by the late KB in the insurance industry?
42. Do you have any photograph(s) of the late Khuda Buksh, which may possibly be used for publication?

Thank you Mr . . . . for sharing your memories and views. Can you tell where and how Khuda Buksh Foundation can approach you for your cooperation, and, also for sharing your memoirs as well as your point of view?

Appendix C

Dialogue of An Insurance Giant[100]

AS THE TWIN-ENGINED Pakistan International Fokker Friendship touched the tarmac of fashionable Chittagong Airport at 4:10 P.M. on 4.11.65, a hurried Deputy General Manager, dressed in dark-gray lounge suit, came out of the plane with a broad smile on his face. Just 45 minutes back, Mr. Khuda Buksh was found sitting tight in his red-carpeted and air-conditioned chamber of Dacca Office, where he worked with the agility of a Fire-brigade Officer'. He dictated sixteen letters, issued half-a-dozen circulars, signed more than three hundred papers, met at least twenty-three visitors, responded minimum twenty one telephone calls, dialed more than seventeen numbers and sent over ten telegrams. His favorite item 'chicken soup' got cold in his five-course-lunch as he reached his residence with hardly 35 minutes to go for the Chittagong-bound-plane to take off on its flight. In an astonishingly hurried manner, he took his lunch while his graceful Begum Sahiba looked bewildered at her illustrious husband who happens to be the number-one-man in Insurance in the country. Mr. Khuda Buksh was taxied to Dacca Air Port by his German-made fabulous Mercedes-Benz and he boarded the waiting plane which carried him to Chittagong City, the beauty-queen of the East, washed by the mighty Bay of Bengal, where his band of lieutenants received him in an atmosphere charged with friendship and cordiality.

On the following day, Mr. Khuda Buksh addressed two meetings – one in the morning and another in the evening, The first meeting was meant for the organization officers and the second meeting was exclusively meant for the agents who are, according to the Deputy General Manager, the pillars and the backbone of the Company. In both the meetings, Mr. Khuda Buksh gave an extempore speech – the phraseology of the speech that he delivered in the morning session different from that of the evening session to a great extent; but the main theme of both the speeches, surprisingly enough, remained one and the same. "Grow more food" was the cry of the Government, and "do more business' was the cry of the Deputy General Manager. Alerting the field officers that the coming days were going to be more crucial as life Insurance business was concerned, the Deputy General Manager counseled 'hard work', 'determined drive' and 'sincere endeavor'. We are still far off from our target set for 1965, but if you work with proper seriousness and determination, nothing under the sun will deter us from achieving our target, Inshallah', he said.

---

[100]Eastern Zone Field Force Bulletin, November, 1965.

In his own forceful, straightforward and characteristic way, he told the agents that they were the prestige of Pakistan since they were striving hard to make a better, richer and fuller Pakistan through life insurance. "We must bring about a fundamental reorientation in our plans to write more and more business", the Deputy General Manager added.

The Deputy General Manager reminded the East Pakistan workers of their target of Rs. 20 crores (200 million) new paid-for business for 1965 and said, "to some it may sound as a legend, to others a miracle or a magic, but to you, I am sure, it is a fact, as solid as a rock, as shining as a star. All that you have to do is plunge into the field with all power and Inshallah victory will be ours." The Deputy General Manager further said," You have only a handful of days before you and it is my earnest appeal to you and to your conscience to utilize every minute in a most befitting manner so that you can exceed your target before the year is out and in doing so, you will only enhance the prestige of Pakistan".

In course of his speech, Mr. Khuda Buksh also referred to the company's All Pakistan Convention to be held at Dacca sometime in early 1966 and asked the field officers and agents to work very hard so that they might get a berth in the Convention, which would be very colourful, jubilant and hilarious one, The Deputy General Manager also expressed his deep sense of gratitude to Messers. Chowdhury, Karim and other field workers of Chittagong for their commendable services towards the company as well as to the cause of insurance.

Penned by : Hossain Mir Musharraf

Appendix D

A Clarion Call[101]

IN THIS SUB-CONTINENT in recent years, under the dynamic and functional leadership of Mr. Khuda Buksh, the great patriarch of the Eastern Federal Union Assurance Company's field-force, we have witnessed what Insurance as a carear can be. In about a decade's time quite a number of freshers in the profession have been writing crores of rupees business per year. Within the last few years the Generalissimo Roshen Ali Bhimjee and his able Commander-in Chief of the Life Business operation, Mr. Khuda Buksh has placed the Eastern Federal on the world map of Insurance. In fact the miracle has happend because Khuda Buksh gave the objective analysis of the career and said truthfully what is the profession. He says:

> Keep your watchful eyes ever vigilant so that no breadwinner of your area of activities dies leaving his family uncared for. Fight out like Hercules the colossus of un-certainty, unrest, of hard times' by offering life assurance protection. Attain belief in the job. Have firm conviction that life assurance is the most noble profession. Have faith that intelligent and honest endeavour never goes unrewarded. You must develop determination and enthusiasm.
>
> Your ambition must touch the star over your head. You must work diligently and persistently towards a particular objective. Plan today your work for tomorrow and do today what you planned yesterday. Make contact with as many people as you can. Spend the major portion of your time in presence of your prospects, act courteously, be tactful in presentation and you will find that it is easier to get than to miss business.

Therefore, when one comes to the profession, let him be not under illusion. In his message to the field workers, Khuda Buksh has very truly said – "Your duty is onerous."

---

[101] *Reprinted from ON TO ULTIMA THULE, by A.F.M. SAFIYYULLAH Insurance Underwriters' Syndicate Dacca (East Pakistan, August, 1967).*

Appendix E

Mymensingh Accords Hearty Welcome To The General Manager

[Following is the full text of the address of welcome read out by Mr. M. A. Qasem, Senior Regional Manager, on the occasion of the General Manager's visit to Mymensingh on Saturday, the 24th Dec., 1966 – Editor][102]

Respected Sir,

We are indeed grateful to you for giving us this unique privilege to accord a most sincere welcome to you in our midst here at Mymensingh and we hasten to express our heartfelt thankfulness for the kindness you have shown to us inspite of your numerous pre-occupations.

To-day is virtually a red letter day for our region. Your very presence to-day, Sir, amongst us is a proof if any were at all needed, of your deep solicitude for us. We cannot but be grateful to you for the extraordinary Humane qualities of your head and heart and the generous manner with which you have always treated us. The very fact that you have kindly agreed to give us your august company here goes out to show how profoundly you love us and hold us in affection.

Sir, you have not only built a reputation for yourself of being the Country's most outstanding Insurance salesman, but it is also due to your most sincere labour and hard endeavour that EASTERN FEDERAL is now the country's largest insurer. You have been very successfully piloting the destiny of the Company and we are rightly proud that to-day EASTERN FEDERAL enjoys an enviable position in the Afro-Asian Countries. We gratefully acknowledge the services that you have been rendering immediately after your joining, by undertaking the enormous and gigantic task of carrying the message of insurance to every nook and corner of the country. You joined the EASTERN FEDERAL in 1952 as its life Manager for East Pakistan. In this capacity, you increased the Life Business of the Company from barely Rs. 25 lacs to 7.51 crores (2.5 million to 75 million) in 1960. You can again justly take pride in the rapid expansion of the company's business, which amounted to Rs. 35 crores (350 million) in 1965. To-day, Sir, EASTERN FEDERAL needs you more than you need EASTERN FEDERAL.

---

[102] EFU Eastern Zone Field Force Review, December 1966.

Sir, we are fully aware of the philosophy of your life. It has always been your guiding principle to serve humanity through insurance. We can assure you Sir, that you will not find us lagging behind from this noble mission. We are determined to complete this year a new paid-for business of at least Rs. 85 lacs of new Life Business from Mymensingh district thereby, diffusing the benefits of insurance to the bulk of the populace and we shall consider no endeavour too great in reaching our goal. God willing, we shall surpass our Target and we shall keep the flag of EASTERN FEDERAL hoisted high on the soil of Mymensingh.

Sir, your very presence amidst us has greatly imbibed us with the spirit of working hard and harder still and we shall leave no stone unturned to discharge the duties assigned to us most faithfully, so that our TARGET for 1966 is not only beaten but we can create an unprecedented record in the history of insurance. Please bless us so that we can come out successful in our mission.

Sir, we do not look upon you only as our Chief, but as our leader also, who is fully aware of our conditions and necessities and with due respect, we approach you to-day with one humble demand for your kind consideration. We shall be extremely grateful to you if you would kindly appoint a Cashier in the Mymensingh Office to collect premiums, to that we can provide still better and more efficient service to our esteemed proponents and policy-holders in our mutual interest.

We beg to subscribe Sir; and thank you once again from the core of our hearts for your kindly affording us this unique opportunity to meet you in a cordial and informal atmosphere.

Most respectfully yours,
Members of the Organisation,
Mymensingh Zone

Appendix F

An Open Letter to All Members of the Field Force

 THE EASTERN FEDERAL UNION INSURANCE CO., LTD.
Territorial Head Office : Dienfa Building, Jinnah Avenue, Dacca—2

An Open Letter to all members of the Field Force

Dated, January 21, 1967

Dear Co-Workers,

The year 1966 is closed and gone. Sweet memories left by it will not, however, be forgotten. It is indeed gratifying to note that once again our Field Force has set up a record in the annals of Insurance Industry by completing over Rs. 450 millions of New Life Business during the year 1966.

I am proud of my lion-hearted Field Force. The entire insurance industry of Pakistan is proud of you. The completion of more than 450 millions of new life business is a great feat, which has demonstrated successfully the adroitness and determination of high order displayed by all the members of our organisation. I fervently look forward to a tremendous boost up in business in the coming years also. I offer my heartiest congratulations to all of you.

Dear Friends, I once again repeat that completion of more than 450 millions of new paid-for business within the course of 12 months is not a mean achievement. It is a great, joyous occasion for each and all of us. You have created a most inspiring record of achievement in modern insurance salesmanship which is the envy and dream of the best of salesmen. Undaunted in crisis, magnificient in action and noble in victory, you are a battalion with your heads held high and spirit undiminished. You have said good bye to 1966 riding on the crest of triumph, glory and fame. I once again take my hats off to you for your most splendid performance. I am really grateful to all of you.

They say increase in new business, increase in premium income, increase of new policies and increase in the strength of the field force have become normal phenomena with EASTERN FEDERAL. But an increase of 10 crores of new business in 1966, over the preceding year's figure of Rs. 35 crores has surprised all and sundry in the country, because this remarkable achievement was made when the Company had already written a very huge amount of business during the previous year. But these outstanding achievements should not be allowed to make us complacent or excessively proud. On the contrary, we should be modest and humble if we want to serve our people with still greater efficiency.

Friends, I am quite aware that you had a very tough time during the last phase of the year, when you all worked round-the-clock with all the might and energy at your command. I am also aware that your wives and children had also sacrificed a lot because you had all plunged into the field day in and day out and they very often missed the pleasure of your sweet company. My heart also goes out to thank them mot sincerely for their noble piece of job. I am proud to say that your company could not have achieved this glory but for their tacit support and encouragement. They were the incentive for our field force to work hard and still harder. My words fail to thank them adequately and it would be my greatest pleasure to remain ever indebted to them.

Friends, I am alive to the fact that human beings require relaxation after hard labour and arrangements are being made in a feverish way to make the forthcoming Convention at Dacca all the more attractive and delightful for your delegates. They will have enough of fun and merriment in the Convention which will be really memorable. The Company's Annual Target for completion of new life business during the current year will be fixed up in the Convention in consultation with your delegates, and you will have to again work with still greater zeal and enthusiam to make 1967 even more successful. You are the architects of a new history and let us all join our hands to create another history in 1967.

I congratulate you all once again most cordially for your wonderful performance during 1966 and wish you and other members of your family a better, richer and fuller life.

Wishing you all the best,

Yours sincerely,

(KHUDA BUKSH)
General Manager.

Appendix G

KHUDA BUKSH IS Commissioned A KENUCKY COLONEL

COMMONWEALTH OF KENTUCKY

WENDELL H. FORD
GOVERNOR

To all to Whom These Presents Shall Come, Greeting:

Know Ye, That _HONORABLE KHUDA BUKSH, DACCA, BANGLADESH_

Is Commissioned A

KENTUCKY COLONEL

I hereby confer this honor with all the rights, privileges and responsibilities thereunto appertaining.

In testimony whereof, I have caused these letters to be made patent, and the seal of the Commonwealth to be hereunto affixed. Done at Frankfort, the 19th day of April in the year of our Lord one thousand nine hundred and 73 and in the one hundred and 81st year of the Commonwealth.

By the Governor

Secretary of State

By _____
Assistant Secretary of State

Appendix H

Rotary News on Khuda Buksh's Death

NUMBER 35, YEAR 1973-74
MAY 14, 1974

BELOVED RTN. KHUDA BUKSH IS NO MORE

The universally-loved Rotarian and the doyen of insurance industry Rtn. Khuda Buksh is no more. A massive heart attack on the 13th May took away this valiant son of the country at the Dacca Medical College Hospital where he was ailing for sometime past.

Rtn. Khuda Buksh began his insurance career 36 years ago. He is the one figure among Bengali Muslims who popularised life insurance among the people. His name itself is an institution and in his own lifetime he became a legendary figure.

Extremely kind-hearted, soft-speaking, gentle and human, Rtn. Khuda Buksh was endowed with the noblest human qualities which endeared him to a large mass of people. In fellow-feeling, fraternal sympathy and empathy for fellow human beings he excelled most.

As a Rotarian, Rtn. Khuda Buksh was a jewel of the Club and was active all throughout. He became a Senior Active member in 1972 and was holding the post of Hony Treasurer for the past two years. His amiable presence in our Club meetings, his humour, his concern for every Rotarian will be sorely missed by our Club. His death is a sad loss to our Club.

His Namaz-e-Janaja was held at Baitul Mukarram after Zohr prayer and he was buried a short while ago at New Azimpura graveyard.

To his grief-stricken wife Mrs. Zubeda, his five sons and one daughter, our Club offers the most heartfelt sympathy and our prayer goes to the Almighty for his soul to rest in peace.

ঢাকা রোটারী পত্রিকা
DACCA ROTARY NEWS

Appendix I

AS I SEE IT

Astryx[103]

We have suffered the sad loss of two of our friends in very quick succession. First, Mr. Khuda Buksh, one of our best talents in the life insurance field. Second, Dr. Mazharul Huq, a typical product of the University of Dacca in its best tradition.

I came to know Mr. Khuda Buksh in October, 1946, in Calcutta on return from the U.K. Mr. Khuda Buksh began his career with Oriental life of Bombay as an agent, but in 1946 he was an inspector. That was a time of great communal unrest in Calcutta. But Khuda Buksh moved about quite unconcerned, cool and composed. He was extremely popular both with Hindus and Muslims. At that time there were very few Muslims employed as inspectors by the Oriental. But he earned it by dint of sheer merit. I found him extremely loyal and helpful to his friends.

On coming to Dacca he joined the Eastern Federal which he built up practically from scratch, and rose to the top but his love of justice and fairness and advocacy for the interests of Bangalees brought him into clashes with Pakistani high-ups, and resigned and then organized another company-Federal life.

Khuda Buksh had an uncanny flair for life insurance business and his organizing ability in the field was, perhaps, incomparable in Bangladesh.

He was soft-spoken and a man of suave manner. He has perhaps, given employment to more Bangalees in insurance than anybody else. His motto of life seemed to be, work and more work to save Bangladesh . . .

I was returning home after my walk one evening when I came across Khuda Buksh not for from my home doing some shopping. As usual, he greeted me effusively, making all kinds of inquiries. He did not look too well, but nothing seemed to be worried about either. He insisted on his giving me a lift. I insisted that I was out for my walk and didn't want a ride. But I could not avoid him that was the last I saw of him.

Khuda Buksh worked his way up and reached the top. People of this type often turn out to be uppish and also snobbish. But Khuda Buksh was a real exception. Because he remembered his early struggles, he was always a good Samaritan to those who had to struggle to make their way in the world.

---

[103] Bangladesh Observer, 3rd June, 1974

One of his teachers in his village middle English school who used to be kind to him, has received from him a handsome monthly allowance for the last forty years or so. Not only that, that gentleman was at least once a year brought to live with him for days together and used to be treated as a son treats his father . . .

Appendix J

A STORY AND FEW QUOTES FROM PUBLICATIONS: 1967-2010

- One chilly evening of January, 1953, possibly first week of the month, I was deeply engaged in my office work, when a big car stopped in front of my office and elderly gentleman stepped down from the car to enquire about the officer over there. I got up from my chair to welcome him and introduced myself, "I am M.A. Rashid. Inspector, EFU Insurance Company in this district of Mymensingh and this is my office." The gentleman was Additional S.P., Head-Quarter and he wanted to talk to me in connection with the death of his son-in-law, Mr . . . . who had life assurance with the Eastern Federal and expired at Dhaka Medical College Hospital due to an accident that took place at Mymensingh in early January, 1953.

    Next morning I hurried to our Dhaka office to report about the death and met Mr. Khuda Buksh., the then Life Manager for East Pakistan. In reply, he told me that he was aware of it and had taken up the matter himself to settle the claim at the earliest possible time, and as a matter of fact the claim was settled in course of reasonable time and the cheque for Rs. 15,000 [$3,150] was handed over by me to the widow, a young mother of three children, aged 3 ½ years, 2 years and 2 or 3 months, toward whom I could not look face to face being overpowered with grief while I was passing the cheque to her trembling hands.

    (M.A. Rashid, "Role of Life Assiurance", in *Symposium on Life Insurance in Pakistan,* ed. A.F.M. Safiyyullah and Mir Mosharraf Hossain, July 1967, pp 59-60)

- Mr. Khuda Buksh is not the most outstanding and sensational Insurance Salesman in Pakistan, he is also an authority on the subject Life Insurance both practical and theoretical . . . Mr. Khuda Buksh is now the country's the most magnetic and dynamic Insurance Executive . . .

    (Page xxv – *Symposium on Life Insurance in Pakistan,* Edited by A.FM. Safiyyullah & Mir Musharraf Hossain, July 1967)

- I found in Mr. Khuda Buksh an image of a patriarch keen for the welfare of family members. Through the reviews and training projects I became known to the EFU men and finally he wanted educational programme to be drawn-up; and I am confident that posterity will remember him for the prophetic role he played as an educator to the vast number of field force who placed faith in his leadership and took insurance as career . . .

    (Page xiii – *Ultima Thule: A loud Thinking of Life Insurance in Pakistan* by A.F.M. Safiyullah, Sept 1967)

- The late Khuda Buksh's role in expanding Life Insurance will be unforgettable.

    (*Dainik Ittefaq* (The Daily Ittefaq), Dacca, Bangladesh 15 May 1974; Comments by Moyeedul Islam, Managing Director, Jiban Bima Corporation, Bangladesh)

- May 13, 1974 . . . Mr. Khuda Buksh, a pioneer in the insurance industry, passed away.

    (Page 101 – *Bangladesh: The First Four Years (From 16 December 1971 to 15 December 1975)* by Nurul Momen; published by The Bangladesh Institute of Law International Affairs, 1980)

- So dedicated. The man was totally and completely devoted to life insurance. Any time of the day and night, any time from morning 'til evening, any time in the house or in the office, the man did not talk anything about but life insurance. He was totally committed to his profession . . .

    (Page 454 – *The EFU SAGA* by Wolfram W. Karnowski; published by M. Yunus, D & Y Printers, Karachi, Pakistan, 2001)

- He (Khuda Buksh) led Eastern Federal Union Insurance Co. Ltd. from almost bankruptcy to a prestigious role in the insurance field not only in Pakistan, but also in Southeast Asia and Africa. No external factors explain these extraordinary increments in performance – his dynamic leadership is the only answer left . . .

    (Challenges of Life Insurance Marketting – Business Applications *by Rizwan Ahmed Farid*; Publication pending, Karachi, Pakistan, 2010)

Appendix K

A Brief Profile of the Contributors

Wolfram W. Karnowski was born in Hamburg, Germany, in 1930. He was closely associated with the late Mr. Roshen Ali Bhimjee and the EFU Group of Companies for the last four decades. He spent six years (1960-1966) with EFU in Karachi, Pakistan, before joining its parent organization, Munich Reassurance Company (Munichre) in Munich, Germany. He retired from Munichre in 1995 as one of its senior executives. Later, he joined the EFU Group in Karachi, Pakistan, as a director and advisor before his retirement. He is the author of two books, entitled *The EFU Saga* and *Roshen Ali Bhimjee Between Tears and Laughter- A Biography*.

Harunur Rashid started his career in insurance by joining EFU as an officer on May 1, 1948. He served EFU as a senior officer, after which he was transferred to the company's General Department and underwent training in all branches of the general insurance business. In 1959, he passed the Associateship of Chartered Insurance Institute (ACII) in London. In 1960, he was appointed a branch manager at Sylhet. He left EFU in 1961 and subsequently served as a manager at Khyber Insurance Limited, a general manager at Eastern Mercantile Limited, a manager at the Great Eastern Insurance Company, the chief manager at the Pakistan Insurance Corporation of East Pakistan and the managing director of Bangladesh Insurance Corporation. He was director of the Karnafuli Bima Corporation, the general manager of Jiban Bima Corporation, the director of Bangladesh Insurance Academy and the Controller of Insurance for the government of Bangladesh. He was also an executive director at United Insurance Company Limited. At present, he is a director at United Insurance Company Limited.

Mosleh Uddin Ahmed started his career as a clerk in EFU in 1961. He joined Federal Life and General Insurance Company in 1969 as an officer and served there for three years. Later, he joined the Jiban Bima Corporation, where he worked until 1984. He served as a general manager at Bangladesh General Insurance Company, a managing director at Loyeds Insurance Company Limited, a managing director at Express Insurance Limited and a joint managing director at Eastland Insurance Company in Bangladesh before his retirement.

A. R. Chowdhury joined EFU in 1948 as an agent, and he served the Company in various capacities in the Chitagong (Bangladesh) field organization. He attended the Company's All Pakistan Insurance Convention held in Karachi in 1963. In 1964, he became a development manager in Chittagong and held that post until the nationalization of the insurance industry. He was a general manager at the Jiban Bima Corporation of the Chittagong region before his retirement in 1984.

Mujib-ud-Daula has had a distinguished career in life insurance that spanned a period of over 50 years. He started his career with the American Life Insurance Company in 1954. He served the Homeland Insurance Company, Eastern Federal Union Insurance Company, Muslim Insurance Company, the Rupsa Jiban Bima Corporation and Delta Life Insurance Company Limited. He was a managing director at Meghna Insurance Company. Under his able leadership, Meghna Life Insurance Company established as one of the leading life insurance companies in Bangladesh. He has traveled to many countries, including Switzerland, West Germany, England and the US. He is a member of the Board of Governors of the Bangladesh Insurance Academy. At present, Mujib-ud-Daula is an adviser for Meghna Life Insurance Company Limited, Dhaka, Bangladesh.

Nazmul Haq Siddiqui started his insurance career as a part-time agent while he was a college student. In 1952, he joined Norwich Union Insurance company as a full-time agent and became an inspector of agencies in National Insurance Company of India. When National Insurance closed its business in Pakistan in 1956 he joined the newly formed Premier Insurance Company of Pakistan and within a short time proved his worth as one of the successful organization builders. In 1958, he was promoted to organizing secretary for the whole of Chittagong division. In 1961, he joined Eastern Insurance Company as assistant life manager and virtually helped to establish the life department of the comany. In 1964, he left the Eastern Insurance and worked for sometimes as life manager for East Pakistan National Security Insurance Company Ltd. In the same year, he joined EFU and managed two divisions, Rajshahi and Chittagong. In 1969, he joined as manager for the Federal Life and General Insurance Company till Bangladesh was born and insurance companies were nationalized. He served as a deputy general manager at Jiban Bima Corporation. He was the managing director of the National Life Insurance Company and a technical Advisor for the Jubilee Insurance Company of the Aga Khan Group in Kenya. He is the author of a book entitled *Jiban Bima (Life Insurance)*. He died on January 19, 2004.

A. B. M. Nurul Haq, M.A., has been associated with the insurance profession for more than four decades. He started his career in insurance with EFU and was the founding secretary and personnel manager of the former Federal Life and General Insurance Company Limited, and he was the secretary and officer in-charge of the former Surma Jiban Bima Corporation. Haq served as a general manager of Jiban Bima Corporation until 1995. He also served as a managing director at Northern General Insurance Company Limited since 1996. Before joining this company, Haq was the managing director of Islamic Insurance Bangladesh Limited. Haq is a well-known, professionally qualified insurance executive in Bangladesh. He has received specialized training on insurance in Karachi, Switzerland, Germany, Japan and Malaysia and has attended many international conferences. He has also presented papers on insurance in general and Islamic insurance in particular in many international seminars and workshops.

His awards include Top Insurance Man (2001 and 2002) by the Bangladesh Journalist Association, Best Islamic Insurance Man (2004) by Financial News Services in Dhaka, Bangladesh. A.B.M. Nurul Haq is the 2007 recipient of the *Bank-Bima* Award for his outstanding contribution to Islamic insurance. He is the president of the Bangladesh Insurance Executive Club (BIEC) and the past president of the Rotary Club of Motijheel, Dhaka, Bangladesh.

Mir Mosharraf Hossain, M.A., LL.B., is a poet, essayist, novelist, journalist, orator and editor. He received his early education in Calcutta. He was the member of Bengali Seminar Committee, Dhaka University and convenor Bengali Language Association Jaganath College, Dhaka, Bangladesh. He was assistant secretary of the Apex Club of Dhaka and an active member of the Pakistan Writer's Guild, Bengali Academy and many other social and academic institutions. He started his career with Homeland Insurance Company. In 1963, he joined EFU as a personal secretary of Khuda Buksh. He was the editor of "Eastern Zone Field Review" and "Spot Light." He translated and prepared a substantial number of leaflets, prospectuses and Tables of Rates in Bengali. He is the author of dozens of publications in Bengali. He was the general manager of Administration and Public Relations at the Jiban Bima Corporation before his retirement.

Abdul Jabbar Mehman started his career as a part-time agent at Muslim Insurance Company and EFU in 1954. He later joined the American Life Insurance Company and rose to the position of agency manager. In 1967, he joined EFU as an agency manager and contributed greatly to the development of business. In 1969, he joined the Federal Life and General Insurance Company. Later he was in-charge of Group Insurance at Jiban Bima Corpoation, Bangladsh. He is presently the editor of the fortnightly "Bank-Bima" magazine. The magazine covers news related to banking insurance, the commerce industry and society in Bangladesh.

Majibur Rahman started his career in insurance as an agent of EFU in 1961. He became a highly by mastering the art of overcoming rejection very quickly. He became an Inspector of EFU in 1965 and was named as one of the "Stars of the Field" in the Zone A of East Pakistan. He was promoted to senior develoment officer in 1966. He served numerous clients who put their faith in insurance and selected EFU for their protection. He was "a giant in procurement of life insurance business for Eastern Federal Union and thereafter in the Jiban Bima Corporation." He was a deputy general manager at the Jiban Bima Corporation and one of the founding directors of Padma Islamic Life Insurance Company Limited in Dhaka, Bangladesh.

Husna Banu Khanam a pioneering cultural activist of the country. She was a musician, artist, writer and professor at the Home Economics College in Dhaka, Bangladesh. She received the national Begum Rokeya Padak Award in 2004 for her contributions to the socioeconomic uplifting of women, establishment of women rights and spread of women's education. She died on May 30, 2006.

Rizwan Ahmed Farid is a well renowned senior marketing professional in the insurance industry in Pakistan. He is the most sought after guest/seminar speaker on account of his knowledge capital and vast experience. He has about fifty years experience in private, multinational and public sectors industrial and financial services marketing, leadership, product design, recruitment, selection, training, and development of human capital. He retired from State Life Insurance Corporation as a senior executive of Marketing and as Principal of the Training Academy in the year 2001. More recently, he served as consultant for Asia Care Health and Life Insurance Company and Dawood Family Takaful Limited.

He has been an outstanding teacher, facilitator and course designer for leadership and executive development programs that help managers in organizational excellence. He has conducted several interactive learning workshops and conferences in the area of customer focus organizational development, team building, performance and productivity problems. Besides, Karachi University, Jinnah University, IBA; Navy and Air Force Officers Mess; and Rotary Clubs; Standard Chartered Bank Ltd., CLU Life Assurance, American Life, Eastern Federal, State Life, all have sought his expertise and opinion by inviting him to many seminars and workshops. He also pioneered Home Service Beema (Micro Life Insurance) in the Eastern Federal Union Insurance Company Ltd. in 1970/72.

Farid designed and taught "Insurance Marketing and Salesmanship" Course for Pakistan Insurance Institute for their Diploma Course. He has published many papers in the Insurance Journal of international repute.

He served as consultant and major contributor for Khuda Buksh Memorial Trust & Foundation, Dhaka, for their forth coming book, *"Khuda Buksh: The Pioneer of Life Insurance in Bangladesh,"* to be published by University Press Ltd., Bangladesh.

Farid has visited USA, UK, UAE, Indonesia, Saudi Arabia, India, and Bangladesh which enhanced his knowledge about financial services marketing around the globe.

An International Consultant based in Karachi, Pakistan, Farid, currently manages human capital, financial services' marketing and field development strategies of Alchemy Technologies Private Limited.

Michael Joseph Pereira obtained a Masters of Science in theoretical physics from the University of Dhaka and then moved to Karachi and to finished a master of business administration. He was selected under the Eastern Federal's Officer's Training Scheme. After training, Pereira joined EFU as a full-fledged officer in March, 1967. He was a member of Khuda Buksh's team at the headquarters in Karachi, Pakistan, from March 1967, until Khuda Buksh retired. Pereira was associated with the life insurance industry for 33 years. In 2000, Pereira retired from his position as executive director at State Life Insurance Corporation in Pakistan. He is now an advisor to Arif Habib Securities Limited in Pakistan.

Naimuddin Khan joined Eastern Federal in 1948. He worked as the superintendent of the company's general department until 1956. He left Eastern

Federal in 1958 and joined the American Life Insurance Company. After Pakistan nationalized the insurance industry, he worked with State Life Insurance Corporation. Khan retired from State Life as Assistant General Manager.

M.A. Chishti is one of the few experts in the field of insurance in Pakistan. He has been associated with the insurance profession for more than six decades and has distinguished himself as an industry spokesman for more than two decades. He started his career as a junior officer in 1947 with the Eastern Federal Union Insurance Company. Later he gained experience with London Lancashire Insurance Company as an office superintendent and with American International Underwriters Group and Employers Liability Insurance as a branch manager. M.A. Chishti has held several leadership positions, including General Manager, New Jubilee Insurance Company in Karachi and Managing Director (1968 to 1975), Standard Insurance Company, a subsidiary of Standard Bank Limited. Following the nationalization of banking and insurance, he joined New Jubilee Insurance as an advisor. Subsequently, he became the managing director of Muslim Insurance Company (1981-1988) and then the managing director of Prime Insurance, a subsidiary of Prudential Group and Delta Insurance, in 1998. M.A. Chishti has written various newspaper articles on insurance in Pakistan and abroad. His books include *Insurance Industry Policies & Practices in Pakistan* (1987) and *How to Sell Insurance* (2000). He also published a book in Urdu (1991). He has been the chairman of the Extent Committee, the chairman of the Merit Committee and the chairman of the Fire Committee. M.A. Chishti also held the position of chairman for the Pakistan Insurance Institute (PII) for four years. "He has devoted his entire life to the improvement and development of insurance industry. His approach has been that of an honest reformer and a frank critic, fearless by exhibiting complete grasp of the subject and logical conduct of his discourse."

Iftekhar Ahmed Hanfi migrated from India to Pakistan in 1947. He excelled in his studies and completed his M.A. in 1960, at which point he joined Eastern Federal. He credits the late Khuda Buksh as his reason for joining the company. He was the regional manager of Eastern Federal. After the nationalization of insurance in Pakistan, Eastern Federal became part of State Life Insurance Corporation. Hanfi later retired from his profession as the development manager of State Life Insurance Corporation in Pakistan.

Abul Mahmood was "one of the legendary figures" of life business in Easten Federal Union Insurance Company prior to nationalization. He hails from West Bengal, India. After completing his education, he completed his British-Indian government service at Kolkata in December 1941. After three years, the Ministry of Industries transferred him to Delhi. After partition, he opted for Pakistan. He came to Pakistan as an employee of his old ministry, which was then called the Ministry of Foreign Affairs. He was involved in several foreign missions. During this time, he became a life insurance agent. Abul Mahmood initially joined Eastern Federal as a part-time agent and later became full-time. He was a deputy manager at Eastern Federal, and he produced large volumes of business for the company's life insurance department in the 1960s. After nationalization, Abul Mahmood joined State Life Insurance Corporation as one of its senior executives. After retiring from State Life, Abul joined EFU General.

Ahkam Siddiqui, a dynamic insurance salesman, became involved in life insurance after completing his education at the University of Aligarh in India. He migrated to Pakistan in 1963 and joined Eastern Federal as an organization officer at Hyderabad. In 1969, he became a division manager at Eastern Federal. Ahkam eventually became the deputy general manager of the Southern Zone of State Life Insurance Corporation in Pakistan before his retirement on July 9, 1999.

M. Fasihuddin migrated from India to Pakistan with his parents in 1948. He earned a Masters Degree in Economics from Karachi University and thereafter he completed LLB. He started his career with the Bank of Bahawalpur. He applied for the Eastern Federal Executive Officers Training Scheme (EOTC) in 1963. Fasihuddin was one of the four persons selected in the first batch among 1,700 applicants of EOTC. After completion of that scheme, Fasihuddin remained in training with various departments for further general training, and, after six months of initial training in Karachi, he was sent to the New India Insurance Company in Mumbai, India, for seven months. During this time, he began to study for the Associateship of the Chartered Insurance Institute (ACII). He passed all tests in just two years, which is the shortest time allowed for completing. He holds the record in Pakistan for having passed seven tests in only one attempt. Fasihuddin became a branch manager in 1972 and subsequently became the rural head looking after Sind and Baluchistan when about 30 branches were opened. Subsequently, Fasihuddin became the deputy managing director of Eastern Federal, and after serving for five years, he requested retirement in 2002. He was a chairman of the Fire Committee for several years and a chairman of the Marine Committee for nearly eight years. He also served at the Karachi Insurance Institute for two years and the Council of Pakistani Insurance Institute until 2002. Fasihuddin has presented several papers at various international seminars in Pakistan and various other countries, including Turkey, Iran, Switzerland, the UK and France. He served as an advisor to EFU for two years before his retirement.

M. B. Qadri, B.A migrated to Pakistan from India in 1965. After serving in a government organization, he joined the insurance industry as an agent. He joined Eastern Federal in June of 1966. Later, he joined the company's research and planning department, where he worked until 1971. After the nationalization of the insurance industry, Qadri joined State life Insurance Corporation. At present, he is head of the training department. His roles include staff training, coordinating membership to various organizations, and sending staff officers to various organizations in order to further develop staff.

Vazir Ali F. Mohammad B. Com., LL.B., is a chartered accountant from the Institute of Chartered Accountants in Pakistan. He joined the Life Department of EFU as an accountant in September of 1967. During his career with EFU, he developed computer accounting systems and was instrumental in introducing cash registers and then National Cash Register (NCR) accounting machines. While he was chief accountant at Eastern Federal, he did all the computerization planning for the company and designed the basic code system that is still in use today. After spending thirteen years in the life and general insurance business as a financial executive, he spent about seven years at the Aga Khan University Hospital and Medical College as an internal auditor. He has over 30 years experience in voluntary community social service and received the Gold Medal Awarded by His Highness the Aga Khan in 1983 for 25 years of Voluntary Community Service. Currently, Vazir is the executive director at the Hashoo Group of Companies.

Mohammed Choudhury has had a distinguished career in general insurance of over 60 years. He started his career in 1947 with Eastern Federal Union Insurance Company in Kolkata. Later, he joined the Norwich Union Insurance Company in Kolkata and was transferred to Karachi. In 1952, he joined the Premier Insurance Company as assistant manager and rose to the position of general manager. He joined the Adamjee Insurance Company in 1977 as a managing director. Under his able leadership, the Adamjee Insurance Company established itself as the top general insurance company in Pakistan. He was a highly respected insurance professional in Pakistan. He was also a director and advisor at the Adamjee Insurance Company before his retirement.

Qazi Anwar Hossain, M.A. (Bengali) is the founder of Publishing house Sheba Prokashoni. Sheba is credited with publishing works of world literature, as well as original work. He created the adult spy-thriller series Masud Rana, modeled after James Bond. There are more then 350 books in this series which has gained a lot of popularity in Bangladesh. Over the span of some forty years, Qazi Anwar Husain has written 371 Rana thrillers. Under his own name and the pen name Bidyut Mitra, he's also produced dozens of adventure books, self-help books, and the 25 Kuwasha titles that are now out of print.

Abdur Razzak has been a leading organizer of the nation's greatest Liberation Movement. Born in 1942, Razzak achieved his M.A. in Political Science from Dhaka University in 1964. He started his career as a public representative after being elected as the Secretary of Fazlul Haq Hall Students Union, Dhaka University in 1963. A versatile charismatic leader with dynamic organizing capacity he emerged as a popular parliamentarian, and took over the responsibilities of different ministries of Government of Bangladesh. He was the member of the Provincial Assembly in 1970 and member of the parliament of the independent Bangladesh in 1973, 1991, 1996, 2001 and 2007. Razzak is graced as vice-chairman of World Peace Council from 1994 to date. Razzak was a minister of water resource 1996-2001. Razzak is now acting as a Presidium Member of Bangladesh Awami League. In Shariatpur-3 (Bhedargonj-Damudaya-Gosairhat) constituency, Awami League nominated candidate is Razzak. He has contributed much in the field of development of Shariatpur and he is a popular leader. There is no rival leader of Abdur Razzak in Shariatpur.

M. Faizur Razzaque obtained his Honors B.A. in Economics from Dhaka University and his Masters in Public Administration from Harvard University, USA. He started his career as a banker in 1965 and later joined the civil service in 1966. He has held a variety of key leadership positions in Bangladesh including Managing Director, Biman Bangladesh Airlines; Chairman, Bangladesh Small and Cottage Industries Corporation; Director General, Bangladesh Television; Chairman, Bangladesh Power Development Board; Secretary, Ministry of Power, Energy and Mineral Resources and Secretary, Bangladesh Election Commission Secretariat. He was an alternative executive director on the Board of Directors of the Asian Development Bank in Manila, the Philippines. In 1991, Razzaque received the highest award in the field of scouting in Bangladesh. After 34 years of government service, he retired and joined the Grameen Bank. He has been the managing director of the Grameen Fund since May 15, 2002. He also serves on the Board of Directors of eleven other Grameen peer companies that work in the fields of telecommunications, information technologies, knitwear, manufacturing and finance.

Rahman M. Mahbub obtained his M.A.(Hons) in English from Jahangirnagar University, Savar, Bangladesh. He teaches English as a senior lecturer at Gono *Bishwabidyalay* (University), Dhaka, Bangladesh. He authored a book of poems translated into Bengali from the originals by William Shakespeare to Robert Frost. He writes poems in Bengali and publishes translations and articles in the *Monthly Gonoshasthya*. Rahman is now working on *Rongdhonu Kanna*, his next collection of poems.

Bazlur Rahim is the fourth son of the late Khuda Buksh. He received his M.A. in Bengali from the University of Dhaka, Bangladesh. He joined *Gonoshasthaya Kendra* (The People's Health Center) as a social worker in 1976. He has been the editor of a monthly socio-health magazine called *Gonoshasthaya* since 1980. During his career, he translated Murry Dickson's book entitled *Where there is no dentist* into Bengali. He is also a co-translator of David Werner's famous book *Where there is no Doctor: Volume 2.*

Muhammad Rahim is the third son of the late Khuda Buksh. He has a Master's of Technology in Mining from the Indian School of Mines in Dhanbad, India, and an MS in Mining engineering from West Virginia University in Morgantown, WV. He immigrated to the US in 1977. He is currently the lead general engineer at a research and development organization in the US Government. Rahim has over 30 years of engineering experience, particularly in ventilation, maintenance engineering system design, and development and configuration management.

Acknowledgments

FIRST, WE WOULD like to pay special tribute to the late Ahmed Ali, who first thought about keeping alive the memory of Khuda Buksh in the mid-eighties by establishing *Khuda Buksh Smriti Sangsad* (Khuda Buksh Memorial Committee) at Dhaka, Bangladesh. We would like to offer heartfelt gratitude to all the contributors. We are grateful to two veteran insurance men, Harunur Rashid from Bangladesh and Rizwan Ahmed Farid from Pakistan. Rashid's interviewee list guided us to plan and progress on the project, while Rizwan's helped us to interview Pakistan insurance personnel. We owe particular gratitude to Mir Mosharraf Hossain and Mosleh Uddin Ahmed. Shuva Rahim and Sara Rahim gave great support by transcribing interview tapes from Pakistan, while Mohammad Nazeeruddin Nazeer helped in transcribing the Urdu comments from the interview tapes.

We are grateful to the late Ataur Rahim for inspiring us on the project. We are also indebted to the late Dr. Asok Banerjee for helping with materials from Kolkata. We pay our respect in memory of them.

We were assisted by a number of persons to whom we owe thanks: Dr. Rezaul Haq, M.A. High, Latifunessa Rashid, Nur Afza Begum, Shanaz Rahim, Mir Obaidur Rahman, Rahman M. Mahbub, Ansaruzzaman Talukdar, Mohammad Ansurazzaman, Mohammad Emranuzzaman, Abdul Awal Majnu, Lutfor Rahman, Subrata Kumar Das, Selima Rahim, Nasreen Rahim, Dr. Zillur Rahim, Javed Bukth, Taniya Bukth, Sajedur Rahim, Asiqur Rahim, Sufia Begum, Raqib Hossain, Kausar Ahmed, Alok Roy and others.

We are thankful to Nazma Akhtar, Subas Mullik, and the associates of Dhanmondi Photo Hut. They helped to improve the quality of old pictures. We extend our thanks to Babuna Faiz who helped us with materials after the death of her mother, Husna Banu Khanum. We owe thanks to the members of Jiban Bima

Corporation and Bangladesh Insurance Academy library for providing material for the book.

We are especially indebted to Dr. Baqui Kahlily who cited an article published in the *Business Chronicle* in 1972 under his joint editorship. We are thankful to him for permission to reprint.

Our heartfelt thanks to Prof. Abdus Samad for translating Bengali interviews to English and Arnab Banerjee for translating few selected topics from Bengali to English. We are greatly thankful for the help of Marcia Trahan who edited the entire translated interviews. Finally, we are grateful for the support of our mother, Zobeda Khatun, our sister Ambereen Islam and brother-in-law Dr. Mahbubul Islam.

Bazlur Rahim
On behalf of the Editorial Board

Index

A

Abbas, Syed Kaiser, 113-114
Abedin, Zainul, 60
Agent(s), 210, 211, 251, 270-271, 275-278, 280, 283-284, 288, 316, 329-330, 337, 341-342, 345-346
Agency, 28, 42, 44, 60, 77, 95, 99, 268
Ahmad, T., 163
Ahmed, Ainuddin, 16, 57, 74
Ahmed, Mosleh Uddin, 16
Ahmed, Tajuddin, 58
Alam, S.F., 129-130, 132, 135
Ali, Ahmed, 30, 40-45
Ali, Atahar, 12, 76
Ali, S. Shamsher, 12
Ali, Wasif, 114, 135-6
Alvi, Mohammad Hussain, 104, 136
American Life Insurance Company (ALICO), 11, 14, 56, 61-2
Ansari, A.R., 82
Awal, Abdul, 85
Awan, S.B., 25
Azam, Shafiul, 28, 68

B

Bangabandhu, 273
Bangladesh, xv-xix, 3-4, 8-9, 11, 15-16, 19-20, 22-23, 27-28, 30-31, 33-34, 37, 42, 44, 46, 48, 50, 52, 56-8, 60, 62-63, 66-67, 70, 75-76, 78, 82-83, 85, 98, 106, 118, 120-121, 123, 137, 146-147, 163, 165-167, 171-172, 175, 182-183, 186, 189-190, 192-193, 195, 197-198, 203, 206, 208, 211-212, 220-221, 223-224, 227, 232, 242, 245, 248-249, 252, 255, 308, 311-313
Battle of Plassey, 246
Bengal, 12, 82
Bengali, xv-xvi, 3-4, 6-7, 9, 11, 13, 19, 27, 37, 48-49, 51, 55-56, 57, 6, 69, 71, 98, 100, 118, 129, 132-133, 144, 147-8, 151, 154, 170, 173, 175, 178, 183, 190
Bengali Muslims, xviii, 247
Bengali nationalism, 55
Bhimjee, Roshen Ali, 5, 7-9, 19, 23, 26, 29-30, 33, 47, 55, 65, 81, 102, 104, 106, 107, 114-115, 118, 120-122, 124, 126, 130, 132, 134-135, 138, 140, 143-144, 151-152, 154, 209, 221, 239, 288, 328, 331, 341

Bhutto, Zulfiquar Ali, 7, 29
British, xv, 52-53, 173, 206, 215, 238, 244, 246-248, 250, 252, 255, 316
British East India Company, 246

C

Calcutta, 4-5, 11-13, 35, 76-77, 125, 146, 176, 185 *See also* Kolkata
Chishti, M.A., 120
Choudhury, Mohammed, 106-107, 115, 146, 148
Choudhury, Hamidul Huq, 61
Chowdhury, A. R., 27
Chowdhury, Zahur Hossain, 51
Chowdhry, S.B., 25, 74
Civil Service of Pakistan (CSP), 102
Cornwallis (Lord), Charles, 246
Crusoe, Robinson, 267

D

Das, Chittaranjan, 249
Dastur, D.K., 77, 237
Dhaka, viii, 3, 8-9, 11-14, 17-20, 23-25, 32, 36-38, 40, 43-44, 54-55, 57, 65, 69, 74, 78, 97, 101-102, 108-109, 111, 117, 125, 135, 146-147, 14-165, 171, 173-174, 177-178, 182, 185, 190, 192, 196, 202-203, 208, 217-219, 221, 223, 229, 234, 237-238, 240, 252
Dhaka Convention (EFU), 65, 115, 118, 126, 134, 220
Dhaka University, 25, 48, 177
Dias, A.J., 97-102, 114, 133
Dienfa Building, 38, 53, 73, 97, 165

E

East Bengal, 4, 69, 77, 170
East Pakistan, 5-9, 12-14, 16, 19, 22-23, 25-26, 29-30, 33, 37, 44, 52-57, 63, 65, 68, 72-73, 75, 77-79, 81-86, 95-96, 100, 103-104, 113-115, 117-122, 129, 131-132, 137-138, 140, 144, 147, 149-153, 170, 177, 179, 190, 221-222, 237-238, 249, 252, 254, 275, 280, 286-289, 297, 309, 317, 330
East Pakistan Co-operation Insurance Society (EPCIS), 22-23
Eastern Federal Union Insurance Company (EFU), xviii-xix, 5, 7-8, 12, 16, 23-24, 27, 31-33, 38-39, 42-48, 52, 65, 72, 75, 77-78, 81-85, 97-98, 102, 104-110, 112-115, 118-119, 124-132, 134-135, 137-144, 146, 149-150, 152, 154, 161, 167-170, 178-179, 187, 304, 316, 326-328, 331-333, 337, 339-34, 342-346
East India Company, 246
EFU Saga, xix, 10, 13, 254, 318

F

Farid, Rizwan Ahmed, 95-96, 209, 344, 349
Fasihuddin, M., 137, 345-346
Father of Insurance, xv, 166-167, 177, 189, 211, 228
Federal Life and General Assurance Company, 9, 15, 19, 21, 30, 32, 33, 38, 49-50, 53, 55, 66, 75, 82, 84, 97, 105, 119, 125, 139, 146
Friedman, Walter A., 211

G

Global Insurance Limited, 48
Great Eastern Insurance Company, 61

H

Habib Insurance Company Limited, 12, 22, 48, 66
Haider, K.F., 29, 73, 77-76
Hakim, Rezaul, 137
Hanfi, Iftekher, 128-129, 133
Haq, A.B.M. Nurul, 38, 48

Haque, Kazi Anwarul, 37
Hasanie, S.A.A., 95-96, 113, 126
Homeland Life Insurance Company, 31-32, 34, 40, 48, 53, 95, 221, 342-343
Hossain, Moinul, 51
Hossain, Dr. Kazi Motahar, 163
Hossain, Mir Mosharraf, 52
Hossain, Kazi Anwar, 163, 346
Hugo, Victor, 56

I

Inspiration, 59, 75, 84, 111, 128, 136, 154, 224, 227-228, 293 *See also* Motivation
Investment, 8, 33, 37, 65, 104, 251, 282, 286, 289, 301, 313
Islam, Ambereen, 177, 201, 317
Islam, Moyeedul, 15, 20, 40, 50, 56, 62, 340
Iven, Erwin C., 5

J

Jaffery, E.A., 104
Jamaluddin, 13, 108, 122
Jatiya Bima Corporation, 50, 53, 55
Jeelani, S.G., 104, 129-130, 288
Jiban Bima Corporation (JBC), xv, xvii, 15, 20, 39, 44, 50, 53, 55, 62, 85, 165, 240, 318. 341
Jiban Bima Tower (Bhaban), 19, 29, 37

K

Kamruzzaman, A.H.M., 15
Karnofuli Bima Corporation, 15 55
Karnowaski, Wolfram W., xix, 13, 209, 254, 318, 325, 340-341
Khaleeli, Abbas, 106, 122, 218
Khan, Ataur Rahman, 50, 65
Khan, Ayub, 6-7, 43, 66, 69, 122, 215, 229, 242, 253
Khan, Habibur Rahman, 292

Khan, Hedayetul Islam, 34
Khan, Naimuddin, 108
Khan, Shafique, 242
Khan, S.R., 67
Khan, Waris Ali, 153
Khan, Yahya, 242
Khanum, Husna Banu, 172, 343, 349
Khatun, Zobeda, 232, 266, 316, 350
Khuda Buksh Memorial Tust & Foundation, xvi, xvii, 75, 96
Khyber Insurance Company, 13, 48, 341
Kolkata, xv, xviii, 16, 27, 63, 70, 76, 78, 165, 172-174, 180-182, 187

L

Leader, xv, 24, 30, 39, 63, 69, 81, 85-86, 95-96, 98, 108, 112-113, 115, 117-118, 121, 138, 144, 153-154, 195, 201, 205, 207, 230, 247, 249, 251, 255, 304, 305, 308
Leadership, 63, 96, 118, 139, 141, 153, 194, 197, 248, 288, 304
Legend, xv, 52, 56, 112, 163, 205, 230, 330
Liberation War, 20, 170
Life Insurance, xv, xviii-xix, 3-6, 9, 13, 22-27, 33, 38, 46-47, 52-53, 60-61, 63, 67, 71, 74, 76-78, 82, 95-96, 98, 101, 106, 108, 113, 115-116, 118-121, 128, 130-131, 136, 143-144, 147-148, 151-152, 183, 189, 206, 208-213, 215, 224, 228, 229, 238, 242, 269-278, 280, 282-285, 287-288, 290, 293, 297-299, 313, 316, 318, 329-330, 337, 339-340, 342-346 *See also* Selling, Premium, Policy

M

Mahbub, Rahman M., 224
Mahmood, Abul, 104, 17-118, 129, 345
Mehman, Abdul Jabbar, 38, 60, 343
Miah, Siddiquallah, 42
Mohammad, Belal, 165

Mohammed, Vazir Ali F., 149, 346
Mohiuddin, Sardar, 76
Monsur Media, 209
Motivation, 84, 105, 129
Mowla, Golam, 57, 62
Mujib-ud-Daula, 31, 342
Munich Reinsurance Company (Munichre), 341
Muslim Insurance Company, 12, 48, 60, 120, 122, 342-3444

N

National Insurance Corporation, 15
Nationalization (Nationalisation), 20, 39, 75, 151, 166, 311-314
Nationalism, 55, 247
Nawaz, Hasan, 195

O

Oriental Government Security Life Assurance Company (OGSLA), xv, xviii, 5, 11. 16, 52, 73, 76, 176, 201, 234, 236-238, 316, 337

P

Pakistan, xv, xviii, 6-7, 12, 15, 18-20, 23, 25, 27, 29, 38, 44, 48, 52-53, 55, 61-62, 65, 67, 78, 83, 95-96, 98, 101-102, 106, 117-118,120-121, 123, 125, 137-138, 141, 144, 146-147, 152, 154, 163, 165, 170, 173, 178, 190, 205-206, 209, 211-212, 215, 220, 237, 239-240, 242, 249-250, 252, 255 272-278, 280-283, 289-290, 293, 296-299, 301, 304, 306, 308-310, 312317, 329-330, 337, 340
Pakistan Administrative Staff College, 25
Pakistan Foreign Service (PFS), 190
Pakistan Insurance Convention, 20, 50, 141, 317, 341

Pakistan Insurance Corporation (PIC), 20, 50, 141, 317, 341
Pakistan Insurance Institute, 344
Pereira, M.J., 97, 229, 344
Pioneer, 177, 224, 242, 250, 284, 340
Policy, 12-14, 18, 20, 28-29, 35, 38, 40-41, 45-46, 58, 60, 64-65, 68-71, 74, 78-79, 98, 108, 121, 147, 163, 168-169, 171, 174, 270
Premium, xvi, 14, 28-29, 38, 42, 53, 58, 62, 64-65, 69, 98-99, 102-105, 118, 125, 131-133, 171, 251, 280, 314, 333
Presidency College, 4, 11,175, 316

Q

Qadri, M.B., 143
Quereshi, D.M., 98
Quereshi, Sharafat Ali, 110

R

Rahim, Md. Ataur, 185, 216, 316, 349
Rahim, Bazlur, xvii, 205,208, 214, 227, 317
Rahim, Dr. Zillur, 199, 203,240,317
Rahim, M.A., 60, 236
Rahim, Sara, 205, 349
Rahim, Shuva, 212, 318, 349
Rahim, Zubaidur, 3-5, 8, 189, 191, 216, 220
Rahman, C.M., 22, 103
Rahman, Habibur, 176, 180-181, 199, 223
Rahman, Habibur, (Justice) 70
Rahman, Mahbubur (Monzu), 180
Rahman, Majibur, 80
Rahman, Sheikh Mujibur, 4, 9, 57, 227
Rahman, Roushanara, 175
Rahman, Shazzadur, xix
Rashid, Harunur, xvi, 11, 44,
Rashid, Quazi Abdur, 63
Rashid, M.A., 177, 195,
Razzak, Abdur, 182, 347
Razzaque, Md. Faizur, 189, 347

Resignation, 13, 19, 26, 61, 80-81, 105, 109, 118, 121, 131, 135, 140-141, 145, 154, 187
Robello, P. M., 55
Role Model, 134, 136
Rotary Club, 51, 54, 56, 178, 218, 220, 343
Rozario, Hubert Arun, 197
Rupsa Jiban Bima Corporation, 15, 55

S

Safiyyullah, A.F.M., 55, 293, 297-299, 339-340
Salam, Abdus, 51
Salesmanship, 195, 269-271, 273, 283-284, 289-290, 293, 297-298, 302
Samad, Quazi Abdus, 72
Samad, M.A., 26, 39. 40, 61, 66
Sandburg, Carl, 231
Sattar, M.A. Abdus (Justice), 30
Sattar, M.A., 55
Selling, 6, 38, 53, 63, 68, 74, 76, 108, 121, 125, 130, 144, 210, 228, 270, 273-277, 282-285, 299
Shaffi, Mushtari, 51, 165
Shyama Charan Edward Institution, 267
Siddiqui, Ahkam, 124, 126, 345
Siddiqui, Hamid Rashid, 99-100
Siddiqui, Motahar, Hossain, 87, 107

Siddiqui, Nazmul Haq, 46, 342
Siraj-ud-Daulah, 246
Six Point, 249
State Life Insurance Corporation (SLIC), 97, 104, 106-108, 117, 124, 128, 143
Surma Jiban Bima Corporation, 15, 55, 62
Swiss Insurance Training Center, 32

T

Tista Bima Corporation, 15, 55

W

Wahiduzzaman, M., 7, 65
Walajahi, S., 49, 97,101-102, 115, 118
West Pakistan, xviii, 5, 13, 18, 23-26, 44, 47, 49, 54-55, 65-66, 81, 103-104, 113-114, 117-119, 123, 134, 137, 14, 147, 150, 152, 179, 189-190, 206, 213, 216-217, 220-221, 238, 249-250, 252, 254-255, 288, 310, 312, 317
Wisaluddin, M., 5, 62, 108, 113, 122
Wizard of Insurance, xv, 52, 71, 77
World War II, 218, 236

Z

Zulqarnain, M., 104

Edwards Brothers Malloy
Oxnard, CA USA
November 10, 2014